The Handbook of Jungian Psychology

The field of Jungian psychology has been growing steadily since the early 1980s and awareness is increasing of its relevance to the predicaments of modern life. Jung appeals not only to professionals who are looking for a more humane and creative way of working with their clients, but also to academics in an increasingly wide range of disciplines.

This handbook is unique in presenting a clear, comprehensive and systematic exposition of the central tenets of Jung's work, which has something to offer to both specialists and those seeking an introduction to the subject. Internationally recognised experts in Jungian psychology cover the central themes in three parts: **Theory**, **Psychotherapy** and **Applications**. Each chapter begins with an introduction locating the topic in the context of Jung's work as a whole, before moving on to an investigation of contemporary developments and concludes by demonstrating how Jung's theories continue to evolve and develop through their practical therapeutic applications.

The Handbook of Jungian Psychology is the definitive source of authoritative information on Jungian psychology for Jungian analysts, psychotherapists, counsellors and related professionals. It will be an invaluable aid to those involved in Jungian academic studies and related disciplines.

Renos K. Papadopoulos is Professor of Analytical Psychology at the Centre for Psychoanalytic Studies of the University of Essex, a training and supervising Jungian psychoanalyst, as well as consultant clinical psychologist and systemic family psychotherapist at the Tavistock Clinic.

The Handbook of Jungian Psychology

Theory, practice and applications

Edited by Renos K. Papadopoulos

Routledge
Taylor & Francis Group

LONDON AND NEW YORK

First published 2006
by Routledge,
27 Church Road, Hove, East Sussex BN3 2FA

Simultaneously published in the USA and Canada by
Routledge
711 Third Avenue, New York, NY 10017

Routledge is an imprint of the Taylor & Francis Group, an informa business

Typeset in Times by Garfield Morgan, Rhayader, Powys, UK
Paperback design by Hybert Design
Paperback cover image: original artwork by Michelle Papadopoulos; digital
enhancement by Olga Papadopoulos

British Library Cataloguing-in-Publication Data
A catalogue record for this book is available from the British Library

Library of Congress Cataloging in Publication Data
The handbook of Jungian psychology : theory, practice, and applications /
edited by Renos K. Papadopoulos.
     p. cm.
  Includes bibliographical references and index.
   ISBN 1-58391-147-2 (hbk) - ISBN 1-58391-148-0 (pbk) 1. Jungian
psychology. I. Papadopoulos, Renos K.
BF173.H333 2006
150.19'54 - dc22

                                                           2005017878

ISBN10: 1-58391-147-2 (hbk)
ISBN10: 1-58391-148-0 (pbk)

ISBN13: 9-78-1-58391-147-2 (hbk)
ISBN13: 9-78-1-58391-148-8 (pbk)

Contents

PART II
Psychotherapy   175

PART III
Applications   261

Notes on contributors

John Beebe, MD, a past president of the C.G. Jung Institute of San Francisco, specialises in problems of personality and character. He is the author of *Integrity in Depth* (1992) and the editor of *Terror, Violence and the Impulse to Destroy: Perspectives from Analytical Psychology* (2003). The founding editor of the *San Francisco Jung Institute Library Journal* and the first US editor of the *Journal of Analytical Psychology*, he continues as a senior adviser to both journals as well as to the *Journal of Jungian Theory and Practice*.

Ann Casement, FRAI, FRSM, is a training analyst with the Association of Jungian Analysts, London, which she represents on the International Association for Analytical Psychology (IAAP) Executive Committee. She is a founding member of the International Neuro-Psychoanalysis Society. She is currently conducting research into statutory regulation at the University of London, writes for *The Economist* and contributes to professional journals, and is an assistant editor on the *Journal of Analytical Psychology*. Her latest book is *Who Owns Psychoanalysis?* (2004).

Joan Chodorow, PhD, is an analyst and faculty member of the C.G. Jung Institute of San Francisco. She lectures and teaches internationally as well as in the United States. A former president of the American Dance Therapy Association, she is the author of *Dance Therapy and Depth Psychology: The Moving Imagination* (1991) and the editor of *Jung on Active Imagination* (1997). Her early papers appear in *Authentic Movement: Essays by Mary Whitehouse, Janet Adler, and Joan Chodorow* (1999) and her forthcoming book is *Active Imagination: Healing from Within*. In addition to papers and books in English, translations in other languages include Bulgarian, Czech, Danish, Dutch, French, German, Hebrew, Italian, Japanese, Korean, Polish, Russian and Spanish.

Warren Colman is a training analyst for the Society of Analytical Psychology and the British Association of Psychotherapists and is a full member of the Society of Couple Psychoanalytic Psychotherapists. He lectures, teaches and supervises in England, Sweden, Poland and Russia and is in private practice in St Albans, England. He is assistant editor of the *Journal of Analytical Psychology* and has published numerous papers on diverse topics, including several on the self.

Christian Gaillard is current president of the IAAP. He has a doctorate in psychology and is a training analyst and former president of the French Society of Analytical Psychology. He is a professor at the Ecole National Superieure des Beaux-Arts in Paris, lecturer at the University René Descartes and at the Institut C.G. Jung in Paris. He founded and directed the *Cahiers de Psychologie de l'Art et de la Culture*, was for a long time co-chief editor of the *Cahiers Jungiens de Psychanalyse*, and is now a member of the international editorial team of the *Journal of Analytical Psychology*, of *Harvest: International Journal for Jungian Studies* and of *Anima*. He has published many articles and book chapters. His book *Jung* (3rd edition 2001) is translated into several languages; other publications include *Le Musée imaginaire de Carl Gustav Jung* (1998), *Les Evidences du corps et la vie symbolique* (2000) and *Donne in mutazione* (2000).

Christopher Hauke is a Jungian analyst practising in London. He is a lecturer in psychoanalytic studies at Goldsmiths College, University of London. He is co-editor (with Ian Alister) of *Jung and Film: Post-Jungian Takes on the Moving Image* (2001) and (again with Ian Alister) of *Contemporary Jungian Analysis* (1988) and the author of *Jung and the Postmodern: The Interpretation of Realities* (2000) and *Human being Human: Culture and the Soul* (2005). His current involvement in film-making links with his next book *What Makes Movies Work? Unconscious Process and the Film-maker's Craft*.

Verena Kast is a training Jungian analyst and former president of the IAAP and of the Swiss Association for Analytical Psychology. She holds a doctorate in psychology from the University of Zurich. She is professor of psychology at the University of Zurich and instructor and training analyst at the C.G. Jung Institute of Zurich. She has published eighteen books in German, three of which – *The Nature of Loving*, *A Time to Mourn* and *The Creative Leap* – have been translated into English. Her works also appear in Chinese, Czech, Danish, Dutch, Greek, Hungarian, Italian, Japanese, Lithuanian, Portuguese, Spanish and Swedish. *Joy, Inspiration, and Hope* (1991) is the first of her books to appear originally in English.

Roderick Main, PhD, is a lecturer in psychoanalytic studies at the University of Essex. He is the editor of *Jung on Synchronicity and the Paranormal* (1997) and the author of *The Rupture of Time: Synchronicity* *and Jung's Critique of Modern Western Culture* (2004) as well as of many book chapters and articles on Jungian psychology and religious studies.

Stanton Marlan, PhD, ABPP, is a Jungian analyst in private practice and a training and teaching analyst for the Inter-Regional Society of Jungian Analysts. He is president of the Pittsburgh Society of Jungian Analysts, and a member of the New York Association for Analytical Psychology. He is an adjunct clinical professor of psychology at Duquesne University, and a diplomate in both clinical psychology and psychoanalysis from the American Board of Professional Psychology. He is a member of the Academy of Psychoanalysis and chairperson of its Mentoring Committee, and has also served on the Board of Directors of the American Board for Accreditation in Psychoanalysis. He is the editor of the *Journal of Jungian Theory and Practice*, the author of *The Black Sun: The Alchemy and Art of Darkness* (2005) and the editor of two previous books on alchemical themes. He has lectured widely in the United States, Europe and Asia. His scholarly interests include archetypal psychology, hermetic philosophy, alchemy and Kabbalah, critical theory, continental philosophy and Asian religions.

Mary Ann Mattoon has practised as a Jungian analyst in Minneapolis, Minnesota since her graduation from the C.G. Jung Institute of Zurich. Since receiving her PhD, she has also taught Jungian psychology at the University of Minnesota and participated in founding the Minnesota Jung Association. Her publications include edited volumes of the proceedings of the Congresses of the International Association for Analytical Psychology.

Renos K. Papadopoulos, PhD, is professor of analytical psychology at the University of Essex, visiting professor at Middlesex University, associate fellow of the British Psychological Society and training analyst of the Independent Group of Analytical Psychologists. He is consultant clinical psychologist at the Tavistock Clinic and a training systemic family psychotherapist. He is the editor of *Harvest: International Journal for Jungian Studies*, was the first chair of the Academic Subcommittee of the IAAP and a founding member of the International Association for Jungian Studies. His publications are in analytical psychology, family therapy, clinical psychology and specialist work with refugees. As consultant to the United Nations and other organisations he has worked with survivors of political violence in many parts of the world.

Andrew Samuels is professor of analytical psychology at the University of Essex, visiting professor of psychoanalytic studies at Goldsmiths College, University of London, honorary professor of psychology and therapeutic studies at Roehampton University and training analyst of the Society of Analytical Psychology. His books have been translated into nineteen languages and include *Jung and the Post-Jungians* (1985), *The Father: Contemporary Jungian Perspectives* (1985), *A Critical Dictionary of Jungian Analysis* (with Bani Shorter and Fred Plaut) (1986), *The Plural Psyche: Personality, Morality and the Father* (1989), *Psychopathology: Contemporary Jungian Perspectives* (1989), *The Political Psyche* (1993) and *Politics on the Couch: Citizenship and the Internal Life* (2001).

Murray Stein, PhD, is a training analyst at the International School of Analytical Psychology in Zurich. He is a founding member of the Inter-Regional Society for Jungian Analysts and the Chicago Society of Jungian Analysts and was president of the IAAP from 2001 to 2004. He has written several books, including *Jung's Treatment of Christianity* (1985), *In MidLife* (1983) and *Jung's Map of the Soul* (1998). He is the editor of *Jungian Analysis* (Open Court) and a publisher (Chiron Publications), where he has edited the Chiron Clinical Series.

Anthony Stevens is a member of the Independent Group of Analytical Psychologists and of the Royal College of Psychiatrists. In addition to his medical degree (Oxford 1963), he has two honours degrees in experimental psychology (Reading 1955; Oxford 1959) and a doctorate in medicine (Oxford 1973) based on research, supervised by the late Dr John Bowlby, on attachment behaviour in Greek orphans. He is the author of twelve books, the last of which is *Archetype Revisited: An Updated Natural History of the Self* (2002).

Foreword

Mario Jacoby

Why a new *Handbook of Jungian Psychology* now, nearly half a century after Jung's death? Over the years, have we not seen already an enormous variety of publications trying to spread his ideas, by describing, explaining, discussing, praising but also criticising their novelty. As some of the important examples, I can mention J. Jacobi, *The Psychology of C.G. Jung* (1939), M.-L. von Franz, *C.G. Jung: His Myth in our Time* (1975), E. Humbert, *Jung* (1983), Polly Young-Eisendrath and Terence Dawson (eds), *The Cambridge Companion to Jung* (1997), Murray Stein, *Jung's Map of the Soul* (1998) and so forth. Yet, by the year 2006 the theme 'Jung' is obviously not exhausted.

On the contrary: this *Handbook* is timely and more than welcome. It is written by a number of experienced and well-known Jungian analysts of the second and third generations, mainly from the English-speaking world. These authors are experts in their special field. All of them have a deep knowledge and respect for Jung's work and begin their individual chapters by grounding their subject matter in Jung's basic findings. After that they take off to deal with more contemporary views and last, but not least, with their own experiences and contributions. Thus the reader can get important insights into Jung's original ideas followed by their practical therapeutic applications and adaptations to the necessities of the present time. On the whole, it is again evident that the rift and animosity between Freudian and Jungian analysts have mellowed considerably. There is more and more convergence between the two main depth psychological approaches, especially where practice is concerned – for better or worse.

It is impossible to address all important themes that this *Handbook* introduces and discusses. In fact, I wish to focus on only one theme because I feel that it offers an original perspective to view the underlying principles upon which Jung's theory is based as well as, it reflects on the individual themes which get treated by the other authors in this book. This theme appears in the long chapter 'Jung's epistemology and methodology', written by the editor of the *Handbook*, Professor Papadopoulos.

In this philosophical essay, which although is dense and weighty, is thorough and very worth grappling with, the author develops the argument that Jung espoused two opposing epistemologies, of which Jung was not necessarily fully aware. Papadopoulos calls these Jung's 'Socratic ignorance and Gnostic knowledge'.

What is meant by 'Socratic ignorance'? Every college student is probably familiar with the famous dictum of Socrates 'I *know* that I know nothing'. In this connection, Papadopoulos mentions among other examples Jung's attitude of 'clearly standing against oversweeping statements of the "nothing but" kind, especially when it comes to dream interpretation'. He quotes Jung: 'Stereotyped interpretation of dream-motifs are to be avoided . . . one is again and again obliged, before each dream to admit to one's ignorance and renouncing all preconceived ideas, to prepare for something entirely unexpected' (Jung 1948, *Complete Works* 8: par. 543). On the other hand, Jung is often also full of sweeping statements and fixed beliefs, and here Papadopoulos speaks of 'Gnostic knowledge or Gnostic epistemology'. Thus, according to Papadopoulos, 'the agnostic and epistemological openness in Jung interchanges with Jung's own Gnosticism which is characterised by his unshakable belief in the correctness of his own assertions and general theories'.

When it comes to the clinical context, this 'Gnostic' epistemology produces an attitude in Jung, which is in complete contrast to his Socratic openness. As Papadopoulos rightly mentions, Jung was also known to have been quite explicitly prescriptive to his analysands, telling them what specific actions and directions to take in their life. There are many examples of this tendency mainly in the letters to people asking him for advice (C.G. Jung: 'Letters', edited by G. Adler and A. Jaffé).

I think that the awareness and differentiation between these opposite epistemologies are very crucial for Jungian scholars as well as for every analyst. Maybe both epistemologies have something good to offer and what is important is for us to be fully aware which one we employ at each given time. On the one hand, the open spirit of Socratic questioning is most useful: Socrates was also called a kind of midwife because, by his questioning, he could bring to life, i.e., to conscious awareness, unquestioned attitudes which were taken for granted. On the other hand, it is also human to need certain convictions in order to stand on a safe enough ground. For most analysts of the early generation, such a pillar of conviction was provided by the complete identification with Jung's ideas. 'Jung always said' was an understandable expression of this attitude, giving much needed reassurance.

This is not so much needed any more at the present time, as it can be seen by the authors of the chapters of this book; they honour Jung's legacy not by parroting him but by developing further the theory and practice of analytical psychology through their own personal approaches. It is for this reason that this *Handbook* constitutes a timely, authoritative and invaluable contribution to the systematic study of the latest trends in Jungian psychology.

Mario Jacoby, PhD
Lecturer, training and supervising analyst at the
C.G. Jung Institute and at the International School
for Analytical Psychology (ISAP) in Zurich

Preface

Renos K. Papadopoulos

This book, the first *Handbook of Jungian Psychology*, is the product of a great deal of intellectual input, analytical sensitivity and sheer labour by many people over a long period of time. Coordinating many eminent authors is a rewarding task although not always easy. There were many difficulties along the way and the final production took much longer than initially planned. I am grateful to all the contributors for their persistence, patience and professionalism. Each one of them worked hard at all stages of the preparation and production of the book.

The strength of a book of this nature depends substantially on the adequate representation of all possible strands of Jungian psychology, both theoretically as well as culturally and geographically. It is my sincere regret that, due to logistical and financial considerations, the majority of contributors come from the UK and the USA. However, in so far as they are leading authorities in their respective fields, I do not believe that the book has suffered in any significant way.

In addition to the contributors, many others have assisted, directly or indirectly, in the final completion of this work. In particular, I am indebted to my colleagues at the Centre for Psychoanalytic Studies of the University of Essex, Professors Andrew Samuels, Karl Figlio, Bob Hinshelwood, Joan Raphael-Leff and Dr Roderick Main, as well as to my colleagues at the Tavistock Clinic, especially Emilia Dowling, Judith Bell and Rita Harris. Mario Jacoby merits particular thanks for agreeing to write the Foreword; despite his many commitments all over the world, he generously accepted this additional task.

Kate Hawes (publisher), Nicola Ravenscroft (production editor), Claire Lipscomb (senior editorial assistant) and Katharine Grummett (marketing executive), all at Routledge, have been most helpful and encouraging, especially at difficult times. Christine Firth did an excellent job as copy-editor, as well as Lisa Footitt who ably compiled the index.

I am also indebted to Bobbi Whitcombe who edited Professor Kast's chapter with expert competence. Bobbi (who completed the MA in Jungian and Post-Jungian Studies at the University of Essex) is a psychodynamic psychotherapist, a writer, a teacher and a freelance editor.

The image on the book cover was a combined product of a painting by Michelle Papadopoulos and digital graphic enhancement by Olga Papadopoulos, my very special daughters! I am grateful to them for their skills as well as the time, effort and dedication they put into this project.

Noel Taylor has been indispensable in his assistance with all computer matters (both software and hardware). His knowledge, efficiency, and patience are most appreciated.

As always, Nina, my wife, has been constantly supportive, encouraging and enormously generous.

These acknowledgements cannot be complete without mentioning the support of my special friends at Essex.

Introduction

Renos K. Papadopoulos

> The more you advance in the understanding of the psyche the more careful you will have to be with terminology, because it is historically coined and prejudiced. The more you penetrate the basic problems of psychology the more you approach ideas which are philosophically, religiously, and morally prejudiced. Therefore certain things should be handled with the utmost care.
>
> (C.G. Jung 1935, *Complete Works* 17: par. 116)

Jung spoke these words of warning during his famous lecture series at the Tavistock Clinic back in 1935. At the same clinic, exactly seventy years later, I am writing this Introduction being fully aware that his words, far from being dated, are still most pertinent today.

In recent years, there has been an astonishing proliferation of Jungian activities on all fronts: publications – journals, books, websites; cultural, artistic and other events; academic courses and projects; associations, conferences and even commercial enterprises. Moreover, the scope of Jungian work has spread much wider than its original clinical and cultural spheres to encompass increasingly more diverse realms – from organisational and human resource management to film criticism and refugee intervention programmes. All these have created a huge body of relevant literature that needs to be digested, re-viewed, re-examined and ultimately deconstructed. In addition, this needs to be put side by side with Jung's original work so that an appropriate comparison and re-evaluation is undertaken in a systematic way. This is a formidable project, indeed.

The timing and conditions for this undertaking seem to be ripe because this vast volume of Jungian material requires systematic attention soon, before it grows even bigger and becomes unmanageable; also, the new phenomenon of academic Jungian studies provides the best possible conditions for this kind of research. It is important to note that the emergence of Jungian (which, of course, includes post-Jungian) studies at universities is a most welcome development in the Jungian world which until recently was dominated exclusively by clinician-analysts. Academic Jungian researchers not only can afford the time, energy and facilities to subject this material to proper scholarly scrutiny but also have a unique position in so far as they are less likely to be tainted by the splits and factionalism that have marked the analytical Jungian community for years.

Therefore, this is an opportune time to undertake such a serious scholarly work in this field in order to refresh it and prepare it to face the new challenges of our current times. One of the key characteristics of this project should be its systematic nature because the Jungian field, almost mirroring Jung's own opus, has been growing 'naturally' (if not haphazardly) without following any plan and without any sequential elaboration of each concept and process that were introduced.

Jung aptly noted that terminology is 'historically coined and prejudiced' and, therefore, it is essential that we pause and re-examine not only Jung's own writings but also all the subsequent Jungian literature in order to investigate their historical 'prejudices' as well as all the other influences that they had been subjected to. Jung was acutely aware that not only the formulations of the theories (and their terminology) can be 'prejudiced' but also the very conceptualisation of what constitutes the subject matter itself, i.e., the 'ideas' about the 'basic problems' can themselves be 'philosophically, religiously, and morally prejudiced'. In effect, Jung's warning suggests the necessity of an essential work that needs to be undertaken well before a clinician or scholar even begins to discuss the validity of any concept or process. This work should be about exploring the very assumptions that theories and techniques are based upon. Without this fundamental groundwork, Jung would warn us that we are likely to accept, unwittingly, a great many assumptions that can be 'prejudiced' not only at the level of logical formulation but also due to 'religious' and 'moral' prejudices. This means that the dangers are not just about the lack of theoretical accuracy or clinical effectiveness but also about espousing, unsuspectingly, a framework whose origin and implications are unknown to us. Without being fully aware of the contexts within which each concept had been developed, it would be easy to stray blindly into pathways that could lead us into unexpected destinations with unpredictable consequences.

Thus, it is imperative that a re-examination of this growing body of Jungian work is undertaken periodically, and this *Handbook* is based firmly on the realisation of the importance of this task. In its extremely modest way, this *Handbook* aspires to contribute to the further development of this project by attempting to offer an authoritative research into some central themes of Jungian psychology. Although no book of this nature can possibly claim to be definitive either in scope or content, every effort has been made to select the most currently relevant themes and to address them in the best possible way by offering a thorough and critical survey of them.

The uniqueness of this *Handbook* is that it has been designed to provide a comprehensive, systematic and competent treatment of some central tenets of Jung's work. Such an enormous undertaking cannot be carried out by any one single author. What is required is a group of specialists who are authorities in their own specific subject matter within Jungian psychology, and this is precisely what this *Handbook* has endeavoured to achieve; that is why the contributors were selected from the most significant contemporary Jungian authors representing, as far as possible, different schools of thought as well as different geographical locations. However, sadly and unavoidably, the great majority of them come from the English-speaking world due to the difficulties in obtaining reliable and inexpensive translation from other languages.

Initially, it was envisaged that the chapters adhere to a uniform structure which would ensure that each topic is treated in the same systematic manner. Moreover, the authors were encouraged to write in a style that is accessible to a wide range of readers while at the same time not being simplistic.

The original uniform structure of each chapter included the following:

- A brief introduction in which the author locates the topic in the context of the Jungian opus and examines its importance and overall relevance.
- A systematic investigation of Jung's actual positions on the topic, including their chronological development, mapping out major revisions within Jung's own writings.
- A clear outline of the range of meanings and definitions of the topic.
- A systematic outline of major innovations, criticisms and developments of the topic which have been introduced by other authors (during Jung's lifetime and after his death).
- An account of the current status and trends for future developments.
- An up-to-date relevant bibliography on the subject.

Most chapters have adhered to this general outline but, inevitably, it is not possible for every theme to be subjected to this same treatment and, therefore, several chapters have deviated from this order, following a structure more appropriate to their subject matter. At the same time, the contributors, true to the Jungian spirit of authenticity, have brought their own individuality into their chapters, thus subverting a blanket uniformity. Even the original intention of keeping all chapters to the same size had to be abandoned, allowing for suitable variations.

A *Handbook* is a concise reference book that addresses a particular subject and this is the first *Handbook* of Jungian psychology. It is divided into three parts: theory, psychotherapy and applications. Needless to say, not all themes that are covered in these chapters can be categorised neatly into these three parts. Nevertheless, creating these categories offers some systematisation of the rich Jungian opus and also provides an opportunity to discuss critically the appropriateness of this very classification. This is done ably by Christian Gaillard at the beginning of his own chapter on 'The arts'.

The first chapter on epistemology and methodology, in a sense, constitutes a commentary on the very conceptualisation and construction of Jung's work and, therefore, it can also be read as an introduction to the *Handbook*. The other chapters use combinations of theoretical and clinical insights to investigate their themes. All chapters are original not only in the way they treat the material but also, being far more than mere review articles, in developing original arguments and introducing creative ideas.

It is impossible to avoid overlaps and even repetitions in a book of this nature. No theme stands on its own. Each one of them is interlinked with the others and it is a commendable achievement of the authors that such overlaps were kept to the minimum. Even where similar topics are discussed in more than one chapter, the reader has the instructive opportunity to observe the differences between them. The authors' task was difficult enough to address their theme in this comprehensive manner, even without being concerned not to encroach onto somebody else's area.

It is hoped that this *Handbook* will not only serve a good purpose in being a reliable reference book, but also stimulate further research in this direction so that the project of periodic systematic re-examination of the Jungian and post-Jungian opus becomes a reality.

Part I

Theory

Chapter 1

Jung's epistemology and methodology

Renos K. Papadopoulos

To begin with, it is important to address the very inclusion of a chapter of this nature in this *Handbook*. This clarification is necessary because Jung is not particularly known for his contribution either to epistemology or to methodology. Jung is widely known mainly for a number of innovations which do not include his epistemological expertise; mostly, these contributions are connected with the content of his theories (i.e., he introduced new theoretical ideas e.g., about the collective unconscious and the archetypes, etc.), his particular approach to psychotherapy (e.g., he advocated not to reject the symptom but to endeavour to find meaning and value in it), and the implications of his ideas to wider existential and cultural considerations. Epistemology and methodology are not areas that are usually associated with Jung. Yet, this chapter will argue that if one were to read Jung in a certain way, one would find important epistemological and methodological insights; moreover, it will be further argued that these insights are of relevance today and they can enrich substantially current debates in these fields.

Difficulties

Several difficulties could be identified in the undertaking of the task of discerning Jung's epistemological contribution. The first has to do with the basic fact that Jung did not write clearly and specifically about epistemology and methodology; whenever he addressed these issues he did so in passing, in the context of writing about something else. This means that his insights on epistemological and methodological matters were interwoven into the very fabric of his theories and his overall psychology and, therefore, would require a special extraction procedure to be brought to light in order to be examined in their own right. Related to this difficulty is another consideration, i.e., by formulating his insights in his usual idiosyncratic language (which was tightly interconnected within his theories), Jung's implications for epistemology are not easily noticeable either by the specialist epistemologists or by the majority of Jungian psychologists; the former would not even look in Jung's writings for this kind of information, and the focus of the latter has been mainly on his innovative contributions to the theory and practice of psychotherapy.

Another difficulty in developing Jung's contribution to epistemology and methodology is that such an activity would seemingly contradict Jung's own strong views about the very essence of his work. Jung is known for being adverse to any suggestion that his theoretical formulation could be separated from his overall psychology. More specifically, he detested the idea that his work could be considered as constituting any 'free-standing' philosophical statement, abstracted, distinct and independent from its clinical-therapeutic context: 'I have set up neither a system nor a general theory, but have merely formulated auxiliary concepts to serve me as tools as is customary in every branch of science' (Jung 1952a: par. 1507).

Evidently, Jung perceived a sharp distinction between two possible ways that his work could be understood: according to the first one, his work was 'empirical' and grounded on solid clinical observations; and, according to the second one, his work was a collection of philosophical speculations and abstractions unrelated to the clinical realities. Throughout his life and in his writings, Jung struggled to gain legitimacy for his work and endeavoured to condemn strongly the latter position and did everything he could to convince others to espouse the former position. However, this sharp distinction presents two difficulties: first, according to the latter view, any philosophical relevance that Jung's work could have possible had was dismissed as being 'philosophical speculation'; this means that this sharp distinction does not allow for any positive appreciation of anything that could be considered even remotely connected with philosophy. Consequently, all possible epistemological and methodological insights were tainted as being philosophical and were, thus, rejected by Jung. Second, surely, this sharp distinction cannot be definitive, regardless of how it is understood. In other words, any comprehension and (more so) any presentation of 'empirical' 'facts' inevitably involves theoretical and philosophical assumptions that need to be taken on board.

This means that Jung's very perception of his work (in terms of this sharp distinction) prevented him (and others after him) from appreciating any contribution he made which could have been construed as being 'philosophical'. More specifically, throughout, Jung was particularly concerned not to venture into anything that he considered that could dilute the validity of his psychological work and in doing so, in effect, he minimised the importance of the epistemological implications of his work. Moreover, it seems that, even when he was aware of the epistemological impact of his formulations, somehow, Jung perceived them as an integral part of his overall theoretical approach (which, indeed, they were) and, consequently, he did not flag out their importance, in their own right.

Accordingly, the main objectives of this chapter are to attempt, first, to argue that Jung indeed had a remarkable epistemological sensitivity and vigilance, second, to delineate those parts of his work that could convey his epistemological awareness and to develop them into a more coherent formulation, third, to trace his epistemological development through the different phases of his career and the way this development interacted with his wider theoretical formulations and with his own life, and finally to examine the present-day relevance of his epistemological contribution in the light of wider developments and current debates in this field. Needless to say, these objectives will have to be scaled down considerably in scope in order to fit within the space limitations of a single chapter.

About epistemology and methodology

Before going any further, it will be important to develop a working understanding of what is meant by epistemology and methodology. As their respective fields are vast and there are many technical definitions of both of them, it will be useful to limit our understanding to a working conception of them, for the purposes of this chapter.

Epistemology is the *logos* of *episteme*. The Greek *logos* is often translated as study, science, discipline, systematic investigation and discourse. In Greek, *episteme* means knowledge but, not surprisingly, it has an interesting history and a wide range of meanings; the Latin equivalent, *scientia*, does not seem to share this rich philosophical past.

Etymologically, *episteme* is related to the verbs *ephistemi* and *epistamai* which mean 'to set or place upon' and 'to know how', respectively. Both verbs refer to standing over or upon (*epi*) implying some king of 'over-seeing' activity. Whereas in English to understand is signified by 'standing under', in Greek it is by standing over, above. The noun *epistema* is 'anything set up, e.g., a monument over a grave' (Liddell and Scott 1869: 575). Therefore, *episteme* could be understood as the act of marking a territory that was observed and comprehended.

There is long debate about the meaning of *episteme* in ancient Greek philosophy (mainly in Plato and Aristotle). This is mainly in connection to its opposition to *techne* (which is often translated as art, craft or practice). In short, the general trend has been to attribute *episteme* to knowledge of pure theory and *techne* to the know-how connected with practice and application. In other words, the predominant tradition has been to equate *episteme* to theoretical knowledge and *techne* to applied technology. This is reflected somehow in the old division between a university and a poly-technic (in Greek *Pan-epistemeion* and *Poly-techneion*). However, this sharp distinction is not always valid. For example, Plato has Socrates clarifying that the knowledge (*episteme*) of health is the medical craft (*techne*) of the physician (*Charmides*, 165c). In other words, according to Socrates, applied and theoretical knowledge are not in a mutually excluding and oppositional relationship.

This debate is not unrelated to Jung's own understanding of knowledge and craft in psychology and psychotherapy. For example, Michael Whan (1987) suggests that Jung's approach transcends the opposition between *episteme* and *techne* and proposes the term *phronesis* as the most appropriate term that characterises the Jungian approach. Thus, for Whan, Jungian therapeutic practice is not based either on 'theoretical knowledge' or on 'technical knowledge' but on an awareness which he terms 'ethical consciousness'. In fact, the ethical consideration has been proposed as a dominant epistemological drive in mental health care, in general (and not only in relation to the Jungian approach) and as superseding the perceived dichotomy between *techne* and *episteme* (Crowden 2003). Needless to say, Jung would have strongly agreed that an ethical stance cannot be divorced from epistemological and technical considerations; indeed, on numerous occasions he emphasised this very point (e.g., Jung 1949: par. 1412, 1934a: par. 315; McFarland Solomon and Twyman 2003; von Franz 1975).

The reference to *episteme* vs *techne* in the context of the Jungian approach is indicative of the complexities involved in delineating boundaries between the various disciplines; these debates, of course, are not limited only to the therapeutic realm. Indeed, the problematic acceptance of knowledge outside the framework of ethical perspectives is universal and it affects most areas of human activity. Characteristically, Levinas proposed the primacy of ethics and maintained that no knowledge was possible without reference to ethical considerations (e.g., Bernasconi and Critchley 1989; Cohen 1986; Levinas 1984). This strong and close relationship between knowledge and ethics makes it imperative to investigate judiciously their boundaries so that their interrelationships can be understood better. Indeed, without this specific understanding, many dangerous confusions and epistemological errors can be committed. For example, this is particularly evident when attempts are made

> to understand and deal with the effects of political violence from exclusively psychological and psychopathological perspectives [without considering] intrapsychic, interpersonal and external dimensions . . . [and without appreciating] the wider political, historical, social, economic, ethical, spiritual and moral perspectives.
>
> (Papadopoulos 2005: 46)

Then, often we tend to become 'prone to get confused and commit methodological and epistemological errors, ending up psychologising the political realm and pathologising human suffering' (Papadopoulos 2005: 46).

Returning to the developing of a working meaning of epistemology, the majority of definitions in non-specialist dictionaries refer to epistemology as 'the theory of knowledge, especially with regard to its methods and validity' (*Oxford English Dictionary*). Other, more technical texts define epistemology as 'the philosophical inquiry into the nature, conditions, and extent of human knowledge' (Sosa and Kim 2000b: ix). Essentially, epistemology is the study of how we know that we know, of what constitutes a valid understanding/explanation/knowledge. A more general definition that would offer a working framework for this chapter would be that epistemology is the systematic investigation of what makes us accept (think/feel) that we know something, of what makes us mark a certain territory as observed and comprehended. This means that epistemology addresses not only the conditions that make the knower know but also the interaction between the knower and the known, as well as the circumstances within which this interrelationship takes place.

Continuing with the etymological approach to definition, methodology is the logos of *methodos*. The Greek word *methodos* is a composite of *meta* and *odos*. *Meta* means after (implying development), and *odos* is the road, the route. Therefore, *methodos* literally means 'a following after' (Liddell and Scott 1869), following a road, adhering to a set way. The *Oxford English Dictionary* (*OED*) defines method as 'a particular procedure for accomplishing or approaching something', and also 'orderliness of thought or behaviour'; hence, methodology (according to *OED*) is 'a system of methods used in a particular field'. This means that methodology refers to the application of the epistemological premises that a person holds at a given time.

In this chapter, methodology will be used to refer to the specific ways that Jung used to apply his epistemology, i.e., the ways he followed which were guided (consciously or unconsciously) by his particular epistemology (cf. also Dieckmann 1991; Penna 2004). In other words, whereas epistemology would be related to his assumptions about sources of knowledge and evidence, methodology would be related to the manner in which Jung applied these insights in the ways he developed his theory and practice.

Jung's epistemological sensitivity

Before investigating Jung's specific epistemological positions and development, it will be appropriate to first establish and emphasise the fact that he had a particularly acute epistemological sensitivity.

An excellent example of this sensitivity and resulting methodology is offered in Jung's essay on *Ulysses* (Jung 1932a). The full title of the essay is '"Ulysses": a monologue' and it is, indeed, Jung's own monologue, recording his own reactions to James Joyce's novel. Jung first writes about his views on the novel and gradually becomes irritated by it. Then, all of a sudden he turns his attention to his own irritation and writes: 'Joyce has aroused my ill will. One should never rub the reader's nose into his own stupidity, but this is just what *Ulysses* does' (Jung 1932a: par. 167). Jung, at this point, stops writing about his subject matter and instead begins to observe himself and his own very reaction;[1] he continues: 'A therapist like myself is always practising therapy – even on himself. Irritation means: You haven't yet seen what's behind it. Consequently we should follow up our irritation and examine whatever it is we discover in our ill temper' (Jung 1932a: par. 168).

Although the analyst reader of Jung's essay will accept this incident as an ordinary example of Jung's awareness of his own countertransference to Joyce's novel, in effect, this is also a clear illustration of Jung's epistemological awareness in so far as Jung attempts to trace back the source of his own assumptions, knowledge and feelings. In fact, the process of countertransference is nothing but an example of an epistemological procedure in action, during psychotherapy. When the analyst tries to catch himself or herself and observes where certain feelings, thoughts or even words said to the analysand come from, to all intents and purposes, the analyst is performing an epistemological tracking (in addition, of course, to attending to a whole lot of other parameters). The attempt to trace back the origin and context of one's own assumptions is the essence of the epistemological procedure and this is what countertransference is about.

In this context, it is worth noting that although it was Freud who first 'discovered' the phenomenon of countertransference (Freud 1910), it was Jung who emphasised its positive contribution to the therapeutic process (e.g., Jung 1916/1948). Freud, for most of his life, considered countertransference as an obnoxious interference of the analyst's pure position as observer of the analysand. On the contrary, Jung appreciated that countertransference is an essential tool through which analysts can trace the source of their own thoughts, feelings and even actions (verbal and otherwise) in relation to their analysands, and it is for these reasons that he recommended that 'the *sine qua non* is the analysis of the analyst, what is called the training analysis' (Jung: *Memories, Dreams, Reflections* (*MDR*), p. 154). Jung proposed the institution of personal analysis (training analysis) for analysts-in-training not so that they become perfect and pure but in order to learn how to learn from their own reactions during the course of their analytical work; in other words, Jung wanted future analysts to know how to know what makes them know.

This example testifies to Jung's epistemological awareness. Moreover, it also shows how Jung put into practice this awareness, i.e., it illustrates his resulting methodology.

In the 'Ulysses' essay, Jung follows up his epistemological awareness with a systematic investigation of the sources of his 'knowledge'. Not only does he catch himself being irritated but also he tries to find out what is the meaning of this irritation. 'Irritation means: You haven't yet seen what's behind it. Consequently we should follow up our irritation and examine whatever it is we discover in our ill temper' (Jung 1932a: par. 168). Once he becomes conscious of the presence of a certain way of reacting (i.e., irritation) he begins to observe himself, by 'practicing therapy even on himself'. In this way, therapy becomes almost synonymous with the very epistemological tracking of one's sources of knowledge.

Another example of Jung's epistemological vigilance is to be found in his views about the uses and abuses of case histories. With incisive perceptiveness, he warned that

> The empirical intellect, occupying itself with the minutiae of case-histories, involuntarily imports its own philosophical premises not only into the arrangement but also into the judgement of the material and even into the apparently objective presentation of data.
>
> (Jung 1935a: par. 548)

This quotation is very important because it demonstrates the degree of Jung's awareness of the complexities of how the knower knows. Philosophy here is not an abstraction or a school of thought one chooses consciously to adhere to. By 'philosophical premises', Jung here refers to the cognitive process that inevitably orders and structures our perception according to various ways that create 'involuntarily' certain premises, assumptions that colour our understanding and make us accept that we have a certain knowledge about something – a patient, in this example. Jung stresses that this structuring process happens at least at three levels – at the very 'presentation' of the (case-) material, at the 'arrangement' and at the 'judgement' of it. Whereas it is evident that our judgements are influenced by certain 'premises' of ours, it is not easily acceptable that there is a certain degree of 'involuntary' interference by some 'philosophical premises' even in the 'apparently objective presentation of data'. Usually, people believe that a 'fact' is a 'fact' and when a therapist presents the 'facts' of the case, it is usually believed that no epistemological colouring (of a substantial degree) is involved in influencing the presentation. The whole tradition of case-history is based on this 'objectivity'. It is remarkable that Jung, at that time, was concerned about the 'objectivity' of such innocuous presentations. This awareness leads Jung to generalise this epistemological process: 'What is the use of even the most accurate and punctilious work if it is prejudiced by an unavowed assumption? Any science worthy of the name must criticize its own assumptions' (Jung 1935a: par. 548). This statement shows that Jung extends his epistemological awareness, as it applies to the analytical situation, to address scientific method in general, thus anticipating current epistemological approaches (cf. Bateson 1979; de Shaser 1982; Keeney 1983; Neil and Kniskern 1982; Selvini-Palazzoli et al. 1978; Watzlawick et al. 1974).

These two examples show Jung's sharp sensitivity to the importance of epistemological considerations, not only in psychotherapy but also in the wider scientific enquiry. Without using the word 'epistemology', Jung demonstrates his epistemological acumen. This can be epitomised by his statement, in 1947, that 'all knowledge is the result of imposing some kind of order upon the reactions of the psychic system as they flow into our consciousness' (Jung 1947: par. 362). Throughout his life and work, Jung displayed a remarkable awareness of these epistemological processes.

Jung: an outline of his epistemological development

Early writings and work

In a letter to Freud, very early in their professional relationship (on 29 December 1906), Jung felt the need to delineate their differences and identified five points on which 'we do not see eye to eye' (McGuire 1974: 14). The first was about the different clinical 'material' Jung was working with ('I am working . . . with uneducated insane patients . . . with Dementia praecox', as opposed to Freud's educated elite of Vienna which Jung did not mention in the letter, but it is implicit); the third was about their differences in experience (Jung was nineteen years younger than Freud), and the fourth was about the 'psychoanalytic talent' that Jung felt that Freud had more 'both in quantity and quality'. As fifth, Jung cited the 'defect' of having not received direct training from Freud and for the lack of contact with his older master. But it is the second one that needs our attention. Jung put it simply, epigrammatically and strongly: 'my upbring- ing, my milieu, and my scientific premises are in any case utterly different from your own' (McGuire 1974: 14).

Jung did not elaborate on any of the issues he stated in his second point (either in the same letter or subsequently in other letters) and Freud, responding on the New Years day (1 January 1907), did not address at all the differences that Jung identified but, instead, implored him, 'I beg of you, . . . don't deviate too far from me when you are really so close to me' (McGuire 1974: 18). In other words, Freud was not prepared to consider their differences, especially at a time when he was too keen to strengthen their closeness both at a professional and at a personal level. Above all, that was a critical time and both were needed to work together to establish and legitimise psychoanalysis. As a result, these differences, so clearly outlined by Jung, were not followed up either by him or Freud again.

What did Jung mean by these differences? Why was he so definitive, writing that he was 'utterly different', not just 'different'? Ultimately, what does he mean by 'scientific premises', here?

In order to address these questions, it is important to be reminded of Jung's life and work until that point. In terms of employment, he was still working at the Burghölzli hospital in Zurich and in terms of writing, the major works he had completed were his doctoral dissertation and his earlier

Zofingia lectures; by that time, he had also completed most of his writing on traditional psychiatric issues and had published his first psychoanalytic paper (in support of Freud's theory of hysteria). At the Burghölzli hospital, in addition to his psychiatric work, Jung was conducting pioneering research in schizophrenia using mainly the Word Association Test.

In so far as he emphasised his differences from Freud (before they even met), Jung showed how strongly he felt about his own identity, not only as a professional but also in terms of his established position with reference to scientific investigation. What was this position and in what way was it related to his epistemological sensitivity?

Zofingia lectures

While he was still a student, Jung gave five lectures (1896–1899) at the Zofingia student society of which he was a member. In these lectures, he addressed issues such as the nature of science, psychology, religion and the nature of scientific enquiry, all from a thoughtful and philosophical perspective. These lectures show the depth of his understanding of epistemological and methodological issues and provide the researcher with a unique opportunity to trace Jung's early philosophical and scientific premises. The positions he developed here were remarkably similar to the ones he held as a mature thinker in his later life, so much so that some authors went as far as claiming that Jung's 'philosophical attitude' revealed in these lectures remained unaltered till the end of his life (Nagy 1991: 12). Such a claim would be rather far fetched because it ignores some important differentiations Jung made during the course of developing his thought; nevertheless, it would be fairly accurate to accept that, with regard to his overall philosophical position, these lectures laid the foundation of most of his subsequent work. Here are some of the basic premises (relevant to this chapter) that he developed in these lectures.

First, in tracing the 'Border Zones of Exact Science', Jung rejects the positions of both 'contemporary sceptical materialist opinion' (1896–1899: par. 63) and metaphysics arguing for the need of a third position in between. At that time he found vitalism to be that third possibility. According to vitalism, life is a vital principle which is distinct from the material realm of physics and chemistry, although connected with it. Throughout, Jung retained this tendency to reject both the mechanistic approach to science as well as the blindly religious approach and always strove to develop a third principle. His early espousal of vitalism was to be replaced successively by other formulas which were never that dissimilar to this initial formulation; however, all of them included a stance which was introduced in these lectures for the first time – a strong emphasis on the primacy of the psychological as an independent realm, not as a product either of mechanistic materialism or of abstract metaphysics.

> The physical phenomena have been studied and threshed out down to the last detail. Metaphysical phenomena are virtually a closed book. Surely it would be valuable to inquire into properties other than those with which we have long been familiar.
>
> (Jung 1896–1899: par. 65)

Second, related to the above, was Jung's emphasis on the personal experience as opposed to 'inductive scientific method' (par. 175).

> The only true basis for philosophy is what we experience ourselves and, through ourselves, of our world around us. Every a priori structure that converts our experience into an abstraction must inevitably lead us to erroneous conclusions [and again] Our philosophy should consist in drawing inferences about the unknown . . . on the basis of *real experience*, and not in drawing inferences about the inner world on the basis of the outer, or denying external reality by affirming only the inner world.
>
> (par. 175)

These quotations demonstrate Jung's sharp epistemological clarity in rejecting either psychologising the world or imposing meaning from exclusively external parameters. This fine delineation was another characteristic in his subsequent epistemology.

Third, it is in the context of the second argument that Jung insisted in emphasising his 'empirical' approach, which was another hallmark of his later methodology. 'All philosophy must have an empirical foundation' (par. 175). His avowal for both the empirical nature of his enquiry as well as the primacy of the psychological created much perplexity. Yet, for Jung these positions were not contradictory. 'The primary concern of empirical psychology is to supply factual documentation supporting the theories of rational psychology' (par. 114).

> The new empirical psychology furnishes us with data ideally designed to expand our knowledge of organic life and to deepen our views of the world . . . Our body formed of matter, our soul gazing toward the heights, are joined into a single living organism . . . Man lives at the boundary between two worlds.
>
> (par. 142)

In later years, this dual emphasis of seemingly opposing methods was to take the form of seeing himself both as an 'empiricist' as well as a 'phenomenologist' (cf. Brooke 1991).

Fourth, another epistemological concept that Jung first introduced in the Zofingia lectures was teleology. This is one of Jung's most important methodological approaches and during these lectures (paradoxically) he connected it with causality. Jung understood this connection as follows: he believed that humans are driven to enquire after the cause of things, so much so that he even spoke about a 'causal instinct'. Inevitably, this instinct 'leads us, a priori, away from all externality to the inwardness of transcendent causes' (par. 224); this is so because 'the chain of cause and effect is infinite' (par. 197) and once one keeps on enquiring after the cause of things one will eventually begin to look for patterns beyond the visible and external. But this kind of enquiry, in effect, is about not just the origin of things but also about their order, their purpose and ultimately their meaning (von Franz 1983: xx). 'The gratification of the need for causal thinking is truth' (par. 171). Behind causality there was an objective purpose:

> Radical subjectivists, i.e., those who regard the world as illusion, and multiplicity as a show of glittering nothingness, deny any objective purpose. That is, they do not acknowledge the existence of any teleology external to man, and instead claim that we ourselves have projected onto the world, out of our own heads, the idea of the purposefulness of nature.
>
> (par. 175)

This means that Jung, even at this beginning stage of his scientific career, held the centrality of teleology not only in relation to human motivation and enquiry but also as a general principle in nature, at large.

The final point that needs to be identified from the Zofingia lectures is Jung's privileging of morality. Following Kant's primacy of morality, Jung criticised science and materialism for 'poisoning morality' (par. 137) and declared that 'no truth obtained by unethical means has the moral right to exist' (par. 138). Jung's strong feelings are reflected in the emphatic language he used in order to press his point; he went as far as advocating 'a "revolution from above" by *forcing* morality on science . . . for after all scientists have not hesitated to impose their scepticism and moral rootlessness on the world' (par. 138). The strong moral foundation of epistemology that Jung established in these lectures was to remain with him till the end of his life. Throughout, he was passionate that no production of knowledge should be placed above ethical considerations. This relates to the earlier discussion of the ethical dimensions of epistemology.

Doctoral dissertation

As it is known, for this dissertation, Jung wrote an account and analysis of his observations of a 15-year-old girl (whom he gave the false initials S.W.) who, as a medium, held spiritualistic séances. In fact, this girl was Helene

('Helly') Preiswerk, who was a relative of Jung's mother. Over a long period of time, Jung investigated, as a participant observer, not only the content of the séances but also Helene's overall progress from an insecure little girl to a self-assertive mature woman. From an epistemological point of view, the main features of his doctoral dissertation were the following four.

First, this was one of the first times that Jung, in a professional context, attempted to look for the meaning behind the external formulations of verbalisations – the focus of his enquiry (in his dissertation) was beyond the expressed language of the medium and on the meaning this language had for her, in her own specific circumstances and context. He did not accept her alleged communications with spirits at face value, but tried to seek the meaning they had for Helene in the context of her own development. For example, he noted that she communicated with certain spirits that were frivolous and superficial and Jung understood this as Helene's need to get in touch with her own childish part which did not have much opportunity to be actualised. Later, he noted that Helene's main 'guide spirit' became another one who was a serious, mature and devout person; Jung understood this as Helene's need to connect with the ideal personality in her which was in the making. All this shows how Jung was keen not to get trapped in the expressed language of the phenomena but to seek the meaning that language had for the person.

Second, and closely connected with the above, is Jung's expressed primacy of the psychological. To put it simply, Jung was not interested in whether the spirits existed or not but he was interested in the psychological meaning and implications of the fact that Helene herself believed that she was communicating with spirits. This approach was going to become a characteristic of Jung's epistemology. Throughout, he emphasised his right to examine the psychological meaning of the phenomena he was investigating, regardless of the nature of the phenomena, always believing that he was not violating the phenomena themselves. By clearly delineating the psychological angle and meaning of these phenomena, Jung gave himself the licence to move into any field and examine their psychological implications; later in his career he was going to follow the same epistemological approach to investigate phenomena that could come under various other headings, e.g., 'insanity', 'religion', 'politics', 'art', etc. Here, in his doctoral dissertation, Jung respecting the nature of the phenomena he was investigating (i.e., spiritualistic), all he was interested in was the psychological impact they had on Helene.

Third, perhaps Jung's most important theoretical innovation, which was also of great epistemological value, was his understanding that Helene's communications with 'spirits' had a teleological function (Haule 1984; Papadopoulos 1980). During her mediumistic career, Helene was contacting different 'spirits' and one of the most important 'spirits' she connected with was that of a person she called 'Ivenes'. It was about Ivenes that Jung said that she was a 'serious' and 'mature person'. Jung observed that by connecting with Ivenes, Helene 'anticipates her own future and embodies in Ivenes what she wishes to be in twenty years' time – the assured, wise, gracious, pious lady' (Jung 1902: par. 116). This means that Ivenes was for Helene what Papadopoulos (1980, 1984) called an 'Anticipated Whole Other', in other words, an other personality in her which anticipated her own wholeness. The important point here is that Jung did not see and understand psychological phenomena in terms of their pathological meaning only, he also appreciated that psychological functioning (including even pathological symptoms) have a certain teleological function, they point to the purpose and goal of one's development. Teleology was to remain one of Jung's most characteristic elements of his epistemological approach.

Finally, in his research for his doctoral dissertation Jung introduced his specific method of participant observation which was to become his characteristic approach to methodology. In the same way that Jung sat in the spiritualistic séances of Helene's both as a participant as well as an observer, so did he continue with the same method in his psychotherapeutic practice as well as in other scientific investigations. This means that he always valued that knowledge was produced by experience and in the context of interaction with others – what modern systemic epistemologists would call 'co-construction' of knowledge (e.g., Coulter 1995; Fulford et al. 2003; Gergen and Davis 1985; Gergen and Gergen 2003; Glaser and Strauss 1967; Hermans and Hermans-Jansen 1995; Sarbin 1986; Young 1997).

Burghölzli

During Jung's period of work at the Burghölzli psychiatric hospital (between 1900 and 1909), this famous institution was the centre of pioneering research. Under the directorship of Professor Eugen Bleuler, the originator of the term 'schizophrenia', a talented team of international clinicians and researchers studied psychotic conditions both from academic research as well as clinical perspectives. First, we will examine the key epistemological features of Jung's psychiatric-therapeutic work of this period and then of his research work.

Continuing on from his doctoral dissertation, one of Jung's main concerns became the search for the meaning of his patients' verbalisations. Again, he did not accept that what his patients said was meaningless because they came from insane people; he did not want to dismiss what they said as just insane talk. Instead, Jung endeavoured to seek the uniqueness of their meaning. Even with chronic patients who were 'completely demented and given to saying the craziest things which made no sense at all' (*MDR*, p. 147), Jung found meaning in what they were saying, 'which had hitherto been regarded as meaningless' (*MDR*, p. 147). For example, one patient used to wail 'I am Socrates' deputy' and Jung found out (by investigating closely her personality and circumstances) that she 'was intended to mean: "I am unjustly accused like Socrates"' (*MDR*, p. 147). Sometimes, by working actively towards developing an understanding of their language Jung was able to produce remarkably positive changes, even 'curing' them, like with the schizophrenic old woman that was hearing a voice whom she called 'God's voice' and Jung told her that '"We must rely on that voice"' (*MDR*, p. 148). By relating to her in a way that was offering not only validation but also bestowing a certain meaning to the meaninglessness of her 'insane' voices, Jung was able to achieve an 'unexpected success' in her treatment (*MDR*, p. 148).

It is important to acknowledge that the emphasis on meaning was not an invention of Jung's, but it was part of the overall ethos and approach developed by Bleuler. Characteristically, A.A. Brill (the American psycho-analyst who was also part of that research group at the Burghölzli) wrote that the psychiatrists at that institution at the time 'were not interested in what the patients said, but in what they *meant*' (Brill 1946: 12). This does not invalidate Jung's contribution but it provides its context; he was able to connect this philosophy to his own approach and, most importantly, to develop it further and reach his unique epistemological positions.

Word association experiment

Many important innovations were introduced at the Burghölzli by the work with and applications of the word association experiment; although the concept of 'complex' is considered to be the most important one, neverthe-less, there are some significant epistemological elements that also emerged from this work and which contributed to the formation of Jung's definition of a knowing person.

To begin with, the actual Word Association Test (WAT) was based on the psychological school of 'Associationism' which, it could said, was a theory of knowledge, i.e., an epistemology. More specifically, the essence of Associationism was that our mental activity is based on associations; i.e., our knowledge and awareness of things is a product of various combi-nations of associations which we have of elements derived from sense experiences. Philosophers throughout the ages developed and updated different theories and laws of association – from Plato and Aristotle to more modern thinkers and psychologists. In psychology, associationism entered via Harvey (1705–1757), Galton (1822–1911) and Wundt (1832–1920). Although Galton and Wundt examined word association as part of their investigations into the field of cognitive functioning, it was Kraepelin (1856–1926), an earlier superintendent at the Burghölzli hospital, who developed the actual WAT and Jung eventually was appointed (by Bleuler) in charge of the programme using this research tool. The Burghölzli pre-occupation with the WAT was not theoretical but applied to abnormal psychology; they were interested in understanding the mechanisms involved in the 'schizophrenic' mind. Bleuler's main contribution in renaming 'dementia praecox' by introducing a new term ('schizophrenia') meant that this condition does not create a 'premature deterioration' but it involves an actual split within the patient's personality and functioning. The WAT was used, in effect, to study the way the schizophrenic patients developed their perception and knowledge in order to trace the way the 'split personality' functions. Their responses to the stimulus words were analysed according to various categories (semantic, phonetic, syntactical and grammatical) and, experimentally, it was possible to identify that inner split. This was found in terms of discerning various themes that formed coherent wholes in the body of their responses. More specifically, Jung found in the responses that certain clusters of ideas and thoughts with a degree of emotional charge formed distinct entities which he termed 'complexes'. Jung did not invent this term but he gave it this specific research definition: 'An emotionally charged complex of ideas becomes so predominant in an individual and has such a profound influence that it forms a large number of constellations . . . all referring to this complex of ideas' (Jung and Riklin 1904: 82). But such a nucleus, a centre in oneself that generated an independent perception and knowledge of things, in effect, represented another 'mind' within an individual. As Jung put it later,

> We are, therefore, justified in regarding the complex as somewhat a small secondary mind, which deliberately (though unknown to consciousness) drives at certain intentions which are contrary to the conscious intentions of the individual.
>
> (Jung 1911: par. 1352)

Therefore, from an epistemological perspective, Jung's theory of complexes enabled him to appreciate that the knowing subject is not a unified entity but it is divided by the various complexes that grip the person. Thus, the complexes created a divided knowing subject according to the various thematical divisions that the complexes formed. This means that by grasping the essential nature of psyche's dissociability (Papadopoulos 1980), Jung was able to increase substantially the complexity of his epistemological grasp of human nature.

'my scientific premises . . .'

It is now possible to return to the questions asked above, in connection with Jung's identification of his differences from Freud. To be reminded, in his letter to his older colleague at the end of 1906, Jung identified three differences: their 'upbringing', 'milieu' and 'scientific premises'. By 'scientific premises', in the context of their respective work, Jung must have meant the specific ways each one of them defined their subject matter and went about investigating it, i.e., their epistemology and methodology. More specifically, by 'scientific premises' Jung must have referred to the way they answered questions such as: what constituted evidence for their investigations? How did they know that they had arrived at knowing something? How did they construe their knowing subjects?

Initially, the reader would be puzzled to read that Jung even before he had developed a close relationship and collaboration with Freud (by the end of 1906), he wrote about his 'scientific premises' in a way that conveyed a certain conviction that he had already formed such 'scientific premises' and, moreover, stating that they were different from those of Freud's. However, the same reader would not be puzzled anymore after reading the outline of Jung's achievements and established epistemological and methodological positions which he had already reached by the end of 1906. Although the correspondence between the two men started only that year (1906) and they did not meet in person until a couple of months later (February 1907), Jung's letter (of December 1906) conveys with clarity his firm belief that their 'scientific premises' were different. In short, Jung's assertion about their differences suggests the following:

1   Jung was aware of the relevance of epistemological and methodological principles (i.e., 'scientific premises') in analytical theory and practice.
2   This awareness was developed well before he met with Freud and, therefore, it was not connected directly with Freudian psychoanalysis.
3   The usual version of their professional relationship, which both Jung and Freud originated and perpetuated, i.e., that Jung started as a mere disciple of Freud's is not accurate as it is not supported by the evidence that these observations in this chapter provide. This means that their version of events must have been developed for other, possibly psychological reasons, related to the dynamics of their personal relationship.

(Papadopoulos 1980, 1984)

Therefore, in the light of this analysis of these observations, it would be difficult to accept the accuracy of Jung's dramatic assessment which he wrote in his autobiography, referring to his break with Freud:

When I parted from Freud, I knew that I was plunging into the unknown. Beyond Freud, after all, I knew nothing; but I had taken the step into darkness.

(*MDR*, p. 225)

These strong words 'unknown', 'nothing' and 'darkness' do not correspond with the evidence that Jung, even before meeting Freud, had established clear epistemological positions, and, moreover, they contradict his own position that was conveyed succinctly in his letter of December 1906. Thus, these words can be puzzling, especially if we take into consideration that his subsequent work (after 1906) did not produce substantial deviations from these epistemological positions; in the following years, Jung introduced, indeed, many important theoretical developments, but in terms of his basic epistemology and methodology, he did not deviate much from the foundations that he had laid by 1906. Why, then, did Jung keep to this false version of events, still writing about them in such a categorical tone nearly half a century later? Why did he keep on perpetuating this myth? In addition to the psychological reasons (which can be extremely powerful and with long-lasting effects), it is possible that Jung retained this conviction because it was based on some partial truth, or at least on something paradoxical.

One way of understanding this puzzle is to accept that Jung's strong words about his (alleged) total ignorance after his break with Freud may refer to another perspective from which Jung saw his own work: it was argued elsewhere (Papadopoulos 1980, 1984) that during the period of his association with Freud (Jung's 'psychoanalytic period') and after his break with Freud (in 1913) there was a disjuncture between Jung's epistemology and his own actual theories; it was only later that Jung was able to develop theories which fitted more appropriately to his already established epistemology. This means that Jung's epistemology preceded his theories. More specifically, during his association with Freud, by and large, Jung went overboard to accept and adopt the Freudian version of psychoanalysis as his own, despite the fact that he did not feel satisfied with it; the fit between his epistemology and the Freudian psychoanalysis was not a good one. Jung felt uncomfortable about this and eventually parted ways from Freud and gradually developed his own language that corresponded better with his already set 'inclinations' and epistemological positions.

Therefore, this version of accounting for the discrepancy between Jung's letter of December 1906 and his categorical assessment (in his autobiography) about the 'darkness' he had stepped into after he left Freud, is based on a distinction between Jung's epistemology (which was the sum of his 'scientific assumptions', which formed the foundations of his approach, and which were, in fact, his 'natural' 'inclination' as to how he approached his work both theoretically and practically) and his 'official' theoretical positions (which referred to the theories that he espoused and identified professionally with). Once such a distinction is made, it is then possible to understand the contradiction between his letter of 1906 (claiming that he had clear positions, and they were different from those of Freud's) and his writing in his autobiography (that after Freud he knew nothing). In other words, Jung was not not telling a truth in his autobiography – he was referring to his explicit theoretical formulations which could identify his professional positions, whereas in his 1906 letter he was referring to his epistemology.

A comparable distinction between Jung's 'official theoretical language' and his own personal 'inclination' was made elsewhere (Papadopoulos 1980, 1984, 2002), where Jung's 'inclination' was articulated in more detail. More specifically, in those studies, Jung's official language was understood to be the result of his professional 'persona', which he felt it was important for him to maintain; in addition (and in contrast), Jung had another perspective on his work which was his epistemological inclination and which was informed by another problematic that was driving his theoretical and professional development. That perspective (his epistemology) was identified as his 'problematic of the other' which referred to his intense interest in the dissociability of the psyche, i.e., in the way various forms of 'other-nesses' were active in one's personality and the ways these 'others' inter-related among themselves and also related to the main body of the personality, to the outside world and to wider collective structures (Papadopoulos 1980, 1984, 2002). In effect, the first two studies (Papadopoulos 1980, 1984)

> proposed a new reading of Jung which was based on the hypothesis that the Jungian opus could be appreciated more fully if it were to be seen as a series of progressive reformulations of his understanding of the Other.
>
> (Papadopoulos 2002: 170)

It was argued that Jung's theoretical development was based on these progressive reformulations of the Other

> from animistic external Other objects [of his childhood, e.g., his 'own' fire, his 'own' stone, his 'own' pebble and carved manikin] to a rather unsophisticated, global internal Other (No. 2 personality), and then from intrapsychic individual functions (complexes) to more collective forms of structuring principles (symbols). The Other-as-archetype represents the pinnacle of Jung's theoretical endeavours as it offers a structuring principle which is also connected with broader cultural and societal perspectives. This reformulation represented a dialectic between the internal and external, specific/individual and general/collective, personal/intrapsychic and societal/symbolic.
>
> (Papadopoulos 2002: 170)

Not only did that approach offer a new 'reading' of Jung which combined almost seamlessly his personal life and preoccupations along with his professional curiosity and career in the context of wider intellectual debates at his time, but also it laid the foundations for an understanding of Jung based on his epistemological astuteness. In other words, the best possible way of understanding the nature of his 'problematic of the other' is in terms of it forming a basis for comprehending the dynamics of the knowing subject, i.e., in terms of epistemology. By endeavouring to dissect the various structures and discourses that inform a person to reach a knowing position, Jung was, in fact, developing an epistemological stance. This means that when Jung was referring to his 'scientific premises' he was referring to his epistemological 'inclination' and his 'problematic of the other' both of which were developed to a considerable degree before even he had met Freud, and before he was exposed to Freud's psychoanalytic theories. Moreover, it was argued that Jung's initial attraction to Freud was based on his assumption that Freud shared the same problematic with him, i.e., had similar epistemological premises. Epistemologically speaking, that was the reason why Jung joined the psychoanalytic movement, hoping to find a more appropriate theoretical language for his own epistemological inclinations. However, when he realised that this was not happening, he left Freud and endeavoured to develop his own psychology which would be more congruent with his already well-developed epistemology.

This reading of Jung's differentiation between his epistemology (which was more basic) and his theoretical formulations (which developed later in his life) offers the means to understand the phrase 'Jung before Freud' which was introduced later (cf. Taylor 1998; Shamdasani 2003).

Although this distinction (between his epistemology and the main body of his theories) resolves the puzzle of the discrepancy between Jung's letter of 1906 and his statements in his autobiography, it still leaves something unclear. Why was Jung not fully aware of this distinction? On the one hand, he had a remarkable clarity about the importance of his epistemology and on the other hand, he seemed to be ambivalent about it. This was perhaps due to his fear that if he was to emphasise too much the epistemological nature of his theories he could have been considered as a philosopher and thus dismissed for not being a serious 'scientist'–psychologist which he wanted to be seen as, in order to gain respectability for his work. Another possibility is that Jung may have taken his epistemology for granted, almost as his 'inclination' and, therefore, as different from (and of lesser importance than) the main body of his theoretical work; according to this perspective, Jung did not consider his epistemology of great importance in its own right, as a free-standing contribution. Certainly, at that time, there was no explicit field of epistemology of psychotherapy to assist him in appreciating the significance of his positions.

Finally, returning to the December 1906 letter, it is also important to appreciate that by grouping all the three differences together – 'upbringing', 'milieu' and 'scientific premises', Jung demonstrated that, even at that early time, he was aware that the 'scientific premises' are not unrelated to one's own personal history ('upbringing') as well as to the wider, collective contexts ('milieu'). This is another important insight that he retained throughout: one's epistemology is not an abstract theoretical construct but is embedded in one's individual and collective realities.

Later writings and work

Although Jung's basic epistemological positions were established by 1906, nevertheless there are some additional insights that contributed to the development of the final epistemological model of his psychology. These include the following:

- the collective dimension of knowledge
- teleology: knowledge in the making
- an epistemology of archetypal teleology.

The collective dimension of knowledge

During his lecturing visit to the United States with Freud in September 1909, in one of his presentations at Clark University (in Worcester, Massachusetts), Jung returned to a piece of research he had conducted with his student Dr Emma Fürst. He had already published a paper on the subject two years earlier (Jung 1907) and, again, he included material from the same study in his Tavistock Lectures more than a quarter of a century later (Jung 1935b). That study offers a clue to the development of Jung's understanding of one of his most significant epistemological insights.

The study, included in Jung's *Collected Works* as 'The family constel-lation' (1909), addresses one application of the WAT. Jung and Fürst administered the WAT to all members of twenty-four families. The two researchers analysed the obtained responses according to the existing 'logical-linguistic criteria' (Jung 1909: par. 1000) which Jung had developed from previous modifications (Jung and Riklin 1904). The findings showed that the differences between and among the response patterns of individual members of a family were not random but occurred in a regular and predictable fashion; they showed that statistically, there were remarkable similarities between the patterns of responses among certain subgroup-ings within families. More specifically, the results showed that children's responses were more similar to their mothers' rather than to their fathers' associations, and that mothers' associations were more similar to their daughters' rather than to their sons' associations.

> The significance of these results is even greater if one appreciates that [this did not happen as a result of] simple repetition of similar words by

different members of the family, due to the given habits or family culture within each family.

(Papadopoulos 1996: 131)

As Jung put it, 'the daughter shares her mother's way of thinking, not only in her ideas but also in her form of expression' (1909: par. 1005); in fact, what is of more relevance is not the shared 'form of expression', which can be a product of learning, but the fact that certain members of the same family share the same 'way of thinking'. This means that these research findings require a closer examination.

The categories of 'logical-linguistic criteria' into which the responses were grouped included 'relations of the verb to the subject', 'definition', 'contrast', 'simple predicate', 'predicate expressing a personal judgment', etc. In other words, these criteria were not addressing superficial similarities; the results were showing how frequently each subject offered a response to the stimulus word that defined it, or was its contrast, etc. This means that the results were showing the pattern of each person's tendency to perceive and structure external stimuli and how they construed logically and linguistically their perceptions. These are not ways that one can copy from another person; these are deeply ingrained mechanisms that convey one's unique ways of cognitive structuring. In effect, this research indicated that within families there must be certain formations that are 'organising structures which are collectively shared' (Papadopoulos 1996: 130). These 'shared unconscious structures' affect the ways that family members structure their perceptions, knowledge, relationships and overall psychological realities. These formations 'could be termed the Collective Structures of Meaning (CSM). This meaning, of course, is not given but is immanent and potential' (Papadopoulos 1996: 136).

Jung was at pains to interpret their research findings. In his 1909 paper, evidently puzzled by their findings, he

> was unable to offer any plausible explanation for these phenomena. Instead, he struggled to fit them within the context of a psychoanalytic language and attributed them to the 'determining influence' of the 'emotional environment constellated during infancy' (Jung 1909: par. 1009).

(Papadopoulos 1996: 131)

On the basis of that research, Jung felt justified to acknowledge 'the determining influence of the family background on [the children's] destiny' (1909: par. 1009), but at that time, confined within his psychoanalytic theoretical framework, he understood that 'background' only in terms of 'the emotional environment constellated during infancy' (Jung 1909: par. 1009). In other words, Jung was able to identify only those elements of these research findings which fitted within his existing psychoanalytic theory, but he must have felt at odds with the underlying 'causal-reductive' epistemology of this piece of psychoanalytic interpretation. As it has been shown, Jung had already a well-developed teleological epistemology.

This means that the family WAT research must have exposed the implications of Jung's distinction between his underlying epistemology and his 'official' theoretical positions; the latter were confined within the Freudian psychoanalytic model and, therefore, were unable to render fully intelligible these findings. More specifically, according to Freudian psychoanalysis, unconscious interactions between people had to be based on projections of one's unconscious material onto another's; there was no room for 'shared' unconscious structures, as this research suggested. Still, evidently unconvinced by the causal-reductive interpretation of his findings, at the end of the paper Jung admits the limitations of his theory (i.e., psychoanalytic theory) and writes: 'We are as yet a long way from general precepts and rules' and, most uncharacteristically, he resorts to extolling the virtues of psychoanalysis like a naive and fervent neophyte: 'Only psychoanalyses like the one published by Professor Freud in our *Jahrbuch*, 1909, will help us out of this difficulty' (Jung 1909: par. 1014).

These findings are of tremendous importance because 'By discovering the . . . patterns of logico-linguistic structuring within pairs in families, Jung, *de facto*, had discovered the intrapsychic interconnection within families as well as the various subgroupings or subsystems' within families (Papadopoulos 1996: 131). From an epistemological point of view, Jung's accidental discoveries in the family WAT research, in effect, indicate that the knowing subject is not just an independent being arriving at knowledge exclusively on the basis of his or her own independent experience. In addition, there are at least two more sources of potential knowledge: first, the interactional and relational patterns of experience; these include the family interactions and transactions as well as the network of inter-projections of unconscious material between members of the same family as well as with the wider sociocultural environment (including what Jung termed 'emotional environment'), and second, the 'shared unconscious structures'; these are structures that are not projected by one person onto another but, nevertheless, are affecting certain subgroups within families. These must be structures of a 'collective' nature that contribute to one's creation of sense and the formation of knowledge.

This paper (of 1909) shows how Jung almost accidentally stumbled across the phenomena of 'shared unconscious structures' which, subsequently, he was to name as 'collective unconscious'. At that time, these phenomena exposed the limitations of his theory and the gap between his epistemology and his theories. Nevertheless, as it was noted, although

> Jung did not pursue this research, and did not work with families again [either clinically or in research] one could argue that the phenomena he

encountered at this stage of his life never left him, instead, they [must have] set him a task to find more appropriate ways of comprehending them. His subsequent development followed that very direction and enabled him to formulate a perspective within which the intrapsychic and collective realms interrelate meaningfully.

(Papadopoulos 1996: 131–132)

The implications of these findings are not limited only to Jung's epistemology; by identifying unconscious shared structures within families, Jung could also be considered as a pioneer of modern family therapy (Garnett 1993; Papadopoulos 1996; Papadopoulos and Saayman 1989).

Teleology: knowledge in the making

Like most of the elements of his epistemological position, by no means, did Jung invent *teleology*, which has a long tradition in philosophy across cultures and time. Jung's contribution was that he located teleology within a specific context along with the other elements of his epistemology and psychological theories.

Teleology refers to the approach that considers phenomena in terms of their *telos*; *telos*, being the goal, end, purpose and fulfilment. As was mentioned above, Jung espoused a teleological approach as early as his Zofingia lectures. At that time, he discerned teleology not only as a method of enquiry but also as a process 'external to man' (Jung 1896–1899: par. 175), as a wider principle in life. Later, in his doctoral dissertation, Jung again employed a teleological approach to understand the spiritualistic phenomena he had observed. He felt that Helene's spiritualistic experiences had a teleological function in that they assisted her psychological development and maturity.

Jung distinguished between two basic methods in approaching psychological phenomena: a 'constructive' or 'synthetic' method and a 'reductive' ('causal-reductive') method. He identified with the former and he considered the latter to be the hallmark of the Freudian approach. Adopting Maeder's understanding of the 'prospective function of the unconscious' (Maeder 1913) and Adler's 'anticipatory function of the unconscious' (Adler 1912), Jung emphasised the 'purposive significance' of the unconscious: 'We conceive the product of the unconscious . . . as an expression oriented to a goal or purpose'; accordingly, he understood that 'the aim of the constructive method . . . is to elicit from the unconscious product a meaning that relates to the subject's future attitude' (Jung 1921: par. 701). In contrast, he considered that 'The reductive method is oriented backwards . . . whether in the purely historical sense or in the figurative sense of tracing complex, differentiated factors back to something more general and more elementary' (Jung 1921: par. 788). Moreover, he understood that

Reduction has a disintegrative effect on the real significance of the unconscious product, since this is either traced back to its historical antecedents and thereby annihilated, or integrated once again with the same elementary process from which it arose.

(Jung 1921: par. 788)

This means that in approaching psychological phenomena, one can either trace them back to their 'origin' into one's own history (reductive method) or endeavour to relate to the purpose and meaning they have in terms of the person's goals and future orientation (constructive method). The constructive method is based on teleology, or according to the Aristotelian terminology – the 'final causality'. We can understand phenomena not only in terms of them being effects to previous causes (this would be the Aristotelian 'efficient causality') but also in terms of their purpose and 'final cause' – their goal. Jung's famous dicta – neurosis 'must be understood, ultimately, as the suffering of a soul which has not discovered its meaning' (Jung 1932b: par. 497) and 'Neurosis is teleologically oriented' (Jung 1943: par. 54) testify to his committed teleological orientation. But Jung did not limit his teleological understanding to his clinical work. He maintained that science at large was adopting teleological principles in approaching its subject matters. For example, he argued that '"function" as conceived by modern science is by no means exclusively a causal concept; it is especially a final or "teleological" one' (Jung 1917: par. 688). Also, he declared boldly that 'Life is teleology *par excellence*; it is a system of directed aims which seek to fulfil themselves. The end of every process is its goal' (Jung 1934b: par. 798).

Therefore, Jung's use of teleology could be categorised into the following four types:

- *therapeutic teleology* – referring to his approach to psychological and psychopathological phenomena in the course of analytical therapeutic work;
- *methodological teleology* – referring to the methodological use of teleology in scientific investigations, in general;
- *human teleology* – referring to the purposeful direction human beings have towards psychological development; and
- *natural teleology* – referring to his understanding that teleology is a law of life.

All four types of teleological understanding have strong implications for Jung's epistemological approach in so far as they suggest an impossibility of complete knowledge in a definitive way, as knowledge is related to a future purpose and goal. This means that, in effect, Jung's epistemological teleology locates knowledge in the very process of generating itself. Thus, it could be said that the production of knowledge for Jung, especially in therapeutic contexts, involves the locating of oneself on the pathway along which teleology is unfolding as a lived experience. Instead of focusing on a final outcome and end product or state, Jung's teleological epistemology favours an approach that accepts, what could be termed, *knowledge in the making*. Accordingly, it is not surprising that Jung repeatedly emphasised the *process* of individuation instead of the final product of individuated state itself. By being connected along with and within the path of teleology one derives a certain meaning and sense which is real and substantial even if it is not definitive and ultimate in terms articulating itself in the format of a logical and rational explanation and definition. Aware of this finer differentiation, Jung used the term 'finality' in this context:

> I use the word finality intentionally, in order to avoid confusion with the concept of teleology. By finality, I mean merely the immanent psychological striving for a goal. Instead of 'striving for a goal' one could also say 'sense of purpose'. All psychological phenomena have some such sense of purpose inherent in them.
>
> (Jung 1916/1948: par. 456)

Jung was evidently concerned that teleology could imply a crude expectation of a definitive goal with an accompanying rational formulation and, consequently, chose to introduce 'finality' in order to address this very idea of *knowledge in the making*.

Therefore, Jung developed further his original understanding of teleology and refined it in the context of his psychological epistemology, which continues to receive appropriate attention (e.g., Horne 2002; Jones 2002; Nagy 1991; Rychlak 1968, 1973, 1984).

An epistemology of archetypal teleology

Having established firmly the teleological intention as the basis of his approach, Jung needed to introduce more elements to support it and render it more applicable, at least to his therapeutic teleology. His initial understanding of the collective structure of knowledge formed a good beginning but it required further elaboration. It was not until the introduction of the archetype that Jung was able to furnish this elaboration.

From an epistemological point of view, Jung's theory of archetypes introduces a complexity that enriches his earlier formulations of teleology, by offering a bridge between the personal realm and the wider collective structures. More specifically, Jung suggests that 'Archetypes . . . manifest themselves only through their ability to *organize* images and ideas' (Jung 1954: par. 440) and 'consciousness . . . rests, as we know, on . . . the archetypes' (Jung 1958: par. 656). Thus, epistemologically speaking, one would not be able to comprehend judiciously the sources of one's knowledge unless one appreciated the organising effect that archetypes have on the knowing process, on one's very consciousness.

This means that, in addition to a reductive process of identifying the various contributing elements in a knowing process i.e., relating to personal history, interpersonal transactions and societal influences (as outlined above), the Jungian approach includes a constructive process that would take into account the archetypal organising influence. Diagrammatically, this could be represented by the dotted-lined arrows that affect not only the individuals (persons A and B in Figure 1.1) but also their interpersonal exchanges and unconscious mutual projections (IE and UP), as well as each person's interaction with their own personal history (PHA and PHB), and the socio-cultural influences (S-CI).

Figure 1.1 requires further clarification. Instead of having one single archetype organising the network of interactions, there is a cluster of archetypes ('Network of Archetypal Images') because archetypes are closely interrelated among themselves and it is seldom that only one, single archetype is activated without other archetypes also participating in the relational network with other individuals (Papadopoulos 1996). Moreover, even in the context of one individual, one archetype does not act on its own but it triggers off related archetypes (in a compensatory or supplementary way). This means that mostly, archetypes affect individuals and groups not in isolation but in clusters/networks/constellations.

There are some additional facets of this process that Figure 1.1 depicts: first, archetypes (or archetypal constellations/networks) can affect not only individuals but also all the relationships and interactions individuals have; these include their interactions with their own personal history, with other individuals and groups, as well as the socio-cultural influences that are exerted on them. Second, it could be argued that although Jung did not emphasise it specifically, it follows from his theories that one's own personal history would not have only a one-way, causal influence on the individual (as the causal-reductive method would dictate); instead, the relationship individuals have with their own past would be affected by the shifting positions and perspectives that the individuals take vis-à-vis their own past. These changes can be the result of various factors, including, of course, the very organising influence of the archetypal constellations which, by their very nature, are not referring to the past but to the future, i.e., the archetypal effect is not retrogressive but prospective, with teleological finality (hence the dotted arrows on the figure are different from all the other arrows, denoting that the archetypal influence is of a different nature than the other kinds of interactions – it is an influence which moves constantly towards a finality). In effect, this means that a Jungian approach would imply (however paradoxical it may sound initially) that 'it is not only the

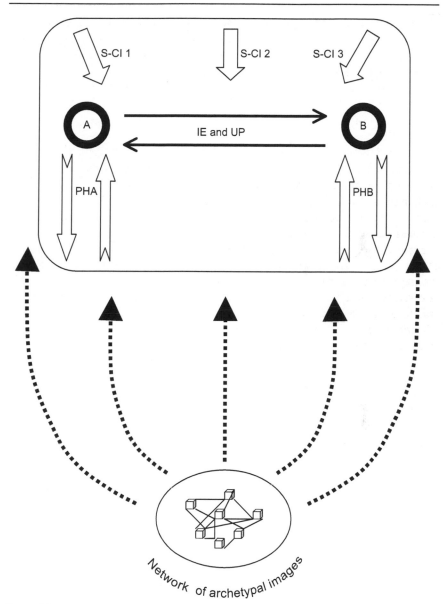

Figure 1.1

past that shapes the present, but also the present that shapes the past'
(Papadopoulos 1996: 158) in a reciprocal manner.

Figure 1.2 depicts the linear model of causal reductive epistemology.
According to this model, A leads to B and then C which means that
phenomenon B is caused by phenomenon A, and C is caused by B. For

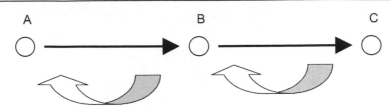

Figure 1.2

example, Jung characterised Freud's understanding of neurosis as linear: one's own childhood (A) causes the formation of one's personality (B) which then causes the neurotic symptoms (C). The therapeutic direction that this model dictates would be the linear route in reverse: the therapist would need to go back to find the causes of the symptom (C) by unravelling the personality (B) which should be carried out by exploring the childhood conflicts (A). Jung accepted the value of causal-reductive epistemology but his argument was that this was not the only model available and certainly not the best one for understanding complex phenomena in the context of their purposive functions, especially when the archetypal involvement is also taken into consideration; for those contexts, Jung felt that it was more appropriate to employ a constructive method that would highlight the function of 'finality': 'When a psychological fact has to be explained, it must be remembered that psychological data necessitate a twofold point of view, namely that of *causality* and that of *finality*' (Jung 1916/1948: par. 456), and 'To understand the psyche causally is to understand only one half of it' (Jung 1914: par. 398).

This means that Jung's understanding of complex psychological phenomena is based essentially on what could be termed an 'epistemology of finality' which may also encompass a linear epistemology. This epistemology of finality would be comparable to what modern systemic family therapists call 'circular' or 'systemic' epistemology' (cf. Becvar and Becvar 2002; Keeney 1983; Papadopoulos 1996, 1998). According to this epistemology, the three positions (A, B and C in Figure 1.2) are related not only in a linear, causal-reductive fashion but also in a way that one affects the other in a constant interaction (as in Figure 1.3), in a circular manner. After all, it should not be forgotten that the pattern of mutual influence is the essence of Jung's alchemical model, where the circle (mandala) was the symbol *par excellence* of wholeness. More concretely, the three positions (A, B and C) are in constant interaction among themselves in so far as the symptom has a further 'final', i.e., purposive function that affects the personality which then affects the way we approach our past.

Another important implication of this new epistemology is that all three positions (A, B and C) do not exist in isolation but are also affected by the activation of archetypal constellations (again, as always with the

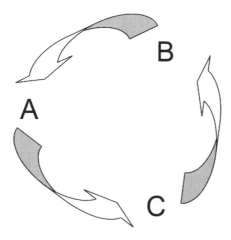

Figure 1.3

archetypes, in a teleological rather than causal-reductive way). This means that the interaction among the three positions is patterned by the wider archetypal networks that affect it. The therapeutic approach in circular epistemologies is not based on the attempt to trace 'the cause' or 'causes' but to connect meaningfully with the contextual *patterns* within which they are located. Jung referred to the 'sense of purpose' rather than clear explanation when he was addressing these relations and clarified that one cannot analyse, translate or interpret the archetype or its influence on the person (in a reductive way) but one has to relate and connect with it (in a constructive, purposive and teleological way):

> Hence the 'explanation' should always be such that the functional significance of the archetype remains unimpaired, so that an adequate and meaningful connection between the conscious mind and the archetype is assured.
>
> (Jung 1940: par. 271)

This sentence is perhaps the best description that Jung offered to describe the relationship between the knowing subject/person and the archetype. First, he places 'explanation' in inverted commas, ensuring that the reader does not confuse this type of engagement (between the subject and the archetype) with the rational process of offering logical explanations. Referring to this unique kind of engagement, many authors have resorted to the traditional distinction between understanding (*Verstehen*) and explanation (*Erklären*) in social sciences (cf. Jaspers 1923/1963; von Wright 1971), i.e., between comprehension/understanding, and logical/rational explanation, and opted for the former (e.g., Brooke 1991; Giannoni 2004; Hillman 1974;

Rauhala 1984; Shelburne 1988). Then, in the same sentence, Jung refers to the 'functional significance' of the archetype which he wishes remains 'unimpaired'. One should be reminded that Jung insisted on extending the meaning of 'function' beyond its usual causal connotation to include the teleological dimension (see above); also he uses the word 'significance' rather than meaning, evidently, in order to avoid any confusion with logical explanation and elaboration. Significance implies immanence, and not a type of objective knowledge. Thus, by 'functional significance' Jung here must be referring to the signification that would emerge from the archetype's engagement and, indeed, relationship with the network of the interacting subject/s, as it is depicted in Figure 1.4.

Although Jung, in the same sentence, addresses only the relationship between 'the conscious mind and the archetype', as it has been shown, none

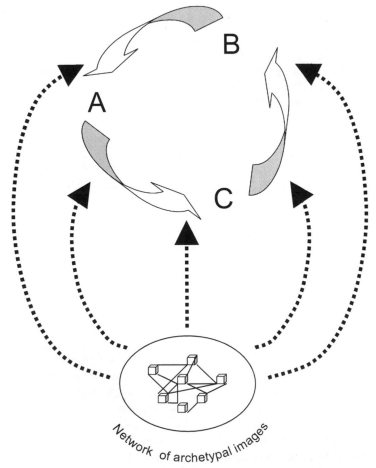

Figure 1.4

of these two are isolated and clearly delineated entities. In so far as both of them involve networks of relationships, the 'functional significance' here must be referring to the meaning that emerges from this engagement with all these interrelationships. Evidently, this meaning would not be a type of meaning that would be bestowed by means of external logical definition or explanation (cf. Mathers 2001).

Finally, Jung clarifies that his preferred relationship between the archetype and the 'conscious mind' should be that of a 'meaningful connection'. The primary characteristic Jung gives to the engagement between the knowing subject with the archetype is that of a 'connection', a relationship, an interaction, a 'meaningful' linkage that is not momentary but endures in time in order to deepen this association; once this 'meaningful connection' is established then a certain pathway is created, a new context is construed and an active process, a living experience begins which could lead gradually to the emergence of a new awareness, a sense of new purpose, thus, a new knowledge. But this knowledge would not be of the usual type of knowledge that a subject has of an object, but a sense of newness, of a shift in position by a person who becomes aware of his/her location within the network of interacting relationships as affected by the activation of the archetypal clusters within their purposive direction.

By examining in detail this sentence by Jung on archetypes, it is now possible to appreciate that what he wants to clearly convey is that the unique engagement (between the knowing subject and the archetype) is not a set of clearly defined logical statements but a living experience that has a purpose and finality, beyond causal-reductive and linear epistemologies. The grip that the archetypal constellation would have on an individual creates a new context, a shift, a new unique *pattern* that shapes and, indeed, patterns one's understanding of oneself, one's relationships with others and one's very sense of identity. This emerging pattern also connects an individual with the wider socio-cultural ecology (which includes the 'Collective Structures of Meaning' – Papadopoulos 1996) as well as with natural ecology in a prospective manner.

Jung used frequently the term *pattern* in relation to archetypes when he was referring to them as connected to 'patterns of behaviour'. Comparing the psychological realm with the biological, Jung used pattern to refer to set combinations of behaviours that are triggered off when a certain instinct is activated. In a parallel way, he argued that the archetype acts in a similar way as it triggers off thoughts, ideas, images, feelings etc., i.e., a series of psychological (in parallel to the biological) elements of human functioning (e.g., Jung 1954: par. 398). The term pattern (be it in the biological or psychological realm) implies a network of interrelationships as opposed to linear causality. The *Oxford English Dictionary* defines pattern as 'a regular or discernible form or order in which a series of things occur', and it is this cluster of interactions that these diagrams depict.

Such archetypal patterning creates a new context within which the individual acquires new perspectives and thinks and feels differently from before. In this way, it could be argued that with the introduction of archetypes, the Jungian epistemology could be considered as 'epistemological contextualism'. Epistemological contextualism asserts that whatever we know is contingent on its context and therefore different contexts set different epistemic standards and conditions (e.g., Annis 1978; Cohen 1998; Sosa and Kim 2000a; Williams 2001).

Thus, the further elaboration that Jung's epistemology underwent by the introduction of his archetypal theory, consisted of all these new considerations that were outlined above and depicted in Figures 1.1 to 1.4. The archetypal patterning pushed Jung's previous incomplete teleological inklings to new ways of formulating his old basic assumptions, articulating them into a new epistemology of archetypal finality which suggests that systemic patterns instead of isolated entities interact to create a new context within which new epistemic conditions arise.

Wider considerations

Pleroma and creatura, archetypes and systems

Gregory Bateson (1904–1980), the English anthropologist and social scientist (who is also one of the founders of systemic epistemology and family therapy) relied heavily on one part of the Jungian epistemology in order to develop his own work, and it would be important to examine the significance of this inter-pollination in relation to Jung's own epistemology. The irony is that this part has been mostly neglected not only by Jungian authors but by Jung himself.

To begin with it is important to be reminded that one of Bateson's many creative and innovative projects was remarkably similar to that of Jung's; he explained it succinctly as follows:

> Freudian psychology expanded the concept of mind inwards to include the whole communication system within the body – the autonomic, the habitual, and the vast range of unconscious process. What I am saying expands mind outwards. And both of these changes reduce the scope of the conscious self. A certain humility becomes appropriate, tempered by the dignity or joy of being part of something much bigger.
>
> (Bateson 1972: 461–462)

Even on the basis of this brief statement, it is possible to see immediately the similarities between Bateson and Jung – both looked for collective structures that affect the ways that individuals formulate their own knowledge;

moreover, both had immense respect for that 'something much bigger' than the individual (cf. Relph 1987). Bateson went about establishing his project by observing a fundamental epistemological flaw in the Cartesian epistemology and used Jung to redress it:

> I think that Descartes' first epistemological steps – the separation of 'mind' from 'matter' and the *cogito* – established bad premises, perhaps ultimately lethal premises, for Epistemology, and I believe that Jung's statement of connection between Pleroma and Creatura is a much healthier first step. Jung's epistemology starts from comparison of difference – *not* from matter.
>
> So I will define Epistemology as the science that studies the process of knowing – the interaction of the capacity to respond to differences, on the one hand, with the material world in which those differences somehow originate, on the other. We are concerned then with an *interface* between Pleroma and Creatura.
>
> (Bateson and Bateson 1987: 18)

'Pleroma' and 'creatura' are not part of the usual Jungian terminology. Jung first introduced these two terms in the long poem *Septem Sermones ad Mortuos* (Seven Sermons for the Dead) which he wrote between 1913 and 1916 (after he broke away from Freud) and circulated privately in 1925; it was published for the general public only in 1967. Jung hardly used these two terms again after this book, although it is understood that they formed the basic building blocks on which he developed further his ideas about archetypes and the collective unconscious (cf. Brenner 1990; Brewer 1996; Fodor 1964; Heisig 1972; Hoeller 1982; Hubback 1966; Jaffé 1972; Papadopoulos 1980; Segal 1992, 1995, 1998).

In the *Septem Sermones*, Jung wrote that pleroma is

> Nothingness [which] is the same as fullness . . . A thing that is infinite and eternal has no qualities, since it has all qualities . . . Therein both thinking and being cease, since the eternal and infinite possess no qualities . . . In the pleroma there is nothing and everything.
>
> (First Sermon)

This means that pleroma does not change.

> What is changeable, however, is creatura . . . The pleroma has all, distinctiveness and non-distinctiveness. Distinctiveness is creatura. Distinctiveness is its essence, and therefore it distinguishes. Therefore man discriminates because his nature is distinctiveness.
>
> (First Sermon)

Bateson commented that

> The pleroma is the world in which events are caused by forces and
> impacts and in which there are no 'distinctions'. Or, as I would say, no
> 'differences'. In the creatura, effects are brought about precisely by
> difference. In fact, this is the same old dichotomy between mind and
> substance . . . I suggest that 'pleroma' and 'creatura' are words which
> we could usefully adopt, and it is therefore worthwhile to look at the
> bridges which exist between these two 'worlds'. It is an oversimpli-
> fication to say that the 'hard sciences' deal only with the pleroma and
> that the sciences of the mind deal only with the creatura. There is more
> to it than that.
>
> (Bateson 1972: 456)

What is this more about?

Bateson was interested in understanding the dimensions of mind beyond
the ordinary human conscious processes and outside the limits of the
human skin, and observed that we can understand the mind also as

> it applies to a much wider range of those complex phenomena called
> 'systems', including systems consisting of multiple organisms or systems
> in which some of the parts are living and some are not, or even to
> systems in which there are no living parts.
>
> (Bateson and Bateson 1987: 19)

His reference to 'something bigger' would resonate with the Jungian
archetypal world which is beyond the individual but also within the person.

But what then is 'a mind', asks Bateson, and adds:

> if this is a useful notion, can one usefully make a plural and speak of
> 'minds' which might engage in interactions which are in turn mental? . . .
> The definition anchors the notion of a mind firmly to the arrangement
> of material parts.
>
> (Bateson and Bateson 1987: 18)

Some of the definition criteria he offers include: 'A mind is an aggregate of
interacting parts or components. The interaction between parts of mind is
triggered by difference . . . Mental process requires circular (or more complex) chains of determination' (Bateson and Bateson 1987: 18–19).

Using the cybernetic principles of feedback, Bateson understands a
system as created by information that is exchanged by its parts within it and
outside it, and defines information as 'the difference which make a difference'. Asking again and again the question 'What do I mean by "my"
mind?', he replies:

I suggest that the delimitation of an individual mind must always depend upon what phenomena we wish to understand or explain. Obviously there are lots of message pathways outside the skin, and these and the messages which they carry must be included as part of the mental system whenever they are relevant.

(Bateson 1972: 458)

Bateson gives the example of 'a tree and a man and an axe' to show that these three form a system of a complete circuit within which differences take place: 'if you want to explain or understand anything in human behavior, you are always dealing with total circuits' (Bateson 1972: 459) which could also include, of course, inanimate objects which belong to the pleroma (e.g., the axe). 'The elementary cybernetic system with its messages in circuit is, in fact, the simplest unit of mind' (p. 459). Following this argument, Bateson writes:

The cybernetic epistemology which I have offered you would suggest a new approach. The individual mind is immanent but not only in the body. It is immanent also in pathways and messages outside the body; and there is a larger Mind of which the individual mind is only a subsystem.

(Bateson 1972: 461)

This 'larger Mind' (with capital M!) would indeed correspond to the Jungian collective unconscious and the epistemological implication would be that the knowing subject is part of a wider knowledge pool with which the individual is in interaction with. So much so, that Bateson went as far as defining a person (what he called a 'self' in inverted commas) 'as a false reification of an improperly delimited part of this much larger field of interlocking processes' (1972: 331). This resonates with Jung's dictum: 'Individuation is an at-one-ment with oneself and at the same time with humanity since oneself is part of humanity' (Jung 1945: par. 227).

Finally, Bateson applied his epistemological premises to comprehend psychopathological states and in so doing, he commented on Jung's own mental state when he was writing the very poem *Septem Sermones*. Jung, many years after the event, wrote that at the time just before writing the poem his 'whole house was filled as if there were a crowd present, crammed full of spirits' (*MDR*, p. 216); Bateson attributed this to Jung's epistemological confusion.

If you get your epistemology confused, you go psychotic, and Jung was going through an epistemological crisis. So he sat down at his desk and picked up a pen and started to write. When he started to write all the ghosts disappeared and he wrote this little book [the *Septem Sermones*].

(Bateson 1972: 455)

Right at the beginning of the poem/book Jung wrote about the distinction between pleroma and creatura and, therefore, it seems that it was that differentiation which brought sanity to his confused 'epistemological crisis'. Bateson wrote that according to 'the vulgar jargon of psychiatry' Jung's 'epistemological crisis' would be called 'psychotic' (Bateson 1972: 455). This means that epistemology is not just an abstract concept but, constituting the very way one organises one's knowledge, it can certainly also affect one's psychological and mental state. It should not be forgotten that Bateson's earlier double-bind theory of schizophrenia was also based on an epistemological perspective (Bateson 1956).

Commenting on Jung's idea that archetypes are 'pleromatic' (Jung 1952b), Bateson wrote: 'It is surely true, however, that constellations of ideas may seem subjectively to resemble "forces" when their ideational character is unrecognized' (1972: 455n). This means that confusion between the archetypal content that interacts with the individual (creatura) and pure archetypes (pleroma) can lead to an epistemological crisis. If an individual appropriates pleromatic material he/she is then in danger of losing discrimination (and difference), and of ceasing to have awareness that he/she is only one interacting part of a wider system; such a misappropriation would not only be illusional but could also be delusional, indeed, as one would identify with the bigger whole, the entire system. Jung referred to this state as psychological inflation, when the archetype takes over one's personality. Without the discrimination and differentiation, there is no information and therefore no system; instead, there is the illusion/delusion that there are just 'forces' that act on their own. Such a condition can lead an epistemological crisis to become even an epistemological breakdown.

As Bateson emphasised, it is the interface between pleroma and creatura that is of importance, it is this interface, the interaction that creates a system that can utilise difference in order to be activated by the information that these differences create. Any alternatives are detrimental both epistemologically and psychologically. The individual cannot be confused with the collective, the archetype cannot substitute the individual. Here lies the unique clue to Jung's use of archetypes that, on the one hand, they can be facilitative and healing in so far as they can enrich the individual personality by expanding its perspectives and opening it up to wider realms, making it aware of 'being part of something much bigger' (Bateson 1972: 462), or, on the other hand, they can flood the personality and take over it in a way that differences between them and the personality become blurred; in the latter case, archetypes would have a detrimental effect on the personality and they would create what could be called a pathological state.

Echoing Jung, Bateson exclaimed that 'A certain humility becomes appropriate, tempered by the dignity or joy of being part of something much bigger (Bateson 1972: 461–462).

Jung's Socratic ignorance and Gnostic knowledge

The last facet of Jung's epistemology that this chapter will examine is a duality of Jung's own approach to epistemological openness.

It has been suggested that one could

> distinguish two opposing epistemologies which Jung, wittingly or unwittingly, actually espoused. The first of those is closer to what could be called 'Socratic ignorance', while the second is essentially a 'Gnostic epistemology'.
>
> (Papadopoulos 1997: 298)

According to the former,

> Jung stands clearly against any oversweeping statements of the 'nothing but' kind, and in the true spirit of Socratic ignorance makes such statements as 'Stereotyped interpretation of dream-motifs is to be avoided . . . Even if one has great experience in these matters, one is again and again obliged, before each dream, to admit to one's ignorance and, renouncing all preconceived ideas, to prepare for something entirely unexpected' (Jung 1948: para. 543) or '. . . clearly, dream-interpretation is in the first place an experience which has immediate validity for only two persons' (para. 539).
>
> (Papadopoulos 1997: 298)

These are characteristic statements of Jung's insistence not to take anything for granted, not to assume any previous knowledge before examining a phenomenon in its own right, not to impose pre-packaged theoretical formulations onto a situation but, instead, retain an openness to examine the uniqueness of each given circumstance. In the clinical setting, this meant that Jung wanted to expose himself to the specificity of each analysand and endeavoured to grasp the meaning of his interaction with him/her at that given time without importing previous biases. This is why he maintained that the dream has meaning only in the context of the analytical interaction, i.e., between the analyst and the analysand.

Socratic ignorance can be understood in two ways. The first refers to Socrates' stance not to possess any wisdom but his only wisdom consisted of his awareness of his own ignorance. An example of this is presented in Plato's *Apology*, where Socrates says,

> Well, although I do not suppose that either of us knows anything really beautiful and good, I am better off than he is – for he knows nothing, and thinks that he knows. I neither know nor think that I know. In this latter particular, then, I seem to have slightly the advantage of him.

The second way of understanding the Socratic ignorance is in terms of the way he applied it in his conversations with others. This refers to his actual method of making use of his 'ignorance'. Characteristically, Socrates tells Theaetetus: 'You forget, my friend, that I neither know, nor profess to know, anything of these matters; you are the person who is in labour, I am the barren midwife' (Plato's *Theaetetus*). By asserting his own ignorance of the subject, Socrates frees himself and his interlocutor to investigate and explore the various underlying assumptions as well as dimensions of the phenomena they were discussing. In other words, his task was by and large epistemological in nature and he likened it to that of the midwife, i.e., to draw out of a person, to facilitate the birth of the knowledge about a certain topic, hence his method was termed 'maieutic' (*maia*, in Greek, being a midwife).

There are striking similarities between the Socratic maieutics and the Jungian approach which did not elude Jung (e.g., Jung 1913: par. 519, 1943: par. 26, 1912: par. 437). In addition to adopting a 'Socratic-ignorance' approach in his analytical clinical work, Jung's insistence that, above all, he was an 'empiricist' and 'phenomenologist' in his wider researches points to the same epistemological openness. He was very proud to quote a comment made about his empirical approach in the *British Medical Journal* (on 9 February 1952), 'a source that would seem to be above suspicion. "Facts first and theories later is the keynote of Jung's work. He is an empiricist first and last." This view meets with my approval' (Jung 1952a: par. 1502). Also, distinguishing between an approach that follows blindly set theories as opposed to his own approach that used theoretical reflection to bind together his empirical findings, Jung expressed his epistemological credo as follows:

> Although I have often been called a philosopher, I am an empiricist and adhere as such to the phenomenological standpoint. I trust that it does not conflict with the principles of scientific empiricism if one occasionally makes certain reflections which go beyond a mere accumulation and classification of experience. As a matter of fact I believe that experience is not even possible without reflection, because 'experience' is a process of assimilation without which there could be no understanding. As this statement indicates, I approach psychological matters from a scientific and not from a philosophical standpoint. In as much as religion has a very important psychological aspect, I deal with it from a purely empirical point of view, that is, I restrict myself to the observation of phenomena and I eschew any metaphysical or philosophical considerations. I do not deny the validity of these other considerations but I cannot claim to be competent to apply them correctly.
>
> (Jung 1938/1940: par. 2)

It is not difficult to identify Jung's 'Socratic ignorance' as it coincides with Jung's own way that he characterised himself and with the way he has been characterised by almost all Jungian authors. What has not been examined often is Jung's opposite epistemological stance that he also followed, evidently without him being aware of its antithetical direction; this was termed 'Gnostic epistemology' (Papadopoulos 1997). According to this epistemology, Jung was by no means open and his researches followed his own pre-established ideas about phenomena and, although he always waved the empiricist 'Socratic-ignorance' banner, in fact, his approach also included closed and predetermined epistemologies.

The most striking single quotation that betrays Jung's Gnostic epistemology is his reply to John Freeman's question (in the famous *Face to Face* interview for BBC Television in 1959) 'Do you now believe in God?', to which Jung replied: 'Difficult to answer. I *know*. I don't believe. I know' (McGuire and Hull 1977: 414).

Jung 'knew' and no further explanation was needed. Such an approach to knowledge was not foreign to Jung and it can be found throughout his writings. However, in so far as he did not ever admit to it, there are no clear quotations in which he actually stated his adherence to this type of epistemology. Instead, his 'Gnostic epistemology' can be traced in his arguments. For example, in his Foreword to Father Victor White's book, Jung claims that

> Psychology, like every empirical science, cannot get along without auxiliary concepts, hypotheses, and models. But the theologian as well as the philosopher is apt to make the mistake of taking them for metaphysical postulates. The atom of which the physicist speaks is not an *hypostasis*, it is a *model*. Similarly my concept of archetype or of psychic energy is only an auxiliary idea which can be exchanged at any time for a better formula.
>
> (Jung 1952c: par. 460)

This sounds a fine expression of epistemological openness; however, as we know, neither Jung nor any Jungian author has ever exchanged the theory of archetypes with a 'better formula' and archetypes are not treaded as models but very much as actual hypostatic entities.

In the very same paragraph, Jung states categorically that 'In reality, . . . individuation is an expression of that biological process . . . by which every living thing becomes what it was destined to become from the beginning' (Jung 1952c: par. 460). There is no hypothetical openness here; Jung declares dogmatically that 'in reality' this is how it is. Moreover, with an equal self-assuredness he pronounces that 'This process naturally expresses itself in man as much as psychically as somatically' and claims that such an assertion 'is by no means a case of mystical speculations, but of clinical observations and their interpretations through comparison with analogous phenomena in other fields'. As if he gets intoxicated by his own words, in the next paragraph he actually goes as far as professing that 'I proceed from facts which everyone is at liberty to verify' (Jung 1952c: par. 461). By boasting this kind of objectivity and external verification, Jung unwittingly abandons his unique epistemology of psychic reality and psychological experiential interactions, and is seduced into adopting positivistic methodologies of the exact sciences which he criticises elsewhere as inappropriate for understanding the uniqueness of psychological phenomena.

At the same time, such categorical claims not only fall very short of their target but also betray Jung's closed system of beliefs. Within the space of two paragraphs he advocates epistemological openness, accepting his theories as working hypotheses and then, he moves to profess his definitive 'knowledge' of phenomena which in a tautological fashion confirm his theories. It is this kind of epistemology that was termed 'Gnostic epistemology' (Papadopoulos 1997); it is the epistemology that provides ready-made answers, offers proclamations and views phenomena within a closed system of beliefs.

Dehing, pointing to 'an internal contradiction in Jung's approach', argues that 'the agnostic empiricist every now and then turns into a prophet. Most of the time Jung's opinions are formulated as hypotheses, but sometimes they become hypostases' (Dehing 1990: 393). Thus, the agnostic and epistemological openness in Jung interchanges with Jung's own Gnosticism which is characterised by his unshakable belief in the correctness of his own assertions and general theories, thus, runs in parallel to his own Socratic ignorance. When Jung adopts this kind of epistemology he implies 'that certain insights are only available to the initiates' (Papadopoulos 1997: 298). This kind of elitism was another characteristic of the Gnostic movement (Lee 1987).

It has been argued that

> the detrimental aspects and implications of Jung's gnosticism have not yet been sufficiently appreciated; besides an elitist attitude, these include a closed system of circular tautology: people believe something to be true and whatever they see around them they judge according to these beliefs, while all the time they also believe that they are open and that their beliefs are based on real evidence. This approach cannot be enriched by new elements and therefore it cannot develop further; the initiates are convinced that their beliefs are absolutely true and correspond with *the* reality. This closed approach not only is self-fulfilling but it also promotes fanaticism.
>
> (Papadopoulos 1997: 299)

This is not surprising because as even Hans Jonas admitted, 'In the gnostic context . . . "knowledge" has an emphatically religious or supernatural meaning and refers to objects which we nowadays should call those of faith rather than of reason' (Jonas 1963/1992: 34); further, he also clarifies that in certain Gnostic authors, 'the "knowledge" is not only an instrument of salvation but itself the very form in which the goal of salvation, i.e., ultimate perfection, is possessed' (p. 35). This confirms that what Jung was after was not just an epistemologically open hypothesis but a transformative kind of knowledge that would have far more than syllogistic functions and characteristics.

The romantic idea of the Gnostic rebels who were against the establishment is only one side of the Gnostic tradition and this is the one that has been favoured by Jung and Jungians. Yet, there are other more unhelpful sides to Gnosticism that have not been taken into consideration seriously, as yet, by Jungian authors. The critiques of Gnosticism that, for example, Eric Voegelin (1968/2005), Manfred Henningsen (1999) and Philip J. Lee (1987) formulated are totally ignored by Jungians who seem entirely satisfied by the Gnostic proclamations to truth that Jung issued. It may be sobering to consider that, for example, the political philosopher Voegelin (1968) characterised both Marx and Hitler as modern Gnostics!

In the clinical context, the opposite to Jung's Socratic ignorance, i.e., his Gnostic epistemology, produces the Jung that, by virtue of feeling justified that he is in touch with the psyche, knows what is good for his clients and prescribes specific actions for them, a practice which is totally opposite to his Socratic openness. For example, Jung was also known to have been quite explicitly prescriptive to his analysands, telling them what specific actions and directions to take in their lives (e.g., Jung, *MDR*, pp. 156f).

Instead of conclusion

In so far as epistemology studies the ways we formulate what and how we know, it should be indispensable for a proper study of psychotherapeutic approaches. Jung's ambivalent stance towards philosophy seems to have prevented him from acknowledging fully the implications of his own epistemological sensitivity. This chapter has endeavoured (within a severely restricted space) to present and discuss some of Jung's epistemological positions that can contribute to the deeper understanding of the theory and practice not only of analytical psychology but also of other psychotherapeutic approaches.

Jung has made a considerable contribution to the epistemology of psychology of therapeutic interactions and it is important that one appreciates his contribution in its totality (i.e., in the way the various parts of it interrelate) and not only in terms of its isolated elements. The last argument that this chapter developed, about Jung's two opposing epistemological positions, does not invalidate his significant contribution. Like all great pioneers, Jung succumbed to the intoxication of his own discoveries and it was only human that there was also a streak in him that wanted to stick to his own theories and propagate them further with the fervour of a zealot. In other words, it is important to appreciate that there are two Jungs, so to speak – the one with an open epistemology and Socratic ignorance who was constructionist and relational, and the other Jung who, following Gnostic epistemology, was, in fact, essentialist and universalist.

Further research in this field is much required in order to locate Jung's contribution in the context of other investigations in the epistemology of psychotherapy (e.g., Barratt 1984; Christou 1963; Clark and Wright 1986; Goldberg 1988; Grünbaum 1984; Haynal 1993; Hogenson 2004; Knorr Cetina 1981, 1999; Mackay 1989; Mills 2004; Orange 1995; Phillips 1996; Ricoeur 1970, 1981; Rorty 1991; Spence 1982; Strenger 1991).

As Jung himself emphasised, it is important to have diversity of views and not only to pursue one-sided perspectives: 'No line of research which asserted that its subject was . . . a "nothing but" has ever made any contribution to knowledge' (Jung 1944: par. 120).

Note

1 This remarkable twist is also discussed, in a different context, by Professor Gaillard in Chapter 14 of this *Handbook*.

References

Adler, A. (1912) *The Neurotic Character*. San Francisco, CA: Alfred Adler Institute, 2002.

Annis, D. (1978) 'A contextual theory of epistemic justification'. *American Philosophical Quarterly*, 15: 213–219.

Barratt, B.B. (1984) *Psychic Reality and Psychoanalytic Knowing*. London: Analytic Press.

Bateson, G. (1956) 'Toward a theory of schizophrenia', in G. Bateson (1972) *Steps to an Ecology of Mind*. New York: Ballantine.

—— (1972) *Steps to an Ecology of Mind*. New York: Ballantine.

—— (1979) *Mind and Nature: A Necessary Unity*. New York: Dutton.

Bateson, G. and Bateson, M.C. (1987) *Angels Fear*. New York: Macmillan.

Becvar, D.S. and Becvar, R.J. (2003) *Family Therapy: A Systemic Integration*, 5th edn. Boston, MA: Allyn and Bacon.

Bernasconi, R. and Critchley, S. (eds) (1989) *Re-Reading Levinas*. Bloomington, IN: Indiana University Press.

Brenner, E.M. (1990) 'Gnosticism and psychology: Jung's *Septem Sermones ad Mortuos*'. *Journal of Analytical Psychology*, 35(4): 397–419.

Brewer, M. (1996) 'Jung's interpretation of Gnostic myths in the light of Nag Hammadi'. *Harvest: Journal for Jungian Studies*, 42(2): 93–116.

Brill, A.A. (1946) *Lectures on Psychoanalytic Psychiatry*. New York: Knopf.

Brooke, R. (1991) *Jung and Phenomenology*. London: Routledge.

Christou, E. (1963) *The Logos of the Soul*. Vienna: Dunquin Press.

Clark, S. and Wright, C. (eds) (1986) *Psychoanalysis, Mind and Science*. Oxford: Basil Blackwell.

Cohen, R.A. (ed.) (1986) *Face-to-Face with Levinas*. Albany, NY: State University of New York Press.

Cohen, S. (1998) 'Contextualist solutions to epistemological problems'. *Australasian Journal of Philosophy*, 76: 289–306.

Coulter, J. (1995) *The Social Construction of the Mind*. New York: Macmillan.

Crowden, A. (2003) 'Ethically sensitive mental health care: is there a need for a unique ethics for psychiatry?' *Australian and New Zealand Journal of Psychiatry*, 37(2): 143–149.

Dehing, J. (1990) 'Jung and knowledge: from gnosis to praxis'. *Journal of Analytical Psychology*, 35(4): 377–396.

de Shaser, S. (1982) *Patterns of Brief Family Therapy: An Ecosystemic Approach*. New York: Guilford.

Dieckmann, H. (1991) *Methods in Analytical Psychology: An Introduction*. Wilmette, IL: Chiron.

Fodor, N. (1964) 'Jung's sermons to the dead'. *Psychoanalytic Review*, 51: 74–78.

Freud, S. (1910) 'The future prospects of psycho-analytic therapy', in *Standard Edition* 11. London: Hogarth Press.

Fulford, B., Morris, K., Sadler, J. and Stanghellini, G. (eds) (2003) *Nature and Narrative: An Introduction to the New Philosophy of Psychiatry*. Oxford: Oxford University Press.

Garnett, R.L. (1993) 'Family resemblance'. *Harvest: Journal for Jungian Studies*, 39: 97–113.

Gergen, K.J. and Davis, K.E. (eds) (1985) *The Social Construction of the Person*. New York: Springer Verlag.

Gergen, M. and Gergen, K.J. (2003) *Social Construction: A Reader*. London: Sage.

Giannoni, M. (2004) 'Epistemological premise, developmental idea, main motivation in Jung's and Kohut's psychoanalysis: looking for some analogies'. *Journal of Analytical Psychology*, 49(2): 161–175.

Glaser, B.G. and Strauss, A.L. (1967) *The Discovery of Grounded Theory: Strategies for Qualitative Research*. Chicago, IL: Aldine/Atherton.

Goldberg, A. (1988) *A Fresh Look at Psychoanalysis: The View from Self Psychology*. Hillsdale, NJ: Analytic Press.

Grünbaum, A. (1984) *The Foundations of Psychoanalysis*. Berkeley, CA: University of California Press.

Haule, J.R. (1984) 'From somnambulism to the archetypes: the French roots of Jung's split with Freud'. *Psychoanalytic Review*, 71(4): 635–659.

Haynal, A. (1993) *Psychoanalysis and the Sciences: Epistemology – History*. London: Karnac.

Heisig, J. (1972) '*The VII Sermones*: play and theory'. *Spring*: 206–218.

Henningsen, M. (1999) *Eric Voegelin: Modernity without Restraint: The Political Religions, the New Science of Politics, and Science, Politics, and Gnosticism* (Collected Works of Eric Voegelin). Columbia, MO: University of Missouri Press.

Hermans, H.J.M. and Hermans-Jansen, E. (1995) *Self-narratives: The Construction of Meaning in Psychotherapy*. New York: Guilford.

Hillman, J. (1974) 'Archetypal theory: C.G. Jung', in J. Hillman (1978) *Loose Ends: Primary Papers in Archetypal Psychology*. Dallas, TX: Spring.

Hoeller, S.A. (1982) *The Gnostic Jung and the Seven Sermons to the Dead*. Wheaton, IL: Theosophical.

Hogenson, G. (2004) 'Archetypes: emergence and the psyche's deep structure', in J. Cambray and L. Carter (eds) *Analytical Psychology: Contemporary Perspectives in Jungian Analysis*. London: Routledge.

Horne, M. (2002) 'Aristotle's ontogenesis: a theory of individuation which integrates the classical and developmental perspectives'. *Journal of Analytical Psychology*, 47(4): 613–628.

Hubback, J. (1966) 'VII Sermones ad Mortuos'. *Journal of Analytical Psychology*, 11(2): 95–112.

Jaffé, A. (1972) *The Creative Phases of Jung's Life*. Dallas, TX: Spring.

Jaspers, K. (1923/1963) *General Psychopathology*. Manchester: Manchester University Press.

Jonas, H. (1963/1992) *The Gnostic Religion*. London: Routledge.

Jones, A.M. (2002) 'Teleology and the hermeneutics of hope: Jungian interpretation in light of the work of Paul Ricoeur'. *Journal of Jungian Theory and Practice*, 4(2): 45–55.

Jung, C.G. (1896–1899) *The Zofingia Lectures*, in *The Collected Works of C.G. Jung*, ed. Sir Herbert Read, Michael Fordham and Gerhard Adler, executive ed. William McGuire, trans. R.F.C. Hull, 21 volumes (hereafter *CW*). Supplementary Volume A. London: Routledge and Kegan Paul; Princeton, NJ: Princeton University Press, 1983.

—— (1902) 'On the psychology and pathology of the so-called occult phenomena', in *CW* 1: pars. 1–165.

—— (1907) 'Associations d'idées familiales'. *Archives de Psychologie*, 7(26): 160–168.

—— (1909) 'The family constellation', in *CW* 2: 466–479.

—— (1911) 'On the doctrine of complexes', in *CW* 2: 598–604.

—— (1912) 'New paths in psychology', in *CW* 7: pars. 407–441.

—— (1913) 'The theory of psychoanalysis', in *CW* 4: pars. 203–522.

—— (1914) 'On psychological understanding', in *CW* 3: pars. 388–424.

—— (1913/1916) *Septem Sermones ad Mortuos*, in S.A. Hoeller (1982) *The Gnostic Jung and the Seven Sermons to the Dead*. Wheaton, IL: Theosophical.

—— (1916/1948) 'General aspects of dream psychology', in *CW* 8: pars. 443–529.

—— (1917) 'Prefaces to *Collected Papers on Analytical Psychology*', in *CW* 4: pars. 670–692.

—— (1921) *Psychological Types*. *CW* 6.

—— (1932a) '"Ulysses": a monologue', in *CW* 15: pars. 163–203.

—— (1932b) 'Psychotherapists or the clergy', in *CW* 11: par. 497.

—— (1934a) 'The practical use of dream analysis', in *CW* 16: pars. 294–352.

—— (1934b) 'The soul and death', in *CW* 8: pars. 796–815.

—— (1935a) 'Editorial for Zentralblatt 8:1', in *CW* 10: par. 548.

—— (1935b) 'The Tavistock Lectures', in *CW* 18: pars. 1–415.

—— (1938/1940) 'Psychology and religion', in *CW* 11: pars. 1–168.

Jung, C.G. (1940) 'The psychology of the child archetype', in *CW* 9i: pars. 259–305.
—— (1943) 'On the psychology of the unconscious', in *CW* 7: pars. 1–201.
—— (1944) *Psychology and Alchemy. CW* 12.
—— (1945) 'Psychotherapy today', in *CW* 16: pars. 212–229.
—— (1947) 'On the nature of the psyche', in *CW* 8: pars. 343–442.
—— (1948) 'On the nature of dreams', in *CW* 8: pars. 530–569.
—— (1949) 'Foreword to Neumann: *Depth Psychology and a New Ethic*', in *CW* 18: pars. 1408–1420.
—— (1952a) 'Religion and psychology: a reply to Martin Buber', in *CW* 18: pars. 1499–1513.
—— (1952b) 'Answer to Job', in *CW* 11: pars. 553–758.
—— (1952c) 'Foreword to Fr. Victor White's *God and the Unconscious* and Werblowsky's *Lucifer and Prometheus*', in *CW* 11: 449–467.
—— (1954) 'On the nature of the psyche', in *CW* 8: pars. 343–442.
—— (1958) 'Flying saucers: a modern myth', in *CW* 10: pars. 589–824.
—— (1961/1995) *Memories, Dreams, Reflections*. London: Fontana.
Jung, C.G. and Riklin, F. (1904) 'The associations of normal subjects', in *CW* 2: 3–196.
Keeney, B.P. (1983) *Aesthetics of Change*. London: Guilford.
Knorr Cetina, K. (1981) *The Manufacture of Knowledge: An Essay on the Constructivist and Contextual Nature of Science*. Oxford: Pergamon.
—— (1999) *Epistemic Cultures: How the Sciences Make Knowledge*. Cambridge, MA: Harvard University Press.
Lee, P.J. (1987) *Against the Protestant Gnostics*. Oxford: Oxford University Press.
Levinas, E. (1984) 'Ethics as first philosophy', in S. Hand (ed.) (1989) *The Levinas Reader*. London: Blackwell.
Liddell, H.G. and Scott, R. (1869) *A Greek–English Lexicon*. Oxford: Clarendon Press.
Mackay, N. (1989) *Motivation and Explanation: An Essay on Freud's Philosophy of Science*. Madison, WI: International Universities Press.
McFarland Solomon, H. and Twyman, M. (2003) *The Ethical Attitude in Analytical Practice*. London: Free Association.
McGuire, W. (ed.) (1974) *The Freud/Jung Letters*. London: Hogarth Press and Routledge and Kegan Paul.
McGuire, W. and Hull, R.F.C. (1977) *C.G. Jung Speaking: Interviews and Encounters*. London: Thames and Hudson.
Maeder, A. (1913) 'Über das Traumproblem'. *Jahrbuch fur psychoanalytische und psychopathologische Forschungen*, 5: 647–686.
Mathers, D. (2001) *An Introduction to Meaning and Purpose in Analytical Psychology*. London: Routledge.
Mills, J. (2004) *Psychoanalysis at the Limit: Epistemology, Mind, and the Question of Science*. Albany, NY: State University of New York Press.
Nagy, M. (1991) *Philosophical Issues in the Psychology of C.G. Jung*. Albany, NY: State University of New York Press.
Neil, J. and Kniskern, D. (eds) (1982) *From Psyche to System: The Evolving Therapy of Carl Whitaker*. New York: Guilford.
Orange, D.M. (1995) *Emotional Understanding: Studies in Psychoanalytic Epistemology*. London: Guilford.

Papadopoulos, R.K. (1980) 'The dialectic of the Other in the psychology of C.G. Jung: a metatheoretical investigation', PhD thesis, University of Cape Town.

—— (1984) 'Jung and the concept of the Other', in R.K. Papadopoulos and G.S. Saayman (eds) *Jung in Modern Perspective*. London: Wildwood.

—— (1996) 'Archetypal family therapy: developing a Jungian approach to working with families', in L. Dodson and T. Gibson (eds) *Psyche and Family*. Wilmette, IL: Chiron.

—— (1997) 'Is teaching Jung within university possible? A response to David Tacey'. *Journal of Analytical Psychology*, 42(2): 297–301.

—— (1998) 'Jungian perspectives in new contexts', in A. Casement (ed.) *The Jungians Today*. London and New York: Routledge.

—— (2002) 'The other other: when the exotic other subjugates the familiar other'. *Journal of Analytical Psychology*, 47(2): 163–188.

—— (2005) 'Political violence, trauma and mental health interventions', in D. Kalmanowitz and B. Lloyd (eds) *Art Therapy and Political Violence: With Art, Without Illusion*. London: Brunner-Routledge.

Papadopoulos, R.K. and Saayman, G.S. (1989) 'Towards a Jungian approach to family therapy'. *Harvest: Journal for Jungian Studies*, 35: 95–120.

Penna, E. (2004) 'Methodological perspectives in Jung's *Collected Works*'. *Harvest: International Journal for Jungian Studies*, 50(1): 100–119.

Phillips, J. (1996) 'Key concepts: hermeneutics'. *Philosophy, Psychiatry, and Psychology*, 3(1): 61–69.

Rauhala, L. (1984) 'The basic views of C.G. Jung in the light of hermeneutic metascience', in R.K. Papadopoulos and G.S. Saayman (eds) *Jung in Modern Perspective*. London: Wildwood.

Relph, A. (1987) 'A Jung–Bateson correspondence'. *Australian and New Zealand Journal of Family Therapy*, 8(1): 1–5.

Ricoeur, P. (1970) *Freud and Philosophy*. New Haven, CT: Yale University Press.

—— (1981) *Hermeneutics and the Human Sciences*. New York: Cambridge University Press.

Rorty, R. (1991) *Objectivity, Relativism and Truth*. Cambridge: Cambridge University Press.

Rychlak, J.F. (1968) *A Philosophy of Science of Personality Theory*. Boston, MA: Houghton Mifflin.

—— (1973) *Introduction to Personality and Psychotherapy: A Theory Construction Approach*. Boston, MA: Houghton Mifflin.

—— (1984) 'Jung as dialectician and teleologist', in R.K. Papadopoulos and G.S. Saayman (eds) *Jung in Modern Perspective*. London: Wildwood.

Sarbin, T.R. (ed.) (1986) *Narrative Psychology: The Storied Nature of Human Conduct*. New York: Praeger.

Segal, R.A. (1992) *The Gnostic Jung*. London: Routledge.

—— (1995) 'The allure of Gnosticism for Jung'. *Harvest: Journal for Jungian Studies*, 41(1): 78–88.

—— (1998) 'Jung and Gnosticism: a reply to Matthew Brewer'. *Harvest: Journal for Jungian Studies*, 44(1): 113–136.

Selvini-Palazzoli, M., Cecchin, G., Prata, G. and Boscolo, L. (1978) *Paradox and Counterparadox*. New York: Jason Aronson.

Shamdasani, S. (2003) *Jung and the Making of Modern Psychology: The Dream of a Science*. Cambridge: Cambridge University Press.

Shelburne, W.A. (1988) *Mythos and Logos in the Thought of Carl Jung*. Albany, NY: State University of New York Press.

Sosa, E. and Kim, J. (2000a) 'Epistemic contextualism', in E. Sosa and J. Kim (eds) *Epistemology: An Anthology*. Oxford: Blackwell.

—— (eds) (2000b) *Epistemology: An Anthology*. Oxford: Blackwell.

Spence, D. (1982) *Narrative Truth and Historical Truth*. New York: Norton.

Strenger, C. (1991) *Between Hermeneutics and Science: An Essay on the Epistemology of Psychoanalysis* (Psychological Issues, Monograph 59). New York: International Universities Press.

Taylor, E.I. (1998) 'Jung before Freud, not Freud before Jung: Jung's influence in American psychotherapeutic circles before 1909'. *Journal of Analytical Psychology*, 43(1): 97–114.

Voegelin, E. (1968/2005) *Science, Politics, and Gnosticism*. Wilmington, DE: ISI Books.

von Franz, M.-L. (1975) *C.G. Jung: His Myth in our Time*. New York: C.G. Jung Foundation for Analytical Psychology.

—— (1983) 'Introduction to Jung, C.G. (1896–99) *The Zofingia Lectures*'. *CW* Supplementary Volume A. London: Routledge and Kegan Paul.

von Wright, G.H. (1971) *Explanation and Understanding*. London: Routledge and Kegan Paul.

Watzlawick, P., Weakland, J. and Fisch, R. (1974) *Change: Principles of Problem Formation and Problem Resolution. New York: W.W. Norton.*

Whan, M. (1987) 'On the nature of practice'. *Spring: An Annual of Archetypal Psychology and Jungian Thought*: 77–86.

Williams, M. (2001) 'Contextualism, externalism and epistemic standards'. *Philosophical Studies*, 103: 1–23.

Young, G. (1997) *Adult Development, Therapy, and Culture: A Postmodern Synthesis*. New York: Plenum Press.

Chapter 2

The unconscious

Personal and collective

Christopher Hauke

The unconscious before we named it

The idea of the unconscious – whether 'collective' or 'personal' – does not, of course, begin with Jung or Freud. The concept of a mind, or spirit or 'will' outside of, and beyond, the everyday 'conscious' mentality of human beings seems – as far as we can tell – to have existed across cultures and throughout human history. In other eras, the degree to which this 'mind' resided in powerful others such as gods, animals, elements like the wind and rivers, or a single God, was emphasised much more than the modern idea that this was an aspect of the minds of human beings themselves. The way that serious attention was paid to dreams seems to be clear evidence of humankind's respect for, and interest in, a non-conscious aspect of mind. But we know from anthropological investigations that the conceptual *separation* between a conscious and an unconscious mind (as we divide them now), is not necessarily the form of understanding shared by humans living far from our own contemporary urban, industrialised lives. For example, Benjamin Paul writes of a case of fugue and mental breakdown in a Guatemalan village woman where the way that her condition was understood was not in terms of conscious and unconscious processes but an understanding advanced by an expert Shaman who attributed her condition to ancestral spirits who were expressing anger at her and her husband's mother and father, and all the grandparents; consequently, what was required of her was not any psychological treatment but a form of penance (Paul 1953/1967: 150–165). Traditional practices such as investigating dreams or ingesting psychotropic drugs in an effort to achieve personal communion with deities – sometimes experienced in animal forms – which would then supply the practitioner with special knowledge to bring back to the world of normal consciousness, bear close comparison to the way that C.G. Jung conceived an 'unconscious' that had something to tell us. Moreover, such ritual practices – whether by individual Shaman, groups at religious ceremonies, or as part of rites of passage – were conducted in an agreed social context. The revelations from the spirit world – or the 'unconscious' – thus carried a shared meaning for the whole group, and one that became established over many generations of repetition of instruction, practice and storytelling. Viewed in this way, we note how development of the idea that humans could usefully access religious and practical knowledge not normally present in the (conscious) mind arose both as an individual and as a collective experience. Contemporary scholarship now emphasises that our human nature as communal beings is every bit as important as our biological being and provides a robust means of examining phenomena which has previously relied solely on biological or evolutionary explanations (cf. Malik 2000). We shall be returning to these speculations about the unconscious when we come to consider Jung's modern reformulation of the collective unconscious early in the twentieth century.

The unconscious just before Freud and Jung

Our contemporary ideas around the personal and collective unconscious also have their roots somewhat earlier than Freud and Jung – partly in Enlightenment thinking (although, ironically, the unconscious mind was rejected as a concept by Enlightenment) and notably in the German Romantic philosophy of Carus, Schopenhauer, von Hartmann and von Schelling. Whyte has written of how, 'The general conception of unconscious mental processes was *conceivable . . .* around 1700, *topical* around 1800, and *fashionable* around 1870–1880' (Whyte 1960: 168–169; emphasis in original). I suggest that earlier literature such as the plays of William Shakespeare (who died in 1616) indicate ideas of inherent conflict between the known and the unknown aspects of our mental processes; this is seen in the depiction of characters such as Hamlet and King Lear. Furthermore, references from one character to another such as 'she doth protest too much' draws attention to a defensive psychological strategy, suggesting that Shakespeare and his audience held an idea of human mentality where the subject was less aware of him or herself, but such hidden 'unconscious' processes were revealed to others through attitude, language and behaviour.

Around a century after Shakespeare, the Enlightenment was, on the one hand, keen to investigate the human soul and so engendered an early psychology. However, the emphasis on rationality and reason above all else tended to hierarchise aspects of our psychology which resulted in emotions and 'irrational' thinking (called 'superstition' among other things) being displaced as inferior activities of the mind. This meant that the notion of an unconscious became devalued if not redundant. Descartes' 'I think, therefore I am' was the summation of our human 'being' depicted as consisting solely of our conscious rational awareness. Where we perhaps notice a precursor of the contemporary unconscious in Enlightenment thinking is in its curiosity about, and search for, the origins of human knowledge and wisdom. From time to time this involved ideas about an ancient, wise early humanity – located in Atlantis or in Egypt or one swept away by Noah's Flood – leaving a few wise minds to pass on such original wisdom to the present day. This speculation and investigation of the depths of human knowledge – beyond and outside conscious rational thinking of the day – also seems to predict an idea of the unconscious. It is as if the hyper-rationalism that began with the scientific Enlightenment engendered a compensatory swerve towards everything the rational mind refused to accommodate. These aspects persisted in the margins of Enlightenment thinking ready to re-emerge when there was space for doubting Enlightenment 'certainties'. They reappeared towards the end of the nineteenth century in the form of beliefs in the paranormal, mediumship, spirit contact and the new psychological ideas of an Unconscious Mind.

However, it is the German Romantics who are the most explicit writers on the unconscious in the fifty years up to the birth of Sigmund Freud (1857–1939), C.G. Jung (1875–1962) and of course, Friedrich Nietzsche (1844–1900). The 'philosophy of nature' founded by Friedrich von Schelling (1775–1854) clearly implied the unconscious as 'the very fundament of the human being as rooted in the invisible life of the universe and therefore the true bond linking man with nature' (Ellenberger 1970/1994: 204). For the eighteenth-century Romantics, attention to the unconscious enabled us to have direct understanding of the universe – and therefore of our 'original' selves – through dreams, mystical ecstasy and poetic imagination. It is no coincidence that these aims and methods were among those used by humankind from the earliest times – a fact that comes together quite explicitly in the psychology of C.G. Jung some seventy years later.

Arthur Schopenhauer (1788–1860) published *The World as Will and Representation* (or *Idea*) in 1819 in which he regarded humankind as being driven by blind, internal forces of which he is barely aware: these were the instincts towards conservation and towards reproduction or the sexual instinct. For Schopenhauer, the Will – an analogy of the unconscious – not only drives many of our thoughts which are often in conflict with our intellect (ego-consciousness), but also causes us to repel unwanted cognitions from consciousness. The similarity to later formulations of the unconscious have been spotted by many such as the writer Thomas Mann, who 'felt that Freud's description of the id and the ego was "to a hair" Schopenhauer's description of the will and the intellect translated from metaphysics into psychology' (Ellenberger 1994: 209). It was then up to Eduard von Hartmann in his book *Philosophy of the Unconscious* (1869) to bring together the early ideas, relabel Schopenhauer's Will the 'unconscious' and relate it specifically to various psychological phenomena such as personality, perception, association of ideas and the emotions as well as investigating the role of the unconscious in language, religion, history and the life of society. He also divided the unconscious into three levels. The first was an absolute, a kind of cosmic unconscious which was the source of the other two forms: a physiological unconscious 'at work in the origin, development, and evolution of living beings, including man' (Ellenberger 1994: 210); and a third, more psychological, unconscious which provides the ground for conscious mental life.

The second level just mentioned corresponds most closely to the formulations of C.G. Carus (1789–1869) who was perhaps the closest influence upon Jung's own formulations of the personal and the collective unconscious. Sounding very much like Jung himself, Carus begins his 1846 book *Psyche* with these words:

> The key to the knowledge of the nature of the soul's conscious life lies in the realm of the unconscious. This explains the difficulty, if not the impossibility, of getting a real comprehension of the soul's secret . . . But if this impossibility is only apparent, then the first task of a science of the soul is to state how the spirit of Man is able to descend into these depths.
>
> (Carus 1846, quoted in Ellenberger 1994: 207)

Carus also distinguished three levels of the unconscious: one that is absolute and unknowable, the second, a type of pre-conscious which influences our emotional life through the vital organs of the body. Consciousness may affect this level of the unconscious which is why, Carus believed, a person's face and body can reflect their personality. The third level of the unconscious corresponds to the repressed material – once conscious feelings, representations and perceptions that subsequently become unconscious. These levels are clear precursors of, respectively, the psychoid unconscious, the collective unconscious and the personal unconscious (the third level) in Jung's structure of the psyche. Carus also mentions characteristics of the unconscious that Jung was later to repeat: the unconscious, unlike the strenuous efforts of the conscious mind, uses little energy and thus does not 'need rest' like consciousness does. It is the source of healing for the mind and body, and it is through the unconscious that we remain in connection with the rest of the world and other individuals.

How different patients gave rise to a different 'unconscious' for Freud and Jung

Freud's formulation of the concept of the unconscious arose out of his and Breuer's work with young women suffering from hysterical symptoms – a diagnosis that was popular in several urban centres of the new psychiatry such as Vienna, Berlin and especially Paris where Charcot and Janet were the leading specialists. The innovation in attitude to these patients and their symptoms was the way in which psychiatry was replacing the idea of organic causes for mental problems with the idea that symptoms were psychological in origin. Through his work, Freud developed what his key patient Anna O. called the 'talking cure'. Freud had tried pure suggestion and hypnosis but found that encouraging patients to say whatever came into their minds by a process of 'free association' enabled him to make links backward to the source or cause of their symptoms. Once such causal links were made and understood, that is, made conscious, the symptoms went away – thus apparently proving there was no organic cause but one arising from some mechanism of psychological trauma. According to this approach, the traumatic experience had been *repressed* in the unconscious because it was unbearable to the conscious mind, and the task of the Freudian psychoanalyst was to trace back, discover and reconstruct the cause like a sort of archaeologist-detective.

However, Freud also wished to establish the science of psychoanalysis as one of the exact sciences of his day and to this end he combined psychological with more materialistic biological theories. Thus, in his first formulations around 1896, he claimed that the repression of a traumatic experience was linked to the repression of instinct – specifically the sexual instinct. From this hypothesis he developed the idea that human psychology – and, eventually, all civilised life – was underpinned by the repression of our instinctual life, and exclusively of our sexual and aggressive instincts. Sexual instinct provided the psychic energy or *libido* (Latin for 'desire') for the psyche which, in its sublimated form, gave rise to human achievements ranging from artistic creativity to intellectual curiosity and scientific inventiveness. Although Freud expanded his theories with the structural model of *ego* (partly unconscious but with conscious functions of reality testing, discriminatory thinking and protection), the unconscious *id* (the instincts or 'the passions') and the *super-ego*, the idea of sexual instinct as the motor of the psyche prevailed. Even his last ideas on *Thanatos* (the psychic drive towards inertia or Death) in constant tension with *Eros* (the life preservative instinct manifested in relatedness) never overrode the centrality of sexuality.

While Freud was working on his theory and method through the treatment of young, 'hysterical' Viennese, bourgeois women, Carl Jung, nineteen years his junior, had abandoned his desire to be an actual archaeologist, trained as a doctor and began working in the famous Burghölzli psychiatric hospital linked to the University of Zurich. He arrived at a time when the director (who became his mentor) was Eugene Bleuler, a psychiatrist enlightened towards the idea that not only were psychiatric problems not necessarily caused by organic disease, but also there was meaning to be found in the utterances and symptoms of such patients despite the way they seemed baffling at first sight. There is another key difference between the early psychiatric experience of Jung and Freud in that the Burghölzli treated many patients suffering from serious psychotic illness. Psychiatry then, as so often now, was managed by men who, by virtue of their education and class, were far removed from the patients they treated. In Switzerland with its cantons and local dialects, apart from their illness, patients were not easily intelligible to their urban upper-class doctors, but both Jung and Bleuler had Swiss countryside backgrounds and had the advantage of being familiar with Swiss peasant dialects thus making them more accessible to their patients even before attending empathically to their patients' words. In addition, it was Bleuler who first distinguished mania (since known as manic-depressive illness or 'bipolar disorder') from *dementia praecox* – the early name for schizophrenia, a term which he introduced. It was Jung's work with these psychotic patients, in addition to others more like Freud's hysterics, that gave him a different insight into the psyche and, eventually, a different conception of the unconscious.

According to Jung (1963/1983), in his autobiography *Memories, Dreams, Reflections*, his interest in and his conceptualising of the unconscious had its earliest roots in three sources: his awareness of his own personality, his interest in psychic phenomena and in the writings of Friedrich Nietzsche. Since his childhood, Jung had an awareness of an inner division which he came to call his 'No. 1' personality and his 'No. 2' personality. The first expressed itself in his day-to-day world of friends, school, family and social play, while his No. 2 personality seemed darker, secretive and more mysterious. It seemed to have its source elsewhere than the world of an intelligent country boy, son of a minister in rural Switzerland. This was the side of his personality connected with dreams as well as fears and fantasies, and it was this insight that provided him with his first awareness of the unconscious. His mother was a highly intuitive woman, possibly with psychic abilities and sensitivities, alongside an otherworldlyness and moods that often accompany this temperament. It was she who seems to have influenced the No. 2 personality and, when he was a young student, Jung became very interested in psychic phenomena to the extent that his PhD thesis was in this area. Using his cousin Helen Prieswerk as a subject, he investigated her apparent abilities as a medium – a trend that was highly prevalent at the time in Europe. In doing so, he became less convinced of her psychic 'powers' and more convinced that the phenomena and knowledge she displayed in trance – which her conscious mind was unaware of – were stemming from her unconscious psyche. Moreover, this was not material known personally to the subject and so implied some sort of cultural collective unconscious. Jung reasoned that unconscious material that emerged from a subject, frequently as dream imagery (not just the trance speeches, as with Prieswerk), could *not* be accounted for through the subject's personal learning or experience; thus, he assumed that this may stem from a collective, general and universal part of the unconscious mind, a collective unconscious derived through aeons of repetition of human cultural imagery and experience that, despite differences in detail, remains typically human with recognisable common qualities and meanings. Jung developed this idea throughout his life, but at its earlier stage it had much in common with ideas stemming from early anthropology such as James Frazer's *The Golden Bough* (1890–1915) which sought to show similarities between human cultures and behaviours previously regarded as bizarre and barely human by those who first encountered them through European colonisation.

Nietzsche was always an influence upon Jung as indeed he was upon Freud – although Freud was not as keen to acknowledge this. Jung regarded the ego as the 'centre of consciousness', but he also absorbed Nietzsche's ideas on the unconscious as the central source for the psyche as a whole, thus utterly relativising the centrality of ego-consciousness. Nietzsche's emphasis on the fact that 'I' do not think thoughts, but 'thoughts think me' and how 'dreaming is a recreation for the brain, which by day has to satisfy the stern demands of thought imposed by a higher culture' (Nietzsche 1878: 24–27) are both picked up in Jung's psychology and his ideas of the personal and collective unconscious. But once Jung began his professional life as a psychiatrist at the Burghölzli, he sought a more scientific method to establish the concept of the unconscious and its processes. To this end he used the Word Association Test, first invented by Sir Francis Galton, which Jung developed through extensive research applying the test to a wide range of psychiatric patients. Initially, Jung used it as a diagnostic tool but later his experiences of using it helped him generate further hypotheses on the nature of human mental processing (Jung 1906a, 1906b; see also Jung 1909).

In quite the reverse direction to the speculative, 'mystical' approach Jung has often been accused of, his word association experiments were very much in line with quantitative approaches used by psychology experiments today. The Word Association Test involved a procedure which Jung adapted, with a colleague, to compile a series of stimulus words that were read to patients who were required to respond as quickly as possible with the first word that came to mind. Their response word and the time it took to reply were all recorded. The results were analysed in an effort to map the emotional blocks that interrupted consciousness in the task. Jung hypothesised that the blocks were evidence of complexes – his word for unconscious knots of affect that distorted rational conscious functioning. Here was experimental evidence for the concept of unconscious repressions that Freud had been developing through his clinical practice in Vienna using his own method of requiring a patient to free associate to the first thing that came into their mind. Analogous to the links made in the Word Association Test, Freud found that his patients' associations could lead them to a core experience, the memory of which had been repressed and kept from consciousness. However, he lacked the more robust (meaning quantitative) evidence of the linking and blocking of ideas that Word Association Tests appeared to provide. Jung sent his findings to Freud and the two began a collaboration that lasted from 1906 until 1912. Central to what they shared was the idea of a personal unconscious which, for Jung, had the complexes as its main content.

Jung's difference becomes apparent

Jung began as a supporter of Freud's psychoanalytic ideas and defended them at conferences and in publications, but he was also an independent thinker and sought to develop what Freud had started, to tackle anomalies and generally expand psychoanalytic theory according to his own experience, new data and insights. Thus, in 1913 he published 'The theory of psychoanalysis' (Jung 1913) in which he expounded Freud's original theory and its development (as Jung sees it) and went on to provide his own expansion of the theory. It is here that we find some of his most succinct statements on the unconscious in a Freudian sense. Although Jung had been pondering his idea of a collective unconscious for some time, this text deals with the unconscious before he formulated the two spheres of the personal and the collective unconscious. For this reason, when Jung refers to the 'unconscious' in the context of psychoanalysis, he means what he later refers to as the *personal* unconscious.

Jung writes about the way in which Freud's early work on hysteria and trauma resulted in

> a concept that was to lead far beyond the limits of the trauma theory. This concept he called 'repression'. As you know, by 'repression' we mean the mechanism by which a conscious content is displaced into a sphere outside consciousness. We call this sphere the unconscious, and we define it as the psychic element of which we are not conscious.
>
> (Jung 1913: par. 210)

One of Jung's innovations occurs soon after this passage. Jung had long been dissatisfied with Freud's dogmatic emphasis on the sexual instinct and infantile sexuality as the sole source of psychic energy or libido. Jung points out that the Latin word 'libido' is used to mean 'hunger' (analogous to the nutrition instinct) and also 'passionate desire' and – along the lines of physics where forces previously seen as separate were now regarded as one 'energy' but channelled into different forms – Jung proposes that sexuality is not the sole source of psychic energy, but that 'libido' is a general psychic energy which may flow in channels serving the sexual, reproductive, nutrition or whatever instinct. This is what is known as his generalised or genetic theory of psychic energy and marks a fundamental break with Freudian psychoanalytic views on the unconscious. Jung notes how neurotics have exaggerated functions that are over-invested with libido:

> The libido is there, but it is not visible and is inaccessible to the patient himself . . . It is the task of psychoanalysis to search out that hidden place where the libido dwells and where the patient himself cannot get at it. The hidden place is the 'non-conscious', which we may also call the 'unconscious' without attributing to it any mystical significance.
>
> (Jung 1913: par. 255)

Furthermore, Jung is explicit in his rejection of the way Freud stretches sexual terminology to encompass infant activities such as sucking: 'this very act of sucking could be conceived just as well from the standpoint of the nutritive function and that, on biological grounds, there was more justification for this derivation than for Freud's view' (Jung 1913: par. 262).

Jung's further views on the unconscious are to be found in this early book which, despite the two examples above, clearly aims to defend the psychoanalytic view – and tries to do so by offering 'improvements'. Jung describes infantile fantasy as part of the unconscious sphere – and intensified in the case of neurotics,

> It never crosses his [the neurotic's] mind that he has still not given up certain infantile demands . . . he indulges in all sorts of pet fantasies, of which he is seldom, if ever, so conscious that he knows that he has them. Very often they exist only as emotional expectations, hopes, prejudices, and so forth. In this case we call them unconscious fantasies.
>
> (Jung 1913: par. 313)

However, even while Jung is seeking to defend psychoanalysis against its detractors, he succeeds in slipping in his own view which Freud, eventually, could not tolerate. This is how he counters the objection, from the famous psychiatrist Gustav Aschaffenburg, 'that the so-called unconscious fantasies are merely suggested to the patient and exist only in the mind of the analyst' (Jung 1913: par. 316):

> only people with no psychological experience and no knowledge of the history of psychology are capable of making such accusations. No one with the faintest glimmering of mythology could possibly fail to see the startling parallels between the unconscious fantasies brought to light by the psychoanalytic school and mythological ideas. The objection that our knowledge of mythology has been suggested to the patient is without foundation, because the psychoanalytic school discovered the fantasies first and only then became acquainted with their mythology. Mythology, as we know, is something quite outside the ken of the medical man.
>
> (Jung 1913: par. 316)

While apparently offering a text in support of Freud's psychoanalysis, Jung is now seen to make a claim for the authenticity of unconscious fantasies, not along the lines of Freudian sexual fantasy or trauma, but in the area – of all things! – of mythology. This is after Jung has already replaced Freud's sexual libido with a generalised psychic energy and dared to question the significance of Freud's pivotal emphasis on infantile sexuality. In citing mythology, Jung may be hinting at the Oedipus fantasy but, in downplaying the element of sexual tension in the Oedipus narrative in favour of its status as a myth *per se*, he is departing from psychoanalysis in a cloud of dust. Although it excited him, the non-scientific, non-biological realm of the mythological was resisted by Freud and underemphasised in favour of bio-evolutionary theorising. Now his 'heir apparent', Carl Jung, brings back myth firmly into the fold of psychoanalytic theory. In doing so he engineers his rejection by the psychoanalysts for not adhering to the party line, but, on the other hand, Jung initiates his own perspective which will come to be known as analytical psychology and launches his key concept of the collective unconscious.

Conceiving of the collective unconscious

Jung had long been dissatisfied with the Freudian conception of the unconscious, but it was not until he was able to formulate his idea of the collective unconscious that he was able to provide a model for the structure of the psyche that not only put the collective unconscious on the map, but also clarified the concept of the personal unconscious along distinctly Jungian lines. Jung reports how he had a dream when on the voyage to the United States with Freud in 1909 which began to answer some pressing questions that he had formulated:

> They were: On what premises is Freudian psychology founded? To what category of human thought does it belong? What is the relationship of its almost exclusive personalism to general historical assumptions?
> (Jung 1963/1983: 185)

In *Memories, Dreams, Reflections* (Jung 1963/1983: 182–183), Jung details the dream which, he tells us, 'became for me a guiding image which in the days to come was to be corroborated to an extent I could not at first suspect' (Jung 1963/1983: 185). The dream involved Jung descending through the layers of a house where each room he entered he identified as progressively older in architectural style. The upper storey had 'a kind of salon furnished with fine old pieces in a rococo style' (Jung 1963/1983: 182), below this the next room dated from the fifteenth or sixteenth century: 'The furnishings were mediaeval; the floors were of red brick' (Jung 1963/1983: 182). Beyond this Jung describes his descent into

a beautifully vaulted room which looked exceedingly ancient. Examining the walls, I discovered layers of brick among the ordinary stone
blocks, and chips of brick in the mortar. As soon as I saw this I knew
that the walls dated from Roman times.

(Jung 1963/1983: 182)

The final layer of the building is a cave – 'Thick dust lay on the floor, and
in the dust were scattered bones and broken pottery, like remains of a
primitive culture' (Jung 1963/1983: 183). Jung reports this dream in the
context of discovering how there were aspects of his inner world and his
theorising about the psyche which he was finding difficult to share with
Freud. He was struggling at the time with his questions about Freud's
psychoanalysis and he tells us how Freud produced a personalised interpretation of the dream, but, for Jung, the dream building meant something
quite different: it suggested something distinct from Freud's model of
the psyche and the original conception of the psychoanalytic project. In
pondering the question of the relationship between the personal and
impersonal-historical, Jung found that

My dream was giving me the answer. It obviously pointed to the
foundations of cultural history – a history of successive layers of consciousness. My dream thus constituted a kind of structural diagram of
the human psyche; it postulated something of an altogether *impersonal*
nature underlying that psyche.

(Jung 1963/1983: 185)

The dream inspired Jung to return to a study of archaeology, myths and the
Gnostics which, in combination with his study of the fantasies of the
patient Miss Miller, eventually led to the publication of *The Psychology of
the Unconscious* (Jung 1912/1916/1952) – arguably Jung's first text of
analytical psychology as distinct from psychoanalysis. Of this book Jung
has written, referring to his time with Freud,

One of my principal aims was to free medical psychology from the
subjective and personalistic bias that characterized its outlook at the
time, and to make it possible to understand the unconscious as an
objective and collective psyche.

(Jung 1956: xxiv)

Defining the personal and the collective unconscious

Once Jung had begun to get to grips with this other, objective, cultural and
collective unconscious it became more pressing, and yet easier, to define

what he meant by the personal unconscious. The collective unconscious is certainly different from Freud's conception, but is Jung's concept of the personal unconscious identical to Freud's? There are similarities: it holds repressed contents and material often of an infantile nature and deriving from the biographical history of the person. Jung says in his revision of the trauma theory of hysteria, that childhood experiences may act as a sort of reminiscence which restricts psychic energy and then provides a form for the stage-managing of hysterical symptoms in the adult. But this is rather different to saying that the childhood experiences *cause* the symptoms; Jung, instead, finds that symptoms have an *aim* or *teleology* (a 'future cause'), and the childhood experience simply provides the *form* by which the patient attempts to solve a crisis in the *present*. He cites the case of a woman who hysterically ran ahead of charging horses in a way that recalled a childhood trauma with a coach and horses, but who in fact was unconsciously driven to this hysterical reaction by a difficult current situation of wishing to be with her lover who was already married. Jung concludes that *'the cause of the pathogenic conflict lies mainly in the present moment'* (Jung 1913: par. 373; italics in original).

A greater clarification of Jung's more or less conventional position on the personal unconscious comes in the 1927 essay 'The structure of the psyche' (Jung 1927).

> The personal unconscious consists firstly of all those contents that became unconscious either because they lost their intensity and were forgotten or because consciousness was withdrawn from them (repression), and secondly of contents, some of them sense-impressions, which never had sufficient intensity to reach consciousness but have somehow entered the psyche.
>
> (Jung 1927: par. 321)

Later, in 'On the nature of the psyche', Jung (1946) details the history of the concept of the unconscious (including those historical precursors I mention above) with the aim of separating out the roles of instinct on the one hand, and will or spirit on the other. Where psyche loses itself in the organic material of the body – i.e., the instinctual sphere – it is so unconscious as to never have access to consciousness and this realm he refers to as the *psychoid*. There is a continuum between the unknown instinct and the image which may become known to consciousness; this is addressed in Chapter 3 of this book (on the archetypes) in more detail. But here is Jung's later, more developed definition of the unconscious as originally conceived in psychoanalysis:

> So defined, the unconscious depicts an extremely fluid state of affairs: everything of which I know, but of which I am not at the moment

thinking; everything of which I was once conscious but have now forgotten; everything perceived by my senses, but not noted by my conscious mind; everything which, involuntarily and without paying attention to it, I feel, think, remember, want, and do; all the future things that are taking shape in me and will sometime come to consciousness: all this is the content of the unconscious. These contents are all more or less capable, so to speak, of consciousness, or were once conscious and may become conscious again the next moment . . . To this marginal phenomenon . . . there also belong the Freudian findings we have already noted.

(Jung 1946: par. 382)

Jung saw the ego as the centre of consciousness, but he also saw the creativity of the unconscious in that the unconscious may influence our conscious thinking and that it is often 'truer and wiser'. The contents of the personal unconscious include the complexes and Jung extends this idea to include personifications or dissociated fragments of personality most clearly seen in our dreams. A further important way of understanding the personal unconscious – and connected with this fragmentation – is Jung's concept of the shadow which may appear in dreams or when the patient projects it onto another person. 'The shadow personifies everything that the subject refuses to acknowledge about himself and yet is always thrusting itself upon him directly or indirectly – for instance, inferior traits of character and other incompatible tendencies' (Jung 1939: par. 513). The shadow is everything that is 'not me', and this might include creative qualities that could benefit the whole personality but have been lost or repressed due to the upbringing or social conditions of the subject. For our purposes in tracking a definition of the personal unconscious it is interesting to note Jung's emphasis that 'the shadow . . . represents first and foremost the personal unconscious, and its content can therefore be made conscious without too much difficulty' (Jung 1950: par. 19) – a statement which reinforces his earlier assertion that, 'The shadow coincides with the "personal" unconscious (which corresponds to Freud's conception of the unconscious)' (Jung 1939: par. 513).

The collective unconscious itself

Jung asserts that consciousness grows out of the unconscious psyche which is older than it – not that the unconscious is merely the remnants of older material. In saying this, Jung refers to a sphere of the unconscious that he defines negatively against the personal unconscious. The collective unconscious is the part of the psyche that is *not* a personal acquisition and has *not* been acquired through personal experience. Its contents have *never* been in consciousness – they are not repressed or forgotten – and they are *not acquired* but owe their existence to a form of heredity. Jung summarises thus:

> My thesis, then, is as follows: In addition to our immediate consciousness, which is of a thoroughly personal nature and which we believe to be the only empirical psyche (even if we tack on the personal unconscious as an appendix), there exists a second psychic system of a collective, universal, and impersonal nature which is identical in all individuals. This collective unconscious does not develop individually but is inherited. It consists of pre-existent forms, the archetypes, which can only become conscious secondarily and which give definite form to certain psychic contents.
>
> (Jung 1936: par. 90)

Jung notes how earlier psychoanalytic theories such as those of Freud and Adler also had an *a priori* general base in the instincts which were similarly impersonal, inherited and universal. In fact, he says, the archetypes are analogous to the instincts.

Before he had settled on the term 'archetype', Jung lectured in 1927 on 'The structure of the psyche' where he formulates his idea of the collective unconscious with evidence along the lines we read in his 1913 revision of Freud's psychoanalysis – namely, the presence of mythological material in his patients' images and dreams. The collective unconscious consists of 'primordial images' and 'mythological motifs' and Jung concludes that our myths, legends and fairy tales are carriers of a projected unconscious psyche. Jung analogises this process to the way in which humans have projected meaningful images onto the stars and 'constellated' them in forms which are then named. He disagrees with the functionalist argument that early man sought to explain natural events by anthropomorphising them. Instead, Jung argues that over millions of years, the psyche, like the body, has adapted to physical events in the environment and produced the mythological material out of a *participation mystique* where the separation of subject and object is not distinct. And it is not the physical phenomena – the thunder or clouds or earthquakes – that remains in the psyche but '*the fantasies caused by the affects they arouse*' (Jung 1927: par. 331; my italics). Bodily functions like hunger and sex similarly produce engrained fantasy images as do dangers, sickness and death. But, above all, it is the most ordinary, everyday events, 'immediate realities like husband, wife, father, mother, child . . . which are eternally repeated, [and] create the mightiest archetypes of all, whose ceaseless activity is everywhere apparent even in a rationalistic age like ours' (Jung 1927: par. 336).

So, the collective unconscious is a record in, and of, the psyche of humankind going back to its remotest beginnings just as we still have ancestral traces in our body morphology and our 'reptilian brain'. But it is far from being,

> a dead deposit, a sort of abandoned rubbish heap, but a living system of reactions and aptitudes that determine the individual's life in invisible ways . . . the archetypes are simply the forms which the instincts assume. From the living fountain of instinct flows everything that is creative; hence the unconscious is not merely conditioned by history, but is the very source of the creative impulse.
>
> (Jung 1927: par. 339)

While being just as relevant for the individual as the personal unconscious, the collective unconscious is, therefore, even more important to take into account when Jung considers the psychological aspects of 'civilised' society – modernity – in general. Freud had linked instinct to 'universal' psychological phenomena when he conceived of the Oedipus complex which also had a mythological expression long before he named it. But his emphasis was reductive and used the myth motif to merely express the ego-development and particular family dynamics of a certain class of individuals. Freud even went as far as rooting the Oedipus in his own fantasy recon-struction of the father-murdering sons of the primal horde in *Totem and Taboo* (Freud 1912–1913), but in the main he specialised in the pathologies of the individual psyche and it is to Jung we turn when we wish to grasp the significance of the modern psyche in general.

Jung points out that since archaic times, the collective unconscious has found its relation with, and expression in, consciousness through various forms of philosophy and religion. But when these forms degenerate under the pressure of rationalism and the epistemological restrictions of science – especially since the end of the medieval period – psyche has fewer and fewer symbolic or ritual ways in which it may be expressed and then tends to get projected collectively as and where it will. A purely personalistic psychology tends to deny and distort this effect: 'Since neuroses are in most cases not just private concerns, but *social* phenomena, we must assume that arche-types are constellated in these cases too' (Jung 1936: par. 98). By the time he was writing the essay to be given as a talk to London doctors in 1936, history – in the form of the rise of the Nazis in Germany – gave Jung the opportunity to see this all too clearly.

> Today you can judge better than you could twenty years ago the nature of the forces involved. Can we not see how a whole nation is reviving an archaic symbol, yes, even archaic religious forms, and how this mass emotion is influencing and revolutionising the life of the individual in a catastrophic manner? The man of the past in us is alive today to a

degree undreamt of before the [First World] war, and in the last analysis what is the fate of great nations but a summation of the psychic changes in individuals?

(Jung 1936: par. 97)

More recently, the figure of Diana, Princess of Wales, and the mass response to her death have been viewed by Jungians as an example of the collective unconscious seeking an object for its projections (Haynes and Shearer 1998). The view I express in *Jung and the Postmodern: The Interpretation of Realities* (Hauke 2000) is the way in which Diana seemed to possess qualities which are ambivalently valued by our contemporary, dominant consciousness; human qualities that are marginalised in certain times are still present in the collective unconscious and will seek a form in which they can be expressed. This is achieved through unconscious projection, and then, as in the case of Diana, a form of 'taking back' the projection through relating to the image – exemplified by those queuing at her funeral who said, 'It is as if I knew her'. The 'knowing' of the Virgin Mary through her image worked in the same way for over a thousand years. Jung claims in making the point that such symbols, were far more common in less rationalistic times than our own. They once functioned for humans and the psyche but have now lost their power to connect consciousness to its roots in the psyche's instinctual base and thus retain for humans a link to Nature and the rest of the (non-human) world.

In another way, the contents of the collective unconscious can have a harmful effect on the ego and the personality when, instead of being projected out into the world, they overwhelm ego-consciousness with their powerful affects and images. This was how Jung viewed psychotic delusions, and, in fact, the universal and mythological character of his seriously ill patients' words and images convinced him of the fact of the collective unconscious. Jung first published material along these lines as early as 1912 (Jung 1912/1916/1952). Dreams, and Jung's own experiences (Jung 1963/1983: 194–225) with active imagination – a type of lucid dreaming where unconscious material arises spontaneously but ego is still 'awake' enough to observe it – provided him with further evidence.

Is there other evidence for the collective unconscious?

The Jungian analyst Anthony Stevens (1995) notes how innate structures – which have been out of fashion for much of the twentieth century due to the prevalence of behaviourism – now seem to feature in many scientific perspectives in biology, psychology and neuroscience. Niko Tinbergen found what he calls 'innate releasing mechanisms' in animals especially when it comes to the relationship between parents and their young. John

Bowlby took this up in his theory of attachment. Noam Chomsky's ideas of 'deep structures' in the brain which give humans the potential for a universal grammatical structure in language despite the vast surface differences in human languages, seems corroborated by more and more evidence. Sociobiology and evolutionary psychology both argue for adaptive psychic structures produced over millennia of evolution which sound very much like what Jung meant by the archetypes of the collective unconscious: 'specialized learning mechanisms that organize experience into adaptively meaningful schemas or frames' (Cosmides 1985, quoted in Walters 1994).

In further support of Jung's views, Stevens also notes how Paul Maclean (1976) demonstrated that mammalian and reptilian parts of the human brain still function in modern human beings. He cites Michel Jouvet's sleep laboratory experiments where he showed that dreams arise from biologically ancient parts of the brain and seem to have a clear evolutionary adaptive function (Jouvet 1975).

However, the most up-to-date investigations into unconscious processes come from the field of cognitive science and its employment of computer modelling and brain imaging to investigate neural substrates of brain function. As Soren Ekstrom writes, 'the speculations by both Freud and Jung left the specific synaptic and neural manifestations of unconscious processes to be inferred' (Ekstrom 2004: 662). Now, Lakoff and Johnson in their book *Philosophy in the Flesh* (1999) have used studies in neuroscience, cognitive linguistics, and neural modelling to conclude that 'most of our thought is unconscious, not in the Freudian sense of being repressed, but in the sense that it operates beneath the level of cognitive awareness, inaccessible to consciousness and operating too quickly to be focused on' (Lakoff and Johnson 1999: 10). Jung's conception of the unconscious combined religion and science, but he clearly anticipated the time when neurological studies would add further scientific evidence to his speculations when he spoke in England in 1935:

> Consciousness is like a surface or a skin upon a vast unconscious area of unknown extent . . . we need a laboratory with very complicated apparatus in order to establish a picture of that world apart from our senses and apart from our psyche . . . very much the same with our unconscious – we ought to have a laboratory in which we could establish by objective methods how things really are when in an unconscious condition.
>
> (Jung 1935/1977: par. 11)

Cognitive science today seems to have the investigative equipment that Jung sought, and which he knew would complement the hundred years of philosophical and psychological speculation on the unconscious psyche that had preceded it.

Concluding thoughts

I often ask myself and my students, 'What would Jung have become if there had not been Freud?' Would he have remained as marginal and perhaps forgotten like C.G. Carus, who so eloquently conceived of the unconscious before either of them? The reason that Jung and Freud became world famous (and Carus did not) seems to lie with the fact that psychoanalysis and analytical psychology are *methods of treatment*. With this new method of treating mental distress, initiated by Freud, depth psychology shifted from being a philosophical theory to being an applied psychological theory that, through its methods, could enlighten and change individuals for the better. With C.G. Jung, the method goes even further in so far as analytical psychology addresses not only individual concerns, but also the way in which these are seen to imply a critique of how the human psyche in general has been affected by social changes in the industrialised West since the Enlightenment. Much like Nietzsche before him, Jung emphasises how on the one hand, modern consciousness has evolved in a specialised way thus enabling the greatest manipulation of the world humans have ever seen. On the other hand, however, neglect of the unconscious has resulted in great losses to humanity in the way that the creative potential of the psyche is, at best, ignored in favour of an assumption that progress may be achieved through the application of conscious rationality alone. At worst, this gives rise to great damage arising from neglect of the relationship between humans and the world and the failure to recognise the projections we place upon it. Thus, Jung's view of the unconscious offers a way of healing not only for the individual soul, but also for the 'soul' of twenty-first-century society in general.

This is far from being a purely sociological project either, because Jung always emphasises the importance of the individual and the development of their full potential in the process he calls individuation. However, in a psychology where each and every individual also carries their own share of the universal, collective unconscious psyche, each individuating subject that fosters the integration of the conscious and unconscious psyche contributes to change in a mass collective sense. In this way I have linked postmodern philosophical and social critique with Jung's psychology in the sense that in both the validation of subjective experience is able to stand authentically and pluralistically beside the claims of the dominant epistemologies that have relied on 'objectivity' alone (Hauke 2000). In another way, the post-Jungian Andrew Samuels (Samuels 1995, 2001) also uses Jungian perspectives to discuss the way in which our political behaviour (including the politics of gender, race and class) may be understood better – and perhaps revitalised out of their cynicism – by paying attention to the psychology of the unconscious. In both cases the use of a psychological perspective – wrongly regarded in modern times as the sole province of individual concerns – is being employed as a new tool of critical social theory analogous to the way in which Frankfurt School theorists once used Freudian ideas. The difference is that myself and Samuels are not welding a depth psychology to social theory, but restoring and amplifying a connection already present in Jung's psychological perspective that has included collective phenomena and has been driven by his need to understand the psychology of collective human behaviour throughout the century in which he lived.

The psychology of C.G. Jung is more vital nowadays than ever before as a way of thinking about, and acting upon, not only individual issues of mental distress as in psychoanalysis, but also the wider implications of psyche in the world. By developing a psychology of the unconscious that has both a personal and a collective aspect, Jung has supplied the theoretical tools which enable psychotherapists – and academics in other fields like film, literature, international relations, art and social policy to name but a few – to offer fresh perspectives on who we are, and where we are heading, at the start of the twenty-first century.

References

Carus, C.G. (1846/1975) *Psyche*. Darmstadt: Wissenschaftliche Buchgesellschaft.

Cosmides, L. (1985) 'Deduction of Darwinian algorithms? An explanation of the "elusive" content effect on the Wason selection task', doctoral dissertation, Department of Psychology and Social Relations, Harvard University.

Ekstrom, S. (2004) 'The mind beyond our immediate awareness: Freudian, Jungian and cognitive models of the unconscious'. *Journal of Analytical Psychology*, 49(5): 657–682.

Ellenberger, H. (1970/1994) *The Discovery of the Unconscious: The History and Evolution of Dynamic Psychiatry*. London: Fontana.

Frazer, J.G. (1890–1915) *The Golden Bough: A Study in Comparative Religion*, twelve volumes. London: Macmillan.

Freud, S. (1912–1913/1983) *Totem and Taboo*. London: Ark/Routledge and Kegan Paul.

Hartmann, E. von (1869/1931) *Philosophy of the Unconscious*, trans. W. Coupland. London: Kegan Paul.

Hauke, C. (2000) *Jung and the Postmodern: The Interpretation of Realities*. London: Routledge.

Haynes, J. and Shearer, A. (eds) (1998) *When a Princess Dies: Reflections from Jungian Analysts*. London: Harvest.

Hunt, R. (ed.) (1967) *Personalities and Cultures: Readings in Psychological Anthropology*. New York: Natural History Press.

Jouvet, M. (1975) 'The function of dreaming: a neurophysiologist's point of view', in M.S. Gazzaniga and C. Blakemore (eds) *Handbook of Psychobiology*. New York: Academic Press.

Jung, C.G. citations: except where a different publication or translation is noted below, all references in the text are to the hardback edition of *The Collected*

Works of C.G. Jung, ed. Sir Herbert Read, Michael Fordham and Gerhard Adler, trans. R.F.C. Hull, 21 volumes (*CW*). London: Routledge and Kegan Paul.

Jung, C.G. (1906a) 'Psychoanalysis and association experiments', in *CW* 2: pars. 660–727.

—— (1906b) 'Association, dream and hysterical symptom', in *CW* 2: pars. 793–862.

—— (1909) 'The association method', in *CW* 2: pars. 939–998.

—— (1912/1916/1952) *The Psychology of the Unconscious. CW* 5.

—— (1913) 'The theory of psychoanalysis', in *CW* 4: pars. 203–522.

—— (1927) 'The structure of the psyche', in *CW* 8: pars. 283–342.

—— (1935/1977) 'The Tavistock Lectures: Lecture 1', in *CW* 18: pars. 1–73.

—— (1936) 'The concept of the collective unconscious', in *CW* 9i: pars. 87–110.

—— (1939) 'Conscious, unconscious and individuation', in *CW* 9i: pars. 489–524.

—— (1946) 'On the nature of the psyche', in *CW* 8: pars. 343–442.

—— (1950) 'The shadow', ch. 2 in *Aion. CW* 9ii: pars. 13–19.

—— (1956) 'Foreword to the fourth Swiss edition', in *CW* 5: xxiv.

Jung, C.G. (1963/1983) *Memories, Dreams, Reflections*. London: Fontana.

Lakoff, G. and Johnson, M. (1999) *Philosophy in the Flesh: The Embodied Mind and its Challenge to Western Thought*. New York: Basic Books.

Maclean, P.D. (1976) 'Sensory and perceptive factors in emotional function of the triune brain', in R.G. Genell and S. Gabay (eds) *Biological Foundations of Psychiatry*, Volume 1. New York: Raven.

Malik, K. (2000) *Man, Beast and Zombie: What Science Can and Cannot Tell Us about Human Nature*. London: Weidenfeld and Nicolson/Phoenix.

Nietzsche, F. (1878) *Human, All Too Human*, trans. H. Zimmern and P.V. Cohn, quoted in Jung, *CW* 5: par. 27.

Paul, B. (1953) 'Mental disorder and self-regulating processes in culture: a Guatemalan illustration', in R. Hunt (ed.) (1967) *Personalities and Culture*. New York: Natural History Press.

Samuels, A. (1995) *The Political Psyche*. London: Routledge.

—— (2001) *Politics on the Couch: Citizenship and the Internal Life*. London: Profile.

Schopenhauer, A. (1819/1958) *The World as Will and Representation*, trans. E.F.J. Payne, two volumes. Indian Hills, CO: Falcon's Wing Press.

Stevens, A. (1995) 'Jungian psychology, the body, and the future'. *Journal of Analytical Psychology*, 40: 353–364.

Walters, S. (1994) 'Algorithms and archetypes: evolutionary psychology and Carl Jung's theory of the collective unconscious'. *Journal of Social and Evolutionary Systems*, 17(3): 287–306.

Whyte, L.L. (1960) *The Unconscious before Freud*. New York: Basic Books.

Chapter 3

The archetypes

Anthony Stevens

Introduction: the place of archetypal theory in the Jungian opus, its importance and overall relevance

With his theory of archetypes operating as components of the collective unconscious, Jung sought to define the living bedrock of human psychology. Virtually alone among depth psychologists of the twentieth century, he rejected the *tabula rasa* theory of human psychological development, wholeheartedly embracing the notion that evolutionary pressures had determined the basic structures and functions of the human psyche. Jung wrote:

> [It is] a mistake to suppose that the psyche of the newborn child is a *tabula rasa* in the sense that there is absolutely nothing in it. Insofar as the child is born with a differentiated brain that is predetermined by heredity and therefore individualized, it meets sensory stimuli coming from outside not with *any* aptitudes, but with *specific* ones.
>
> (Jung 1936/1954: par. 136)

The archetypes form the substrate on which these specific aptitudes proceed.

> There is no human experience, nor would experience be possible at all, without the intervention of a subjective aptitude. What is this subjective aptitude? Ultimately it consists of an innate psychic structure which allows men to have experiences of this kind. Thus the whole nature of man presupposes woman, both physically and spiritually. His system is tuned into woman from the start, just as it is prepared for a quite definite world where there is water, light, air, salt, carbohydrate, etc. The form of the world into which he is born is already inborn in him as a virtual image. Likewise, parents, wife, children, birth, and death are inborn in him as virtual images, as psychic aptitudes. These *a priori*

categories have by nature a collective character; they are images of parents, wife, and children *in general*, and are not individual predestinations. We must, therefore, think of these images as lacking in solid content, hence as unconscious. They only acquire solidity, influence, and eventual consciousness in the encounter with empirical facts, which touch the unconscious aptitude and quicken it to life. They are, in a sense, the deposits of all our ancestral experience, but they are not the experiences themselves.

(Jung 1928: par. 300)

'All these factors, therefore, that were essential to our near and remote ancestors will also be essential to us, for they are embedded in the inherited organic system' (Jung 1928/1931: par. 717).

Apart from Jung, nearly all other twentieth-century psychologists and psychoanalysts, as well as sociologists and anthropologists, focused on the myriad ways that individuals differed from one another and attempted to account for these differences in terms of the cultural and social influences they had been subjected to in the course of growing up. In opposition to this view, Jung held that a truly scientific psychology must start from what human beings had in common before the study of individual differences could proceed with any hope of reaching meaningful or valid conclusions.

This inevitably brought him into conflict with Sigmund Freud. Whereas Freud insisted that the unconscious mind was entirely personal and peculiar to the individual and made up of repressed wishes and traumatic memories, Jung maintained that there existed an additional phylogenetic layer (the 'collective unconscious'), which incorporated the entire psychic potential of humankind. Support for this notion came from the studies Jung conducted with his colleagues at the Burghölzli Hospital in Zurich into the delusions and hallucinations of schizophrenic patients. They were able to demonstrate that these contained motifs and images that also occurred in myths, religions, and fairy tales from all over the world (Jung 1956). Jung concluded that there must exist a dynamic substratum, common to all humanity, on the basis of which each individual builds his or her own experience of life, developing a unique array of psychological characteristics. In other words, the archetypes of the collective unconscious provided the basic themes of human life on which each individual worked out his or her own sets of variations.

The archetype is thus Jung's basic concept, in that its significance for analytical psychology is comparable to that of gravity for Newtonian physics, relativity for Einsteinian physics, or natural selection for Darwinian biology. It is one of the most important ideas to emerge in the twentieth century, possessing far-reaching implications for both the social and the natural sciences.

The chronology of Jung's ideas concerning archetypes: the major developments and modifications within Jung's own writings

The intuition that there is more to the psyche than individual experience could possibly put there began in Jung's childhood when it struck him that there were things in his dreams that came from somewhere beyond himself – for example, the very first dream he could remember, which occurred when he was 3, of an underground phallic god (Jung 1963: 25–26).

Jung's researches at the Burghölzli Hospital under Eugen Bleuler, the great authority on schizophrenia, served to confirm this early childhood intuition. He became convinced that some universal structures must exist which are common to both the mind and the brain of all men and women and that they must underlie all human experience and behaviour.

Jung first referred to these universal structures as 'primordial images' in 1912 – a term he borrowed from Jakob Burckhardt – and later, in 1917, as 'dominants of the collective unconscious'. His first use of the term 'archetype' is in his essay 'Instinct and the unconscious' originally published in 1919 (1929: par. 270).

This change of nomenclature occurred because, with time, Jung recognised that the manifestations of the universal dominants were not restricted to images but occurred in ideas, feelings and experiences as well as in characteristic patterns of behaviour. As a result, 'archetype' gradually supplanted 'primordial image' in his writings, though for some years he tended to use both terms interchangeably.

This lack of precision laid him open to the charge of Lamarckism – namely that, like Freud, he subscribed to the discredited theory of Jean-Baptiste Lamarck (1744–1829) that experiences acquired by one generation could be transmitted genetically to the next. Some passages written by Jung lend credence to this criticism, as, for example, when he talks of archetypal experiences as being 'engraved' upon the psyche by repetition through the millennia of human existence. 'Endless repetition has engraved these experiences into our psychic constitution, not in the form of images filled with content, but at first only as *forms without content*, representing merely the possibility of a certain type of perception and action' (1936: par. 99; Jung's italics).

There is no difficulty with Jung's statement that archetypes represent only the *possibility* of certain types of perception or action, but no contemporary biologist could go along with the assertion that endless repetition has *engraved* archetypal experiences into the psychic constitution. In Jung's defence it can be argued that he used such terms figuratively rather than scientifically and he was later at pains to correct the impression that he believed in the inheritance of actual experiences rather than in the inheritance of the *capacity* to have them.

However, it was not until the publication of his essay 'The spirit of psychology' (1947; revised in *CW* 8 as 'On the nature of the psyche', 1954) that he finally freed himself of the Lamarckian taint, making a clear distinction between the deeply unconscious and therefore unknowable and irrepresentable *archetype-as-such* (similar to Kant's *das Ding-an-sich*) and the archetypal images, ideas and behaviours that the archetype-as-such gives rise to. It is the archetype-as-such (the *predisposition* to have certain experience) that is inherited, not the experience itself.

This proposition is fully in accord with modern biological usage and is no more Lamarckian than the statement that children are innately disposed to acquire speech or to run on two legs. As Jung himself insisted in his Foreword to Esther Harding's *Woman's Mysteries* (1955), the term archetype

> is not meant to denote an inherited idea, but rather an inherited mode of psychic functioning, corresponding to the inborn way in which the chick emerges from the egg, the bird builds its nest, a certain kind of wasp stings the motor ganglion of the caterpillar, and eels find their way to the Bermudas. In other words, it is a 'pattern of behaviour'. This aspect of the archetype, the purely biological one, is the proper concern of scientific psychology.
>
> (Jung 1949: par. 1228)

Such statements clearly link archetypes with instincts and Jung fully acknowledged this relationship, describing archetypes as the *source* of the instincts, 'for the archetypes are simply the forms which the instincts assume' (1927/1931a: par. 339). Or to put it another way: 'the archetypes are the unconscious images of the instincts themselves . . . they are *patterns of instinctual behaviour* (1936: par. 91; Jung's italics). Or again: 'The primordial image might suitably be described as *the instinct's perception of itself*, as the self-portrait of the instinct' (1919/1929: par. 277; Jung's italics). Ultimately, it is probable that instinct and archetype share a common irrepresentable, transcendent source, rather than one being the source or version of the other.

The link between archetypes and instincts would go some way to explain the empirical finding that archetypes are experienced as 'numinous' – to borrow Rudolf Otto's (1917) term – possessing awesome power and energy, as when the God archetype is activated. Thus the archetype is 'a *dynamism* which makes itself felt in the numinosity and fascinating power of the archetypal image' (1947/1954: par. 414; Jung's italics).

In addition to drawing parallels from biology and religion, Jung was fond of making a crystallographic analogy, comparing the form of an archetype to the axial system of a crystal,

> which, as it were, preforms the crystalline structure in the mother liquid, although it has no material existence of its own. This first

appears according to the specific way in which the ions and molecules aggregate. The archetype in itself is empty and purely formal, nothing but a *facultas praeformandi*, a possibility of representation which is given *a priori*. The representations themselves are not inherited, only the forms, and in that respect they correspond in every way to the instincts, which are also determined in form only. The existence of the instincts can no more be proved than the existence of the archetypes, so long as they do not manifest themselves concretely. With regard to the definiteness of the form, our comparison with the crystal is illuminating inasmuch as the axial system determines only the stereometric structure but not the concrete form of the individual crystal. This may be either large or small, and it may vary endlessly by reason of the different size of its planes or by the growing together of two crystals. The only thing that remains constant is the axial system, or rather, the invariable geometric proportions underlying it. The same is true of the archetype. In principle, it can be named and has an invariable nucleus of meaning – but always only in principle, never as regards its concrete manifestation. In the same way, the specific appearance of the mother-image at any given time cannot be deduced from the mother archetype alone, but depends on innumerable other factors.

(Jung 1938/1954: par. 155)

Jung had no hesitation in linking the archetypes to structures in the brain:

every man is born with a brain that is profoundly differentiated, and this makes him capable of very various mental functions, which are neither ontologically developed or acquired . . . This particular circumstance explains, for example, the remarkable analogies presented by the unconscious in the most remotely separated races and peoples.

(Jung 1916: pars. 452–453)

Hence the extraordinary correspondence of cultural artefacts occurring throughout the world. 'The universal similarity of human brains leads us then to admit the existence of a certain psychic function, identical with itself in all individuals; we call it the collective psyche' (Jung 1916: par. 454).

With hindsight, this seems such a reasonable position to adopt that future generations will find it hard to understand why Jung's proposal encountered as much opposition as it did. In addition to the entrenched antagonism of academics wedded to the Standard Social Science Model (the SSSM, which is deeply hostile to the idea that biology or innate structures could have a part to play in human psychology), Jung also suffered a blistering attack from the Freudians, who, usurping the high scientific ground, dismissed him as a crank and a mystic. It is ironic that now, at the beginning of the new century, Jung's theory of archetypes, first proposed in the form of 'primordial images' nearly a hundred years ago, is being rehabilitated by the new disciplines of evolutionary psychology and evolutionary psychiatry, while Freud's scientific credentials have been seriously impugned (Macmillan 1997; Webster 1995).

To sum up, archetypes form the basis of all the usual phenomena of human existence and we inherit them as part of our genetic endowment. They are the phylogenetic (evolutionary) foundations on which ontogenesis (individual development) proceeds. An individual's entire archetypal inheritance makes up the collective unconscious, whose authority and psychic energy is co-ordinated by a central nucleus which Jung termed 'the Self' or 'the archetype of archetypes'.

Definitions, origins and meanings

Like all profound ideas, the archetypal hypothesis is not entirely new. Its origins go back at least as far as Plato and probably further. Jung himself recognised this when he described archetypes as 'active living dispositions, *ideas in the Platonic sense*, that pre-form and continually influence our thoughts and feelings and actions' (1938/1954: par. 154; italics added). For Plato, 'ideas' were pure mental forms originating in the minds of the gods before human life began, and, as a consequence, they were supraordinate to the objective world of phenomena. They were *collective* in the sense that they embody the *general* characteristics of a thing rather than its *specific* peculiarities. This applies to animals and plants as well as to objects and ideas. The human fingerprint, for example, is instantly recognisable for what it is on account of its characteristic configuration of contours and whorls. Yet every fingerprint has a configuration unique to its owner: which is why those who turn their hands to burglary must remember to wear gloves if they hope to escape detection and arrest.

Archetypes similarly combine the universal with the individual, the general with the unique. While they are common to all humanity, they are nevertheless manifested in every individual in a manner peculiar to him or her.

Jung took the term 'archetype' from the *Corpus hermeticum*, where God is referred to as τό 'αρχέτυπον φως (the archetypal light). In *De divinis nominibus* Dionysius the Areopagite brings out the essential paradox between the universal and the particular by comparing the archetype with an official seal:

> That the seal is not entire and the same in all its impressions . . . is not due to the seal itself . . . but the difference of the substances which share it makes the impressions of the one, entire, identical archetype to be different.
>
> (quoted by Jacobi 1959: 34)

Jung also found the term in *Adversus haereses* by Irenaeus: 'The creator of the world did not fashion these things directly from himself but copied them from archetypes outside himself.' Although St Augustine does not use the word 'archetype' he nevertheless speaks of '*ideae principales*, which are themselves not formed . . . but are contained in the divine understanding' (Jung 1934/1954: par. 5).

The other important influences on Jung's development of the archetypal concept were Kant and Schopenhauer. Kant argued that we cannot know what we add to or subtract from the real world in the act of perceiving it. We experience the world in the way we do because of the nature of our perceptual apparatus and because of the *a priori* categories of time and space which condition all our perceptions. These given and inescapable factors function like tinted spectacles which we cannot remove and which, as a result, colour every observation that we make.

Throughout Jung's work there are recurring references to Kant's *Critique of Pure Reason* and its assertion that 'there can be no empirical knowledge that is not already caught and limited by the *a priori* structure of cognition'. Jung equated this *a priori* structure with the archetypes. Even more influential than Kant was Schopenhauer, who described what he called 'prototypes' as 'the original forms of all things'. They alone, he maintained can be said to have true being, 'because they always are, but never become nor pass away' (Jarret 1981).

While fully acknowledging his debt to these earlier thinkers, Jung was to conceive of the archetype as no mere mental abstraction but as a dynamic entity, a living organism, endowed with generative force, existing as a 'centre' in the central nervous system and actively seeking its own expression in the psyche and in the world. Repeatedly, Jung stressed that the archetype was not an arid, intellectual concept, but a living, empirical entity, charged not only with meaningfulness but also with *feeling*. 'It would be an unpardonable sin of omission', he wrote, 'were we to overlook the *feeling value* of the archetype. This is extremely important both theoretically and therapeutically' (1947/1954: par. 411; Jung's italics). Psychology, he maintained, is the only science that has to take 'feeling-value' into account, for feeling 'forms the link between psychic events on the one hand, and meaning and life on the other' (Jung 1961: par. 596). In other words, the archetype is 'a piece of life', 'a living system of reactions and aptitudes' (1927/1931a: par. 339) and 'it is connected with the living individual by the bridge of emotion' (1961: par. 589).

There is some disagreement about the etymology of the term. Archetype is a Greek word signifying an original or prototype from which copies are made.

> The first element 'arche' signifies 'beginning, origin, cause, primal source and principle,' but it also signifies 'position of a leader, supreme

rule and government' (in other words a kind of 'dominant'); the second element 'type' means 'blow and what is produced by a blow, the imprint of a coin . . . form, image, copy, prototype, model, order, and norm' . . . in the figurative, modern sense, 'pattern, underlying form, primordial form' (the form for example 'underlying' a number of similar human, animal or vegetable specimens).

(Schmitt, quoted by Jacobi 1959: 48–49)

However, van der Hammen (1981) suggests that the Greek noun τύπος signified a mould and the idea that it is something 'produced by a blow' is incorrect. It is this sense of a 'mould' or a 'matrix' that informs Goethe's idea of the *Urbild* or 'original plan' on which he believed all animals and all plants to be based. Even Charles Darwin felt obliged to use the term archetype in approximately the same sense in *The Origin of Species* (1859), where he argued that selection occurred through a series of slight modifications to a persistent or stable pattern:

> if we suppose that an early progenitor – the archetype as it may be called – of all mammals, birds, and reptiles, had its limbs constructed on the existing general pattern . . . we can at once perceive the plain significance of the homologous construction of the limbs throughout the class.

Parallels and developments

Although the term 'archetype' did not originate with Jung, the sense in which it is now current has been very largely determined by his usage of it. Just how valuable the concept proves to be in practice can be judged from the manner in which researchers in other disciplines keep rediscovering the hypothesis and re-announcing it in their own terminology. When reading the work of contemporary authorities on anthropology, biology or psycholinguistics, one often comes across passages which could have been written by Jung. Thus the French molecular biologist and Nobel laureate, Jacques Monod, wrote in his book *Chance and Necessity* (1971): 'Everything comes from experience, yet not from actual experience, reiterated by each individual with each generation, but instead from experience accumulated by the entire ancestry of the species in the course of its evolution.' Jung expressed exactly the same notion when he described archetypes as 'the deposits of all our ancestral experiences, but they are not the experiences themselves' (1928: par. 300).

Admittedly, some of the earlier discoveries of the archetypal hypothesis predated Jung's announcement of the 'primordial image' and these were known to him; others occurred in the course of his lifetime; but many have surfaced since his death.

Thus, nineteenth-century mythology had discovered numerous 'motifs' as recurring in the myths of humankind, and the anthropologist Lucien Lévy-Bruhl (1857–1939) maintained that certain *représentations collectives* characterised the psychology of primitive peoples. The ethnographer Adolf Bastian (1826–1905), who travelled extensively throughout the world recording the folklore of diverse cultures, noted the existence of universal themes which he called 'primordial thoughts' or 'elementary ideas' which nonetheless manifested themselves in local forms ('ethnic ideas') peculiar to the group of people he happened to be studying; while in the field of comparative religion, Hubert and Mauss (1909) described the recurrence of universal beliefs and doctrines, calling them 'categories of the imagination'.

Of particular interest is the work of Claude Lévy-Strauss, the advocate of structuralism in anthropology, who studied the unconscious infrastructure of the patterns typical of human social, economic, political and cultural life. For Lévy-Strauss all forms of social life were a projection of universal laws responsible for regulating the unconscious activities of the psyche. Other related concepts are the 'social instincts' of Charles Darwin (1809–1882), the 'faculties' of Henri Bergson (1859–1941) and the 'isomorphs' postulated by the Gestalt psychologist Wolfgang Köhler (1887–1967).

In biology, a clear parallel to Jungian archetypes exists in Ernst Mayr's (1974) 'open programmes', which prepare animals and plants to respond appropriately to environmental changes – as when furry animals moult at the onset of summer, or plants reach upwards towards the sun when put in the shade by tall neighbours.

The anthropologists Robin Fox and Lionel Tiger, both of Rutgers University, have applied ethological concepts to the study of human social behaviour and maintain that the basic functions responsible for such behaviour are encoded in the 'biogrammar' (Tiger and Fox 1972) which each individual is born with and which develops in appropriate ways during the course of the human life cycle.

The amazing readiness with which young children in different cultures learn to speak the language or dialect of their parents is considered by the psycholinguist, Noam Chomsky (1965), to be dependent upon the activation of an innate 'language acquisition device' within the central nervous system incorporating the 'deep structures' upon which all languages proceed.

Most important for the empirical foundations of archetypal theory and its future applications are the parallels which are apparent in the new sciences of ethology (the study of animals in their natural habitats), evolutionary psychology and evolutionary psychiatry (Stevens 1982, 2002; Stevens and Price 2000a, 2000b).

In the late 1940s, the ethologists, Niko Tinbergen and Konrad Lorenz, proposed that the repertoire of behaviours with which each animal species is equipped is dependent upon *innate releasing mechanisms* in its central nervous system which are primed to become active when appropriate stimuli – called 'sign stimuli' – are encountered in the environment. When these stimuli are met, the innate mechanism is released, and the animal responds with a 'pattern of behaviour' which is adapted, through evolution, to the situation. Comparison of ethological findings with those of Jungian psychology make it clear that both disciplines are studying the same archetypal phenomena, but from opposite ends: Jungian psychology is focused on their introverted psychic manifestations, while ethology has examined their extroverted behavioural expression. The two approaches richly complement one another in such fundamental areas as bonding between parents and children, sexual desire and gender differences, court-ship and mating, co-operation and hostility between individuals and groups, and the development of the individual through the course of the human life cycle (Stevens 1982, 2002). Further evidence in support of the archetypal hypothesis comes from cross-cultural studies of human com-munities throughout the world (Brown 1991; Eibl-Eibesfeldt 1971; Ekman 1973; Fox 1975; Murdock 1945), from cross-cultural studies of dreams (Hall and Domhoff 1963; Hall and Nordby 1972; Stevens 1995) and from Booker's (2004) mammoth study of plots in stories and myths.

Since the early 1980s, evolutionary psychologists and psychiatrists on both sides of the Atlantic have detected and announced the presence of neuropsychic propensities which are virtually indistinguishable from arche-types. Gilbert (1997) refers to them as 'mentalities', Gardner (1988) as 'master programmes' or 'propensity states', while Wenegrat (1984) borrows the sociobiological term 'genetically transmitted response strategies'. Buss (1995) refers to 'evolved psychological mechanisms', Nesse (1987) to 'pre-pared tendencies', and Cosmides and Tooby (1989) to 'multiple mental modules'. These evolved propensities or modules are held responsible for psychosocial goals and strategies that are shared by all members of the species, whether they be healthy or ill. 'Ultimately', wrote Jung, 'every individual life is at the same time the eternal life of the species' (Jung 1938/ 1940: par. 146).

The independent discovery of the archetypal hypothesis – or something very like it – by workers in such a rich diversity of disciplines bears eloquent testimony to its empirical validity. Although Jung's original insights into the existence of innate structures in the human psyche arose out of reflection on his own dreams and experiences and out of his study of psychotic patients, abundant corroborative evidence has been derived from careful examination of patterns of behaviour as they manifest themselves in diverse human societies and different species of animals. Evolutionary psychiatry is exploring the implications of two major archetypal systems derived from Chance's (1988) *hedonic* and *agonic* modes, one concerned with attachment, affiliation, care-giving, care-receiving and altruism; and one concerned with rank, status, discipline, law and order, territory and possessions (Stevens and Price 2000a). Broadly, these two social archetypal systems correspond to Jung's *Eros* and *Logos* principles. This is potentially a major contribution to Jungian psychology, which has neglected the societal ramifications of human archetypal propensities, largely on account of Jung's introverted psychological type – an orientation shared by many of his followers.

In conclusion, there do indeed appear to be universal forms of instinctive and social behaviour, as well as universally occurring symbols and motifs (Jung 1956; Jung and von Franz 1964; Stevens 1998a). These forms have been subject to the essentially biological processes of evolution no less than the anatomical structures on whose homologous nature Charles Darwin based his theory.

Examples

The terminological confusion implicit in Jung's interchangeable use of the term 'archetype' and 'primordial image' is apparent when one searches his *Collected Works* for examples of archetypes in action. Thus he describes archetypal *events* (e.g., birth, death, separation from parents, initiation, marriage, the union of opposites, etc.), archetypal *figures* (e.g., mother, child, father, God, trickster, hero, wise old man, etc.), archetypal *symbols* (e.g., sun, moon, water, mandala, cross, fish, horse, snake, etc.) and archetypal *motifs* (e.g., the Apocalypse, the Deluge, the Creation, the night sea journey, etc.).

It is undeniable that all such events, figures, symbols and motifs are part of the age-old experience of our species, but there are difficulties in Jung's use of such terms as 'the archetype of the snake', 'horse' or 'fish'. The 'image' of each of these creatures is certainly universal but to what extent are we justified in concluding that this universality is due to the existence of an innate 'archetype-as-such' giving rise to the image? How far is it due to the ubiquitous existence of such creatures in the outer world? Jung would say that the *archetype-as-such* is at once an innate predisposition to form such an image and a preparation to encounter and respond appropriately to the *creature per se* in the environment. But nowhere does he examine in detail how this correspondence between creature and image comes about and is reproduced in each individual. A possible explanation of how this may occur in relation to the snake archetype has been offered by Stevens (1998a). That innate factors are involved seems highly probable, and there is evidence to support this idea. For example, primates reared in isolation from all other animals tend to display fear on first encountering snakes but not when first encountering mammals. Snake and spider phobias are commonly found by psychiatrists among people living in urban environments where such creatures no longer constitute a dangerous threat

(Stevens and Price 2000a). However, Jung's neglect of these issues, together with his loose application of the archetypal concept, induces a degree of cognitive dissonance among his more perceptive readers.

The most profound influence of archetypal functioning on the experience of the individual is the manner in which archetypes are held to control the human life cycle. Jung postulated that as we mature we pass through a programmed sequence which he called *the stages of life*. Each stage is mediated through a new set of archetypal imperatives which seek fulfilment in both personality and behaviour – being parented, exploring the environment, playing in the peer group, meeting the challenges of puberty and adolescence, being initiated into the adult group, accomplishing courtship and marriage, child-rearing, gathering, hunting and fighting, participating in religious rituals and ceremonials, assuming the responsibilities of advanced maturity, old age and the preparation for death. In addition to the Self, the psychic nucleus responsible for co-ordinating this lifelong sequence, Jung postulated other structures which play crucial roles in the psychic development and social adjustment of everyone. These include the persona, shadow, anima and animus.

Archetypal actualisation and psychological development

The archetypal units making up the collective unconscious possess the dynamic property of seeking their actualisation in the reality of life – that is to say, in the behaviour and personality of the individual as the life cycle unfolds within the context of the environment. In his essay 'Mind and earth' (1927) Jung wrote: 'Archetypes are systems of readiness for action, and at the same time images and emotions. They are inherited with the brain-structure – indeed, they are its psychic aspect' (1927/1931b: par. 53). This conception of the archetype as the common source of both behavioural and psychic events was a contribution of great theoretical significance, for it enabled psychology to move beyond the quagmires of vitalism and epiphenomenalism which had hitherto hampered the progress of all those who sought to explore the mysterious relationship between the body and the mind.

Archetypal actualisation determines the degree to which the over-riding goal of *individuation* is achieved. Actualisation (Jung also spoke of 'evocation' and 'constellation') of an archetype seems to proceed in accordance with the laws of association worked out by psychologists at the end of the nineteenth century. Two of these laws are particularly apposite: they are the *law of similarity* and the *law of contiguity*. Thus, for example, the mother archetype is actualised in the child's personal psyche through the *contiguity* of a female caretaker whose characteristics are *similar* enough to the innate anticipations of the maternal archetype for the child to perceive her and experience her as 'mother'. In this manner, the mother archetype is activated or 'evoked' in the collective unconscious and, as the attachment relationship develops, is built into the personal psyche of the child in the form of the mother *complex*. Complexes are functional units which make up the personal unconscious, just as the collective unconscious is composed of archetypes.

All archetypes are actualised in this way: 'The constellated archetype is always the primordial image of the need of the moment', wrote Jung.

> Although the changing situations of life must appear infinitely various to our way of thinking, their possible number never exceeds certain natural limits; they fall into more or less typical patterns that repeat themselves over and over again. The archetypal structure of the unconscious corresponds to the average run of events. The changes that may befall a man are not infinitely variable; they are variations of certain typical occurrences which are limited in number. When therefore a distressing situation arises, the corresponding archetype will be constellated in the unconscious. Since this archetype is numinous, i.e., possesses a specific energy, it will attract to itself the contents of consciousness – conscious ideas that render it perceptible and hence capable of conscious realization.
>
> (Jung 1911–1912: par. 450)

Because of its dynamism the actualised archetype may have a powerful impact on the conscious personality. This imposes an ethical responsibility on the ego and can, in adverse circumstances or in susceptible individuals, result in mental illness.

> When a situation occurs which corresponds to a given archetype, that archetype becomes activated and a compulsiveness appears, which, like an instinctual drive, gains its way against all reason and will, or else produces a conflict of pathological dimension, that is to say, a neurosis.
>
> (Jung 1936: par. 99)

Archetypal actualisation is thus at the core of Jung's understanding of developmental psychology, both healthy and abnormal. Psychopathology occurs when archetypal strategies malfunction as a result of environmental insults of deficiencies at critical stages of development (Stevens and Price 2000a).

Some attempts have been made to revise Jung's position on the hereditary nature of archetypes, Petteri Pietikainen (1998) preferring to conceive them as 'culturally determined functionary forms' and George Hogenson

(1999) as 'the emergent properties of the dynamic developmental system of brain, environment and narrative'. These suggestions would appear to make a semantic confusion between the archetype-as-such and the archetypal ideas, motifs, images and behaviours the archetype-as-such gives rise to. To accept their definitions would be to offend against Occam's Razor. It would relegate the brain once more to the outdated status of a 'general purpose processing mechanism' and would erode the hermeneutic elegance of Jung's hypothesis (Stevens 1998b, 2002).

The psychoid archetype and the *unus mundus*

The archetype possesses a fundamental duality: it is both psychic and non-psychic, both 'spirit' and 'body', for the archetype is the essential precondition of all psychophysical events:

> the archetypes are as it were the hidden foundations of the conscious mind, or, to use another comparison, the roots which the psyche has sunk not only in the earth in the narrower sense but in the world in general.
>
> (Jung 1927/1931b: par. 53)

To this non-psychic aspect Jung gave the term 'psychoid' archetype and it represents his boldest contribution to the resolution of the body–mind problem.

To illustrate what he meant by the non-psychic or 'psychoid' aspect of the archetype, Jung drew an analogy with the electromagnetic spectrum. The part of the spectrum which is visible to us (i.e., the ultra-violet end) represents those psychic processes of which we are conscious. The invisible infra-red end of the spectrum corresponds to the unconscious biological aspect of the archetype which is identical with 'the physiology of the organism and thus merges with its chemical and physical conditions' (1947/1954: par. 420).

Jung proceeded to propose not only that archetypal structures were fundamental to the existence and survival of all living organisms but also that they were continuous with structures controlling the behaviour of inorganic matter as well. The archetype was no mere psychic entity but 'the bridge to matter in general' (1947/1954: par. 420). It was this psychoid aspect of the archetype which was to exercise the imagination of the physicist and Nobel laureate, Wolfgang Pauli (1955), who believed it made a major contribution to our ability to comprehend the principles on which the universe has been created.

In an attempt to describe the unitary reality which Jung believed to underlie all manifest phenomena, he resurrected the ancient term *unus mundus* – the eternal ground of all empirical being. He conceived archetypes to be the mediators of the *unus mundus*, responsible for organising ideas and images in the psyche and for governing the fundamental principles of matter and energy in the physical world. Embracing Jung's conception, Pauli argued that the archetype could provide the 'missing link' between the physical events which are the legitimate study of science on the one hand and the mind of the scientist who studies them on the other. Thus, the archetypes which order our perceptions and ideas are themselves the product of an objective order which transcends both the human mind and the external world.

In adopting this standpoint, Pauli was reaffirming the position adopted by the German astronomer, Johannes Kepler (1572–1630), who ascribed his delight in scientific discovery to a process of 'matching' whereby he linked 'inner ideas', already implanted in his mind by God, with the external events which he perceived through his senses. Kepler actually referred to the 'inner ideas' as 'archetypal' and saw them as the necessary foundation of all knowledge. 'For, to know is to compare that which is externally perceived with *inner ideas* and to judge that it agrees with them.' Our sensory experiences 'call forth intellectual notions that were already present inwardly; so that which formerly was hidden in the soul, as under the *veil of potentiality*, now shines therein in actuality' (Kepler 1619, quoted by Pauli 1955). The parallel between Kepler's 'inner ideas' which lie 'under the veil of potentiality' and Jung's 'primordial images' is clear.

A further significant parallel drawn by Pauli and Jung, working in collaboration, is between analytical psychology and quantum physics. Just as Jung's enquiry into the structure and function of the psyche had led him to postulate the existence of dynamic 'irrepresentables' (archetypes), so research in quantum physics has given rise to the postulate of similar 'irrepresentables' (elementary particles) constituting matter and defying all space–time descriptions. Could these two areas of research be approaching the same aspects of reality? 'When the existence of two or more irrepresentables is assumed', wrote Jung, 'there is always the possibility – which we tend to overlook – that it may not be a question of two or more factors but of one only' (1947/1954: par. 417).

Another eminent physicist, Werner Heisenberg, came, towards the end of his life, to see the fundamental aspects of nature not as residing in the particles themselves but in the 'symmetries' which the particles form. Perceiving the parallel between Heisenberg's 'symmetries' and Jung's 'archetypes', the physicist David Peat has argued: 'These fundamental symmetries could be thought of as the archetypes of all matter and the ground of material existence. The elementary particles themselves would be simply the material realization of these underlying symmetries' (Peat 1987: 94).

Just as the elementary particles are maintained by a dance that transcends the world of matter, so too, is mind sustained by dynamics that

lie beyond both mind and matter. Beyond mind and matter are therefore patterns and symmetries that have a generative and animating
effect.

(Peat 1987: 111–112)

Evidently, biology must function as a bridge between these two sets of
symmetries, and it is conceivable that this could be provided by symmetries
within the structure of DNA or by molecular symmetries responsible for
neuronal and synaptic events in the brain and central nervous system,
which are being studied by the molecular biologists.

The dance transcending the worlds of mind and matter is responsible,
in Jung's view, for the phenomenon of 'meaningful coincidence', which
he called *synchronicity*: 'a coincidence in time of two or more causally
unrelated events which have the same or similar meaning' (1952: par. 849) –
as when one dreams of the death of a distant relative the very same night as
she dies. There can be no causal connection between the two events, yet a
personally impressive acausal connection is established through their shared
meaning.

Synchronicity, Jung believed, is the expression of an *acausal orderedness*
dependent upon archetypal functioning. Such an acausal archetypal order is
apparent in the properties of the prime numbers as well as the discon-
tinuities of physics, and it must, ultimately, be responsible for the meaningfulness implicit in the coincidence of associated mental and physical
events. Jung wrote: 'I have a distinct feeling that number is the key to the
mystery, since it is just as much discovered as it is invented. It is a quantity
as well as a meaning' (von Franz 1974). He understood number to be the
'most primitive element of order in the human mind' and defined number
psychologically as 'an archetype of order which has become conscious' (von
Franz 1974: 45).

In his eighties Jung began to work on the first five integers, but shortly
before his death, he gave his notes to his friend and colleague Marie-Louise
von Franz, saying: 'I am too old to be able to write this now, so I hand it
over to you' (von Franz 1974: ix). As a result, von Franz undertook an
exhaustive investigation of number archetypes acting as dynamic organising
principles in both psyche and matter. She published her findings in *Number
and Time* (1974) and her work represents a significant extension of the
archetypal hypothesis of Jung and Pauli.

The parallel between von Franz's search for the primal archetypes
inherent in numbers and Chomsky's search for linguistic universals has
been examined by the physicist Charles Card (1991a, 1991b, 2000), and he
has reformulated a general archetypal hypothesis as follows:

All mental and physical phenomena are complementary aspects of the
same unitary, transcendental reality. At the basis of all physical and

mental phenomena there exist certain fundamental dynamical forms or patterns of behaviour which may be called number archetypes. Any specific process, physical or mental, is a particular *representation* of certain of these archetypes. In particular, the number archetypes provide the basis for all possible symbolic expression. Therefore, it is possible that a neutral language constructed from abstract symbolic representations of the number archetypes may provide highly unified, although not unique, descriptions of all mental and physical phenomena.

(Card 2000)

Card evidently feels that this general archetypal hypothesis may prove to be of the highest significance for physics and for the epistemological foundation of our scientific world view. In his most recent publication Card (2000) has proposed that archetypal theory could form the basis of a contemporary philosophy of nature.

Since archetypes precondition all existence, they are manifest in the spiritual achievements of art, science and religion, as well as in the organisation of organic and inorganic matter. The archetype thus provides a basis for a common understanding of data derived from all sciences and all human activities – not least because of its implications for epistemology (the study of knowledge *per se*).

The scientific potentials of archetypal theory have been examined by Cohen (1975), Hogenson (1999), McDowell (1999), Maloney (1999), Routh (1981), Sabini (2000), Shelborne (1988) and Walters (1994), its integration with sociology has been advanced by Gray (1996), its philosophical significance has been explored by Nagy (1991), and its implications for religious studies have been outlined by MacLennan (2005), Stevens (1986, 1998a) and Stevens and Price (2000b) and for the psychology of warfare and terrorism (Stevens 2004), while Robertson (1995) has carried the discussion of the archetypal hypothesis beyond the biological and physical sciences to the very foundations of mathematics. The concept is so fundamental that it is being taken out of the hands of Jungians and its implications are being worked out by theorists and practitioners in other disciplines. This is as it should be, for Jung never argued that his psychology was definitive or final. The full implications of archetypal theory have yet to be realised.

References

Booker, C. (2004) *The Seven Basic Plots*. London and New York: Continuum.
Brown, D.E. (1991) *Human Universals*. New York: McGraw-Hill.
Buss, B.M. (1995) 'Evolutionary psychology, a new paradigm for psychological science'. *Psychological Enquiry*, 6(1): 1–30.

Card, C.R. (1991a) 'The archetypal view of C.G. Jung and Wolfgang Pauli, part I'. *Psychological Perspectives*, 24: 19–33.

—— (1991b) 'The archetypal view of C.G. Jung and Wolfgang Pauli, part II: the relevance of the archetypal hypothesis to physics'. *Psychological Perspectives*, 25: 52–69.

—— (2000) 'The emergence of archetypes in present-day science and their significance for a contemporary philosophy of nature', in B. Goertzel, A. Coombs and M. Germine (eds) *Mind in Time*. Creskoll, NJ: Hampton Press.

Chance, M.R.A. (1988) 'Introduction', in M.R.A. Chance (ed.) *Social Fabric of the Mind*. Hillsdale, NJ: Erlbaum.

Chomsky, N. (1965) *Aspects of the Theory of Syntax*. Cambridge, MA: MIT Press.

Cohen, E.D. (1975) *C.G. Jung and the Scientific Attitude*. New York: Philosophical Library.

Cosmides, L. and Tooby, J. (1989) 'Evolutionary psychology and the generation of culture, Part II. Case study: a computational theory of social exchange'. *Ethology and Sociobiology*, 10: 51–97.

Darwin, C. (1859) *The Origin of Species by Means of Natural Selection*. London: John Murray.

Eibl-Eibesfeldt, I. (1971) *Love and Hate*. London: Methuen.

Ekman, P. (1973) 'Cross-cultural studies of facial expression', in P. Ekman (ed.) *Darwin and Facial Expression: A Century of Research in Review*. New York: Academic Press.

Fox, R. (1975) *Encounter with Anthropology*. London: Peregrine.

Gardner, R. (1988) 'Psychiatric syndromes as infrastructure for intra-specific communication', in M.R.A. Chance (ed.) *Social Fabrics of the Mind*. Hillsdale, NJ: Erlbaum.

Gilbert, P. (1997) 'The evolution of social attractiveness and its role in shame, humiliation, guilt and therapy'. *British Journal of Medical Psychology*, 70: 113–148.

Gray, R.M. (1996) *Archetypal Explorations: An Integrative Approach to Human Behaviour*. London and New York: Routledge.

Hall, C.S. and Domhoff, B. (1963) 'A ubiquitous sex difference in dreams'. *Journal of Abnormal and Social Psychology*, 66(3): 278–280.

Hall, C.S. and Nordby, V.J. (1972) *The Individual and his Dreams*. New York: New American Library.

Hogenson, G. (1999) 'Evolution, psychology and the emergence of the psyche', presentation at the National Conference of Jungian Analysts in Santa Fe, New Mexico, October.

Hubert, H. and Mauss, M. (1909) *Mélanges d'histoire des religions*. Paris: Alcan.

Jacobi, J. (1959) *Complex, Archetype, Symbol*. London: Routledge and Kegan Paul.

Jarret, J. (1981) 'Schopenhauer and Jung'. *Spring*: 201.

Jung, C.G. (1911–1912) 'The battle for deliverance from the mother', in *CW* 5ii.

—— (1916) 'The structure of the unconscious', in *CW* 7: pars. 442–521.

—— (1919/1929) 'Instinct and the unconscious', in *CW* 8: pars. 263–283.

—— (1927/1931a) 'The structure of the psyche', in *CW* 8: pars. 283–342.

—— (1927/1931b) 'Mind and earth', in *CW* 10: pars. 49–103.

Jung, C.G. (1928) 'The relations between the ego and the unconscious', in *CW* 7: pars. 202–406.

—— (1928/1931) 'Analytical psychology and *Weltanschauung*', in *CW* 8: pars. 689–741.

—— (1934/1954) 'Archetypes of the collective unconscious', in *CW* 9i: pars. 1–86.

—— (1936) 'The concept of the collective unconscious', in *CW* 9i: pars. 87–110.

—— (1936/1954) 'Concerning the archetypes, with special reference to the anima concept', in *CW* 9i: pars. 111–147.

—— (1938/1940) 'Psychology and religion', in *CW* 11: pars. 1–168.

—— (1938/1954) 'Psychological aspects of the mother archetype', in *CW* 9i: pars. 148–198.

—— (1947/1954) 'On the nature of the psyche', in *CW* 8: pars. 343–442.

—— (1949) 'Foreword to Harding: "Woman's Mysteries"', in *CW* 18: par. 1949.

—— (1952) 'Synchronicity: an acausal connecting principle', in *CW* 8: pars. 816–968.

—— (1956) 'Foreword', in *CW* 5. London: Routledge and Kegan Paul.

—— (1961) 'Healing the split', in *CW* 18.

—— (1963) *Memories, Dreams, Reflections*. London: Routledge and Kegan Paul; New York: Random House.

Jung, C.G. and von Franz, M.-L. (eds) (1964) *Man and his Symbols*. London: Aldus.

Kepler, J. (1619) *Harmonices Mundi*, Book IV. Augsburg.

McDowell, M.J. (1999) 'Relating to the mystery: a biological view of analytical psychology'. *Quadrant: Journal of the C.G. Jung Foundation for Analytical Psychology*, 29(1): 12–32.

MacLennan, B.J. (2005) 'Evolution, Jung, and theurgy: their role in modern neoplatonism', in J.F. Finamore and R. Berchman (eds) *Plato Redivivus: History of Platonism*. New Orleans, LA: University Press of the South.

Macmillan, M. (1997) *Freud Evaluated: The Completed Arc*. Cambridge, MA and London: MIT Press.

Maloney, A. (1999) 'Darwin and Jung in a new psychiatry'. *San Francisco Jung Institute Library Journal*, 18: 11–22.

Mayr, E. (1974) 'Behavior programs and evolutionary strategies'. *American Scientist*, 62(6): 650–659.

Monod, J. (1971) *Chance and Necessity*. New York: Alfred A. Knopf.

Murdock, G.P. (1945) 'The common denominator of culture', in R. Linton (ed.) *The Science of Man in the World Crisis*. New York: Columbia University Press.

Nagy, M. (1991) *Philosophical Issues in the Psychology of C.G. Jung*. Albany, NY: State University of New York Press.

Nesse, R.M. (1987) 'An evolutionary perspective on panic disorder and agoraphobia'. *Ethology and Sociobiology*, 8(3): 73–84.

Otto, R. (1917/1950) *The Idea of the Holy*. Oxford: Oxford University Press.

Pauli, W. (1955) 'The influence of archetypal ideas on the scientific theories of Kepler', in C.G. Jung and W. Pauli, *The Interpretation of Nature and the Psyche*. London: Routledge and Kegan Paul.

Peat, F.D. (1987) *Synchronicity: The Bridge between Matter and Mind*. New York: Bantam.

Pietikainen, P. (1998) 'Archetypes as symbolic forms'. *Journal of Analytical Psychology*, 43(3): 325–343.

Robertson, R. (1995) *Jungian Archetypes: Jung, Gödel, and the History of Archetypes*. York Beach, ME: Nicolas-Hays.

Routh, V. (1981) 'Jungian psychology and evolutionary theory: an enquiry into the relation of psyche to phylogenesis', unpublished dissertation, Brunel University, Uxbridge, Middlesex.

Sabini, M. (2000) 'The bones in the cave: phylogenetic foundations of analytical psychology'. *Journal of Jungian Theory and Practice*, 2: 17–33.

Shelburne, W.A. (1988) *Mythos and Logos in the Thought of Carl Jung*. Albany, NY: State University of New York Press.

Stevens, A. (1982) *Archetype: A Natural History of the Self*. London: Routledge and Kegan Paul; New York: William Morrow.

—— (1986) 'Thoughts on the psychobiology of religion and the neurobiology of archetypal experience'. *Zygon*, 21(1): 9–29.

—— (1995) *Private Myths: Dreams and Dreaming*. London: Hamish Hamilton.

—— (1998a) *Ariadne's Clue: A Guide to the Symbols of Humankind*. London: Allen Lane.

—— (1998b) 'Response to P. Pietikainen'. *Journal of Analytical Psychology*, 43(3): 345–355.

—— (2002) *Archetype Revisited: An Updated Natural History of the Self*. London: Brunner-Routledge; (2003) Toronto: Inner City.

—— (2004) *The Roots of War and Terror*. London and New York: Continuum.

Stevens, A. and Price, J. (2000a) *Evolutionary Psychiatry: A New Beginning*, 2nd edn. London: Routledge.

— (2000b) *Prophets, Cults, and Madness*. London: Duckworth.

Tiger, L. and Fox, R. (1972) *Imperial Animal*. London: Secker and Warburg.

van der Hammen, L. (1981) 'Type-concept, higher classification and evolution'. *Acta Biotheoretica*, 30: 5.

von Franz, M.-L. (1974) *Number and Time*. Evanston, IL: Northwestern University Press.

Walters, S. (1994) 'Archetypes and algorithms: evolutionary psychology and Carl Jung's theory of the collective unconscious', unpublished paper, Department of Psychology, Simon Fraser University, Burnaby, British Columbia.

Webster, R. (1995) *Why Freud was Wrong: Sin, Science, and Psychoanalysis*. London: HarperCollins.

Wenegrat, B. (1984) *Sociobiology and Mental Disorder*. Menlo Park, CA: Addison-Wesley.

Chapter 4

The shadow

Ann Casement

One does not become enlightened by imagining figures of light, but by making the darkness conscious.

(Jung 1967: 265)

Introduction

The concept of the *shadow* is one of Jung's great contributions to psychology which he adapted early on in the twentieth century from Freud's original division between the light and dark sides of the human psyche. According to Jung, when the *shadow* is activated, usually through projection, it is charged with *affect* and takes on an autonomous life of its own beyond the ego's control. It is possible to depict Jung as a *structuralist* thinker who was not so much interested in creating a highly systematised metapsychology, but who was, instead, concerned with the interrelationships between different psychic phenomena. As a result, he did not develop clear-cut definitions of the latter and this included his thinking about *shadow*. Inextricably linked to this concept is that of *compensation* so that *shadow* – both individual and collective – is compensatory to a consciously held attitude.

In a classical Jungian analysis, problems related to *shadow* are thought to be the first to need attention. These largely arise from the realm of *personal shadow* which may be conceived of as the repository of all the aspects of a person that are unacceptable or distasteful to them. As a clinician, one encounters a variety of *shadow* phenomena which include envy, aggression, greed, laziness and jealousy (the latter being one that is particularly hedged around with shame). This is by no means an exhaustive list. However, it is important to note that *shadow* is not always negative, for instance, where the more positive side of the individual is repressed and consequently lives in the *shadow*. In these instances, the ego plays an essentially negative role while a *positive shadow* projection may be activated by an admired or liked outer object, for example, in the analytic setting where the *wounded healer* archetype often gets constellated with the analyst having to carry the analyand's 'healer' projection until the latter can reclaim and own it for him or herself.

Many aspects of the *personal shadow* may be traced back to the relationship to the parents or parental surrogates and siblings. An individual who has a huge *shadow* problem with jealousy may have felt excluded from the parental relationship. Equally, there may be an attractive high-achieving older sibling to whom the individual has felt unfavourably compared or a spoilt younger sibling who is the centre of attention in the family.

The resulting *shadow* problem from such family dynamics plays an important part in the individual's life and will often carry over into relationships with the opposite sex where excessive jealousy can become a destructive force. This will infiltrate the individual's other interactions and may cripple their functioning as a well-adapted social being. In analysis, *personal shadow* problems of this kind will manifest in the transference where the patient/analysand may experience the analyst as an excluding parent or as a rival either to be competed with or be subservient to. The latter kind of transference can evoke a powerful countertransference on the analyst's part in the form of feelings of superiority or of being the all-wise one.

Jung gives an example of this kind of *transference/countertransference* in his analysis of a philosophy student. He diagnosed the patient as having a father fixation which led her to seek out a male analyst like her father with whom she could jostle intellectually, and, at the same time, force into a superior position making him into an object of admiration. Jung writes that her authentic self lay hidden behind her persona of 'the supremely wise, very grown-up, all-understanding mother-daughter-beloved' (Jung 1953b: 159).

The patient had experienced the oedipal triumph in winning father from mother at an early age so that father became the idealised parent and mother the patient's *shadow* rival. Jung's evident countertransference irritation with the patient is an expression of the latter. *Personal shadow* transference/countertransference would need to be worked through in the early part of the analysis, but behind this can lie an archetypal oedipal conflict emanating from the *collective unconscious*. The latter is the innate, non-personal part of the psyche which is the realm of archetypal imagery that expresses itself symbolically.

Jung points to the fact that the kind of analysis that is advocated in analytical psychology is nothing other than the scientific rediscovery of an ancient truth which is the healing power of catharsis or cleansing. This comes about as a result of the analytic work during which the patient begins to become aware of their darker side and can confess to it. As Jung expresses it: 'The first beginnings of all analytical treatment of the soul are to be found in its prototype, the confessional' (Jung 1954: 55). Through the observation of images and feelings that detach themselves from the invisible realm of the unconscious, repressed and forgotten *shadow* contents manifest themselves. According to Jung, the individuating process invariably starts off by the patient's becoming conscious of their *shadow*, which is experienced at first as the inferior personality made up of everything that does not fit with conscious demands. This is a gain, albeit a painful one, as it gives the person substance. There has to be a dark side in order for a person to become whole and by becoming conscious of that they remember they are human like everyone else.

Apart from the *personal shadow* there is also the *collective shadow* of which history provides many examples. The most notorious example from the twentieth century was the projection of *collective shadow* by the Nazis into the Jews, who could then be portrayed as inferior or evil beings to be exterminated. As Jung says: 'In Hitler, every German should have seen his own shadow, his own worst danger' (Jung 1964: 223).

The phenomenon of *shadow* also varies from one culture to another so that what is acceptable in the United States may not be in Japan. This may vary within the same culture at different times in history so that in English society at one time good manners and social status were paramount. Nowadays that would be considered rather old-fashioned as other priorities such as a more egalitarian society have superseded them.

A further aspect, touched on above, is that of *archetypal shadow* which would emanate from the archetypal or mythological realm of the *collective unconscious*. In Jung's thought this would be equated with evil. A more detailed exploration of this will be undertaken later in the chapter.

Jung's writings on *shadow*

Jung acknowledged Freud as the medical man who at the turn of the nineteenth century showed that reason was not the ruler in the human psyche but that human nature was instead steeped in an abysmal darkness. Since then psychotherapy has explored this darkness in one way or another.

In *Memories, Dreams, Reflections*, Jung wrote of a personal encounter with the *shadow* in December 1913, while he was going through his 'creative illness'. As Ellenberger expresses it: 'the intermediate period from 1913 to 1919 was that of a *creative illness* . . . a period of intense preoccupation with the mysteries of the human soul' (Ellenberger 1970: 672). At this time, he had a dream in which he killed the heroic Siegfried at the behest of a brown-skinned savage. He was distraught with grief when he awoke but came to see the latter as an aspect of the 'primitive' *shadow* at whose urging he now had to let go of his heroic, idealised conscious attitude. An alternative view of this dream could relate Siegfried to the child Sabina Spielrein yearned to have with Jung. She was his first psychoanalytic patient which resulted in both parties becoming embroiled in powerful erotic transference/countertransference enactments.

In Jung's writings, *shadow* from the personal unconscious is said to be projected onto a person of the same sex, whereas projections onto persons of the opposite sex are thought to emanate from the *anima/animus* and lead to confrontation with contra-sexuality and the *collective unconscious*. This is touched on below in an example from Jung's (1956) *Symbols of Transformation*, an early work frequently updated by him. Jung tended to do a cut-and-paste job when he was revising, and, in the process, would completely rewrite large passages of text. In the earliest version of this work, which was then entitled *The Psychology of the Unconscious* and published in 1912, there is no mention of *shadow*, which came later in his theory, and the word used instead was *complex*. In the later *Symbols of Transformation*, Jung writes: 'I have frequently observed in the analysis of Americans that the inferior side of the personality, the "shadow", is represented by a Negro or Indian' (Jung 1956: 183). This is in reference to the patient whose material he was studying in the book, a young American woman, who was being treated by Jung's colleague, Théodore Flournoy. Jung thought the Aztec figure in one of her dreams could not be a *shadow* aspect of herself as it was a male figure so that it must instead be regarded as a masculine component of her personality.

It is important to note with regard to the above that Jung was a man of his time when the kind of thinking he puts forward in connection with *shadow* representations was acceptable, even taken for granted. Post-Jungians take a very different approach to this and would not automatically assume that a black person in a white person's dream was a *shadow* figure or vice versa. Their thinking has also changed about seeing *shadow* figures as not only associated with persons of the same sex. In other words, a male may be equally a *shadow* figure for a woman as a female can be for a man.

The book Jung wrote after this was *Psychological Types* (published in 1921). Although this work contains only three references to *shadow* in the index, the whole work centres around that concept. It was, in part, inspired by William James's characterisation of two temperaments: the *tough-minded* and the *tender-minded*, each of which is the *shadow* of the other. In *Psychological Types* Jung developed his theory of two attitudes: the *extravert* and the *introvert* who are equally each other's *shadow*. The *extravert* is orientated to the data supplied by the outer objective world. The *introvert*, on the other hand, relates to data supplied by the inner subjective world. Jung marries the concepts of *introvert* and *extravert* to the four functions of *thinking*, *feeling*, *sensation* and *intuition* and points to how Darwin, as an extraverted thinker, would be the *shadow* of Kant as an introverted thinker.

In the same work, Jung examines the Apollonian and Dionysian aesthetic that Nietzsche applied to the ancient Greeks, who saw the latter as being

caught in a conflict between the two. According to Nietzsche, the antagon-
ism between them – the domesticated Apollonian and the barbarian nature
of the Dionysian – could be bridged only by art. An important new work,
Nietzsche and Jung: The Whole Self in the Union of Opposites by Lucy
Huskinson (2004), demonstrates Nietzsche's enormous contribution to
Jung's central concepts. For instance, she relates Nietzsche's *Übermensch* to
Jung's *self*, both of which are involved in confrontation with the *shadow*.
Compare Nietzsche's: 'For a shadow came to me – the most silent, the
lightest of all things once came to me! The beauty of the Superman came to
me as a shadow' with Jung's: 'the shadow contains the self. Behind the
shadow looms up the self' (Huskinson 2004: 103).

The most concerted attempt Jung made to define the concept of *shadow* is
in his book, *Aion*. A summary of what he writes in that may be useful here
in order to orientate the reader towards this central Jungian idea.

To start with, Jung briefly touches on the difference between the *personal
unconscious* and the *collective unconscious*. The contents of the former are
acquired during the individual's lifetime; whereas those of the latter are
from the realm of the archetypes. The ones that are experienced empirically
most frequently, usually through projection, are those of the *shadow* and
the *anima/animus*.

As has been said above, in a classical Jungian analysis it is problems to
do with the personal *shadow* where 'it represents first and foremost the
personal unconscious' (Jung 1959a: 10) that are initially worked on and
Jung says that no one can gain any insight into themselves or acquire self-
knowledge without first tackling their *shadow*. He alludes to this as a moral
problem and says that it is a huge challenge to the ego-personality requiring
painstaking work over a long period of time.

Some aspects of the *shadow* are more resistant to being assimilated to
consciousness since they are lived through powerful affect by way of
projection onto another. Where there is complete failure to gain insight into
the phenomenon, the outer world becomes increasingly impoverished and
illusory, and, in extreme cases, the individual is trapped in an autistic
condition isolated from the environment. This is because the shadow is
being lived through projection and the outer world becomes a replica of the
person's unknown side. In this way, one may speak of someone being afraid
of their own shadow.

This more severe manifestation 'when it appears as an archetype' (Jung
1959a: 10) belongs in the realm of the *collective unconscious* and represents
an encounter with evil. This results in a shattering experience for the person
gazing into the face of absolute evil. However, Jung does point to the fact
that the contents of the *personal unconscious* or *shadow* are merged with the
archetypal contents of the *collective unconscious* and bring the latter into
consciousness with them when *shadow* is activated. Evil then may result
from the fusion of a negative parental introject with the dark side of the *self*

which results in the introject becoming infused with archetypal power. This might be encountered in analysis through an archetypal negative father transference being constellated and then projected onto the analyst, who is consequently experienced as a bullying tyrant.

The individual who lives through projection is convinced that it is others who have all the bad qualities and who practise all the vices. Therefore, it is *they* who are wrong and *they* who must be fought against. On the other hand, the individual who succeeds in shouldering some of the burdens of the world and seeing that whatever is wrong with the world is not unrelated to themselves becomes a serious problem to him or herself. As Jung says, only the individual who learns to deal with his/her own *shadow* has done something real for the world for no one can see straight if they do not see themselves.

In this same work, *Aion*, he goes on to talk about the necessity for the individual's welfare of embodying the *shadow* in consciousness. In this way, if a feeling of inferiority is conscious there is a chance of correcting it. If, on the other hand, it is repressed and isolated from consciousness, it remains uncorrected and liable to erupt in a moment of unawareness. This explains why the most carefully laid plans may go awry or well-meaning intentions may turn out badly as the mere suppression of *shadow* is not the answer.

When the *shadow* results in neurosis it becomes considerably intensified and it then becomes a necessity for the individual to find a way for the conscious personality and *shadow* to live together. Suppression is of little use and the reconciliation of the two poses a major problem both for the individual and for society at large but it is a problem that must be engaged with if the person is to become more than two-dimensional.

Jung equated the inferior function with *shadow* as it is hedged around with a great deal of autonomy and affect and has the character of an instinct. Jung's thinking on typology posited that there are four functions: thinking, feeling, intuition and sensation. In his model, the first two are the rational functions lying at either end of a vertical continuum; while the second two are the non-rational ones which are located at different ends of a horizontal line. 'Jung went on to postulate that the superior function had its opposing inferior function in the one at the other end of a vertical spine' (Casement 2001: 151). However, the individual who has achieved rational orientation at the expense of not integrating the inferior function into their conscious personality may, according to Jung, remain as ignorant of themselves as an infant because 'the fourth would not come' (Jung 1958a: 166). The 'fourth' here refers to the least differentiated function which is, as a consequence, the least conscious one and brings with it unconscious, archetypal contents when it is activated. Jung even says that the inferior function is identical with the dark side of the personality which is the door into the unconscious.

There are various traps any individual may fall into, one of which is identifying with the *shadow*. A person of this kind will always prefer to make an unfavourable impression on others and will create obstacles for himself where none exist. However, the opposite way of living can equally be a trap – that is, identification with the *persona*, which is the outer front one presents to the world. If this becomes too much part of the individual's identity then the person is condemned to live a false self identical with their own inauthentic biography. The temptation to identify with what one seems to be is great because, as Jung says, 'the persona is usually rewarded in cash' (Jung 1959b: 123).

He writes at some length equating the inferior function with *shadow* and says the individuation process is invariably started by the individual becoming conscious of the *shadow*. It is the inferior function that acts autonomously towards consciousness and that cannot be harnessed and controlled. Individuating may come about only through the realisation of *shadow* which does not mean giving into one's Mr Hyde side, but, instead, of struggling with it so that in place of a neurotic dissociation of that aspect, there is a real attempt to bring it into consciousness. Jung was impressed by the Jekyll and Hyde story and made frequent reference to it in his own writings.

Neurosis, according to Jung, is an inner cleavage – a state of being at war with oneself. What drives individuals to this state is the suspicion of being two people in opposition to each other – the *shadow* and the *ego*. To illustrate this, Jung quotes Faust's saying that two souls are housed within his breast.

If the individual cannot reconcile these two aspects then it can lead to a neurotic split in the personality and Jung says that the healing of this split is a religious problem. Just as Christian teaching exalts forgiveness of one's enemy in an external situation, this needs to be turned inward by the individual in learning to live with the enemy within and to call the wolf one's sibling. However, Jung warns against seeing this as simple as in reality the acceptance of the shadow-side of human nature verges on the impossible as this means coming to terms with what is unreasonable, senseless and even evil.

However, as Jung points out, the dangers of not undertaking this super-human struggle is that a weak ego can identify with the transcendent *self* if the *shadow* has not been sufficiently realised. This in turn leads to the inflation of the ego with consequent delusions of omniscience and omni-potence – the ultimate road to madness. Just as the *self* may be seen as the inner God-image so Jung (1953b) says in *Two Essays on Analytical Psychology* that the devil is a variant of the *shadow* archetype.

Jung saw in alchemical symbolism an analogy with the *individuating* process, that is, the way in which individuals may become themselves undivided, distinct from others and whole. Jung equates the *nigredo*, the first stage of the work in alchemy, with the encounter with the *shadow* in psychology. This is the stage of melancholy and stasis when everything comes to a standstill. The *shadow* presents a fundamental contrast to the conscious personality as a positive virtue is usually the result of a victory over the corresponding vice. Indeed, for Jung the problem of opposites called up by the *shadow* plays the decisive role in alchemy since it leads to the ultimate union of opposites in the archetypal *hierosgamos* or higher marriage. When the conflict is brought into consciousness it leads to the recognition of an alien other in oneself. The alchemists named this Mercurius, which they conceptualised as God, daemon, person, thing and as psyche as well as soma. In other words, as the source of all opposites.

Jung points to Christ and the infernal or chthonic side of the self as autonomous images and says our psychic conditions are derived from these archetypal figures in the *collective unconscious*. From this standpoint, Jung points to Christ as the archetype of consciousness and Mercurius as the archetype of the unconscious.

The alchemical text, the *Chymical Wedding*, written by the seventeenth-century alchemist Christian Rosencreutz, was concerned with the transformation and union of the royal pair depicted in it but it was also concerned with the moral development of the individual undertaking the alchemical work. This is based on the union with the *shadow* and the problem of opposites that become constellated and in turn activate opposing archetypal contents in the *collective unconscious*. This process results in *numinous* or awesome experiences.

According to Jung, Mercurius signifies by its very nature the unconscious itself and is also by nature both active and passive. In alchemy, the active or 'ascending' part of him is called Sol or King and the passive or 'descending' part Luna or Queen. This duality of light and shadow in alchemy is for Jung also the duality of psychic life. Alchemy may be seen as a subversive force compensating for the purified imagery of medieval Christianity. In a similar way, it could be said that dynamic psychology led to the lifting of the repression of sexuality of the nineteenth century. Jung goes on to say: 'The arcanum of alchemy is one of those archetypal ideas that fills a gap in the Christian view of the world, namely, the unbridged gulf between the opposites, in particular between good and evil' (Jung 1963: 473).

The conflict that ensues from confrontation with the *shadow* in both alchemy and analytical psychology must eventually result in a union or *coniunctio*, the term Jung borrows from alchemy. It is a struggle that has to be lived through and experienced and cannot be abolished by rational means or repression, as the latter means that it lives in the unconscious, and, in that way, is all the more subversive to the conscious personality. The *shadow* is synonymous with the primitive aspects of the psyche to which reason means nothing.

If, through analysis, a coniunctio results then what was hidden behind the conventional mask – i.e., the *shadow* – is raised to consciousness and integrated with the ego. This means, according to Jung, a move in the direction of wholeness as the assimilation of the *shadow* gives a person body as the animal sphere of instinct emerges into consciousness.

This is the only way that humans can develop as repression leads to dissociation in an attempt to get rid of the *shadow*. As opposed to that one-sided way of living, individuals have to learn to live with the *shadow* without it leading to a series of disasters. Recognition of the *shadow* leads to humility and genuine fear of what lies in the depths of humanity. It is ignorance of this that is the most dangerous thing for humans.

The meanings and definitions of shadow

Personal shadow

Three kinds of *shadow* were touched on above – *personal, collective* and *archetypal* – and these will now be elaborated further. It is important to bear in mind that these are not three entirely discrete entities but that there is a large degree of overlap between them as there is in everything in Jung's schema.

The *personal, collective* and *archetypal shadow* may be seen at work in the complex relationship between Jung and Freud. This, of course, does not mean that their complex relationship can be reduced to an interaction of shadow projections; however, it would be useful to be used for illustration purposes. With regard to *personal shadow*, the relationship started with a mutual projection of positive *shadow* contents as each filled an important gap in the other's work. Freud needed Jung's work on the Word Association Test to underwrite his theory of unconscious contents and Jung needed Freud's ideas on the latter to bolster his work on complexes.

In 1906 Jung wrote that even a superficial glance would show how indebted he was to the brilliant discoveries of Freud. In his turn, Freud unreservedly acknowledged the services rendered to the spread of psycho-analysis by the Zurich School, particularly by Jung and Bleuler (who was Jung's director at the mental hospital where he worked).

The long correspondence between the two men over the next seven years charts the increasing *positive shadow* projections between them in the form of growing mutual regard, affection and the sharing of confidences and ideas. This gradually changed until the final descent into the negative side of the *shadow* that grew between the two and destroyed both their friendship and their working collaboration.

This splitting of *shadow* into 'positive' and 'negative' may be clinically insightful as it can throw light on where and how an idealising transference arises as well as a demonising one. This can be specially useful in working with borderline patients who often manifest powerfully split transferences in the course of analysis.

In 1907, Jung wrote fulsomely about Freud's *Gradiva* claiming that it was magnificent and that he gulped it in one go. Freud reciprocated by saying that he was very much surprised to hear that he was the rich man from whose table Jung could glean a few crumbs.

Later in 1907 Jung admitted to Freud that his admiration for the latter bordered on being a religious crush. However, by 1912 relations between the two were increasingly fraught and Freud eventually wrote to Jung denying that he was trying to tyrannise him intellectually.

Jung responded by saying that Freud's technique of treating his pupils like patients or sons and daughters was a blunder and was motivated by the fact that Freud could then remain on top as the father. In 1913, Freud finally proposed that they abandon their personal relations to which Jung assented saying he never thrust his friendship on anyone. He ended with: 'The rest is silence' (McGuire 1974: 540).

The relationship between the two thinkers was in essence a *shadow* one which was to a large extent based on the attraction of opposites. The latter always carries the potential for turning into repulsion so that a *positive shadow* projection may end up becoming a negative *shadow* one. In Freud and Jung's case there were a number of *shadow* components to their inter- action: they came from different cultures and generations; they functioned in quite disparate ways with Freud having extraverted feeling as his primary function and Jung introverted intuition. In addition, there was a strong homo-erotic element to the relationship accompanied by unresolved father– son transference feelings. Freud called Jung his heir apparent and Jung projected the disappointed longings from his relationship to his own father into Freud.

Collective shadow

In his writings, Jung refers to a 'collective shadow figure . . . which . . . is in part descended from a numinous collective shadow figure' (Jung 1959b: 262). A terrifying example in recent history of a take-over of large numbers of people by *collective shadow* is that of the Nazi movement. Again, this claim does not mean that the entire Nazi movement can be reduced to a psychological level of explanation based on the *shadow*; however, it is instructive to look at this disturbing phenomenon from the perspective of Jung's theory of the shadow. Many fell under the spell of the Nazi move- ment and Jung's ambiguous relationship to it over a period of time seems to suggest that he was also affected. His actions between 1933 and 1940 in relation to the Nazis have been the subject of a great deal of controversy. Some of the main sources for this are catalogued in Ann Casement's *Carl Gustav Jung* (2001) where different viewpoints are expressed by writers such as Geoffrey Cocks, James and Thomas Kirsch, Micha Neumann and Andrew Samuels. However, as this chapter is about *shadow*, only the critical comments will be highlighted in it.

Jung provoked most criticism in his role as editor of the *Zentralblatt*, a psychotherapy journal published in Germany. An article he wrote for the journal on the distinction between Jewish and German science was attacked by many people outside Germany as it echoed the claims put forward by the Nazis to underwrite the Nazi regime. A brief reference from it will serve to make the point. Jung states that perceptive people have for a long time recognised that science would only benefit from recognising that there is a difference between German and Jewish psychology. The impact of this statement was made the greater by the inclusion in the same issue of an article by Matthias Göring full of pro-Nazi rhetoric. In this way, Jung's remarks could be used to underwrite the racist claims of the Nazi regime.

Jung's involvement with the Nazi movement is well documented in Cocks' (1997) book *Psychotherapy in the Third Reich: The Göring Institute*, where the latter holds a middle position between condemning him outright while also pointing to his lack of judgement in making statements like the one above. He stresses what he sees as disturbing ambiguities in Jung's thought and 'asserts that uncritical admirers of Jung have tried to render harmless the latter's assertions at a politically sensitive time' (Casement 2001: 107).

Cocks disagrees with the kind of statement that claims that Jung was purposefully engaging with the shadow of prejudice in order to destroy it. He asserts that such a judgement not only naively ignores the multiplicity of motives that lie behind any human action but also turns a blind eye to Jung's early lack of criticism of Hitler and the negative effects that had.

Jung's attitude also created difficulties between himself and his close colleague, Erich Neumann. The latter eventually opted for the inner connection to Jung over and above their differences as Jew and Christian. However, his son, the psychoanalyst Micha Neumann, takes a different view, claiming that Jung had a blind spot towards the Jews because of the complicated father–son relationship with Freud but also because of the strong elements of religious content in the Nazi ideology. Neumann claims that Jung unconsciously identified with Nazi symbols, ideology and anti-semitism and 'believed in the positive collective "Germanic soul," to which he felt he belonged' (Maidenbaum and Martin 1991: 276).

Another contributor to the above work, Andrew Samuels, in his book *The Political Psyche* (1993), says that the *shadows* surrounding Jung are going to linger as they want psychological attention paid to them. Apart from criticising Jung for his part in Nazi-run psychotherapy and the *Zentralblatt*, Samuels is also critical of two other aspects in Jung's approach, for instance, his attempt to found a cultural psychology akin to Nazi thinking. This, linked to his fascination with the question of leadership, has its roots in

German Romantic philosophy which, when activated, can unleash powerful forces in the psyche. 'In Zurich in 1946 Jung admitted to Rabbi Leo Baeck that he had "slipped up"' (Casement 2001: 114). This brief excursion away from the central theme of shadow has been introduced to throw some light on Jung's complicated relationship to Nazism. Dazzled by the mythological charisma combined with the world dominance exhorted by the latter, Jung appears to have fallen prey to a *shadow* power complex.

Another example of the destructive potential of *collective shadow* is portrayed in Joseph Conrad's *Heart of Darkness*.

> The white colonialist, Kurtz, . . . is confronted with the Colonial Ego's tyrannical control and exploitation of the Congo and becomes totally identified with it. This is a sort of psychic inflation that can overcome anyone who is exposed to powerful forces in the environment, which can then activate the darkest recesses of *shadow* in the individual's unconscious. By enacting rather than integrating his *shadow*, Kurtz unleashed deeply destructive forces both in himself and in the community he created. The Congo was rendered savage by the colonialists who exploited it and who unleashed evil by the projection of their collective *shadow* onto it.
>
> (Casement 2003: 44; original italics)

Archetypal shadow

The God-image or 'archetype of Deity' as Jung (1958b) expresses it in his book *Answer to Job*, is 'an *antimony* – a totality of inner opposites – and this is the indispensable condition for his tremendous dynamism, his omniscience and omnipotence' (Jung 1958b: 7). In this late work, Jung sets out to show nothing less than the *shadow* side of Deity and to demonstrate that the Old Testament Yahweh and Satan are two sides of the same God. The book was the culmination for Jung of many years of struggle with this problem. As he reports in *Memories, Dreams, Reflections*, Jung (1963/1983) dreamt that he was in the gloomy courtyard of the beautiful medieval Gymnasium at Basel. From there he went through the big entrance and saw before him the cathedral of Basel with the sun shining on the roof of coloured tiles. This impressive sight was topped by God sitting above the cathedral on his throne. Jung thought it was beautiful and was filled with wonder at the perfection and harmony of the world. Suddenly, unexpectedly, God dropped a vast faeces on the cathedral and smashed it to pieces. This was so shattering that Jung woke up.

For Jung this was the revelation of the *shadow* of the Christian God. In *Answer to Job*, Jung concludes that Yahweh's harsh treatment of Job brought about through the initiative of his son, Satan, brought Yahweh to the realisation of Job's moral superiority in relation to himself. 'In this respect the creature has surpassed the creator' (Jung 1958b: 43). This situation gives rise to the need for real reflection and this is where, according to Jung, Sophia, or feminine wisdom, steps in. Through 'her' reinforcement of the need for reflection, Yahweh decides to become man as he recognises he has done wrong. As so often with the eruption of *shadow*, there is the possibility of the attainment of the feminine goal of completeness as opposed to the masculine one of perfection.

Jung goes on to say that even when God is incarnated as Christ he shows a lack of self-reflection. Only in the despairing cry from the Cross – 'My God, my God, why hast thou forsaken me?' – does his human nature attain divinity as he drinks to the dregs what he made his servant Job suffer. According to Jung, in this supreme moment is given the answer to Job.

From the human point of view, says Jung, Yahweh's *shadow* is revolting with his touchiness and suspiciousness and two-faced behaviour when he pointed to the tree of knowledge while at the same time forbidding Adam and Eve to eat of it. In this unconscious way, states Jung, Yahweh precipitated the Fall.

Major innovations, criticisms and developments of the concept of shadow

Jung's criticism of the Christian doctrine of evil as a *privatio boni* (i.e., absence, privation of the good) lies at the centre of the thesis he expounds in *Answer to Job*. In this way, evil is denied absolute existence and how then can one speak of good if there is no evil? If the latter has no substance then good, too, must remain shadowy and evil becomes a mere privation of good. Jung saw life as an energic process that needs the opposites and good and evil as simply the moral aspects of this natural polarity.

It is this central thesis of Jung's that was debated at length between himself and the English Dominican priest, Father Victor White, reported by Ann Conrad Lammers (1994) in her book *In God's Shadow: The Collaboration of Victor White and C.G. Jung*. Jung bemoaned the fact that other theologians saw him as an atheistic metaphysician rather than as an agnostic psychologist. In contrast to this, he felt that in Father White he had finally met a member of the clergy who could grasp what he (Jung) was trying to say.

The two men struggled for several years to find a resolution to their diverging views on the problem of the *privatio boni*. In a letter that White wrote to Jung, which is reproduced in Gerhard Adler's (1976) *C.G. Jung Letters*, he states that the *privatio boni* is dogma or a statement of Christian truth that affects all value-judgements. Jung, on the other hand, asserts that the dogma arises out of Christianity's elevation of God to be the source of ultimate good but that this does not empirically justify theological judgement that God is either good or evil. He is, instead, transcendental which means that he is beyond human logic. White responded he could think of no single empirical example of evil in which the *privatio boni* is not verified. Jung contested this by claiming that Christianity gets out of its inherent dualism by denying the existence of evil.

Jung went on to say that the *privatio boni* is an archetypal symbolic truth and challenged White to show him how many people have finished their dealings with the devil so that they be can rid of the Christian symbol. It is the symbolic conflict with the *shadow* represented in Christianity as Christ versus Satan that points the way to the unity of the self in God. For Jung, Satan is Christ's *shadow* but according to Catholic dogma Christ knew everything so could not have a *shadow*.

In his book, *God and the Unconscious*, White (1982) summarised his view by saying that he understood the Jungian concept of the assimilation of the shadow as signifying the supplying of some absent good in the form of consciousness.

The differences between the two men proved irreconcilable and they parted, although they never broke with each other completely. White had varying reactions to *Answer to Job*. He eventually reproached Jung for publishing it, for it made his own position difficult in his Order and in the wider Catholic community. Ann Lammers gives a more detailed account – too complex to go into here – in her book *In God's Shadow*. This work includes the correspondence cited above between White and Jung. White's final work expressed his strong disagreement with Jung's views in *Answer to Job*. Nevertheless, he wrote to Jung saying that though he felt their ways must part, he would never forget nor lose what he owed to Jung's work and friendship. There continued to be some correspondence between them until White died of cancer in 1960.

In the 1950s, Paul Radin's (1956) work on the *Trickster* in American Indian mythology served to underwrite Jung's concept of *collective shadow*. For Jung, the *Trickster* is synonymous with *collective shadow* and the alchemical figure of *Mercurius* in being sly, mischievous and able to change shape. In Radin's book, Jung wrote a commentary called 'On the psychology of the trickster-figure', in which he says that the trickster haunts the mythology, carnivals and picaresque tales of all ages as it is an archetypal structure.

Christianity rid itself of this emblem of pagan wantonness which was subsequently repressed into the unconscious and lived as the *collective shadow* of civilised human beings. It would occasionally reappear in different forms such as the Italian commedia dell'arte, in alchemy, and in Radin's trickster cycle where *shadow* is preserved in its pristine form before the achievement of a higher state of consciousness by the American Indian. This mythological tale can be told only once the latter stage has been achieved so that: 'It was only to be expected that a good deal of mockery and contempt should mingle with this retrospect' (Jung 1959b: 263).

A critique of the way Jungian writers have approached the concept of *shadow* is to be found in a paper written by Jocelyne James, a graduate of the MA course in Jungian and Post-Jungian Studies at Essex University, England. For instance, she takes up von Franz's statement that 'the shadow is simply the whole unconscious' (James 2000: pages unnumbered). As James says, if this is the case then it could embrace the whole of human history, evolution and culture. Although she demonstrates her awareness of the efficacy of vagueness with regard to defining *shadow*, James also, by implication, appears to be making a Popperian point that if something can explain everything then it cannot be subject to being falsified and lies outside the realm of being tested empirically. But throughout his writings, Jung lays claim to being an empiricist so that von Franz's statement would seem to run contrary to Jung's.

James also challenges Jungians (including myself) who have written on this topic to produce research that will critically reflect on the clinical application of *shadow*. She questions why and tentatively suggests a number of possibilities: that analytical psychologists may still be struggling to comprehend the concept as it evokes a quagmire of epistemological problems. She also points to a popular book on the subject, Zweig and Wolf's (1997) *Romancing the Shadow*, which emphasises sex and potency. James's thesis opens the way to the last section of this chapter, which looks at trends for future developments.

An account of the current status and trends for future developments

The term *shadow* is in constant usage among analytical psychologists but as James (2000) says in her thesis, there is need for a more detailed differentiation than von Franz's assertion that the term *shadow* is simply a mythological one referring to everything in a person that cannot be named. One writer who has tried to elucidate this in relation to the 'helping professions' is Adolf Guggenbühl-Craig. He talks of the *charlatan shadow* that may be constellated in an analyst when the need arises to say difficult things to a patient. At this point, the analyst may become either sadistic or flattering to the patient. Examples of the latter may be the following sorts of interpretation: extolling the positive aspects of the archetype of the queen to a power-hungry woman or lack of courage may be interpreted as positive introversion on the part of a patient. Both interpretations feed the patient's narcissism as does encouraging a lack of a dutiful response to an ageing mother as a liberation from mother's negative animus. Care needs to be taken by the analyst in walking the thin line between enabling the patient to value his or her own psychic needs without encouraging narcissism. The latter can lead to collusion on the part of the patient so that the serious business of analysis degenerates into its *shadow*. In this way, 'The deeper value of psychic development is betrayed' (Guggenbühl-Craig 1971: 74).

Another *shadow* aspect of the profession is the abuse of the search for meaning. Unfair or disloyal behaviour towards spouse, friend or relative may be exalted as self-realisation and the workings of the unconscious. In promoting him or herself as the Great Healer, an analyst may lay claim to transcendental knowledge. 'Like a little god the analyst sees everything clearly . . . there is no longer any tragedy; any incomprehensible horror' (Guggenbühl-Craig 1971: 77).

Guggenbühl-Craig (1971) also points to the obvious polarity that can develop in any relationship of healer/patient where the former is identified with being all-powerful and the latter carries the *shadow* of the regressed, fearful child. With society's demand for greater accountability on the part of practitioners in the 'helping professions', abuses of power are increasingly being brought out in the open. In this way, instead of analysis holding up the mirror to society's *shadow*, society has for some time been holding up the mirror to the *shadow* in analytic work.

Even though working through the *shadow* is such a feature of Jungian analysis, particularly the classical approach, it is nevertheless widely evident in the analytical psychology world, not least in the destructive splits that are such a conspicuous part of Jungian professional organisations around the world. In 1995 I was commissioned by the *Journal of Analytical Psychology* to write an article on the splits that have been a feature of the evolution of analytical psychology as a profession in the United Kingdom. In the 1970s, difficulties within the Society of Analytical Psychology led to the formation of what came to be known as the 'Adler Group' and finally to a breakaway movement. A middle group had also been forming over the previous seven years and several of its members tried hard to prevent the split that eventually took place. Kathleen Newton, an analyst from this middle group, had the foresight to point to 'the disastrous impact that a split would have, both for the present but also for the future in hardening defensive attitudes and fostering mutually antagonistic projections' (Casement 1995: 335).

Thomas Kirsch's (2000) narrative account of the world-wide Jungian movement, *The Jungians: A Comparative and Historical Perspective*, also features splits in many analytical psychology groups. These splits may, in part, be seen to be a destructive acting-out of *shadow*, although there are clearly many other factors involved – not, by any means, all destructive. Nevertheless, reflection on its own internal *shadow* is probably the most important work to be done within the analytical psychology movement, particularly if it is to be able to offer any enlightenment to the world at large in its on-going struggle with *shadow* in all its aspects.

References

Adler, G. (ed.) (1976) *C.G. Jung Letters*. London: Routledge and Kegan Paul.

Casement, A. (1995) 'A brief history of Jungian splits in the United Kingdom'. *Journal of Analytical Psychology*, 40(3): 327–342.

—— (2001) *Carl Gustav Jung*. London: Sage.

—— (2003) 'Encountering the shadow in rites of passage: a study in activations'. *Journal of Analytical Psychology*, 48(1): 29–46.

Cocks, G. (1997) *Psychotherapy in the Third Reich: The Göring Institute*. New Brunswick, NJ: Transaction.

Ellenberger, H.F. (1970) *The Discovery of the Unconscious: The History and Evolution of Dynamic Psychiatry*. New York: Basic Books.

Guggenbühl-Craig, A. (1971) *Power in the Helping Professions*. Dallas, TX: Spring.

Huskinson, L. (2004) *Nietzsche and Jung: The Whole Self in the Union of Opposites*. Hove, UK: Brunner-Routledge.

James, J. (2000) 'The shadow: a critical enquiry into the significance of the concept of the shadow in analytical psychology', unpublished MA thesis, Essex University.

Jung, C.G. (1953a) *Psychology and Alchemy*. London: Routledge and Kegan Paul.

—— (1953b) *Two Essays on Analytical Psychology*. Princeton, NJ: Princeton University Press.

—— (1954) *The Practice of Psychotherapy: Essays on the Psychology of the Transference and Other Subjects*. London: Routledge and Kegan Paul.

—— (1956) *Symbols of Transformation: An Analysis of the Prelude to a Case of Schizophrenia*. Princeton, NJ: Princeton University Press.

—— (1958a) *Psychology and Religion: West and East*. London: Routledge and Kegan Paul.

—— (1958b) *Answer to Job*. Bollingen Foundation New York. Princeton, NJ: Princeton University Press.

—— (1959a) *Aion: Researches into the Phenomenology of the Self*. Princeton, NJ: Princeton University Press.

—— (1959b) *The Archetypes and the Collective Unconscious. Part One*. London: Routledge and Kegan Paul.

—— (1963) *Mysterium Coniunctionis*. London: Routledge and Kegan Paul.

—— (1963/1983) *Memories, Dreams, Reflections*. London: Fontana.

—— (1964) *Civilization in Transition*. London: Routledge and Kegan Paul.

—— (1967) *Alchemical Studies*. London: Routledge and Kegan Paul.

—— (1971) *Psychological Types*. London: Routledge and Kegan Paul.

Kirsch, T. (2000) *The Jungians: A Comparative and Historical Perspective*. London: Routledge.

Lammers, A.C. (1994) *In God's Shadow: The Collaboration of Victor White and C.G. Jung*. New York: Paulist Press.

McGuire, W. (ed.) (1974) *The Freud/Jung Letters*. London: Hogarth Press.

Maidenbaum, A. and Martin, A. (1991) *Lingering Shadows: Jungians, Freudians, and Anti-Semitism*. Boston, MA: Shambala.

Radin, P. (1956) *The Trickster: A Study in American Indian Mythologies. With Commentaries by Karl Kerényi and C.G. Jung*. London: Routledge and Kegan Paul.

Samuels, A. (1993) *The Political Psyche*. London: Routledge and Kegan Paul.
White, V. (1982) *God and the Unconscious*. Dallas, TX: Spring.
Zweig, C. and Wolf, S. (1997) *Romancing the Shadow: How to Access the Hidden Power in your Dark Side*. London: Thorsons; New York: Ballantine.

Recommended further reading

Berry, P. (1982) 'The training of shadow and the shadow in training', in P. Berry, *Echo's Subtle Body: Contributions to an Archetypal Psychology*. Dallas, TX: Spring.

Bly, R. (1988) *A Little Book on the Human Shadow*, ed. W. Booth. New York: HarperCollins.

—— (1989) *The Human Shadow*. Lecture in New York (audio video). New York: Sound Horizons.

Brinton Perera, S. (1986) *The Scapegoat Complex: Toward a Mythology of Shadow and Guilt*. Toronto: Inner City.

Conger, J. (1988) *Jung and Reich: The Body as Shadow*. Berkeley, CA: North Atlantic Books.

Dalal, F. (1988) *Jung: A Racist*. Dallas, TX: Spring.

De Shong Meador, B. (1992) *Uncursing the Dark: Treasures from the Underworld*. Wilmette, IL: Chiron.

Edinger, E. (1986) *Encounter with the Self*. Toronto: Inner City.

Eliade, M. (1990) *The Symbolism of Shadows in Archaic Religions*, in D. Apastolos-Cappodona (ed.) *Symbolism, the Sacred, and the Arts*. New York: Crossroad.

Fechner, G. (1991) *The Shadow is Alive*. Dallas, TX: Spring.

Giegerich, W. (1991) *The Advent of the Guest: Shadow Integration and the Rise of Psychology*. Dallas, TX: Spring.

Guggenbühl-Craig, A. (1970) *Must Analysis Fail through its Destructive Aspect?* New York: Spring.

—— (1971) *Power in the Helping Professions*. New York: Spring.

Henderson, J. (1990) *Shadow and Self: Selected Papers in Analytical Psychology*. Wilmette, IL: Chiron.

Hillman, J. (1964) *Suicide and the Soul*. Dallas, TX: Spring.

—— (1979) *The Dream and the Underworld*. New York: Harper Row.

Hollis, J. (1996) *Swamplands of the Soul: New Life in Dismal Places*. Toronto: Inner City.

Johnson, R. (1991) *Owning your Own Shadow: Understanding the Dark Side of the Psyche*. New York: HarperCollins.

Mattoon, M.A. (ed.) (1987) *The Archetype of Shadow in a Split World. Proceedings of the Tenth International Congress for Analytical Psychology*. Einsiedeln, Switzerland: Daimon Verlag.

Scott Peck, M. (1983) *People of the Lie: The Hope for Healing Human Evil*. London: Arrow.

Stein, M. (1995) *Jung on Evil*. London: Routledge.

von Franz, M.-L. (1991) 'The realisation of the shadow in dreams', in C. Zweig and J. Abrams (eds) *Meeting the Shadow*. New York: Tarcher/Putnam.

—— (1995) *Shadow and Evil in Fairytales*. Boston, MA: Shambala.

Whitmont, E. (1991) 'The evolution of the shadow', in C. Zweig and J. Abrams (eds) *Meeting the Shadow*. New York: Tarcher/Putnam.

Zweig, C. and Abrams, J. (eds) (1991) *Meeting the Shadow: The Hidden Power of the Dark Side of Human Nature*. New York: Tarcher/Putnam.

Chapter 5

Anima/animus

Verena Kast
Translation edited by Bobbi Whitcombe

The topic in the Jungian opus

The theory of the individuation process is the key concept of Jungian therapy. The goal of individuation is to become more and more who we really are, distinct from others and yet in relationship to others. This process is a series of confrontational dialogues between us and the world, the human beings to whom we are related and bound and the inner world of the complexes and the archetypes. An essential part of this process, according to Jung, is that a man becomes conscious of his anima, and a woman of her animus, in order to differentiate him or herself from it, and not be dominated by it. The relationship with the anima – which in Jung's oeuvre is given more attention than the animus – gives vitality, creativity and flexibility.

It is greatly to Jung's credit that he continually emphasises that 'female' elements exist in every man, just as 'male' elements are in every woman, and that these elements also need to be acknowledged. Jung's concept of the anima and the animus has enabled many individuals to accept themselves as they are and not as they should be according to rigid gender stereotypes. On the other hand, in describing anima and animus, Jung is basically using the established gender stereotypes of his time to define what is female and what is male.

The concept of anima and animus has become quite popular because it explains falling in love and 'inexplicable' fascinations with an other onto whom we find ourselves projecting anima or animus, or both; it explains 'impossible' love, and also why we behave sometimes in a relationship in a way we do not intend to and do not understand because, for example, we take on the role of an anima that someone is projecting onto us.

A systematic exploration of Jung's views

The discovery of the anima

In his autobiography Jung (1961) writes about his discovery of the anima. After the break with Freud, in a vulnerable phase, he felt the need to get in touch with his fantasies. He visualised a descent beneath the earth. In one of these visualisations he encountered an old man with a white beard, who explained that he was Elijah. With him was Salome, a beautiful young girl, who was blind. A strange couple: Salome and Elijah, belonging together from all eternity – and with them was a black serpent. Jung explains later that couples like this – old man and young girl – are often found in such 'dream wanderings', as in mythological tales.

Jung calls Salome an anima figure, Elijah the wise old prophet. He feels 'distinctly suspicious' of Salome, and he 'stuck close to Elijah because he seemed to be the most reasonable of the three' (Jung 1961: 181). Out of Elijah developed Philemon, an inner figure of great importance for Jung for many years – a kind of inner guide who 'taught me psychic objectivity, and the reality of the psyche' (Jung 1961: 183). Nowadays we would call Philemon an animus figure, a representation of the archetype of the wise old man. Even when Jung is talking only about the anima figure and the wise old prophet, his fantasy can be seen as a personification of the couple, animus and anima, being constellated in his psyche.

Exploring the idea of the anima further, he later found himself arguing with an inner female voice which told him that what he was writing was art – not science. He entered into a dialogue with this female voice, which he identified as the voice of one of his female patients, but he concluded that this female was more than an internalised figure: she spoke for parts of his unconscious. This was an important experience of the anima – and through his dialogue with this anima figure, Jung developed the technique of active imagination, which allows us to express unconscious material and to change it. Jung did not always agree with his anima figure – he found her irritating and he felt suspicious about her. This might be the reason why his early definitions of the anima are not as enthusiastic as the later ones.

Jung explains the relationship of this inner figure to the collective unconscious by its archetypal nature and calls it an anima figure; he concludes that women must experience an equivalent, the animus, personified by a male figure.

Why does he use these Latin terms: *anima*, the soul, and *animus*, the spirit? They are words which are more or less interchangeable: the ancient Greeks and Romans thought that when someone dies the *soul*, which is the principle of life, leaves the body – but it is also possible to say that the *spirit* has departed. In the history of the humanities there are many theories about the soul and spirit, from the ancient Greeks onwards. Concepts of the soul and spirit vary depending on the view of humanity in the culture concerned. Quite often, anima and animus belong together. For St Augustine, for example, the anima or soul is bound to the body, while the animus has the power of insight, and is able to understand not only about the soul and the body but also about God.

Jung's development of the concept

In 1916 Jung describes anima and animus as a part of the structure of the psyche which is complementary to the *persona* (Jung 1916/1966: par. 507). Whereas he describes the persona as 'a compromise formation between external reality and the individual', he explains that 'the anima would thus be a compromise formation between the individual and the unconscious world, that is, the world of historical images, or "primordial images"'. So a man who behaves in a very masculine way (his persona) would have a very feminine anima.

He explains this more precisely in the *Visions Seminar* of 1925, quoted in the glossary in *Memories, Dreams, Reflections*: 'The animus and the anima should function as a bridge, or a door, leading to the images of the collective unconscious, as the persona should be a sort of bridge to the world' (Jung 1961: 392). The function of animus and anima is to make a connection with the depths of the psyche.

The complications start when Jung tries to describe the content of the anima:

> If I were to attempt to put in a nutshell . . . what it is that characterises the animus as opposed to the anima, I could only say this: as the anima produces *moods*, the animus produces *opinions* . . . But in reality the opinions are not thought out at all; they exist ready made, and they are held so positively and with so much conviction that the woman never had the shadow of a doubt about them.
>
> (Jung 1928/1966: par. 331)

This begins to seem confusing: is Jung describing anima and animus, or a specific stage of anima and animus, when the ego complex has not yet separated either from the mother complex (moods) or from the father complex (opinions)? In the same section we find the following statement:

> The animus is the deposit, as it were, of all woman's ancestral experiences of man – and not only that, he is also a creative and procreative being . . . He brings forth something we might call the . . . spermatic word. Just as a man brings forth his work as a complete creation out of his inner feminine nature, so the inner masculine side of a woman brings forth creative seeds which have the power to fertilise the feminine side of man.
>
> (Jung 1928/1966: par. 336)

This statement turns up constantly in feminist discussions as evidence that Jung's concept of anima and animus sees a man as having an even more inspiring feminine nature than a woman, with an internal *femme inspiratrice*, but suggests that he actually denied women any natural creativity. Further, we might question whether Jung was unable to accept the fact that men are not able to give birth to a child – so he suggests that a man at least has an inner feminine nature, which can bring forth a complete creation, without the need for a real woman. Thus we are hurled into the midst of the gender debate. Indeed, the statement could be understood that way. But if we start with the idea that men and women each have both an anima and an animus (a post-Jungian development of the theory), this statement takes on a completely different meaning. We are closer to the ancient Greeks' idea that the spirit inspires the soul and through this interplay things are brought into being.

However, the problem of gender issues, combined with a slight devaluation of women and the idealisation of the anima, is implicit in this concept. It seems undeniable that Jung conflated the gender stereotypes of his time with the notion of anima and animus as archetypes.

In 1925, in his essay on marriage, Jung says, 'Every man carries within him the eternal image of woman; not the image of this or that particular woman, but a definitive feminine image' (Jung 1925/1972: par. 338). Further, women carry with them the eternal image of the masculine. Here Jung is pointing to the archetypal nature of anima and animus, and he is talking about projection of these inner figures onto real women and men. This is the common definition of animus and anima.

In the same text Jung also speaks about the projection of anima and animus as a matter of fascination and falling in love with another, which is sometimes a good basis for a relationship, but more often may arise from deep-seated emotions and connected fantasies, and cause problems due to idealisation, lack of fulfilment and disillusion – though these are very often experienced as 'fate'. The anima can create the most profound personal understanding or initiate the best risk ever taken in a person's life (Jung 1934/1976: par. 62). The same could be said of the animus. At this point, Jung is no longer speaking about anima and animus being the opposite of the persona.

In 1927 in the text 'Mind and earth', he explores the development of anima and animus (Jung 1927/1974: pars. 71–76). In puberty, a new archetype gets constellated: in a man it is the archetype of the woman, the anima, and in the woman the archetype of the man, the animus. Anima and animus have been hidden by the imago of the parents, and highly influenced by this imago. The more the youth is influenced by the parental imagos, the more the choice of the beloved will be a positive or negative replacement of the parents. This, according to Jung, is a general phenomenon. It seems to be important to see that animus and anima are based on the parental archetype and the parental complexes, and that Jung sees the change in adolescence not only as the experience of the sexual drive, but also as a spiritual experience of attraction governed by the images of anima and animus which are projected.

Jung observes that there are some patterns in the projection process:

> The animus likes to project itself upon 'intellectuals' and all kinds of 'heroes' (including tenors, artists, and sporting celebrities). The anima has a predilection for everything that is unconscious, dark, equivocal and unrelated in woman, and also for her vanity, frigidity, helplessness, and so forth.
>
> (Jung 1946/1971: par. 521)

In 1936 in the text 'Concerning the archetypes and the anima concept', Jung continues the developmental path and argues that the young man has to free himself from the anima fascination caused by his mother (Jung 1936/ 1976: par. 146). For the first half of life, young people can bear the loss of the anima, but for the second half of life, the loss of the relationship to the anima causes 'a diminution of vitality, flexibility and of human kindness' (Jung 1936/1976: par. 147).

For the process of individuation, which is a central part of Jungian theory, it is necessary to understand one's anima or animus, in order to distinguish the conscious personality from these archetypal influences. If they remain unconscious, they may behave as autonomous complexes, with negative effects. If they are brought into consciousness, they make creativity possible, adding meaning to life. This differentiation between ego and anima/animus is what Jung called the 'masterpiece' of analysis (Jung 1934/1976: pars. 61–64).

In the same text of 1934, he emphasises the idea of the anima and animus being archetypes: 'With the archetype of the anima we enter the realm of gods . . . everything that the anima touches becomes numinous – unconditional, dangerous, taboo, magical' (Jung 1934/1976: par. 59). And he describes the animus as the archetype of meaning, the anima as the archetype of life (Jung 1934/1976: par. 66).

In 1936 Jung defends his concept of animus and anima by reference to the idea of the *syzygy*, concluding from the evidence in many different mythologies of the divine couple, united by a sacred marriage, that this motif is as universal as the existence of men and women (Jung 1936/1976: par. 134). He postulates that in the syzygy the archetypal union of the parents is expressed, the mother corresponding to the anima. These archetypal images of the syzygy, or fantasy-images, according to Jung, are more real than the apperception of the reality, and therefore become the apperception of the reality, especially the reality of the parents (Jung 1936/1976: pars. 135–136).

In 1950, in *Aion*, Jung is describing his concept again under the title the 'Syzygy of anima and animus' (Jung 1950/1976: pars. 20ff.). In this text he declares that in the anima and the animus figures the autonomy of the collective unconscious is expressed. 'The projection-making factor is the anima, or rather the unconscious as represented by the anima' (Jung 1950/ 1976: par. 26). This text also makes it clear that anima and animus can be realised 'only through a relation to a partner of the opposite sex, because only in such a relation do their projections become operative' (Jung 1950/ 1976: par. 42). In the same text Jung qualifies this statement, pointing to the fact that not all the contents of the anima or animus are projected, and that many of them appear in dreams and can be brought into consciousness only by the process of active imagination (Jung 1950/1976: par. 39).

If anima and animus become conscious, as far as is possible, and the individual is no longer dominated by them, there will be fewer illusions in relationships, and a wider range of emotional and cognitive experiences will be possible – and with that comes the possibility of better bonding. These developments are able to take place in any emotional relationship to an 'other'. Nowadays we would question the notion that the realisation of the anima and animus only takes place in a relationship to a partner of the opposite sex. We find today that human beings of the same sex may carry the images of anima or animus.

In 1954, in *Mysterium Coniunctionis*, Jung makes some important final remarks about anima and animus.

> In so far as the spirit is also a kind of 'window on eternity', immortal as animus rationalis, it conveys to the soul a certain influxus divinus, . . . and the knowledge of a higher system of the world, wherein consists precisely its supposed animation of the soul.
>
> (Jung 1954/1968b: par. 338)

And: 'If products of the anima (dreams, fantasies, visions, symptoms, coincidences) are assimilated, digested and integrated, this has a beneficial effect on the growth and nourishment of the soul' (Jung 1954/1968b: par. 83).

And again in this, his last book, Jung stresses the idea that the animus compensates female consciousness, which he identifies with 'eros', while the anima compensates male consciousness, identified with 'logos' (Jung 1954/ 1968a: pars. 218–227). Here he is also struggling with the idea of a more solar consciousness in men and a more lunar consciousness in women. Let us review for a moment the background to this idea. In *Aion*, Jung claims that the anima corresponds to the eros of the mother, the animus to the logos of the father. For Jung, eros means psychic relatedness, while logos means differentiation, objective knowledge and intellectual judgement.

> The positive aspect of the animus expresses . . . spirit, philosophical or religious ideas in particular, or rather the attitude resulting from them. So the animus also (like the anima) is a mediator between the unconscious and consciousness and is a personification of the unconscious . . .

Just as the anima gives relationship and relatedness to a man's consciousness, so the animus gives to a woman's consciousness a capacity
for reflection, deliberation and self knowledge.

(Jung 1950/1976: par. 33)

A brief summary

When Jung wrote about what the animus and anima have in common,
he was writing about archetypes that function as mediators between consciousness and the unconscious, especially by means of the imagination.
The dynamic-creative aspect of the anima and the animus archetype is
described. The dynamic-creative aspect, however, is characteristic of every
archetypal constellation.

Anima and animus can be seen as representing the unconscious at a given
moment.

The effect of animus and anima on the ego is one of fascination and
disquieting stimulation – a numinous experience – which is also characteristic of archetypal situations.

Animus and anima are often discovered in the form of projections onto
other persons. Since they represent the central contents of the unconscious,
these projections make the projector very dependent on the person to whom
they are attached. It is very difficult for that person not to behave in keeping
with the projection, leading to stereotypical assumptions about patterns of
behaviour such as 'the way women are'. Once a projection that has been cast
on you dissolves, you are left feeling as if you have just been taken apart.
You realise that you were not what it was all about – that it was not you as
an individual, but rather you as a carrier of anima or animus.

As animus and anima are experienced mainly in relationships between
men and women, and because Jung did not introduce the idea of archetypes
earlier, but talked about the anima and animus complementing the persona,
his theory can be seen as a reflection and confirmation of gender stereotypes. On the other hand, in the 1930s, it must have been refreshing for
women, in the context of the theory of individuation, to get in touch with
the 'male' aspects of their personality.

When Jung identifies the individual's anima or animus – even though he
considers these at the same time to be archetypes – with the principles of
eros and logos, it is easy once again to produce a gender stereotype. And it
seems slightly strange to identify the anima with the male Greek god Eros.
Another questionable identification is that of anima with 'feeling' – we
would say 'emotion' nowadays – and animus with thinking, 'cognition'
today, again because of the old gender stereotypes they imply.

It is interesting to note the references to the motif of the *syzygy*, and to
the archetype of the *coniunctio*. In this conjunction, the male–female
dichotomy is overcome, and a balance is achieved between the feminine and

masculine aspects within the psyche. This seems crucial to Jung to allow creativity and to engender the process of becoming oneself.

There is an aspect of developmental psychology connected with this concept, which Jung did not clearly explain. When he found 'his' anima in his imagination, Jung was suspicious. The earlier definitions of anima and animus foreground the pathological element. We could conclude that at this time his anima was contaminated with his mother complex. There are some definitions where Jung claims that the parents are the first human beings onto whom we project anima and animus (Jung 1954/1968a: par. 226); thus anima and animus are influenced by these complexes, which makes them 'difficult' or may even give them a pathological element. This might be the reason why Jung, at a later stage, gives a more positive meaning to anima and animus, having separated more fully from his mother and father complexes. He also argues in a more psychological way, saying that these psychic functions have a positive effect when integrated as far as possible, and a negative effect when rejected or only remaining in projection.

Further, when Jung in his later texts refers to the spirit as the 'window to eternity', which is able to animate the soul, this is distinct from individual psychology, and the animus–anima concept becomes a gender-neutral one, based on the humanities: that is to say, with the realisation of anima and animus human beings are also connected to the *anima mundi* and the possibility of enlightenment about the principle of life itself.

The concept in practice

A theory develops not only through people's building and rebuilding it, but also through daily use. In the use therapists make of the Jungian anima–animus theory, the theory is sometimes simplified, or even falsified: anima is referred to as the female aspects of a man, animus as the male aspects of a woman. This is talking in terms of gender-role stereotypes, which disregard the archetypal aspect of the concept. We also find analytic jargon and bias: the anima, except in a case of anima posession, or perhaps a case of the 'free-floating anima', is accorded respect, even reverence. The concept of animus on the other hand is often used to minimise a woman's accomplishments – even by women themselves: 'She just has a good animus', someone will say, meaning that she has lost a lot of her femininity. The criticism implied in the comment that a woman's standpoint is 'animusy' can silence a woman unless she has developed so much autonomy that she questions the jargon – which then naturally suggests her animus again! What the man sees in the woman as his shadow, which is also the shadow of the patriarchy, is often designated as 'negative animus'. Nor must we forget the confusion about father complex and animus. Destructivity in women (and also in men), which can be the consequence of many difficult complex-constellations, is often wrongly attributed to the negative animus.

Major innovations, criticisms, development

Almost all Jungians who have published papers have something to say about this basic concept. It touches a wide range of interests: the process of individuation, the development of the Self, the infantile origins of the Self, transference-countertransference and the analytic relationship, the fascination that mythological symbols can hold for us, the archetypal basis of relationships, love and separation processes. I will therefore mention only a few of the innovations, criticisms and developments.

During Jung's lifetime, it was not so much criticism of this concept which led to many different approaches to this part of his work, but rather the working out of the phenomenology of these archetypal figures in mythological material. For example, Marie-Louise von Franz made a study of fairy tales, showing their relevance to clinical cases, especially in connection with the individuation process. In her writings she explored how wide-ranging the phenomenology of the anima and animus is, and she repeatedly emphasised the positive aspect of the animus, without denying the negative one. 'The animus can personify an enterprising spirit, courage, truthfulness and, in the highest form, spiritual profundity' (von Franz 1968: 195).

Emma Jung (1967) in her book *Animus and Anima*, which is based on a talk she gave in 1931, is also dealing very much with the phenomenology, in connection with mythological symbols, and some clinical implications. However, this account is basically a description of how 'the modern woman' and 'the modern man' in the 1930s understands or should understand themselves in relation to Jung's new theories, and be grateful for this new approach. Even when in her text the woman, the feminine and the anima are all mixed up, the text imparts an atmosphere of change.

Esther Harding (1932) wrote a remarkable book about the implications of the anima–animus theory on women. She shows how anima and animus are at work in everyday life, in relationships and in fantasies. One of the main topics she deals with is the impact the projection of the anima has upon a woman – in present-day terminology we could even speak about projective identification – and she gives advice as to how a woman can free herself from these projections. She sees it as a cultural problem, that men project their anima onto women, and women behave as they are supposed to behave due to this projection. When a woman is able to free herself from this projection she takes responsibility for herself: she is a self-aware, self-assured woman. This book shows how important the concept of the anima was for the emancipation of women in the 1930s.

At a later stage, some took a more questioning approach to this concept. Hillman (1985) investigates the concept of the anima, and tries to sort out the different aspects of the idea. He rejects the notion of contrasexuality and criticises the dichotomies which are forced upon the anima, such as conscious–unconscious, persona–anima, anima–animus, because, if it is seen this way, the anima is only part of the 'tandem', and thus has no right to exist in herself, which suggests that if a man is identified with a very male persona, he has as compensation a strong anima.

The reason the anima is seen as one of a pair, Hillman observes, is to be found in the connection to the syzygy, the male–female divine couple. This is a polarity which is intrinsic, but it leads Hillman to the conclusion that anima and animus trigger each other. Soul and spirit call for each other; if we are in touch with the anima, we are also in touch with the animus. He sees the psychic experience of the syzygy as psychic-spiritual inspiration. Commenting on Jung's definition of anima as the archetype of the 'feminine' (Jung 1949/1976: par. 356), and the archetype of 'life itself', Hillman (1985) concludes that these archetypes are equally important for males and females. He rejects the idea that an archetype can be gender specific. He also points to the fact that in clinical work we find images of the anima in women, and also emotions which are connected with the anima in women.

Samuels (1989) argues that there is no feminine principle. He suggests that differences in feminine or masculine psychology are due to culture and society. Hillmann and Samuels both reject the idea of contrasexuality, but accept the archetypal aspect of anima and animus.

Gordon (1993) claims that the anima figure is possessed by both men and women. She sees the difference as being in the relationship to the anima: men relate to it through projection onto a woman, a woman through identification with it. Gordon also points out that the anima is different from the woman, and notes the confusion among Jung and some of his followers whereby woman and anima are sometimes seen as interchangeable. She sees in the anima an archetypal, cultural and collective influence. She also makes a distinction between 'mother' and 'anima', saying that mother is the elemental character, and anima the transformative character. Here she is referring to Neumann's concept, but also to myths and fairy tales, where the anima lures the hero into the world, far away from mother, while mother tries to keep him at home.

Young-Eisendrath and Wiedemann (1987), in *Female Authority: Empowering Women through Psychotherapy*, discuss a model of animus development in which women may be seen to be fighting the 'deficit model' of femininity and an internalised sense of the inferiority of women. It is a book rich in clinical examples; the authors put forward a model of psychotherapy with women which works with the 'animus complex'. For them, the interpersonal relationship is essential for the development of the personality. The model for animus-development in building up the female Self is very interesting; more research could and should be done in this area.

Giegerich (1994) discusses the position of the animus theory in Jungian psychology. At the outset, he notes a lack of interest in this aspect of the theory. He comments that the animus has a negative connotation, in that it seems to have been invented in a mechanical way as the opposite of the anima. His conclusion is that the concept of the animus itself is born out of the negative animus and therefore it is questionable whether women are able to develop animus qualities. He even doubts whether there is such a thing as the animus, claiming that psychological terms must be derived from the phenomenology of the soul. Giegerich connects the animus with thinking – and feels that as a concept it needs further development in Jungian psychology.

My own work (Kast 1984) has been to explore the idea of the syzygy, the anima and animus seen as a couple. Working with people in mourning, I found that acceptance of death is easier for those who are aware of the fantasies underlying their relationships. Such individuals understand which fantasies bound them to their partner when their relationship was most vital and which aspects of their own personality their partner enlivened. These people feel robbed by their partner's death, but they are also aware of what cannot be taken from them in their partner's death. The crucial work in mourning is often the laying bare of the fantasies contained in the relationship. These fantasies, which change in the course of a lifetime, can reveal the meaning of the relationship in terms of an individual's development and life. Underlying these fantasies about the relationship are mythological images of the sacred marriage, such as the unions celebrated by Shiva and Shakti, or Zeus and Hera. In my discussion of the myths of sacred marriage, I demonstrate how human relationships, depicted in narratives, dreams, fantasies and literature, mirror the relationships of such divine couples. I also postulate the idea that both men and women possess anima and animus, and that anima and animus very often can be experienced in unconscious material as a couple. This also has a clinical implication: if there is an imbalance in the anima–animus relationship, we can ask what kind of anima figure could be touched by the relevant animus figure and work it out through imagination.

In the paper 'Animus and anima: spiritual growth and separation' (Kast 1993) I discuss the development of anima and animus, moving from the fusion with mother and father complexes (Kast 1997) to the representation of anima and animus figures which are much less influenced by these complexes.

Individuation requires not only the integration of anima and animus but also a separation from one's parental complexes. Here one needs to separate emotionally from one's actual parents as well as psychologically from one's parental complexes. A human resource available to those of us engaged in the difficult process of separation is the storehouse of archetypal parental images. These can aid us in differentiating ourselves from our own parents. Further resources that are crucial to the process of separation are the archetypes of anima and animus, which orchestrate the process in a very organic way. At the beginning of a phase of separation (of which there seem to be many), anima and animus figures are mixed up with father and mother complexes, thus obscuring their identity and function. For quite some time, animus and anima are influenced by individual father and mother complexes. But at their core is always a spark of the more essential, archetypal animus and anima figures, which lead the ego complex into a journey of separation from the parental complexes.

During the course of a research project, looking at about 600 dreams, I found various categories of anima and animus, which show the relation to the father and mother complexes but also demonstrate the possiblities of development into independent anima and animus figures (Kast 1993).

The categories were:

- Authority figures: teachers, politicians (male and female), priests and priestesses, kings and queens. Such figures closely resembled images of father and mother.
- Brother/sister figures (with an archetypal quality).
- Mysterious strangers: nixies, gypsies, travellers from outer space, death as brother/sister, gods and goddesses. This included a subcategory of animal bride or bridegroom.
- Wise old man/woman.
- Unknown girl/boy. These figures, often connected with the archetype of the divine child, seem to represent developmental stages of the anima/animus; new configurations of anima/animus are often first symbolised as an unknown child.

In my discussion of these different categories with colleagues and students, the impression grew that, strictly speaking, only the mysterious stranger (including wise old woman/man and divine child) qualified as an animus/anima figure. But some aspect of the mysterious stranger is always present in the other categories as well. This recognition has the following important implication for therapy.

If we interpret an authority animus/anima figure as deriving strictly from the father/mother imago and the authority complex, our interpretations will be one-sided, and we will fail in our task of helping the analysand with the problem of separation from the parental complexes. Indeed, such interpretations may even confirm the analysand's bonds to the father/mother complex by reinforcing the idea that nothing will ever change. By recognising the dimension of the mysterious stranger through work with fantasies and imagination, our interpretations can open up the complexes, shed light on the mystery and offer some hope. New paths are cleared for potential growth and development. I am persuaded that the authority-animus/anima – and to a lesser extent the brother/sister-animus/anima – are figures that overlap and may conceal a number of different dimensions. Thus interpretation should lead to the analysand's recognising and experiencing the various dimensions and nuances contained potentially within the complex image.

If we see in these images only individual fathers, mothers, sisters and brothers, the unconscious is reduced to the status of a family grave. (Naturally, the basic father and mother complexes have an effect on the image of the mysterious stranger as well.) But if we are able to entertain a dimension of ambiguity, we open the ego complex to the influx of the collective unconscious and we may help people discover realms in their psyche that are not determined by relationships to father, mother and siblings. In the process, we help in the discovery of the individual's spirituality.

Daniela Heisig, in her thesis at the universities of Bonn and Zurich in 1994, investigated the hypotheses of Hillmann, Gordon, Kast and others empirically through her inquiry into whether the anima is gender specific. Her research was done with dreams from different dream data banks. Heisig combined two methods: dream interpretation in a group using the method of amplification, and a qualitative-quantitative content analysis. The results were compared using statistical methods. This demonstrated that the archetypal image of the anima can be experienced in dreams of both men and women.

The figure of the anima differs from other female figures in dreams in a number of ways: the characteristics of the figure can be categorised as evincing fascination, strangeness, radical fervour, wisdom, bringing about the initiation of transformation, and helping in a dangerous situation. These categories, at my suggestion, were identified and elaborated. So the anima as the mysterious stranger could be subdivided into anima as guide, anima as guide to transformation, and anima as stranger. The results were published in a book (Heisig 1996).

Ellen Heinke (2000) in her thesis at the University of Zurich also uses statistical methods to attempt to verify the hypothesis that both men and woman can experience what is called 'animus'. She devised a questionnaire, starting with Jung's own central definitions of the anima and animus. She used this questionnaire for semi-structured interviews with experts – senior and junior analysts, with equal numbers of women and men. From these interviews she formed categories of answers, which have been statistically elaborated with NMDS (nonmetrical moredimensional scaling). The results are very interesting: I have never seen so many facets of the animus in one publication – all collected from our colleagues. The results showed that there is a difference between Jung's concept of the animus and the average view of the experts. The animus is not seen as being gender specific, but there are differences between men and women as to what is expected from the experience of it. There are far more positive emotions associated with the animus than in Jung's account; in particular, 'being animated' is associated with the experience of animus.

Anne Springer (2000) proposes in an article to give up the constructs of anima and animus, as complexes and also as archetypal structures. She found the concept was not helpful, especially in clinical work with homosexual female patients. Springer views a feminine homosexual development as a successful mode of living, an example of successful individuation, and not necessarily as a pathological development, even when the animus has not been experienced in a sexual relationship with a man. Springer criticises the contrasexual construct of anima and animus. The reactions published in the *Journal of Analytical Psychology* by Braun and Wilke (2001) show in a very clear way what different views of this concepts there may be: Braun and Wilke do not want to give it up, but to differentiate it. However, they do not deny that a homosexual development can be a form of successful individuation.

Hopcke (1989) has explored the concepts of anima and animus in relation to male homosexuality. He finds that the variables of sexual identity, such as anatomical gender, socio-cultural sex-roles and sexual orientation, have become confused in Jungian psychology. He suggests that personal experience and an awareness of archetypes are important, and 'proposes that the sexual orientation of an individual is determined through a complex interaction of the archetypal masculine, the archetypal feminine and the archetypal androgyne' (see Christopher 2000).

Current views and trends for the future

Many of the difficulties and misunderstandings in this area have resulted from individuals referring to different definitions from different stages in Jung's own development of this concept. However, perhaps we could agree about the following: Jung never maintained that archetypes are gender specific. It follows that anima and animus must exist in persons of both sexes. Empirical research seems to indicate the same.

Jung wrote that the animus corresponds to 'masculine consciousness' (logos) and the anima to 'feminine consciousness' (eros). This easily leads to the conclusion that women are the very opposite of men, which was in keeping with the prevailing psychological views of the 1930s. In speaking of *eros* as 'making connections and establishing relationships' and *logos* as 'making distinctions, speaking one's opinions, discerning', Jung's thought conformed to traditional sex-roles (Jung 1954/1968a: par. 218).

More recently, feminist psychologists have taken the view that the making of connections and establishing relationships is central to the role of women and to be valued as such (Gilligan 1982). But we are nonetheless aware that both sexes need the talent both for relationship and for discrimination. In other words, it makes no sense to assume that autonomy comes naturally to one sex any more than it does to assume that relationship comes more naturally to the other. In addition, we must surely ask whether it makes any sense to speak of consciousness as being 'male' or 'female'. I doubt this, and support the above argument – which, interestingly, is corroborated by the findings of modern neurobiology (Damasio 1999).

Jung did maintain that the anima compensates male consciousness and the animus female consciousness, assuming that the first occasion in a boy's life for projections was the mother, and that in the girl's life, the father. But this arises from a fundamental misunderstanding, for originally – in most cases – the girl, like the boy, bonds with the mother. We see again how the psychology of women is so often based on that of men.

In sum, anima and animus are archetypes, but they are not gender specific – both can be constellated in men as well as women, and they often appear in tandem, as couples. However, even when we agree that anima and animus are archetypes, there may be some disagreement about archetypes themselves.

I understand archetypes, or archetypal fields, to be ordering or structuring principles, common to all human beings, which allow us to register information and emotion – usually in images – as having meaningful connections. They also promote meaningful and life-preserving behaviour and action in any given situation. I am not talking about a static order or structure, but about one which is continually renewing itself in the sense of a self-organisation of the psyche in response to the body and the outer world. The archetypal images, and the stories that are linked to them, are very stable in their narrative core, but have a pronounced capacity for marginal variation. These archetypal images are mediated and coloured by our complexes (Jung 1957/1971: par. 856), that is, our internalised patterns of relating, and are also influenced by the current social climate.

I understand complexes as generalised, internalised episodic relationship patterns which always imply an emotionally toned collision between a significant other and the ego as it is at any given time.

I would speak of anima and animus as archetypal images and archetypal experiences only when numinous female or male figures appear, for example in dreams; they are emotionally highly charged and they produce an intense feeling that makes possible a sense of transcending everyday life. That would correspond with the archetypal experience as Jung describes it.

Anima and animus regulate relationship in the widest sense, relationship to a 'thou', to 'the other', above all love relationships, erotic and sexual, but also relations between the ego and the inner world of fantasies. We could even call them archetypes of relationship and bonding. From the point of view of psychological development, anima and animus are to start with linked to the parental complexes, and are obviously coloured by them. The impulses connected with the animus and anima archetypes lead to an age-appropriate separation of the ego-complex from these complexes, bringing us closer to the individual personality, to the Self, and perhaps even to images of being in relationship to something like an Anima Mundi. Phenomenologically, anima and animus then appear as the mysterious, fascinating stranger, and provoke emotionally an atmosphere of moving towards major changes.

Future developments

I do not think that some views of this subject are right and others are wrong. When we look at these concepts from other perspectives, we find different opinions of them. Indeed, having different experiences ourselves with anima and animus, we may prefer some aspects of the theory, and neglect others.

We need more interviews with experts, with Jungian analysts, which could then be analysed in an empirical way. We should find out what the concept means personally to the analyst, and in which clinical key situations they find the concept of use. We could explore whether it is more of a clinical concept or, rather, the individual's vision of humanity, which naturally also has an influence on their clinical theories and work.

We need to do more empirical research to find out whether men and women possess anima and animus, whether there are statistical differences in the experience of these specific archetypal situations in men and in women, and in what situations we find the image of the anima and animus as a couple.

In connection with animus and anima we are necessarily referring a good deal to projection. We should investigate this connection further. Perhaps we should talk more about 'resonance'. I have gained the impression that very often there is a resonance between different archetypal fields, especially anima and animus in people who are in close contact with each other, but also in individuals' relationship with nature, with art, with intellectual concepts – and the concept of projection seems to be too static to explain the interchange. In this respect we will also, no doubt, be challenged by the findings of neuroscience.

References

Braun, C. and Wilke, H.-J. (2001) 'Bye-bye anima'. *Analytical Psychology*, 32: 53–65.

Christopher, E. (2000) 'Gender issues: anima and animus', in E. Christopher and H. McFarland Solomon (eds) *Jungian Thought in the Modern World*. London: Free Association.

Damasio, A.R. (1999) *The Feeling of What Happens: Body and Emotion in the Making of Consciousness*. New York: Harcourt Brace.

Giegerich, W. (1994) *Animus-Psychologie*. Frankfurt a/M, Germany: Lang.

Gilligan, C. (1982) *In a Different Voice: Psychological Theory and Woman's Development*. Cambridge, MA: Harvard University Press.

Gordon, R. (1993) *Bridges*. London: Karnac.

Harding, E. (1932) *The Way of all Women*. New York: Longmans, Green.

Heinke, E. (2000) 'Das Animus-Konzept C.G. Jungs aus der Sicht Analytischer Psychologinnen und Psychologen. Eine empirische Untersuchung', unpublished thesis, University of Zürich.

Heisig, D. (1996) *Die Anima: Der Archetyp des Lebendigen*. Zürich and Düsseldorf: Walter.

Hillman, J. (1985) *Anima: An Anatomy of a Personified Notion*. Dallas, TX: Spring.

Hopcke, R. (1989) *Jung, Jungians and Homosexuality*. Boston, MA: Shambhala.

Jung, C.G. (1919/1966) 'The structure of the unconscious', in *CW* 7: pars. 442–521.

—— (1925/1972) 'Marriage as a psychological relationship', in *CW* 17: pars. 324–345.

—— (1927/1974) 'Mind and earth', in *CW* 10: pars. 71–76.

—— (1928/1966) 'The relations between the ego and the unconscious', in *CW* 7: pars. 202–406.

—— (1934/1976) 'Archetypes of the collective unconscious', in *CW* 9i: pars. 1–86.

—— (1935) 'The Tavistock Lectures', in *CW* 18: pars. 1–415.

—— (1936/1976) 'Concerning the archetypes and the anima concept', in *CW* 9i: pars. 111–147.

—— (1946/1971) 'The psychology of the transference', in *CW* 16: pars. 353–539.

—— (1949/1976) 'The psychological aspects of the Kore', in *CW* 9i: pars. 306–383.

—— (1950/1976) *Aion. CW* 9ii.

—— (1954/1968a) *Mysterium Coniunctionis. CW* 14i.

—— (1954/1968b) *Mysterium Coniunctionis. CW* 14ii.

—— (1957/1971) 'Synchronicity: an acausal connecting principle', in *CW* 8: pars. 816–968.

—— (1961) *Memories, Dreams, Reflections*. New York: Random House.

Jung, E. (1967) *Animus und Anima*. Zürich: Rascher.

Kast, V. (1984) *Paare: Wie Götter sich in Menschen spiegeln*. Stuttgart: Kreuz, trans. (1986) *The Nature of Loving: Patterns of Human Relationship*. Wilmette, IL: Chiron.

—— (1993) 'Animus and anima: spiritual growth and separation'. *Harvest*, 39: 5–15.

—— (1997) *Father–Daughter, Mother–Son: Freeing Ourselves from the Complexes that Bind Us*. Shaftesbury: Element.

Samuels, A. (1989) *The Plural Psyche*. London: Routledge.

Springer, A. (2000) 'Überlegungen zur weiblichen Homosexualität'. *Analytical Psychology*, 31: 26–38.

Stein, M. (1998) *Jung's Map of the Soul*. La Salle, IL: Open Court.

von Franz, M.-L. (1968) 'The process of individuation', in C.G. Jung (ed.) *Man and his Symbols*. Garden City, NY: Doubleday.

Young-Eisendrath, P. and Wiedemann, F. (1987) *Female Authority: Empowering Women through Psychotherapy*. New York: Guilford.

Chapter 6

Psychological types

John Beebe

Introduction

It has not always been clear to students of Jung's analytical psychology what his famous 'types' are types *of*. The commonest assumption has been that they refer to types of *people*. But for Jung, they were types of *consciousness*, that is, characteristic orientations assumed by the ego in establishing and discriminating an individual's inner and outer reality. For psychotherapists, an understanding of these different natural cognitive stances can be invaluable in the daily work of supporting the basic strengths of their clients' personalities and of helping a particular consciousness to recognise its inherent limitations. The understanding of individual differences communicated on the basis of this theory can reduce a client's shame at areas of relative ego weakness and diminish the client's need to buttress the ego with strong defences that complicate treatment.

Jung's position on psychological types

Ever since his landmark self-defining text, *Wandlungen und Symbole der Libido* (1912), it had been Jung's understanding that the movements of the psyche observable in analysis tend toward consciousness. He had already recognised that consciousness is not expressed uniformly in the same way in every person. Rather, Jung conceptualised consciousness as centred in an ego that expressed its ability to orient the psyche through different basic *attitudes* and *functions*.

Jung arrived at the germ of this point of view in the midst of his studies on word association, undertaken at the Burghölzli Mental Hospital beginning about 1902. In 'The association of normal subjects', written with Franz Riklin, Jung describes how the associations produced in the subjects by calling out a series of 400 different stimulus-words can be shown to be affected by unconscious complexes. But even in this earliest research, Jung recognised that 'one principal factor is the individual character'. He and Riklin wrote:

From our experiments, two easily recognizable types emerge:

(1) A type in whose reactions, subjective, often feeling-toned experiences are used.
(2) A type whose reactions show an objective, impersonal tone.

(Jung 1973: 148)

As late as September 1913, in a lecture delivered to the Psychoanalytic Congress in Munich, Jung, now turning his attention to the psychopathology observed in clinical work, still observed two basic types of 'relations to the object' (and the self), that of the 'hysteric', whose 'centrifugal' extraversion 'displays as a rule an intensity of feeling that surpasses the normal', and that of the 'schizophrenic', in whom, on account of a 'centripetal' introversion, 'the normal level is not reached at all' (Jung 1971: 499–500).[1] This added another dimension beyond presence of complexes to the problem of analysing the subjectivity of consciousness, a problem that other observational sciences, including experimental psychology, had already recognised as 'the personal equation', a term Jung now adopted to describe his developing area of study (Shamdasani 2003: 30–31).

In the next seven years, with the help of Hans Schmid-Guisan and Toni Wolff, Jung began to unpack his typological theory. The correspondence with Schmid-Guisan particularly helped him to examine and get past his preliminary equation of feeling with extraversion and thinking with introversion. His close associate Toni Wolff made him aware that beyond extraversion–introversion and thinking–feeling, which so far organised the psyche along strictly rational grounds, there was another axis of orientation altogether that his theory would need take into account, the 'irrational' axis of sensation–intuition. (Jung himself seems to have recognised that the difference between his original thinking–feeling axis and Wolff's sensation–intuition axis was that the first pair of functions are deployed in a rational way to interpret experience, whereas the latter merely apprehend what is already given to us by the outer or inner world, and hence do not use any optional process of cognition or evaluation: see Marshall 1968.) By the time he came to write *Psychological Types* in 1919 and 1920, he had already envisioned a sophisticated system of analysis of types of consciousness characterised by four main dichotomies: extraversion–introversion, thinking–feeling, sensation–intuition and rational–irrational. It was this system that he continued to defend for the rest of his life and that has informed all subsequent work on Jung's psychological types.

Definitions

In *Psychological Types*, Jung understands there to be four *functions of consciousness*, which he names *sensation*, *thinking*, *feeling* and *intuition*.

These terms did not originate with Jung; rather, they were culled from the history of psychology, and they carry the ghost of earlier meanings placed on them by many physicians and philosophers, e.g., Hippocrates' four temperaments: Melancholic, Sanguine, Choleric and Phlegmatic. Jung's theory of psychological types resembles in some ways the eighteenth-century faculty psychology developed by theorists such as Christian von Wolff and Thomas Reid, according to which the mind consists of various powers or capacities, called faculties. One of these faculties had been *willing*, which became for Schopenhauer the essential attribute of the *unconscious* mind. Freud and Adler would develop this theme in their theories of wishing and over-compensation. Their idea of the ego was an agency that needed to defend itself against knowing too much about the willing of the unconscious mind, and whose faculties could therefore best be described as defences, even if those defences enabled the psyche to pursue its true aims in disguise, as it were.

Jung, consistent with his greater emphasis on the possibilities of consciousness, accepted the will as part of the ego (Jung 1971: 486), and concentrated on the functions the ego needs to orient itself to any reality with which it must cope. To understand reality, he reasoned, we need a function of consciousness that *registers reality as real*: this he called the *sensation* function, which delivers to us the sensation that something *is* (Jung 1968: 11). Then, he said, we need a function to *define* for us what we are perceiving when we notice that something is there: this he called the *thinking* function. Next, he understood that we need a function that *assigns a value* to the thing that we have perceived and named; this is called the function of *feeling*.[2] Finally, he realised that we require a function to enable us to divine *the implications or possibilities* of the thing that has been empirically perceived, logically defined and discriminatingly evaluated: this he called the intuitive function.

Jung found it easier to define the first three functions than the fourth. On one occasion, he said,

> Sensation tells us that a thing is. Thinking tells us what the thing is, feeling tells us what it is worth to us. Now what else could there be? One would assume one has a complete picture of the world when one knows there *is* something, *what* it is, and what it is *worth* [original italics].

He added immediately:

> But there is another category, and that is time. Things have a past and they have a future. They come from somewhere, they go to somewhere, and you cannot see where they came from and you cannot know where they go to, but you get what the Americans call a hunch.
>
> (Jung 1968: 13)

That ability to get, and to a certain degree to trust, the hunch is what Jung meant by *intuition*. That he understood what it means to trust this essentially irrational process of perception is part of Jung's appeal to people who are naturally disposed to use their intuition to orient themselves to reality.

Jung held that feeling and thinking are *rational* functions, and that sensation and intuition are *irrational* functions. He did not sustain the faculty psychologists' opposition between reason and passion. Jung understood 'feeling' as a rational process, that is, as neither affect (or what we sometime call 'feelings') nor the result of more unconscious emotion-based processes, even though he admitted our complexes are 'feeling-toned'. Rather, Jung made clear that he took the process of assigning feeling value to be an ego-function that was just as rational in its operation as the process of defining and creating logical links (thinking).

Jung also recognised that sensation, even though it is the evidential basis for our empirical reality testing, is as irrational a process as the intuitive one that delivers our 'hunches' to us. As a moment's reflection will demonstrate, we do not rationally choose what we manage to see, hear, smell, taste or grasp with our sense of touch. By linking feeling with thinking as rational functions, and sensation with intuition as irrational functions of consciousness, Jung broke with the nineteenth-century habit of lumping feeling with intuition as marking a 'romantic' temperament and thinking with sensation as the unmistakable signs of a 'practical' disposition. Rather, in *Psychological Types*, he convincingly makes the case that consciousness is for all of us the product of both rational and irrational processes of encountering and assessing reality.

The concept of introversion was by now fully liberated from its earlier confusion in Jung's writings with both thinking and objectivity, just as extraversion was freed from its former fixed association with feeling and subjectivity. In *Psychological Types*, Jung states that

> The extravert is distinguished by his craving for the object, by his empathy and identification with the object, his voluntary dependence on the object. He is influenced by the object in the same degree as he strives to assimilate it.
>
> (Jung 1971: 317)

By contrast,

> the introvert is distinguished by his self-assertion vis à vis the object. He struggles against any dependence on the object, he repels all its influences, and even fears it. So much the more is he dependent on the idea, which shields him from external reality and gives him the feeling of

inner freedom – though he pays for this with a very noticeable power
psychology.

(Jung 1971: 317–318)

Jung's use of personification here – his reference to the introvert and the
extravert – needs some deconstruction. Read literally, as too many have
read him, he seems to be saying that introversion – 'the inward-turning of
libido' – and extraversion – 'the outward-turning of libido' – characterise
different kinds of people. Elsewhere in the book *Psychological Types* he
implies that we all use both processes, that there is an extravert and an
introvert in each of us. How this can be finally becomes clear when he uses
the now famous terms not as nouns but as *adjectives*, to define the way in
which the various functions of consciousness happen to be deployed in a
particular individual. In turn, he takes up the description of extraverted
thinking, extraverted feeling, extraverted sensation, extraverted intuition,
introverted thinking, introverted feeling, introverted sensation and introverted intuition, noting that these 'basic psychological functions seldom or
never have the same strength or degree of development in the same
individual' and that as 'a rule, one or the other function predominates, in
both strength and development' (Jung 1971: 346). The implication, however, is that all eight of these distinct cognitive processes exist, at least to
some degree, in every one of us. The origins of what is nowadays called 'the
whole-type eight-function model' of personality (Geldart 1998; Clark 2000;
Haas et al. 2001) are therefore plainly laid out in *Psychological Types*.

What Jung means by the *introverted* use of a function comes across in his
personified notion of someone 'dependent upon the idea'. He explains that
he employs the term *idea* 'to express the *meaning* of a primordial image'
(Jung 1971: 437), that is to say, an archetype. An introverted function,
therefore, is one that has turned away from the object and toward the
archetypal 'idea' that the object might be most closely matched to. This
archetypal idea, residing in the inner world, can be understood as a profound
thought, a value, a metaphorical image, or a model of reality, depending
upon whether the introverted function is thinking, feeling, intuition or sensation. When an introverted function is used to orient to something external,
it is in the end the comparison to the archetype, not the stimulating object or
situation itself, that finally commands the attention of the function. This can
seem like a withdrawal from the object itself.

Introverted sensation, as a process, is thus 'guided by the intensity of the
subjective sensation excited by the objective stimulus' (Jung 1971: 395).
That means that the person strongly identified with the use of this function
will react immediately to the internal, bodily sensations caused by, for
example, the food served at a meal, so that the distension of his stomach, or
the degree of pepper in the meal, even the audibility of others at his table,
may turn out to be more determinative of his happiness at a dinner party

than the carefully assembled company that the host or hostess has arranged for the gathering. This is because a dissonance with the archetype of the good meal has been constellated by the excessive stimulation. This process is not usually visible. When someone has been using the introverted sensation function primarily,

> seen from the outside, it looks as though the effect of the object did not penetrate into the subject at all. This impression is correct inasmuch as a subjective content does, in fact, intervene from the unconscious and intercept the effect of the object. The intervention may be so abrupt that the individual appears to be shielding himself directly from all objective influences.
>
> (Jung 1971: 396)

Introverted sensation, of course, can be just as guided by a visual cue: the films of Alfred Hitchcock, who seems to have used this function in a dominant way, dazzle us with the uncanny power of seemingly ordinary images to stimulate unexpected, archetypal reactions.

Those who make abundant use of an introverted function – introverted intuition, say, or introverted feeling – can nevertheless be perceived by others as depreciating the object. Jungian case studies sometimes seem, when introverted intuition is taking the lead, to leave the patient behind in a maze of mythological 'amplifications'. The poet Rilke, who seems to have known that his sensibility was masked by a strong introverted feeling, is said to have written to a new mistress, 'I love you, but of course it's none of your business'.

A particularly difficult introverted function, from the standpoint of personal relations, is *introverted thinking*, because when the object of introverted thinking is a person, 'this person has a distinct feeling that he matters only in a negative way'. Often, 'he feels himself warded off as something definitely disturbing' (Jung 1971: 383). The object, when this function is being used, *is* being avoided because the person using this function is 'building up his world of ideas, and never shrinks from thinking a thought because it might prove to be dangerous, subversive, heretical, or wounding to other people's feelings' (Jung 1971: 384). The ideas that are encountered, however, are archetypal ideas that may be out of common circulation, but which can be far more profound and appropriate to the actual definition of a situation than the accepted dictates of conventional extraverted thinking. These 'new' thoughts are, however, very difficult to articulate, and the introverted thinking function frequently goes on refining its conceptions when the patience of others has been exhausted: it does not know when to stop.

Introverted intuition, as a function, is concerned 'with the background processes of consciousness', and for the person using that function in a differentiated way, 'unconscious images acquire the dignity of things' (Jung 1971: 399). This is the one type of consciousness that naturally 'apprehends the images arising from the *a priori* inherited foundations of the unconscious'. That is, rather than thinking about, experientially comparing, or feeling the archetype that arises in relation to a situation, the introverted intuitive function becomes directly aware of the archetype as an image, as if 'seeing' it: introverted intuition is therefore the function responsible for visionary experience, which often seems 'mystical' to others.

Introverted feeling, by contrast, can only feel the archetypal image of a situation. It cannot see it. The hoary Indian story of the three blind men and the elephant takes on more meaning if one considers that India is a country where introverted feeling seems to predominate in collective consciousness. Thus, all of the blind men (there are as many as six in some versions, and sometimes they come from a city in which all of the inhabitants are blind) could be said to represent the introverted feeling function, literally feeling its way slowly around the archetype, the elephant in their midst. Necessarily, a thinking definition of that experience at any moment will be partial – 'It's a rope', 'It's a snake', 'It's a great mud wall' – but the *process* never ceases until the elephant is felt entirely. It is important to realise that when the introverted feeling function is, for example, feeling 'bad', it is feeling the entire archetypal category of 'bad' and is not likely to quit until that archetypal badness is felt through. As Jung says,

> The depth of this feeling can only be guessed – it can never be clearly grasped. It makes people silent and difficult of access; it shrinks back like a violet from the brute nature of the object in order to fill the depths of the subject. It comes out with negative judgments or assumes an air of profound indifference as a means of defence.
>
> (Jung 1971: 387)

Perhaps we all get into our introverted feeling when we are depressed. The important thing to grasp, in understanding introverted feeling, is that archetypes can be *felt* every bit as much as they can be thought about, directly intuited, or experienced somatically. As Jung puts it,

> The primordial images are, of course, just as much ideas as feelings. Fundamental ideas, ideas like God, freedom, and immortality, are just as much feeling-values as they are significant ideas.
>
> (Jung 1971: 387–388)

The extraverted functions, as Jung has already been quoted as informing us, tend so completely to merge with the object as to identify with it. They often end up without adequate distance from the stimuli that are presented to them. In the case of *extraverted feeling*, these are the feelings – that is, the emotions and prejudices – of others, and often of society at large, so that the personality of a person strongly identified with this function 'appears adjusted in relation to external conditions. Her feelings harmonize with objective situations and general values' (Jung 1971: 356). The woman led by extraverted feeling in her 'love choice', Jung tells us, will see to it that 'the "suitable" man is loved, and no one else' (Jung 1971: 356). On the other hand, no type is more capable of appreciation and sympathy.

Similarly, *extraverted thinking* tends to become enamoured of established ideas, frequently neglecting the duty to think freshly about what is being expressed and the language that is really appropriate to it. There is no brake, therefore, against insisting that these ideas should govern everyone's behaviour. As Jung puts it, the person strongly identified with this function 'elevates . . . an objectively oriented intellectual formula . . . into the ruling principle not only for himself but for his whole environment'. On the other hand, this most characteristic function of the Enlightenment period must have guided John Locke in establishing principles of government that many in the West still believe have universal applicability – as well as Mozart in elaborating musical ideas that everyone soon could follow.

Extraverted sensation, as a cognitive process, seeks 'an accumulation of actual experiences of concrete objects' (Jung 1971: 363) and the function can become, in the moment, so riveted on the reality 'out there' that it cannot recognise that other things may also be happening at that same time: this is a function perfect for watching a basketball game, but it may not notice that someone is about to say or do something unexpected.

Extraverted intuition can become so engaged with the possibilities of its objects that for the person strongly identified with this function, it is 'as if his whole life vanished in the new situation' (Jung 1971: 368). To use a metaphor to describe what is really an unmediated, instinctive process, this function operates like a traffic signal, indicating with its green light when it is time to proceed to develop something, with its red light when it is time to stop, and with its yellow light when one must proceed with caution. A significant problem is that people without a similar degree of development of extraverted intuition may not perceive the presence of any signal at all and thus cannot understand why the person led by such intuitions is rushing ahead, stopping, or pausing when he does. And extraverted intuition's failure to heed sensation cues can undermine the actualisation of the possibility being pursued.

In *Psychological Types*, Jung offered the all-important notion of a selective *differentiation* of the various functions of consciousness as the key to the different degrees and styles of consciousness individual people display. As he puts it in his 79-page section of definitions at the end of the book,

> Differentiation means the development of differences, the separation of parts from the whole. In this work I employ the concept of

differentiation chiefly with respect to the psychological *functions*. So long as a function is still so fused with one or more other functions – thinking with feeling, feeling with sensation, etc. – that it is unable to operate on its own, it is in an archaic condition, i.e., not differentiated, not separated from the whole as a special part and existing by itself. Undifferentiated thinking is incapable of thinking apart from other functions; it is continually mixed up with sensations, feelings, intuitions, just as undifferentiated feeling is mixed up with sensations and fantasies, as for instance in the sexualization (Freud) of feeling and thinking in a neurosis.

(Jung 1971: 424–425)

As long as a function is undifferentiated, moreover, it cannot be deployed in the conscious manner of a directed mental process that is truly under the control of the ego, and capable of being applied to tasks and goals:

Without differentiation direction is impossible, since the direction of a function towards a goal depends on the elimination of anything irrelevant. Fusion with the irrelevant precludes direction; only a differentiated function is *capable* of being directed.

(Jung 1971: 425)

These passages hold the key to why, in the first English translation (by H.G. Baynes) of *Pyschologische Typen*, the work bore the subtitle, 'or, The Psychology of Individuation' (Jung 1921, 1923). One way to understand what Jung meant by *individuation* is *the progressive differentiation of the various psychological functions of consciousness*. For, as he puts it elsewhere in the Definitions section, 'Individuation is a process of *differentiation* (q.v.) having for its goal the development of the individual personality'. It is 'an extension of the sphere of consciousness, an enriching of conscious psychological life' (Jung 1971: 450).

Since Jung also believed that individuation, i.e., the development of consciousness, is a *natural* process, he felt that there was a way to describe its orderly unfolding in all of us, and he used his idea of psychological types to offer certain developmental guidelines. These guidelines have been mostly ignored outside the narrow circle of those who are interested in the theory of psychological types, but they are most important, as they hold the key to much of what happens in psychotherapy when a personality starts to develop.

Jung believed that we all get a head start in individuation through a natural tendency to differentiate at least two function-attitudes out of our total potential complement of eight.[3] The two function-attitudes that most naturally tend to differentiate early in our development of ego-consciousness will not be the same for each individual. Because they develop so early, they appear to be innate, although later 'falsification of type' as a result of environmental influences can distort the individual's typological bent (Benziger 1995). Sixteen psychological type profiles can be distinguished simply on the basis of which of the eight function-attitudes turns out to be the most differentiated – the 'superior' function – and which the next most differentiated – the 'auxiliary' function.

Jung found that '[f]or all the types met with in practice, the rule holds good that besides the conscious, primary function there is a relatively unconscious, auxiliary function which is in every respect different from the nature of the primary function' (Jung 1971: 405–406). Since he also believed that 'naturally only these functions can appear as auxiliary whose nature is not *opposed* to the dominant function' (the emphasis is mine), feeling, for instance, 'can never act as the second function alongside thinking' nor sensation alongside intuition. Rather, if with respect to differentiation someone's first, or superior, function is on the rational axis (i.e., is either thinking or feeling) then that individual's auxiliary function will have to come from the irrational axis (be either sensation or intuition).

A superior thinking function will thus be paired with only one of two possible other functions in the course of normal type development – either an auxiliary sensation or an auxiliary intuition. Similarly, a superior sensation function, being on the irrational axis, will take as its auxiliary a function from the rational axis, meaning that it can be paired only with thinking or feeling. The following possibilities naturally emerge:

Superior/Auxiliary
Feeling/Intuition
Feeling/Sensation
Thinking/Intuition
Thinking/Sensation
ntuition/Feeling
Intuition/Thinking
Sensation/Feeling
Sensation/Thinking

This scheme is the basic model for the differentiation of the eight function-attitudes into different types of people. Given that each of the leading functions can be either extraverted or introverted (for instance, feeling/intuition could describe the typology of a person with either 'introverted feeling with auxiliary intuition' or 'extraverted feeling with auxiliary intuition'), it follows that, typologically speaking, there are at least sixteen kinds of people.

Even this differentiation does not, unfortunately, clarify the problem of whether there is any difference in *attitude* between the first two functions in an actual individual. The clinician should be aware that Jung's text has been interpreted in two different ways by later commentators. Apparently seizing on Jung's assertion that the secondary function is 'not antagonistic to' the primary one, Jo Wheelwright (1982) concluded that the first two functions would have the same attitude with respect to extraversion and introversion. Isabel Briggs Myers, on the other hand, took Jung's subsequent statement, that the auxiliary function is 'in every respect different from the nature of the primary function', to mean that the auxiliary must differ from the superior function in attitude (I. Myers and P. Myers 1980: 18–21).

It should be noted that Jung took for granted that most consciousnesses are so *un*differentiated that even the auxiliary function is rarely more than 'relatively unconscious'. Too fine a distinction regarding the attitude of the auxiliary would not have made a great deal of sense to him: everything besides the superior function was still more or less unconscious anyway. He spoke of a shadowy tertiary function, and a fourth, 'inferior' function to which he gave a special status, as a source of problematic, 'touchy' reactions because of its especial closeness to the unconscious. This *inferior function* is 'the function that lags behind in the process of differentiation' (Jung 1971: 450). Often a source of shame, the inferior function is conceived of as being carried by the anima in a man, and the animus in a woman, in contrast to the superior function, which is identified with the persona.

The inferior function will always be the other pole of the typological axis (whether rational or irrational) on which the superior function falls; so a superior thinking function will be plagued by an inferior feeling function, superior sensation by inferior intuition, superior intuition by inferior sensation, and superior feeling by inferior thinking. Moreover (and here there is more agreement in the Jungian tradition) if the superior function is introverted, the inferior function will be extraverted; and if the superior is extraverted, the inferior function will be introverted. The axis between the superior and inferior functions is what I have called the 'spine' of personality. There are eight possible spines, shown in Figure 6.1 as vertical lines. If one imagines each of these line diagrams as a stick figure representing a person who is facing the reader, the auxiliary function appears as the figure's 'right hand', which will be to the reader's left. The different figures that share the same superior function are shown in pairs, as two figures side by side, with identical spines but different auxiliary functions, making sixteen standpoints in all.

These are the famous sixteen 'types' of personality that most people are referring to when they use the term 'psychological types': they have been described as the 'MBTI types' by those who have learned to recognise the superior and auxiliary functions with the help of the Myers-Briggs Type Indicator. However, I prefer to call them 'type profiles'. Using Jung's rules for type differentiation and understanding Isabel Briggs Myers' notion of 'good type development' (K. Myers and Kirby 2000), it is clear that the differentiation of a strong natural superior and accompanying auxiliary function that is different in every respect is the starting point for further differentiation. The other function-attitudes operate largely out of awareness until and unless they become conscious in the course of development.

Innovations, criticisms and developments

Although types were carefully studied by many of the analysts who were trained directly by Jung, including Meier (1959), Henderson (1970) and Wheelwright (1982), the most important development of psychological types within analytical psychology came from Jung's close associate, Marie-Louise von Franz (1971/1998), who systematically studied the inferior function for each of the types. She also clarified the relation of the inferior function to Jung's transcendent function, pointing out that if the inferior function is made conscious, then the relation to the unconscious changes and the personality is unified (see also Beebe 1992: 102–109). She explained that Jung's hierarchy of first, second and third functions implies a relative order in which the functions can be differentiated in the course of a psychotherapy, although she indicated that once the superior function has been established one can choose whether to develop the second or third function next. No one, however (and Jung also says this), can simply take up the inferior function directly and develop it. Not only does it tend to 'stay low' (E. Osterman, personal communication, 1972), it cannot be approached effectively until the first three functions have been differentiated.

I pursued this line of thought by clarifying the archetypal constraints around the development of the function-attitudes in the course of development (for a discussion of my ideas about this, see Harris 1996: 65–76). Noting that the superiority of the leading function derives from its association with the hero archetype, I went on to identify the archetypal figures that carry the other three functions in the hierarchy that Jung and von Franz established. Following the evidence of dreams and also movies in which the auxiliary and tertiary functions are often symbolised as an older and younger person of the same sex, as the figure identified with the superior function, I have concluded that the auxiliary function is carried by a stable parental figure (usually a father in a man and a mother in a woman) and the tertiary function by an unstable child figure, given to cycles of inflation and deflation (*puer aeternus* in a man, *puella aeterna* in a woman). Although von Franz spoke broadly of the fourth, inferior function as 'the door through which all the figures of the unconscious come' (1971/1998: 67), I have identified the fourth function, experienced by the ego as a problematic aspect of itself, not with the shadow, but with the anima and animus. It is the *other* four functions, I believe, that constitute the shadow of the first four, a shadow accentuated by the process of differentiation that allows the first four to develop and become conscious function-attitudes.[4]

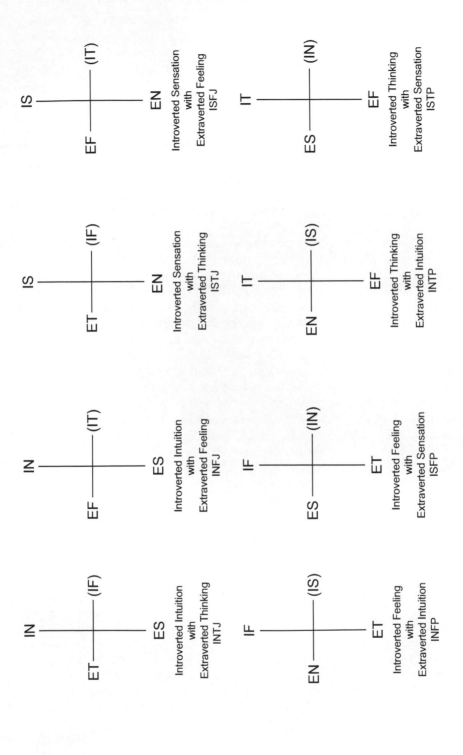

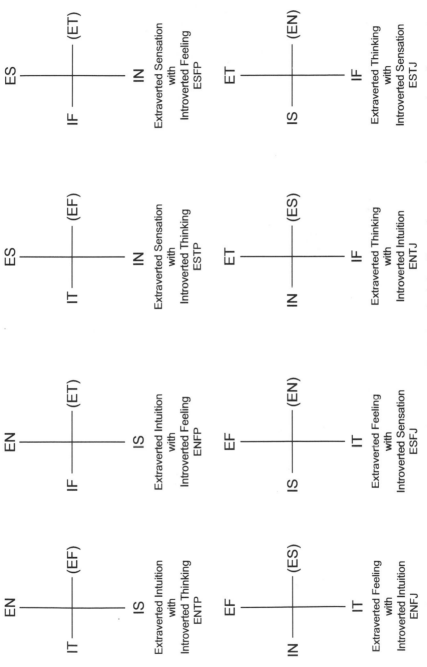

Code: E = extraverted; I = introverted; N = intuition; S = sensation; T = thinking; F = feeling. Tertiary functions are shown in parentheses. By convention, the four letter MBTI codes list the irrational function before the rational one, regardless of which is the superior and which the auxiliary; the P and J refer to whether the leading extraverted function is irrational (perceiving) or rational (judging).

Figure 6.1

Thus, someone with superior extraverted thinking and auxiliary introverted sensation will have introverted thinking and extraverted sensation strongly in shadow, and when that person develops tertiary extraverted intuition, introverted intuition will be rejected and become an aspect of the shadow. From this perspective, even the inferior function has a shadow: in the case of this individual, who would have an inferior introverted feeling, carried by the anima, a shadow of extraverted feeling could be found.

In this way, I was able to conceptualise a first typology of the shadow (although Naomi Quenk (1993), not long after, produced her own typological model of the shadow in the book *Beside Ourselves*). According to the model of typology I have developed (Beebe 2004), specific archetypes carry the shadows of the first four functions: the Opposing Personality (carrying the shadow of the Hero), the Senex or Witch (shadow of the Father or Mother), the Trickster (shadow of the Puer or Puella), and the Demonic/Daimonic Personality (shadow of the Anima/Animus). Figure 6.2 shows how this model organises the basic archetypal complexes as part-personalities that express themselves through their individual function-attitudes.

My model implies that development of all eight function-attitudes will involve a significant engagement with each of the archetypal complexes, and a differentiation of each function out of its archetypal manifestation. In integrating one's typology, the issues associated with each archetypal complex must be faced, exactly as in classical individuation, which has been conceived as the progressive integration of the collective unconscious through engagement with a series of archetypal figures. Moreover, as Papadopoulos (1992 vol. 2: 6) pointed out, the model provides a rational basis for analysing archetypal interactions between individuals on the basis of typology. Recognising correlations between functions and complexes in an individual patient can be very helpful to the therapist, especially when encountering markedly altered states of mind in patients. At such times the therapist can often help to re-establish ego strength in the patient by speaking the language of the patient's superior function rather than mirroring the typological idiom of the possessing complex (Sandner and Beebe 1995: 317–344). An account of the way Jung worked with an analytic patient whose reality testing was overwhelmed by an irruption of intuitive religious imagery reveals how he used his understanding of typology to guide an intervention that helped her recover her natural sensation type orientation (von der Heydt 1975). In less florid, but nevertheless demanding, borderline and narcissistic conditions, function-attitudes that are in shadow for a client can be associated with archetypal defences of the self, and it advances therapy to understand their precise character (Beebe 1998b).

Other noteworthy contributions to the conceptual and clinical elucidation of the theory of psychological types have been as follows:

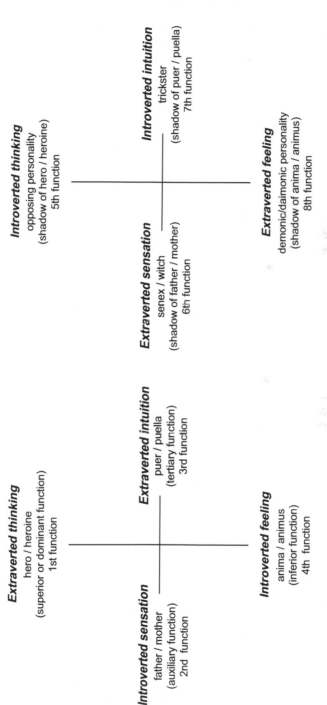

Figure 6.2 An illustration of Dr John Beebe's arrangement of the eight functions of consciousness

© John Beebe, MD, 2004

- Meier's (1959) exposition of the transference-countertransference in terms of a 'rotation' of the analyst's typological mandala to bring his or her orientation into attunement with the analysand's.
- Mann, Siegler and Osmond's (1968) discussion of the different relations to time among the different functions (sensation, in their view, being present oriented, feeling being past oriented, intuition future oriented, and thinking having a continuous time line through past, present, and future).
- Marshall's (1968) clarification of 'rational' and 'irrational' through his conceptual analysis of the functions (sensation and intuition revealed to be 'functions of the given' and thinking and feeling as 'functions of option').
- James Hillman's (1971/1998) well-drawn distinctions between aspects of the feeling function and affect, the anima, and the persona, and his discussion of the role of inferior feeling in synchronistic phenomena.
- William Willeford's (1975, 1976, 1977) insistence on the 'primacy' of feeling in the hierarchy of functions (because it is the function that discriminates affect).
- Shapiro and Alexander's (1975) phenomenological analysis of the characteristic 'moves' of extraversion (merger with the object) and introversion (matching with the archetype) in creating experience.
- Groesbeck's (1976) examination of the role of the analyst's tertiary and inferior functions in the constellation of the 'wounded healer' archetype during analysis.
- Kirsch's (1980) demonstration that introverted therapists tend to interpret dreams on the subject level and extraverted therapists on the object level.
- Sabini's (1988) discussion of the therapist's inferior function.
- Hill's (1998) discussion of the typology of the anima.

All of these writers have appreciated and extended the therapeutic possibilities of Jung's typological formulations.

Another significant line of development of the theory of psychological types has been in the area of standardised testing to determine one's type and level of type development. Although in the 1940s Jo Wheelwright, together with his wife, Jane Wheelwright, plus Horace Gray and later John Buehler, produced the first paper-and-pencil type test, the Gray-Wheelwrights Jungian Type Survey (JTS), and did pioneering research with this instrument (Mattoon and Davis 1995), it was really the Myers-Briggs Type Indicator (MBTI) developed by Isabel Briggs Myers and her mother Katherine Briggs, who were not Jungian analysts, that put standardised type testing on the map internationally. The MBTI, developed in earnest from 1942 and finally licensed in the 1960s, has become one of the most popular psychological instruments in the English-speaking world and is starting to be used in translation in other countries (see Quenk 2000 for an up-to-date description). It is regularly used by career counsellors to assess the 'type' of clients looking for work that suits them as well as in human resource and personnel departments all over the world. A Center for Applications of Psychological Type in Gainesville, Florida maintains a large statistical database of test results. In the United States, the Association for Psychological Type, which has more than 4000 members, hosts conferences sharing experience and research based on the use of the MBTI, and there are similar organisations in other countries. There is also a version of the MBTI test for children, the Murphy-Meisgeier Type Indicator for Children (MMTIC). All of these paper-and-pencil tests involve forced choices constructed according to Jung's 'bipolar assumption' that we cannot think and feel, or take in sensation and use intuition, at the same time. In 1980, Jungian analysts June Singer and Mary Loomis offered their own test, the Singer-Loomis Inventory of Personality (SLIP), which does not build on this assumption; instead it assesses the level of development of each of the eight function-attitudes separately (Loomis 1982). A comparison of test findings, undertaken to determine the extent of agreement between the JTS, MBTI and SLIP was published in 1994.

> Results found that the MBTI and the JTS both indicated extraversion-introversion with substantial agreement, sensing-intuition with moderate agreement, and thinking-feeling with limited agreement. Evidence was equivocal for the instruments' ability to indicate dominant function. It appears that the SLIP measures different constructs than either the MBTI or the JTS, so that little support was found for Singer and Loomis' challenge to Jung's bipolarity assumption.
>
> (Karesh et al. 1994: 30)

The popularity of the MBTI has resulted in a spate of publications, the *Journal of Psychological Type*, the *Bulletin of Psychological Type*, *The Type Reporter* and *TypeFace* among them. Myers also is responsible for the terms 'judging' and 'perceiving' as less loaded synonyms for 'rational' and 'irrational', although the test itself confines its J and P descriptors to the characterisation of the leading extraverted function. Myers also introduced the notion of 'good type development' to suggest a progressive differentiation of the functions according to the hierarchy of superior, auxiliary, tertiary and inferior. In recent years, a controversy has developed as to whether the third and fourth functions continue the alternation of attitudes (with respect to extraversion or introversion) begun by the first two functions. A regularly alternating pattern is espoused by both Grant et al. (1983) and Brownsword (1988), whereas the MBTI Manual suggests that the auxiliary, tertiary and inferior are all opposite in attitude to the dominant.

Important attempts to integrate the empirical discoveries of those who have developed the MBTI test into the clinical and conceptual tradition of analytical psychology have been made by Angelo Spoto (1995), John Giannini (2004) and myself (Beebe 1984). There have also been attempts to link the eight Jungian function-attitudes and sixteen MBTI type profiles to a new notion of temperament (Keirsey and Bates 1984; Berens 1998), Sheldon's body types (Arraj and Arraj 1988), the DSM-IV personality disorders (Ekstrom 1988), the Neo-PI 'Big-5' Personality Factors (McRae and Costa 1989; Wiggins 1996; Scanlon 1999), and the 'multiple intelligences' of cognitive psychology (Gardner 1983; K. Thompson 1985; Goleman 1995). The types have been linked to religious orientation (Ross 1992) and moral decision-making styles (Beebe 1992, 1998a; Burleson 2001). Within academic psychology, Kagan (1994, 1998) has recognised Jung's contributions to a theory of temperament but warned of the problems inherent in trying to understand these issues without a grasp of inherent physiology as well as psychology. There have also been attempts to correlate Jung's types with occult traditions of characterology, such as the enneagram and astrology.

Current status and trends

Type is still a 'hard sell' among many analysts. A study published by Plaut (1972) revealed that less than half of Jungian analysts use type in their clinical work.[5] Those who do often rely on test results rather than clinical observation to establish the 'type diagnosis'. Many of these analysts are unaware that the Association for Psychological Type considers it unethical to type someone simply on the basis of their results on the MBTI, which is after all only an 'Indicator'. There must be at least a follow-up interview in which the results of the test are explained with a proviso along the lines of, 'this is the type the test *indicates*, and you can see if it really fits you'. Nevertheless, Annie Murphy Paul (2004) has severely criticised the way the MBTI has been used by teachers and career counsellors to assign identities to individuals.

In psychotherapeutic circles, sadly, few clinicians can even recognise the eight function-attitudes, confusing introverted feeling with introverted intuition, not knowing the difference between extraverted and introverted thinking and so on. (Sharp's (1987) book is an excellent remedial primer.) Many do not really understand the difference between introversion and extraversion as processes in the self. (This is helpfully addressed in Lavin's (1995) article.) One place type theory has taken limited, but promising, hold in clinical work is in the area of couple therapy and marriage counselling. Therapists who have explained the types to their clients have often reported that the results are very satisfying, in terms of creating appropriate expectations between the partners and helping them to adjust their communication styles. There can be no real advance in the understanding of Jung's most subtle and far-reaching contribution to ego psychology, however, until many more analytical psychologists become much more type-literate than they are nowadays. Then we can hope for some interesting research that follows up the implications of Jung's theory of psychological types, research that can also move our understanding of the actual path of individuation forward.

Notes

1 The terms 'extraversion' and 'introversion' were apparently adapted from Binet's terms 'externospection' and 'introspection' (Binet 1903, cited by Oliver Brachfeld in Ellenberger 1970: 702–703).
2 Carolyn Fay (1996) has suggested this be called 'feeling value'.
3 'Function', strictly, refers to the four functions of consciousness – sensation, thinking, feeling and intuition – whereas 'attitude' suggests the habitual way the attention is directed – whether extraverted or introverted – when the psyche acts or reacts (Jung 1971: 414). In the type literature, it is common to identify the extraverted and introverted deployment of a function when specifying it; hence rather than speaking of four functions and two attitudes, people nowadays speak of eight function-attitudes (H. Thompson 1996). These eight cognitive modes offer a total complement of possibilities for conscious orientation that can potentially be differentiated as we individuate.
4 Here, I have followed Myers, and not Wheelwright, in finding that the auxiliary function is different in attitude from the superior function, and have asserted that the attitudes of the functions alternate in the course of their differentiation, so that if the first, superior, function is extraverted, the auxiliary function will be introverted, the tertiary extraverted, and the inferior introverted.
5 Bradway and Detloff (1978) established the incidence of the different psychological types among Jungian analysts, and Bradway and Wheelwright (1978) studied the relation of the psychological type of the analyst to the analysts' actual analytical practices, finding, for instance, that extraverts tend to use typology more than introverts in making connections and interpretations with their patients and that typology is used more often by San Francisco than by London Jungian analysts.

Bibliography

Arraj, J. and Arraj, T. (1988) *Tracking the Elusive Human*, Volume 1. Chiloquin, OR: Inner Growth.
Beebe, J. (1984) 'Psychological types in transference, countertransference, and the therapeutic interaction', in N. Schwartz-Salant and M. Stein (eds) *Transference/ Countertransference*. Wilmette, IL: Chiron.
—— (1992) *Integrity in Depth*. College Station, TX: Texas A&M University Press.
—— (1998a) 'Toward a Jungian analysis of character', in A. Casement (ed.) *Post-Jungians Today*. London: Routledge.
—— (1998b) 'Review of Donald Kalsched's *The Inner World of Trauma: Archetypal Defenses of the Personal Spirit*'. *Quadrant*, 28(1): 92–96.
—— (2004) 'Understanding consciousness through the theory of psychological

types', in J. Cambray and L. Carter (eds) *Analytical Psychology*. Hove, UK: Brunner-Routledge.

Benziger, K. (1995) *Falsification of Type*. Dillon, CO: KBA.

Berens, L. (1998) *Understanding Yourself and Others: An Introduction to Temperament*. Huntington Beach, CA: Temperament Research Institute.

Binet, A. (1903) *L'Etude expérimental de l'intelligence*. Paris: Schleicher.

Brachfeld, O. (1954) 'Gelenkte Tagträume als Hilfsmittel der Psychotherapie'. *Zeitschrift für Psychotherapie*, 4: 79–93.

Bradway, K. and Detloff, W. (1976) 'Incidence of psychological types among Jungian analysts, classified by self and by test'. *Journal of Analytical Psychology*, 21(2): 134–146.

Bradway, K. and Wheelwright, J. (1978) 'The psychological type of the analyst and its relation to analytical practice'. *Journal of Analytical Psychology*, 23(3): 211–225.

Brownsword, A. (1988) *Psychological Type: An Introduction*. Nicasio, CA: Human Resources Management Press.

Burleson, B. (2001) *Pathways to Integrity: Ethics and Psychological Type*. Gainesville, FL: Center for Applications of Psychological Type.

Clark, P. (2000) 'Work and the Eight Function Model'. *Bulletin of Psychological Type*, 23(7).

Costa, P. and McCrae, R. (1985) *The NEO Personality Inventory Manual*. Odessa, FL: Psychological Assessment Resources.

Ekstrom, S. (1988) 'Jung's typology and DSM-III personality disorders: a comparison of two systems of classification'. *Journal of Analytical Psychology*, 33(4): 329–344.

Ellenberger, H. (1970) *The Discovery of the Unconscious: The History and Evolution of Dynamic Psychiatry*. New York: Basic Books.

Fay, C. (1996) *At the Threshold* (video cassette). Houston, TX: C.G. Jung Educational Center.

Gardner, H. (1983) *Frames of Mind*. New York: Basic Books.

Geldart, W. (1998) 'Katharine Downing Myers and whole MBTI type – an interview'. *The Enneagram and the MBTI: An Electronic Journal* http://tap3x.net/EMBTI/journal.html (February 1998).

Giannini, J. (2004) *Compass of the Soul: Archetypal Guides to a Fuller Life*. Gainesville, FL: Center for Applications of Psychological Type.

Goleman, D. (1995) *Emotional Intelligence*. New York: Bantam.

Grant, W.H., Thompson, M.M. and Clarke, T.E. (1983) *From Image to Likeness: A Jungian Path in the Gospel Journey*. Ramsey, NJ: Paulist Press.

Groesbeck, C. (1978) 'Psychological types in the analysis of the transference'. *Journal of Analytical Psychology*, 23(1): 23–53.

Haas, L., McAlpine, R. and Hartzler, M. (2001) *Journey of Understanding: MBTI© Interpretation Using the Eight Jungian Functions*. Palo Alto, CA: Consulting Psychologists Press.

Harris, A. (1996) *Living with Paradox: An Introduction to Jungian Psychology*. Pacific Grove, CA: Brooks/Cole.

Henderson, J. (1970) 'Inner perception in terms of depth psychology'. *Annals of the New York Academy of Sciences*, 169: 664–672.

Hill, G. (1998) 'Men, the anima, and the feminine'. *San Francisco Jung Institute Library Journal*, 17(3): 49–61.

Hillman, J. (1971/1998) 'The feeling function', in M.-L. von Franz and J. Hillman, *Lectures on Jung's Typology*. Woodstock, CT: Spring.

Jung, C.G. (1912) *Wandlungen und Symbole der Libido*. Leipzig and Vienna: Franz Deuticke.

—— (1921) *Psychologische Typen*. Zurich: Rascher.

—— (1923) *Psychological Types, or, The Psychology of Individuation*, trans. H.G. Baynes. New York: Harcourt Brace.

—— (1968) *Analytical Psychology: Its Theory and Practice*. New York: Pantheon.

—— (1971) *Psychological Types*, trans. R.F.C. Hull. Princeton, NJ: Princeton University Press.

—— (1973) *Experimental Researches*, trans. L. Stein and D. Riviere. Princeton, NJ: Princeton University Press.

Kagan, J. (1994) *Galen's Prophecy: Temperament in Human Nature*. New York: Basic Books.

—— (1998) *Three Seductive Ideas*. Cambridge, MA: Harvard University Press.

Karesh, D.M., Pieper, W.A. and Holland, C.L. (1994) 'Comparing the MBTI, the Jungian type survey, and the Singer-Loomis Inventory of Personality'. *Journal of Psychological Type*, 30: 30–38.

Keirsey, D. and Bates, M. (1984) *Please Understand Me: Character and Temperament Types*. Del Mar, CA: Prometheus Nemesis Books.

Kirsch, T. (1980) 'Dreams and psychological types', in I. Baker (ed.) *Methods of Treatment in Analytical Psychology*. Stuttgart, Germany: Bonz Verlag.

Lavin, T. (1995) 'The art of practicing Jung's psychological types in analysis', in M. Stein (ed.) *Jungian Analysis*. La Salle, IL: Open Court.

Loomis, M. (1982) 'A new perspective for Jung's typology: the Singer-Loomis Inventory of Personality'. *Journal of Analytical Psychology*, 27(1): 59–70.

McCrae, R. and Costa, P. (1989) 'Reinterpreting the Myers-Briggs Type Indicator from the perspective of the Five-Factor Model of Personality'. *Journal of Personality*, 57: 17–40.

Mann, H., Siegler, M. and Osmond, H. (1968) 'The many worlds of time'. *Journal of Analytical Psychology*, 13(1): 33–56.

Marshall, I. (1968) 'The four functions: a conceptual analysis'. *Journal of Analytical Psychology*, 13(1): 1–32.

Mattoon, M. and Davis, M. (1995) 'The Gray-Wheelwrights Jungian type survey: development and history'. *Journal of Analytical Psychology*, 40(2): 205–234.

Meier, C. (1959) 'Projection, transference, and the subject-object relation'. *Journal of Analytical Psychology*, 4(1): 21–34.

Myers, I. and Myers, P. (1980) *Gifts Differing: Understanding Personality Type*. Palo Alto, CA: Consulting Psychologists Press.

Myers, K. and Kirby, L. (2000) *Introduction to Type Dynamics and Development*. Palo Alto, CA: Consulting Psychologists Press.

Papadopoulos, R. (ed.) (1992) *Carl Gustav Jung: Critical Assessments*. London: Routledge.

Paul, A.M. (2004) *The Cult of Personality*. New York: Free Press.

Plaut, F. (1972) 'Analytical psychologists and psychological types: comment on replies to a survey'. *Journal of Analytical Psychology*, 17(2): 137–151.

Quenk, N. (1993) *Beside Ourselves: Our Hidden Personality in Everyday Life*. Palo Alto, CA: Consulting Psychologists Press.

Quenk, N. (2000) *Essentials of Myers-Briggs Type Indicator Assessment*. New York: John Wiley.

Ross, C. (1992) 'The intuitive function and religious orientation'. *Journal of Analytical Psychology*, 37(1): 83–103.

Sabini, M. (1988) 'The therapist's inferior function'. *Journal of Analytical Psychology*, 3(4): 373–394.

Sandner, D. and Beebe, J. (1995) 'Psychopathology and analysis', in M. Stein (ed.) *Jungian Analysis*. La Salle, IL: Open Court.

Scanlon, S. (ed.) (1999) 'The MBTI and other personality theories: Part 2 – "The Big Five" and the NEO-PI'. *The Type Reporter*, 72.

Shamdasani, S. (2003) *Jung and the Making of Modern Psychology: The Dream of a Science*. Cambridge: Cambridge University Press.

Shapiro, K. and Alexander, I. (1975) *The Experience of Introversion: An Integration of Phenomenological, Empirical, and Jungian Approaches*. Durham, NC: Duke University Press.

Sharp, D. (1987) *Personality Types: Jung's Model of Typology*. Toronto: Inner City.

Singer, J. and Loomis, M. (n.d.) *The Singer-Loomis Inventory of Personality: Experimental Edition* (booklet). Palo Alto, CA: Consulting Psychologists Press.

Spoto, A. (1995) *Jung's Typology in Perspective*. Wilmette, IL: Chiron.

Thompson, H. (1996) *Jung's Function-Attitudes Explained*. Watkinsville, GA: Wormhole.

Thompson, K. (1985) 'Cognitive and analytical psychology'. *San Francisco Jung Institute Library Journal*, 5(4): 40–64.

Von der Heydt, V. (1975) 'A session with Jung', *Harvest*, 21: 108–110.

von Franz, M.-L. (1971/1998) 'The inferior function', in M.-L. von Franz and J. Hillman, *Lectures on Jung's Typology*. Woodstock, CT: Spring.

Wheelwright, J.B. (1982) 'Psychological types', in J.B. Wheelwright, *Saint George and the Dandelion*. San Francisco, CA: C.G. Jung Institute of San Francisco.

Wiggins, J. (ed.) (1996) *The Five-Factor Model of Personality: Theoretical Perspectives*. New York: Guilford.

Willeford, W. (1975) 'Toward a dynamic concept of feeling'. *Journal of Analytical Psychology*, 20(1): 18–40.

—— (1976) 'The primacy of feeling (Part I)'. *Journal of Analytical Psychology*, 21(2): 115–133.

—— (1977) 'The primacy of feeling (Part II)'. *Journal of Analytical Psychology*, 22(1): 1–16.

Chapter 7

The self

Warren Colman

SECTION 1: JUNG

Introduction

Since Jung viewed the self as both the centre and the totality of the psyche, it has a strong claim to be regarded as the central concept of his entire psychology. The self is the goal towards which the process of individuation strives. It represents psychic wholeness and the process by which self-division may be healed.

The psychology of the self is also the psychology of religious experience. Jung's work on the self is at the heart of his investigations into the religious function of the psyche and the varying ways that this has manifested in the historical consciousness of the West. From the early 1920s onwards, he drew frequent comparisons between the self and the divine and, especially in his later work, emphasised that 'the spontaneous symbols of the self, or of wholeness, cannot in practice be distinguished from a God-image' (Jung 1951: par. 73). Jung thus regards God-images as symbolic representations of the self.

Individuality and the mediation of the opposites

Despite or, perhaps, because of its importance, the concept of the self emerged only gradually in Jung's writings and his first major statements about it do not occur until the 1928 version of 'The relations between the ego and the unconscious'. If we go back to the 1916 version of this essay we find Jung using the concept of 'individuality' in the place of what he later termed 'the self'. These statements illuminate the intimate link between the self, as the essence of individuality, and individuation as the process by which that individuality may be realised. In this early model, Jung contrasts 'the individual' with 'the collective' in both its conscious and unconscious forms. Between the individual and the collective he places the persona as the 'outward attitude' that is oriented towards the external world of collective consciousness and the anima as the 'inward attitude', that is oriented towards the internal world of the collective unconscious.[1] He defines 'individuality' as 'the innermost core of ego-consciousness and of the unconscious alike' (Jung 1916: par. 507). It is thus intimately linked with the ego (as the centre of consciousness) but also distinct from the ego since it is also at the core of the unconscious.

Jung's picture of the psyche at that time can be tabulated in the following way, showing how the individual is placed at the 'mid-point' of psychic life:

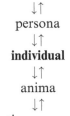

collective consciousness/external reality
↓↑
persona
↓↑
individual
↓↑
anima
↓↑
collective unconscious

He writes that 'The individual stands, as it were, between the conscious part of the collective psyche and the unconscious part' (Jung 1916: par. 507). He also emphasises that the individual is made of elements which are in themselves collective and universal but whose particular arrangement constitutes their uniqueness. Individuality is thus 'particular and universal at once' (1916: par. 505).

These pairs of opposites (conscious/unconscious, individual/collective, particular/universal) are examples of what Jung later came to see as a defining feature of the self as a *complexio oppositorum*. The process of individuation, however, resolves that state of inner conflict and opposition into a *coincidentia oppositorum*, a union of opposites which brings about wholeness. Jung explores this theme further in *Psychological Types* (published in 1921). There he speaks of 'the possibility of separating out an individual nucleus' from the opposing functions which, if unsuccessful, leads to 'the dissolution of the individuality into pairs of opposites' and 'disunion with oneself' (Jung 1921/1950: par. 174). And, in the first specific reference to the self as an entity distinct from the ego, he writes of 'a differentiation of the self from the opposites' as something which brings relief (healing) from inner conflict (1921/1950: par. 183).

It is apparent from Jung's references to Eastern philosophy and religion at this time (especially in *Psychological Types*) that his development of the concepts of the self and the opposites were heavily influenced by similar concepts in the Eastern tradition. For example, Buddhism, Chinese philosophy and the Upanishads all contain clear references to the 'mediation of the opposites'. Jung later acknowledged the influence of Eastern philosophy in general and the Upanishads in particular in his choice of the term 'self' to designate the 'supraordinate' or 'suprapersonal' centre of the personality which is, at the same time, 'the totality of man, the sum total of his conscious and unconscious contents' (Jung 1938/1940: par. 140).

Mandalas and the 'Pool of Life'

The account of this period in Jung's life given in *Memories, Dreams, Reflections* (1963) shows how much these ideas owed to his own 'confrontation with the unconscious', a severe state of inner turmoil and conflict into which he was pitched following his break with Freud. Towards the end of this period (1916), Jung began painting mandalas but only gradually began to understand their significance.

> During those years between 1918 and 1920, I began to understand that the goal of psychic development is the self . . . I knew that in finding the mandala as an expression of the self I had attained what was for me the ultimate.
>
> (Jung 1963: 222)

Jung continued painting mandalas during the 1920s but the climax of this development came in a dream of the 'Pool of Life' in 1927 in which the city of 'Liver-pool' is represented as a typical mandala. In this dream Jung came to a broad square in the centre of the city where many streets converged.

> In the centre of the square was a round pool and in the middle of it a small island. On it stood a single tree, a magnolia. It was as though the tree stood in the sunlight and was at the same time the source of light.

Looking back at the end of his life Jung commented:

> The dream brought with it a sense of finality. I saw that here the goal had been revealed. One could not go beyond the centre. The centre is the goal, and everything is directed towards that centre. Through this dream I understood that the self is the principle and archetype of orientation and meaning. Therein lies its healing function . . . The dream depicted the climax of the whole process of development of consciousness. It satisfied me completely, for it gave a total picture of my situation.
>
> (Jung 1963: 224)

This account of Jung's own profound mystical experiences bears out the evidence from his published writings that the major period of development of his ideas about the self took place between 1921 and 1928. The 'Pool of Life' dream must have been contemporaneous with Jung's revision of what became 'The relations between the ego and the unconscious' and the addition of the section on 'Individuation' (Jung 1928). Almost the entire corpus of Jung's subsequent work can be seen as the working out of ideas – and experiences – which were already in place at that time. While there is considerable development over the next twenty-five years, there is scant evidence of modification of his basic ideas. Rather Jung's subsequent work elaborates in ever more profuse detail the symbolic iconography of Western religious thought through which the phenomenology of the self can be traced. Only in his final work on alchemy, *Mysterium Coniunctionis* (1954) (to which I will refer later) is there evidence of a shift in view concerning the relations between the ego and the self.

Totality and centre

It is in the 1928 additions to the *Two Essays on Analytical Psychology* that we find the first definition of the self as the 'totality' of the psyche which recurs, essentially unchanged, throughout his writings:

> Conscious and unconscious . . . complement one another to form a totality which is the self. According to this definition the self is a quantity that is supraordinate to the conscious ego. It embraces not only the conscious but also the unconscious psyche, and is therefore, so to speak, a personality which we *also* are.
>
> (Jung 1928: par. 274)

At the same time, he continues pursuing the theme of the self as individuality and the achievement of one's own uniqueness: 'in so far as "individuality" embraces our innermost, last and incomparable uniqueness, it also implies becoming one's own self. We could therefore translate individuation as "coming to selfhood" or "self-realization"' (1928: par. 266). This process is also seen as having to do with the achievement of a *centre* of the personality which transcends the opposites; this centre is also defined as the self (1928: par. 389). Echoing the earlier model which places 'individuality' in the centre of the personality, he refers to transformations

> which have as their goal the attainment of the mid-point of personality . . . [This] centre of personality no longer coincides with the ego, but with a point midway between the conscious and the unconscious. This would be the point of a new equilibrium, a new centering of the total personality, a virtual centre.
>
> (Jung 1928: pars. 364–365)

Clearly, this refers to Jung's own experiences of mandalas such as the 'Pool of Life' in which the total figure is organised round a centre which exerts a numinous 'pull' and is both defining of and defined by the whole. At several points in his later writing, Jung returns to the paradox of the self as both totality and centre. In the introduction to *Psychology and Alchemy* (written in 1944) he states:

> I call this centre 'the self' which should be understood as the totality of the psyche. The self is not only the centre, but also the whole circumference which embraces both conscious and unconscious; it is the centre of this totality, just as the ego is the centre of consciousness.[2]
>
> (Jung 1944: par. 41)

Archetype and symbol

A further paradox arises from the fact that Jung increasingly refers to the self as an *archetype* from the early 1940s onwards. Notwithstanding that he regards it as the *central* archetype, there remains the difficult question of how the self can be both the totality of the psyche and one of the archetypal contents *within* the psyche.[3] This problem can best be approached by considering some of the difficulties inherent in the notion of the self as totality. By its very nature, the totality of the self is inexperiencable since the greater part of it is unconscious and therefore unknown to us. Jung repeatedly insists on this radically unknown quality of the unconscious: since everything known is a content of consciousness, the very idea of the unconscious presupposes all that is unknown and, since it is unknown, we cannot have any knowledge of its nature or its limits. All that we can say about it is said on the basis of its manifestations in consciousness. With regard to the self, these manifestations take the form of archetypal *symbols* which, for Jung, are the best possible representation of an unknown psychic fact (Jung 1921/1950: par. 814). The self is necessarily represented through symbols since it cannot be represented in any other way: 'the conscious mind can form absolutely no conception of this totality, because it includes not only the conscious but also the unconscious psyche, which is, as such, inconceivable and irrepresentable' (Jung 1942/1948: par. 230).

In other words, Jung studies the 'empirical manifestations' of the self, its archetypal symbols, as a means of gaining 'clues' as to its essential nature which, nevertheless, remains inherently out of reach. At the same time, the nature of these symbols and the numinous, mystical experiences with which they are associated produce a sense of wholeness (totality) which is unarguable and self-validating. As we have seen, Jung knew about such mystical religious experiences at first hand; as a scientist, however, he was at pains to attempt to analyse them objectively. The idea that mystical experience is the result of a shift in centre from the ego (which is the centre of consciousness) to the self (which is the centre of conscious *and* unconscious) is actually one of his most brilliantly original insights, offering an explanation of the very unexplainable quality of such experiences.

Experience and concept

This means that there are three levels of argument in Jung's discussion of the self. The first level is that of direct experience. At the end of his final work, Jung addresses the inherent impossibility of the task he has undertaken in this respect:

> It is not worth the effort to try to describe [the] totality character [of experiences of the self]. Anyone who has experienced anything of the sort will know what I mean, and anyone who has not had the experience will not be satisfied by any amount of description. Moreover there are countless descriptions of it in world literature. But I know of no case in which the bare description conveyed the experience.
>
> (Jung 1954: par. 799)

The second level is the phenomenological analysis and classification of symbolic representations of the self. This constitutes the major part of Jung's work. Such symbols provide experiential indicators of what the self may be like as well as acting as powerful attractors and motivators towards the goal of the individuation process. Although these symbols may indicate totality, they most frequently have the quality of 'centre' and convey the deeply satisfying sense of an ineffable and inviolable core to the personality. Such symbols include those of the 'supraordinate personality' e.g., king, hero, prophet, saviour (Jung 1921/1950: par. 790) and 'the geometrical structures of the mandala containing elements of the circle and quaternity, namely circular and spherical forms . . . and quadratic figures divided into four or in the form of a cross' (Jung 1951: par. 352). The numinosity of these symbols enables Jung to assert that 'the self is no mere concept or logical postulate; it is a psychic reality', albeit one that 'is inconceivable except in the form of symbols' (Jung 1942/1948: par. 233) and 'does not allow of scientific proof' (Jung 1928: par. 405).

The third level of argument is the point of view of abstract, intellectual argument and here Jung equally insists that the self *is* merely a 'postulate'. That is, we may speculate intellectually about the nature of the self but its unconscious, infinite aspect precludes us from any actual definition. In the 1950 definition added to *Psychological Types*, Jung is careful to make this distinction: 'in so far as the total personality, on account of its unconscious component, can be only in part conscious, the concept of the self is, in part, only *potentially* empirical and is to that extent a postulate'. Thus Jung emphasises the distinction between *concept* and *experience*, between an intellectual 'objective' view and a phenomenological 'subjective' one.

The organising principle of the psyche

Occasionally, and especially in his later work, Jung refers to the self as the 'organizer of the personality' (Jung 1958: par. 694) or the 'ordering principle' of the collective unconscious (Jung 1951: par. 304, 1954: par. 373). This is also implicit in his experience of the healing function of mandalas with their geometric structure. This idea exists on the borders of 'experience' and 'concept' since while it is an abstraction, it is made on the basis of symbolic experience. These distinctions will be important in considering the various strands of post-Jungian thinking on the self.

The God-image

The distinction between concept and experience is also important in relation to the connection Jung makes between the self and the 'God-image'. Jung claims that psychologically speaking, God is an archetype in that there has to be an 'imprint' or 'type' in the psyche that corresponds to the manifold images of God found throughout world history (Jung 1944: par. 15). Nevertheless, Jung also insists that

> Psychology . . . is not in a position to make metaphysical statements. It can only establish that the symbolism of psychic wholeness coincides with the God-image, but it can never prove that the God-image is God himself, or that the self takes the place of God.
>
> (Jung 1951: par. 308)

Thus, while acknowledging the experiential and phenomenological identity between God-image and symbol of the self, Jung also maintains a strict *conceptual* distinction between the self and God 'as such'.[4] Just as 'the self' is only a conceptual name for a psychological reality which gathers together the symbolic experiences of the archetype and the idea of the totality to which they refer, so God is a conceptual name for a metaphysical reality of which psychology can say nothing.

The Christian God-image

While Jung retained some interest in the Eastern religious tradition, from the mid-1920s onwards, it was the Christian God-image (together with alchemy) that seems to have had the major hold on his own imagination.[5] As both God and man, according to Jung, Christ serves as a symbol of the unity of conscious and unconscious and the relation between the ego and the self. He is both unique, limited and human and, at the same time, the infinite universality of the Divine.

From one point of view, Christ represents a totality in that 'anything that a man postulates as being a greater totality than himself can become a symbol of the self' (Jung 1942/1948: par. 232). However, as an image of perfection, Christ lacks a dark side and is therefore not a *complete* totality. Jung felt strongly that good and evil were a pair of opposites that needed to be united in the self, just as much as conscious/unconscious or unique/universal and that the suppression of the dark side of the self in Christianity had led to the appalling outbreaks of violence and evil of Jung's own time, the first half of the twentieth century. In his later work, especially in *Aion* (1951) and 'Answer to Job' (1952), Jung emphasised this opposition of light and dark, Christ and Anti-Christ, ego-consciousness and archetypal Shadow as a critical problem of opposites in the Western God-image and, *pari passu*, the self.

Ego and self

In his earlier work, Jung always emphasises the littleness of the ego in relation to the self and the collective unconscious. In 1928 he uses the vivid image of the conscious personality being 'pushed around like a figure on a chess-board by an invisible player' (Jung 1928: par. 250). He also compares the relation of the ego and the self to the earth revolving round the sun (1928: par. 405) and in a similar image, in 1940, says that 'the ego stands to the self as the moved to the mover' (Jung 1940/1954: par. 391). The self is 'a more compendious personality that takes the ego into its service' (par. 390) and which 'dwarfs the ego in scope and intensity' (Jung 1946/1954: par. 430).

However, while 'the self exists from the very beginning, [it] is latent, that is unconscious' (Jung 1935/1944: par. 105n.34); individuation is the process of bringing this latent self to consciousness. This makes the self seem more like a child struggling to be born out of the womb of the unconscious. While there is an inherent urge to self-realisation, the ego is also needed as a sort of 'midwife' and it is, after all, into the world of ego-consciousness that the self is born. This leads to a subtle shift in the way Jung talks about the relation between ego and self so that the ego, despite its absurd littleness in the face of cosmic infinity, is also seen to be at the centre of the process of individuation, its activity being crucial to the realisation of the self. This shift is most apparent in his final work, *Mysterium Coniunctionis* where the ego is described as 'the condition of the unconscious coming into being' due to the 'the world-creating significance of . . . consciousness' (Jung 1954: par. 131). Referring to 'the identity of God and ego' in India, he now identifies the personal atman with the ego rather than the self (1954: par. 131). Jung is aware of the seeming contradiction with previous writings and that he now appears to be defining the ego as he previously defined the self. He argues that

[The ego] is an essential part of the self, and can be used *pars pro toto* when the significance of consciousness is borne in mind. But when we want to lay emphasis on the psychic totality it is better to use the term 'self'.

(Jung 1954: par. 133)

This shift may indicate an important development in Jung's own self-consciousness. Earlier in life, he had been painfully aware of the split in himself between ego and unconscious and the emergence of the realigned centre of the self had brought with it a deep sense of wholeness, which also carries the meaning of 'healing' and 'holy' (Jung 1935: 137). In *Memories, Dreams, Reflections* he recalls how, from the age of 12 or thereabouts, he had thought of himself as two different persons – the 'No. 1' personality of his everyday outward life and a greater, more important but very private 'Other' that he called 'No. 2' (Jung 1963: 50 and *passim*). Perhaps, late in life, he had achieved something of the greater integration he had always sought between his 'No. 1' and 'No. 2' personalities and, as a result, his ego felt closer to and more accommodated with the self. As a result, the earlier sharp distinction between ego and self is softened since the more individuated the ego, the more indistinguishable it becomes from the self.

Outline summary of range of meanings

In summary, Jung's major definitions of the self include the following:

- individuality
- mid-point between conscious and unconscious
- union of opposites
- totality of the psyche
- centre of the psyche
- archetype
- wholeness
- organising principle.

SECTION 2: POST-JUNGIAN DEVELOPMENTS

Jung's major focus of interest was in the development of the self in the second half of life. He left it to others to work out a detailed psychology of the ego and of the first half of life in which ego development is a predominant feature. This also involved developing more detailed theories about the relation *between* ego and self. This task was approached in very different ways by two of Jung's most important early followers, Erich

Neumann and Michael Fordham, who each worked out their own theoretical models during the 1940s and 1950s.

Neumann: the ego-Self axis

In *The Origins and History of Consciousness* Neumann (1949/1954) argues that ego-consciousness emerges out of an original state of oneness which is expressed in the image of the uroboros (the snake swallowing its tail). The uroboros represents the original state of the Self before individual consciousness has arisen, a state of primary oneness and non-differentiation.[6] Neumann relates this to the way the child is held entirely within the 'containing round of maternal existence' (1973: 14), suggesting a parallel between the mother/infant relationship and the ego/Self relationship – i.e., 'the mother represents the self and the child the ego' (Neumann 1959: 129).

Because the mother fulfils for the child so many of the functions which will later be carried out by the Self, Neumann suggests that 'the mother, in the primal relationship, not only plays the role of the child's Self but actually *is* that Self' although he also distinguishes between this 'relatedness-Self' and the child's own 'body-Self' (Neumann 1973). In this early state of relatedness, the mother stands at once for the child's relationships to its own body, to its Self, to the thou and to the world. As development proceeds, the child achieves more autonomy and, as a result, the Self is withdrawn from the mother to the person of the child: 'it is with this formation of a unitary Self that the human child is truly born' (1973: 28).

The ego-Self axis: the Self as an unconscious personality

Neumann uses the term 'ego-Self axis' to describe the nature and quality of the connection between ego and Self. One of the difficulties of this term is that it leads to a tendency to think of ego and Self as separate 'entities', that is, the notion of the Self as a totality becomes eroded and the Self comes to be seen as equivalent to the unconscious or the centre of the unconscious. For example, at one point Neumann refers to 'the systems of consciousness and the unconscious and . . . the corresponding centres of the ego and the Self' and then has to add a footnoted caveat that (usually) 'the Self is the centre not of the unconscious but of the entire psyche' (Neumann 1973: 47n.1).

It is certainly not always easy to distinguish between the unconscious and the self especially since, at the beginning of life, when ego-consciousness has not developed, there is as yet no distinction to be made since the *whole* self is unconscious of itself. Yet as soon as the ego emerges out of the self, that from which it has emerged is no longer the whole self but only the unconscious *part* of the self. So as soon as it is possible to speak of a tension of opposites, such opposition must be understood as being between ego (consciousness) and the unconscious, not between ego and self.

Many Jungian writers fail to grasp this point and so continue to speak of 'ego/self conflict' even when speaking of adult development and the 'second half of life' individuation process (e.g., Beebe 1988; Samuels 1985: 92; Whitmont 1969: 220). In all these cases, the Self is being thought of not as the centre and totality of the entire personality but as a kind of personification of the unconscious part of the personality with which the ego is in conflict. For Jung these were conflicts between the conscious (ego) and unconscious which, through the operation of the transcendent function issued in the achievement of a mid-point between the opposites – i.e., the self. That is, in Jung's model, the self is the *outcome* of this conflict and is superordinate to it. If the Self is seen as one party to the conflict, what superordinate principle can there be to resolve it?

The trouble here is that the metaphorical language of image and symbol is not distinguished from the abstract language of theoretical speculation (Fordham 1963; Young-Eisendrath and Hall 1991). So the fact that the self *appears* in personified form does not actually mean that the self *is* a separate personality that comes into conflict with the ego. When the self is reified in this way (by equating the symbol with that which is symbolised), the inexpressible mystery of the All is scaled down into something more like an internal object relationship.

Neumann's model lends itself to this through the linkage of Unconscious = Mother = Self. Edinger provides a telling and influential example of this kind of conceptual confusion when he argues that since the self includes everything that we are, the self also *accepts* everything that we are (Edinger 1960: 10) – rather like an ideal mother? This also has an unfortunate tendency to lead towards an idealised view of the Self as wholly good, a Self that is wise and good and knows what is best for us. Willeford (1987: 150ff.), for example, refers to 'the self that knows what is good for itself'. Although there clearly are examples of something which 'knows better' than the ego, this rather begs the question of all the more destructive compulsions which also afflict the ego. If these do not belong to the self, what else is there to which they can belong? The same problem can be found in Beebe (1988) where a 'self' separate from either ego or Self has to be proposed in which to place destructive-ambivalent 'trickster' elements of the personality. By contrast, Kalsched (1996) grasps the nettle and attributes the immensely powerful malevolent force of the internal 'protector/persecutor' to the dark side of the Self, a notion fully in accord with Jung's picture of a self made up of good *and* evil.

Perhaps the most extreme version of the tendency to narrow down conceptions of the self occurs in an article by Weisstub (1997). Weisstub draws attention to the tendencies I have mentioned not only to regard the ego as separate from the self but also to equate the self with maternal/

feminine aspects and therefore proposes a solution in which the self might be regarded simply as the 'feminine' principle of being, with the ego as the 'masculine' principle of doing. Here, the move away from the totality has become explicit but, as McGlashan points out in his response, 'The whole balance and integrity of Jung's creative view of the psyche is thus disastrously impoverished' since Jung's idea of a transcendent self has been done away with (McGlashan 1997: 454).

The intentional Self

As in most of the controversies that have arisen about the nature of the self, some of the confusions about the Self as a separate personality derive from Jung. But although Jung describes the self as a 'more compendious personality that takes the ego into its service', he nevertheless questioned the existence of anything like a personality in the unconscious. (Jung 1940: par. 507; Fordham 1985: 42). Jung seems to have been speaking in a metaphorical way about the experiential sense which the ego may come to have of the Self but, again, there has been a tendency to literalise and reify this view. Whitmont, for example, while putting the 'intentions' of the self in inverted commas, nevertheless refers to 'the demands and expectations of the self' (1969: 220) and its 'emotional value system and goals', over and above those of the ego, clearly seeing these as structural elements in the personality rather than simply metaphors.

At the other extreme of this controversy is Young-Eisendrath, who argues that the notion of an archetypal Self refers to an abstract-design level of analysis (the 'logical postulate' level of Jung's thinking) and is therefore beyond experience or conscious knowledge/awareness (Young-Eisendrath and Hall 1991; Young-Eisendrath 1997a). She warns that 'not only are there many epistemological errors in assuming that such an overarching principle has its own subjectivity, but we may sound as though we can know the unknowable in saying that the Self has intentions, views and desires' (Young-Eisendrath 1997a: 162).

Nevertheless, one of the most readily attested and commonly occurring experiences attributed to the Self is that of the 'inner voice' which seems to 'know' better than the conscious ego (Humbert 1980). Experiences of synchronicity can also give a powerful indication of some kind of greater purpose and meaning. The idea of the intentional self is probably due to a linking of these deeply convincing inner experiences with Jung's more abstract ideas of a self-regulating, homeostatic psyche which has an urge to individuate and throws up images, dreams and even behaviours which act as compensations to a one-sided consciousness.

The extreme limitations of ego-consciousness (in comparison with the infinite totality of the Self) mean that even if there were an intentional self, the ego could form little or no conception of it. The implications of the indefinable and incomprehensible nature of the self are stressed by Huskinson (2002) who, drawing on the philosopher Levinas, describes the self from an experiential point of view as an overpowering and violent Other that impresses its permanent supremacy on the ego. This enables her to encompass experiences such as Humbert's (1980) 'inner voice' and Redfearn's (1977) 'inspiring effect' while also allowing for the potentially devastating impact that the Self may have, particularly on an ego that is resistant to the unknown Other.

Fordham: primary self and deintegration

Fordham, writing in 1963, anticipates some of Young-Eisendrath's arguments in his proposal that there is a fundamental incompatibility between Jung's definition of the self as the totality and his alternative definition of the self as an archetype. For Fordham, all *experiences* of the self must derive from the self-as-archetype; it is impossible to *experience* the totality since the totality of the Self is defined by Jung as 'ego + archetypes' whereas any experience of an archetypal reality cannot, at the same time, include the part that is doing the experiencing – i.e., the ego. The totality as such, he argues, is therefore not so much unknowable as *inexperiencable*, i.e., outside the realm of experience. In this sense the self-as-totality can *only* be a theory or postulate and it is hypostatised thinking to assert that the self is a thing which exists (Fordham 1963: 22).

Fordham's preference for the totality definition of the self arises from his own concept of the primary self, which he introduced in 1947, to describe the initial condition of the self at birth. Like Neumann, he took his starting point from the suggestion by Jung that the self has somehow always been there, even though it only comes into conscious awareness in the second half of life. However, from the start, Fordham took a radically different approach, concentrating on the direct observation of actual children (and later infants) and formulating theoretical hypotheses on the basis of these observations.

Although Fordham and Neumann both postulated the existence of an original totality of the self at birth, their conceptions of it were diametrically opposed. Fordham's conception overturned the prevailing idea of primary union between mother and infant which formed the basis for Neumann's idea that the mother functions as ('is') the infant's Self. On the contrary, Fordham argued that the initial condition of the infant is a psychosomatic integrate – it is the *infant*, not the mother, who is the Self. In order for this primary integrate to come into relationship with the environment (initially the mother) in the first place, a process of 'unfolding' must be initiated which Fordham termed 'deintegration'.

Deintegration was conceived as the active contribution by the infant in bringing about states from which it was previously assumed he passively began. Thus the idea that mother-infant togetherness is created by the mother alone is done away with and attention is focused on what the baby does to help bring this about.

(Fordham 1971: 86)

Thus, Fordham consistently argued in favour of a notion of 'children as individuals' (Fordham 1969), active autonomous beings who play a significant role in creating the maternal environment in which they find themselves.[7] At each point of relating to the environment the infant deintegrates in 'readiness' for experience which is then, in turn, reintegrated into an increasingly complex and differentiated self. Fordham proposes that the process of deintegration/reintegration leads to the formation of an inner world composed of ego and archetypes which together make up the totality of the self. Each archetype is itself a 'deintegrate' or 'part-self' which, however partakes of the qualities of the self: 'A deintegrate is endowed with and is continuous with the self' (Fordham 1985: 54). He regards the typical individuation process of the second half of life as one in which the ego becomes *aware* of the deintegrating self: these 'experiences of the self' are themselves the outcome of processes of deintegration and reintegration through which the ego comes into a deeper relation to the total self of which it is a part.

Pluralism and multiplicity

In the decade or so following Jung's death, an increasing rigidity and dogmatism seems to have set in among many of his close followers, particularly in Zurich so that the idea of the Self became reified and deified.[8] This was one of the factors leading to a counter-reaction spearheaded by James Hillman in the early 1970s. Hillman emphasised the multiple, shifting and fluid nature of personality over against the emphasis on integration, unity and order – all functions typically attributed to the self. Since the self is so heavily associated with synthesis, it is conceptually antithetical to an emphasis on 'elaboration, particularising, complication' (Hillman 1981: 129). In Hillman's psychology, the central role of the self has therefore been replaced with an emphasis on *soul* (anima), the deepening of imaginal experience. The wholeness of the personality is seen not in terms of integration leading to a state of unity but in terms of inclusiveness – the development of a capacity to embrace multiplicity. As Adams (1997: 113) puts it, 'in this respect, the purpose of analysis is not individuation but animation'.

Samuels, from his own perspective of an 'anti-hierarchical' pluralism is also critical of the elevation of the self to a privileged 'hierarchical' position in traditional Jungian parlance. In its place he suggests an *ad hoc* hierarchy in which the pre-eminence of the self is 'only one version among many possible versions'. From this point of view the self 'in its function as "container" of the scintillae and luminosities of psyche . . . competes for importance with those contents themselves' (Samuels 1989: 13). Samuels can only be thinking of the self-as-archetype among other archetypes here: from the point of view of the totality, the self is, by definition, the totality of the 'scintillae and luminosities'. Alternatively, it may be that he is not so much thinking about the actual nature of the self but merely how it is *thought about* in 'Jungian parlance'.

While not necessarily accepting Samuels' pluralism, many other analysts recognise the shifting, multiple nature of self and identity. For example, Willeford (1987) maintains a view of the self as neither fixed nor stable and manifesting itself in disorganisation as much as organisation. Redfearn (1985) has also paid detailed attention to shifts in the 'I'-feeling between different parts of the personality, the 'many selves' for which he proposes the generic term 'sub-personality'. Like the pluralists, he is suspicious of order, harmony and symmetry, always looking for the shadow 'Not-I' elements of the self which have been left out. 'For all stages of development there is a mandala which includes more complex and more profound opposites' (Redfearn 1985: 127).

Constructivism: objective self vs. sense of self

Constructivism, like Hillman's (1981) imaginal psychology and Samuels' (1989) pluralism, is strongly influenced by postmodern trends of thought which question the existence of 'grand narratives' and essentialist structures outside of the immediacy of lived experience. Constructivism emphasises the active process of meaning-making from which our sense of the world emerges: the reality of both the world and the self is not given but is always self-constructed within a particular social and relational context (Harré 1979; Maturana and Varela 1980).

In Jungian psychology, the constructivist perspective has been separately developed by Louis Zinkin in England and Polly Young-Eisendrath in the United States. Both of them critique the idea of a substantive, objective self in favour of an emphasis on the *sense* of self and how this arises in lived experience. Both of them agree that 'the self only comes into existence through interaction with others' (Zinkin 1991: 6). The self is therefore not a given but something which has to be acquired 'within a context that includes culture, language and other persons' (Young-Eisendrath and Hall 1991: xii).

This view challenges both Neumann and Fordham, each of whom assume the existence of an *a priori* self at the start of life which unfolds in the course of development. For Zinkin the idea of the self as a pre-given entity is a reification. He is therefore more interested in that aspect of Jung's thought which sees the self as a *goal* to be achieved (through individuation) rather than as the source from which ego-consciousness arises.

In this respect, Young-Eisendrath is less radical than Zinkin, who seems to have been interested *only* in the experiential aspect of the self and not at all in the abstract, intellectual 'postulate' level. Eisendrath uses the term 'self' in both senses. In the experiential sense, the self, for her, is interchangeable with 'individual subjectivity'. However, in the 'logical postulate' sense, the self is an archetypal *'predisposition . . .* to form a coherent image . . . the image of the individual embodied subject around which an ego complex will form'. This predisposition can be defined in terms of four 'invariants of subjectivity': coherence, continuity, a sense of agency and affective relational patterns. Since these features exist in all cultures everywhere they may justifiably be regarded as archetypal. This is a very abstract view in which 'the Self' is being thought about as a category like 'the body' or 'the eye'. It is non-essentialist because the principles underlying the organisation of the self at the 'design' level are not thought to have any substantive existence. The archetypal Self is only a *principle* of transcendent coherence – it would no more be possible to 'experience' it than to experience our DNA. This is not to close the door on a sense of the numinous: Young-Eisendrath also refers to transcendent coherence as 'that unity of life that is not personal and may be called God, Tao, Buddha Nature, a central organising principle (of the universe) or other names' (Young-Eisendrath 1997b: 54).

Blueprint and incarnation

Although the constructivist viewpoint rejects the notion of an *a priori* self, Young-Eisendrath's position is not in all respects opposed to the notion of a 'blueprint' for development since this is implied in the concept of a *predisposition*. Since no one would argue with the proposition that the self depends on a particular context for its realisation, the contrast with essentialist viewpoints is not as great as might be thought. Furthermore, although her main emphasis is on the self-as-archetype, she also suggests the self is 'a gathering of (multiple) subjectivities', that its realisation involves the inclusion of 'Not-I' elements into the 'I' – a nod in the direction of self as totality. But once the self is thought about in this way, it must presumably include not only the archetype of subjectivity but *all* predispositions to act and perceive in any universally occurring manner. This, again, narrows the gap between Young-Eisendrath's constructivism and the biologically based essentialism of Anthony Stevens (1982).

For Stevens, the link between the Self and DNA is more than a metaphor: the human genome constitutes an *a priori* programme of development for 'the total archetypal system – what Jung termed the Self' (Stevens 1982: 76).[9]

Where Young-Eisendrath concentrates on the predisposition for subjectivity, Stevens looks at the total range of predispositions for human living, drawing particularly on Waddington's theory of epigenesis as developed by Bowlby – the occurrence of universal patterns of development. In terms of Fordham's distinction, Young-Eisendrath takes the 'self-as-archetype' position while Stevens takes the 'self-as-totality' position but both of them are interested in demonstrably universal features which can thereby be attributed to the collective Self.

This kind of *collective* 'blueprint', though, is very different from the notion of the Self as constituting an *individual* blueprint in which the individuation process is seen as the 'incarnation' of inherent potential. The danger of this view is that it can lead either to a form of determinism or else to the notion of an intentional self. In this respect Stevens is very different from Young-Eisendrath, speaking of the self as 'an invisible guide or mentor' which 'never stops prompting and advising' (Stevens 1982: 66 and 142).

The fundamental difference between constructivist and essentialist views of the self concerns the issue of whether the self is *created* (through culture and context) or *discovered* (as the realisation of *a priori* potential). Attempting to reunite this typical pair of Jungian opposites, Colman (1999) has pointed out that the self that is 'made' cannot just be *any* self but must be one that is in accord with the innate characteristics of the individual which act as limiting factors on the range of potential realisations available. While the number of possible realisations is unknown, and perhaps unknowable, it cannot be infinite. The self is not a blank slate. Thus, 'context' is not only cultural but also biological. At both the collective level and the individual level, we must conclude that the self is discovered through the process of its own creation.

Current status and future developments

Since the mid-1990s there has been a spate of articles in the *Journal of Analytical Psychology* and elsewhere, reviewing Jung's theory of archetypes in the light of current developments in related fields of science such as evolutionary biology, neuroscience, cognitive science and physics (Tresan 1996; Hogenson 1998, 2001; Saunders and Skar 2001; McDowell 1999, 2001). The specific application of some of these ideas to the self has already been explored by Salman (1999) and Colman (2000) and it is likely that future thinking on the Self will take them further.

At the risk of oversimplification, the common thread in these new ideas involves the explanation of complex behaviour as the emergent properties of self-organising dynamic systems. This means, as Hogenson says, that it is no longer necessary or viable to claim that the archetypes 'exist' somewhere, as some kind of structural entity. Salman draws attention to a comment of Jung's made in 1957 which shows him thinking very much along these lines: 'So far I have found no stable or definite centre in the unconscious and I don't believe such a centre exists' (Serrano 1966: 50; quoted in Salman 1999: 73). Zinkin (1987) has also pointed out that Jung did not believe in the absolute existence of individual entities: 'the ambiguity and confusion we have struggled with in the self results from Jung's never seeing it as a fixed entity with a constant boundary and definite size or as having an inside or an outside' (Zinkin 1987: 124). Instead, Zinkin, drawing on the example of the hologram concludes that, 'movement is primary and the appearance of forms as they emerge from the movement is secondary' (1987: 124).

This puts the emphasis on the self as the continuous process of the psyche in which archetypal forms appear as emergent properties (including archetypal images of the self). This view does away with several of the paradoxical difficulties which have dogged theoretical understanding of the self to date. For example, there is now no contradiction between the self as an organising principle (archetype) and the self as the totality since there is no need to distinguish between the organisation/system and that which is organising it. The self is rather the self-organisation of the totality of psychic functioning. This, in turn, includes the capacity to create meaning and pattern, enabling us to organise elements of our experience into archetypal imagery and behaviour. The 'centrality' of the self in the psyche is merely a metaphorical way of referring to its importance, as in the phrase 'of central importance'. There is no need to posit a 'directing centre' (as Neumann does) to explain the existence of meaning, purpose and order in psychic life. The idea of a 'directing centre' is an example of what Daniel Dennett (1991) calls 'the Cartesian Theatre'. By this Dennett means the 'homuncular fantasy' of some kind of 'Central Meaner' who is the subject of consciousness. This is the self which 'does not exist', as Jung well knew and as the Buddhists, with their concept of 'no-self', have been teaching for centuries. It is no coincidence that Young-Eisendrath, who is so critical of the notion of a substantive Self with its own intentionality, is a practising Buddhist.

The self is therefore not a structure *in* the psyche (Gordon 1985), but rather the structure *of* the psyche, not a fixed structure but one which is ever fluid and changing yet maintains its continuity by means of self-organisation. This opens the way for the kind of multiplicity so valued by the pluralists without foreclosing on some kind of inherent archetypal organisation – it is just that the archetype is no longer seen as *a priori* but as constellated through the process of self-organisation (Saunders and Skar 2001).[10]

Similarly, there is no longer the same difficulty over 'parts' and 'wholes' since an emergent property of the self is not in any sense a 'part' of it. So the fact that the self gives rise to images of its own process through self-reflexive activity does not mean that the source of such images is an 'archetype' which can be only a part-self, as Fordham argues.

This is not to suggest that, in the future, some single uncontested theory of the self will finally emerge. Nor must we forget that the self is not merely a theoretical matter but also an overwhelming experience of the *mysterium tremendum*. It is not a problem to be solved but a mystery to be explored. In so far as it is the core of our individuality as well as the totality of what makes us human, it has an irreducible element of uniqueness. For this reason, each investigator will experience and conceptualise it differently and different aspects of Jung's 'subjective confession' will assume greater or lesser importance. Continuing theoretical diversity is not merely a sign of confusion and muddle but an indication of health and vitality.

Notes

1 'The inner personality is the way one behaves in relation to one's inner psychic processes; it is the inner attitude, the characteristic face that is turned towards the unconscious. I call the outer attitude, the outward face, the persona; the inner attitude, the inward face I call the anima' (Jung, 1921/1950: par. 803).
2 This in turn refers to a saying about God as 'a circle whose centre is everywhere and the circumference nowhere' (*CW* 6: par. 791 and n. 74). The paradox is beautifully expressed by the seventeenth-century Polish mystic, Angelus Silesius, quoted by Jung in *Aion* (1951):

> God is my centre when I close him in
> And my circumference when I melt in him

3 This issue is examined in depth by Fordham (1985).
4 cf. 'the self can be distinguished only conceptually from what has always been referred to as '"God" but not practically' (Jung 1954: par. 778).
5 In *Psychology and Religion: East and West* (*CW* 11), 475 pages are devoted to Western (Judeo-Christian) religion while 135 pages are devoted to the East. If one includes the 300-odd pages of *Aion* (*CW* 9ii) which is entirely concerned with Gnosticism and Christianity, the proportions are even more striking.
6 Neumann and other, mainly 'classical' Jungians, capitalise 'Self' to distinguish it from its ordinary usage (as in 'me, myself') which is more to do with the ego. However, the editors of the English translation *Collected Works* decided against capitalisation and, in this chapter, I have tried to follow their usage except when discussing those authors who specifically refer to 'Self' with a capital 'S'.
7 In his later work, on the basis of observational infant research, Fordham came to question that there ever is an early stage of mother–infant union as such. Rather, states of union do occur but they are transient states in an ongoing rhythmic oscillation of deintegration and reintegration.
8 As an example of rigid dogmatism, von Franz is reported to have said that Jung's psychology was 'final and fixed at his death, and no subsequent interpretation of theory could or should be either superimposed upon or incorporated within it' (Bair 2004: 770, n. 69). As an example of deifying the self, see Edinger (1987, 1996) who seems to take religious doctrine as an almost literal narrative of individuation in which the terms 'God' and 'Self' are interchangeable. At times,

he seems almost to deify Jung himself, suggesting that 'Jung is the new Aion' (Edinger, 1996: 192).

9 Stevens (1982) goes so far as to equate the genome with God, obscuring the distinction between the god-image and God Himself. 'The eternal quality universally attributed to Him', he says 'is an expression of the miraculous durability of the archetype of archetypes, the human genome'.

10 McDowell (2001) takes a contrary view, arguing that the principles of self-organisation are 'pre-existing'.

References

Adams, M.V. (1997) 'The archetypal school', in P. Young-Eisendrath and T. Dawson (eds) *The Cambridge Companion to Jung*. Cambridge: Cambridge University Press.

Bair, D. (2004) *Jung: A Biography*. London: Little, Brown.

Beebe, J. (1988) 'Primary ambivalence towards the self: its nature and treatment', in N. Schwartz-Salant and M. Stein (eds) *The Borderline Personality in Analysis*. Wilmette, IL: Chiron.

Colman, W. (1999) 'Creation and discovery: finding and making the self'. *Harvest*, 45(1): 52–69.

—— (2000) 'Models of the self in Jungian thought', in E. Christopher and H. McFarland Solomon (eds) *Jungian Thought in the Modern World*. London: Free Association.

Dennett, D. (1991) *Consciousness Explained*. London: Penguin.

Edinger, E. (1960) 'The ego-self paradox'. *Journal of Analytical Psychology*, 5(1): 3–18.

—— (1987) *The Christian Archetype: A Jungian Commentary on the Life of Christ*. Toronto: Inner City.

—— (1996) *The Aion Lectures: Exploring the Self in C.G. Jung's 'Aion'*. Toronto: Inner City.

Fordham, M. (1963) 'The empirical foundation and theories of the self in Jung's works', in M. Fordham (1980) *Analytical Psychology: A Modern Science*. London: Academic Press; revised version in M. Fordham (1985) *Explorations into the Self*. London: Academic Press.

—— (1969) *Children as Individuals*. London: Hodder and Stoughton.

—— (1971) 'Maturation of ego and self in infancy', in M. Fordham (1980) *Analytical Psychology: A Modern Science*. London: Academic Press.

—— (1985) *Explorations into the Self*. London: Academic Press.

Gordon, R. (1985) 'Big self and little self'. *Journal of Analytical Psychology*, 30(3): 261–271.

Harré, R. (1979) *Social Being: Theory for Social Psychology*. Oxford: Blackwell.

Hillman, J. (1981) 'Psychology: monotheistic or polytheistic', in D. Miller (ed.) *The New Polytheism*. Dallas, TX: Spring.

Hogenson, G.B. (1998) 'Response to Pietikainen and Stevens'. *Journal of Analytical Psychology*, 43(3): 357–372.

—— (2001) 'The Baldwin effect: a neglected influence on C.G. Jung's evolutionary thinking'. *Journal of Analytical Psychology*, 46(4): 591–611.

Humbert, E. (1980) 'The self and narcissism'. *Journal of Analytical Psychology*, 25(3): 237–246.

Huskinson, L. (2002) 'The Self as a violent Other'. *Journal of Analytical Psychology*, 47(3): 437–458.

Jung, C.G. (1916) 'The structure of the unconscious', in *CW* 7: pars. 442–521.

—— (1921/1950) *Psychological Types. CW* 6.

—— (1928) 'The relations between the ego and the unconscious', in *CW* 7: pars. 202–406.

—— (1935) *Analytical Psychology: Its Theory and Practice. The Tavistock Lectures.* London: Routledge and Kegan Paul, 1968.

—— (1935/1944) 'Individual dream symbolism in relation to alchemy', in *Psychology and Alchemy, CW* 12: pars. 44–331.

—— (1938/1940) 'Psychology and religion', in *CW* 11: pars. 1–168.

—— (1940) 'Conscious, unconscious and individuation', in *CW* 9i: pars. 489–524.

—— (1940/1954) 'Transformation symbolism in the Mass', in *CW* 11: pars. 296–448.

—— (1942/1948) 'A psychological approach to the dogma of the Trinity', in *CW* 11: pars. 169–295.

—— (1944) 'Introduction to the religious and psychological problems of alchemy', in *Psychology and Alchemy, CW* 12: pars. 1–43.

—— (1946/1954) 'On the nature of the psyche', in *CW* 8: pars. 343–442.

—— (1951) *Aion. CW* 9ii.

—— (1952) 'Answer to Job', in *CW* 11: pars. 553–758.

—— (1954) *Mysterium Coniunctionis. CW* 14.

—— (1958) 'Flying saucers: a modern myth', in *CW* 10: pars. 589–824.

—— (1963) *Memories, Dreams, Reflections.* London: Routledge and Kegan Paul.

Kalsched, D. (1996) *The Inner World of Trauma: Archetypal Defenses of the Personal Spirit.* London and New York: Routledge.

McDowell, M.J. (1999) 'Relating to the mystery: a biological view of analytical psychology'. *Quadrant: Journal of the C.G. Jung Foundation of Analytical Psychology*, 29(1): 12–32 (also available online as 'Jungian analysis and biology' in *Cogprints*).

—— (2001) 'Principle of organisation: a dynamic-systems view of the archetype-as-such'. *Journal of Analytical Psychology*, 46(4): 637–654.

McGlashan, R. (1997) 'Comment on Eli Weisstub's "Self as the feminine principle"'. *Journal of Analytical Psychology*, 42(3): 453–455.

Maturana, H.R. and Varela, F.J. (1980) *Autopoiesis and Cognition: The Realization of the Living.* Dordrecht: Kluwer Academic.

Neumann, E. (1949/1954) *The Origins and History of Consciousness.* London: Routledge and Kegan Paul.

—— (1959) 'The significance of the genetic aspect for analytical psychology'. *Journal of Analytical Psychology*, 4(2): 125–137.

—— (1973) *The Child: Structure and Dynamics of the Nascent Personality.* London: Hodder and Stoughton.

Redfearn, J. (1977) 'The self and individuation'. *Journal of Analytical Psychology*, 22(2): 125–141.

—— (1985) *My Self, My Many Selves.* London: Academic Press.

Salman, S. (1999) 'Dissociation and the Self in the magical pre-Oedipal field'. *Journal of Analytical Psychology*, 44(1): 69–86.

Samuels, A. (1985) *Jung and the Post-Jungians*. London: Routledge and Kegan Paul.

—— (1989) *The Plural Psyche*. London: Routledge.

Saunders, P. and Skar, P. (2001) 'Archetypes, complexes and self-organisation'. *Journal of Analytical Psychology*, 46(2): 305–323.

Serrano, M. (1966) *C.G. Jung and Herman Hesse: A Record of Two Friendships*. New York: Schocken.

Stevens, A. (1982) *Archetype: A Natural History of the Self*. London: Routledge.

Tresan, D.L. (1996) 'Jungian metapsychology and neurobiological theory'. *Journal of Analytical Psychology*, 41(3): 399–436.

Weisstub, E. (1997) 'Self as the feminine principle'. *Journal of Analytical Psychology*, 42(3): 425–452.

Whitmont, E.C. (1969) *The Symbolic Quest: Basic Concepts of Analytical Psychology*. Princeton, NJ: Princeton University Press.

Willeford, W. (1987) *Feeling, Imagination and the Self: Transformations of the Mother–Infant Relationship*. Evanston, IL: Northwestern University Press.

Young-Eisendrath, P. (1997a) 'The self in analysis'. *Journal of Analytical Psychology*, 42(1): 157–166.

—— (1997b) *Gender and Desire: Uncursing Pandora*. College Station, TX: Texas A&M University Press.

Young-Eisendrath, P. and Hall, J. (1991) *Jung's Self-Psychology: A Constructivist Perspective*. London and New York: Guilford.

Zinkin, L. (1987) 'The hologram as a model for analytical psychology', in H. Zinkin, R. Gordon and J. Haynes (eds) (1988) *The Place of Dialogue in the Analytic Setting: The Selected Papers of Louis Zinkin*. London and Philadelphia, PA: Jessica Kingsley.

—— (1991) 'Your self: did you find it or did you make it', unpublished paper for discussion at the Analytic Group of the Society of Analytical Psychology, 4 November.

Part II

Psychotherapy

Chapter 8

Transference/countertransference

Andrew Samuels

Some general issues

In his *Autobiographical Study*, Sigmund Freud wrote this:

> One day I had an experience which showed me in the crudest light what
> I had long suspected. It related to one of my most acquiescent patients,
> with whom hypnosis had enabled me to bring about the most mar-
> vellous results, and whom I was engaged in relieving of her suffering by
> tracing back her attacks of pain to their origins. As she woke up on one
> occasion she threw her arms around my neck. The unexpected entrance
> of a servant relieved us of a painful discussion, but from that time
> onwards there was a tacit understanding between us that the hypnotic
> treatment should be discontinued. I was modest enough not to attri-
> bute the event to my own irresistible personal attraction, and I felt that
> I had now grasped the nature of the mysterious element that was at
> work behind hypnotism. In order to exclude it, or at all events to
> isolate it, it was necessary to abandon hypnotism.
>
> (Freud 1925: 27)

As we know, Freud initially thought he had been experienced as the
woman's first boyfriend in adolescence and subsequently came to think that
what was being 'transferred' onto him was a feeling for the first love
object(s) in the client's childhood. In this autobiographical vignette, there is
much on which to speculate from today's vantage point, not least upon
what the content of the 'painful discussion' between hypnotist and subject
might have been. The roots of psychoanalysis do lie in hypnotism and
worries about there being too much 'suggestion' at play in clinical work,
leading to the establishment of 'neutral', 'abstinent' and 'blank screen' ways
of working stem from this aetiology; thence there is an ongoing professional
denial of the part played by suggestion in psychotherapeutic treatment (e.g.,
Moore and Fine 1990: 196–197). Contemporary relational approaches to
psychoanalysis might allow for doubts about Freud's own doubts about his

'irresistible personal attraction'. By now, the therapist's role in the construction of the client's transference is a much theorised phenomenon. I bring in these up-to-the minute considerations as an illustration of my belief (Samuels 1980, 1989) that an exciting and fulfilling way to study the evolution of theory in depth psychology is to begin with the most conflictual and disputed contemporary issues and work backwards, as it were.

It is no mere play of words to state that the very theme of transference-countertransference excites the most extreme transferences and countertransferences. This is true in psychotherapy generally and Jungian analysis may even be seen as a special case illustration of the trend. Intense anxiety surrounds the question of whether Jung did or did not have an adequate conception of transference. Sometimes, he can be understood as dismissing its importance: transference is a 'hindrance' and 'you cure in spite of transference and not because of it' (*CW* 18: 678–679). At other times, such as the moment when he sought to reassure Freud of his orthodoxy (*CW* 16: par. 358), he is very keen to stand up and be counted as a reputable psychoanalyst who has fully understood the centrality of the idea of transference as the 'alpha and omega of analysis'; Freud apparently told him that he had 'grasped the main thing' (see Perry 1997: 141–163; Samuels 1985: 182–183 for a full discussion of this ambivalence of Jung's). Of course, many spiritual directors and doctors had long known about the risks of exciting and responding to amatory feelings in the course of their work and, like Freud in his early years of practice, tended to regard the phenomenon as a danger. Freud may well have been the first to want to know why such processes occurred and he does not seem to have been particularly frightened of them – in fact, with his idea of the 'transference neurosis' he made it possible for therapists to transform what had been seen primarily as a problem into the very thing that made depth work possible. Nevertheless, the penumbra of transference-as-danger remains with psychotherapy and we find even broad-minded psychoanalytic commentators (e.g., Symington 1986: 112) claiming that it is only the painful and difficult things that get transferred; if it is not negative, no need to transfer it. As we will see below, nothing could be more different from the Jungian tradition with regard to transference.

The key role played by transference-countertransference dynamics and understandings in psychotherapy practice reflects a recognition by practitioners that there are many things that are not ordinary about the psychotherapy relationship. But the not ordinary features are, even today, in spite of huge and sophisticated shifts in theory and practice, often boiled down to the apparently inevitable tendency of clients to experience their therapists as parental figures, along Freudian lines. Hence the emotional states associated with transference reflect those of the child–parent relationship – dependency, fear of abandonment, jealousy of siblings, incestuous desire and so on. Jung's insight, often cited by Jungians, that transference is a natural, multifaceted phenomenon that is widespread in culture is over-looked. In the Jungian therapeutic tradition, there is much more to transference than its infantile or regressive version (see Kirsch 1995: 170–209) and it would be a feature of much Jungian analysis that what look like 'parental projections' would be closely interrogated by therapist and client to make sure it was not a clichéd understanding at work.

The reason why infantile transferences do so often seem to be in play has to do with the nature of what Freud (e.g., 1900: 4–5) called 'primary process', meaning the typical ways in which the unconscious functions, overlooking the rules of space, place and time. The therapeutic space becomes the site of nursing, the therapeutic relationship the place for repair of a nursing experience that did not work out well, and present-day time is overlooked in favour of the time of infancy. It is claimed that the very act of asking for help will constellate or bring into being a regressive, infantile transference – but critics of this view (well summarised in Totton 2000: 134–166) have pointed out that the social structure of the therapy rela-tionship, rather than its assumed morphological similarity to childhood, is also at work; not all seemingly infantile transferences are infantile, many have to do with what is felt about and projected onto psychological experts and mental health professionals (Hauke 1996; Papadopoulos 1998).

Thinking about what lies beyond childhood when it comes to transference-countertransference, Jung was perhaps the first therapist to understand that what the client sees and experiences in the therapist, whether as a positive or negative feature, is connected, via projection, with the client's own self or personality just as it is, as a whole, rather than in its infantile aspects. Hence, an admiring or idealising (in a positive way) transference projection will lead to the client appearing to discover in the therapist aspects of personality – wisdom, tolerance, sensuality, imagination, intellect – that do not belong to, or do not only belong to, the therapist. Here, Freud's 'modesty' is also needed. Post-Freudian theorising about the self and self psychology (e.g., Kohut 1971) has taught us that idealisations are not only negative and defensive features of psychic life. Idealisations are ways in which someone discovers something about him or herself but in a projected form, so that another person carries these qualities. The projection has been necessary because the client is not yet ready to own their own strength and beauty. Maybe this is because they are caught in self-sabotage, or maybe they have had experiences in life that either contradict their more positive features, or make it impossible to claim them. Now, whether the problem is self-sabotage or life experiences such as being born into a poor family and hence not having received much education, a client can quite easily start to experience the therapist as preternaturally wise. Equally often, something different happens and images are projected onto the therapist which make the therapist seem to be a critical, distant, undermining and (socially) super-cilious individual.

All of this is transference and *both* the unrealised gold *and* the unrecognised shit of a life will find their concrete form in the lived experience of the transference. The reference to shit is meant educatively because of the need to recall that, in transference projections, the client will often or usually encounter material from his or her own shadow – 'the thing a person has no wish to be', in Jung's words (*CW* 16: par. 470) – but, according to the notion of the shadow, actually is. In the example just given, what if the critical, distant, undermining and supercilious personification is a part of the client's shadow? Much more work needs to be done on the linkages between shadow and transference because of a possible confusion in which 'bad objects' and 'shadow projections' get conflated, especially in the writings and work of those Jungian analysts who have identified very closely with psychoanalysis (wherein there is a huge literature on bad objects but none on the shadow). For example, positive aspects of a person's selfhood can reside in their shadow as well as negative aspects. This has to do with super-ego functioning (if I might bring in a Freudian concept to amplify a Jungian one). Say a person has had an hyper-religious upbringing in which all lights must be hid under bushels and it is just not 'done' to celebrate oneself. This person will grow up with ordinary and realistic self-esteem in their shadow – and the transference projection will be the first step in the breaking of the shadow's iron grip on the flowering and rounding out of the personality of that individual.

In so far as there is a generic Jungian tradition in connection with transference and countertransference, the following tensions exist within it.

First, there is a tension between an understanding of transference-countertransfernce that gives it an important but *limited* place in any consideration of the therapeutic process as a whole, and one that considers *everything* that takes place in therapy as connected with transference-countertransference and subsumed into it. Proponents of the latter view (everything is transference-countertransference) argue that, due to the special features of the therapy set-up and also the ubiquity of transference as already noted, there is no relationship possible in psychotherapy without an importation of features from outside that relationship. Those who disagree point out that, if everything were to be considered transference-countertransference, there would be little point in having such specialised terminology at all. We could simply refer to 'interactional dialectic' (Fordham 1979: 208) or 'conversation' (Hobson 1985). Terms like transference or countertransference would be reserved specifically for highly neurotic, borderline or psychotic phenomena in therapy.

My own view is that it is necessary to state explicitly what is not transference in the therapy relationship; this provides a sensible basis for delineating what is transferential in the general sense of having been imported into the two-person therapy relationship from the subjectivity of the client. So, again in my opinion, it remains necessary to mention the 'real relationship' or 'treatment alliance' and to distinguish these from the transference-countertransference dynamics of the therapy relationship while allowing for massive overlap and influencing of one kind of relationship by the other. Jung insisted that therapy rests upon a dialectical relationship – i.e., one comprised of a dialogue, important and transforming for both persons and involving a hypothetical equality of the participants, in the sense of spiritually equal in the eyes of God (and, I would add, potentially equal as citizens within the state). This has greatly deepened our understanding of the real relationship and the treatment alliance. Jung is a profound precursor to contemporary psychoanalytic and other interest in the relational base of psychotherapy. Jung's crucial contribution was to stress that both therapist and client are involved in the process as individuals and that both have conscious and unconscious reasons and motives for being there. Implicitly, he raises the complex questions that have increasingly become explicit in contemporary theorising about the clinical process of psychotherapy: what does the therapist do to evoke the transference? And what in the therapist contributes even to a usable (i.e., non-neurotic) countertransference response to the client's transference?

The *second* tension is over the presence of archetypal, as opposed to personal, factors in transference-countertransference material. The discussions on this point quickly become theological. It is said that all transference must be personal, in the sense that only personal expressions of inner world content are possible – i.e., the collective unconscious is indivisible from the personal unconscious (Williams 1963). While intellectually impressive, this position may also be a debating device. For what is usually meant by archetypal transference is that the transference does not emanate from a personal experience – for example, of parenting. Rather, the content that is transferred onto the therapist is of a more general, 'typical' kind. So the wise (or stupid) therapist may be more accurately understood as a transference image to do with the typical, perennial, structuring features (its *sine qua non*) of the healing situation, and not a regressive, personal theme in the client. Certainly, for there to be an experience of a wise or stupid therapist there have to be persons involved. But to claim the whole thing as 'personal' is really a political move given the ideological wars that have taken place in Jungian psychology and analysis since (and before) Jung's death (see Samuels 1985 for an account both reliable and provocative of the division of post-Jungian analytical psychology into three schools: Classical, Developmental and Archetypal; see Young-Eisendrath and Dawson 1997: 89–222 for an extended illustration of what these schools mean in terms of actual analytical and therapeutic practice).

To say that all transferences are truly personal was a mighty fusillade in such a war. On the other hand, it needs to be borne in mind that many apparently archetypal transferences, for example, dreams of the therapist in an impressive guise as a god-like figure or as the acme of masculinity or femininity may be additionally understood as having personal roots in the presence or absent virtues of parental figures in childhood. Working the field between personal and archetypal transference requires very intricate and flexible interpretative strategies, a capacity in the therapist to stay with confusion and an excess of competing ideas, and an acceptance by all that there is a tension here that resists closure.

The *third* tension concerns whether transference is better understood as a cul-de-sac or blind alley that it may be necessary to explore before turning back, having mapped all its nooks and crannies and feeling able to disregard it as a highway for future development – or whether going into the transference as comprehensively as possible is a road (or *the* road) to further personality integration and individuation. Of course, these two positions are often overlapping and it may be necessary to work on a transference issue for some time, understanding it as something that has to be 'cleared', as it were, and also as tending to promote growth and development. One could express this tension in terms of the difference between 'ghosts' and 'ancestors'. You cannot ignore the ghosts of the past but, once encountered and noted, ghosts may not be as much use in the establishment of a life-enhancing and firm-enough identity as ancestors would be. Transference-driven explorations of the past or of the unconscious situation in the client in the present may play a part in converting ghosts into ancestors, transforming our cul-de-sac into a highway pointing in the direction of psychic richnesses in the future.

The *fourth* tension concerns whether transference is truly a natural phenomenon (as Jung claimed) or more something induced by the therapeutic situation. In the latter viewpoint, there is a cultural and even a political aspect to transference. To my mind, this latter, more socially sensitive understanding of transference is a necessary one and has the added advantage that it does not in any way vitiate the effectiveness of transference analysis as an essential component of healing. But we have to be honest here and accept that whatever we do influences everything that goes on in our clinical settings. If the client is required to attend for analysis four or five times per week, it is disingenuous to claim that the requirement itself has nothing at all to do with the often far greater intensity of transference feeling experienced by such clients compared to the experience of clients in once weekly therapy. Those who advocate intensive analysis of the transference might bear in mind that their advocacy helps to bring the transference into being as a phenomenon originating in the therapist. Extra sessions may not be bringing out features of the transference-countertransference that less intensive therapy fails to bring out; they might be putting something *in* that is very far from being a natural additive. There has been little discussion in psychotherapy generally of these considerations.

The *fifth* tension concerns the interweave between transference projection and 'reality' and how the therapist handles that interweave. Let us say that the client feels that the therapist does not like him. The therapist is aware of this feeling on the part of the client but, search as he might, he cannot find such dislike of the client in himself. It is a transference. (The therapist may be wrong about this and his self-analysis deficient but let us give him the benefit of the doubt for the moment and for the sake of the discussion.) So it is a transference. What is our therapist to do? There are a number of therapeutic strategies he might follow. The therapist may be open to naming the feeling but not to taking this very much further, a state of constructive indifference (constructive because the therapist's theoretical position is that to go into the transference would be a cul-de-sac, as described above), a deliberate decision on the part of the therapist. Or the therapist might recognise that the client has this feeling, accept it without contradicting it but be thinking in terms of exploring and interpreting the feeling (e.g., as a projection) at a later stage. Plaut (1956) referred to this as 'incarnating the archetypal image' and had in mind that the therapist would neither confirm nor deny the feeling in himself, nor explain the mechanisms of transference or projection, nor amplify the material by educating the client via references to the ambivalence of mythological father figures to son figures (Chronos, Uranos, Zeus, Laius, Pharoah, Herod). The next possibility would be to work in the knowledge that this feeling exists and allow for its influence on all aspects of the therapeutic relationship. For example, if the clinical material is somewhat thin, this may be due to the client's reluctance to put forth sensitive and precious things to one whom he feels does not like him.

The last possibility is that the therapist will want to work with this transference for as long and as deeply as seems possible and be alert to related transferences. In fact, the therapist may have long desired such material to emerge, believing, along with James Strachey (1934) and many contemporary post-Jungian analysts, that these here-and-now transferences are gold dust for the clinician. There are many things to consider here. Some have alleged that, far from being a mutative (i.e., change inducing) technique, here-and-now transference interpretations have become an addiction, a sign of hopeless narcissistic preoccupation on the part of the therapist (Peters 1991). Mockingly, references are made to 'you mean me' interpretations (N. Coltart, personal communication 1993). My own position is to try to judge each case on its merits. Sometimes, when the clients refer to a workplace superior who does not like them, they do mean their boss. At other times, a here-and-now interpretation that the boss is a disguised referent for the therapist is valid. In both cases, one hopes that there is some exploration of the client's lifelong and present-day psychological experiences of social superiority and inferiority in the work and other settings but, so it is argued, the incorporation of the figure of the analyst will make the dialogue much more earthy and full of life.

Jung's conception of transference and countertransference

Jung's overall position was that the therapeutic relationship must be distinguished from a medical or technical procedure and that therapy will take a different course according to the particular combination of therapist and client. Hence it is not surprising that Jung's attitude to transference varied so much. As we saw, on the one hand, it is the central feature of therapy and, on the other, little more than an eroticised hindrance to therapy. Jung shows greater consistency when it comes to counter-transference and has been recognised as one of the pioneers of a general movement in psychotherapy to regard the emotional, fantasy and bodily states of the therapist as being of importance for a deeper understanding of the client's situation. Up until the 1950s, psychoanalysis, following Freud, tended to regard countertransference as invariably neurotic, an activation of the analyst's infantile conflicts and an obstacle to his functioning (Freud 1910, 1913). To the contrary, Jung wrote in 1929 that 'You can exert no influence unless you are subject to influence . . . The patient influences [the analyst] unconsciously . . . One of the best known symptoms of this kind is the countertransference evoked by the transference' (*CW* 16: par. 163). In sum, Jung regarded countertransference as 'a highly important organ of information' for an analyst (par. 163). Jung accepted that some counter-transferences were not so benign, referring to 'psychic infection' and the dangers of identifying with the patient (*CW* 16: pars. 358, 365).

Contemporary post-Jungian analytical psychology has assiduously pursued this interest of Jung's in countertransference as usable in the service of the client's development. For surveys of this see Samuels (1989: 147–159) and especially the outstandingly comprehensive review by Sedgwick (1994). Let me give a flavour of such thinking by outlining my own position, which owes much to Dieckmann (1974), Fordham (1978), Plaut (1970) and Schwartz-Salant (1984).

We can state that there are numerous countertransferences that are not primarily neurotic on the part of the therapist without ruling out the existence of an omnipresent neurotic 'bit', even in such usable counter-transferences. My thinking is that there are two rather different sorts of clinically usable countertransference, though both may be seen as com-munications from the client, who is therefore an ally in the work in this respect.

Suppose, after a session with a particular client, I feel depressed (this may be a single occurrence or part of a series). Now I may know from my own reading of myself that I am not actually depressed and certainly not seriously depressed. I may conclude that the depressed state I am in is a result of my close contact with this particular client. It may be that the client is feeling depressed right now and neither of us was aware of it. In this instance, my depression is a reflection of his or her depression. I call this phenomenon (my depression) an example of 'reflective countertransference'.

But there is another possibility. My experience of becoming a depressed person may stem from the presence and operation of such a 'person' or personification in the client's psyche. The client may have experienced a parent as depressed, and my reaction precisely embodies the client's emotionally experienced parent. I have become part of the client's inner world. I emphasise 'inner' here because I am not attempting any kind of factual reconstruction that would discover a depressed parent. Sometimes there is no person as such. Indeed, the depressed parental image may be symbolic of a depressive theme active in the client's psyche – the client may project his current, present-day depression onto the past, onto the historical figures of his parents. This entire state of affairs I have come to call 'embodied countertransference' and I distinguish it from reflective countertransference.

In this model, considerable emphasis is laid on the distinction between, on the one hand, my reflecting of the here-and-now state of my client, feeling what he or she is unconscious of at the moment, and, on the other hand, my embodiment of an entity, theme or person of a long-standing inner world nature. However, one problem for the analyst is that, experientially, the two states may seem similar and perhaps many usable countertransferences are both reflective and embodied.

Though this is just one model among many, I think many Jungian analysts and therapists who have considered countertransference have become aware that what has been termed 'the countertransference revolution', in which practitioners are legitimised in regarding their own subjective states as somehow linked to the client's, may have gone too far. Perhaps we have become a bit too glib and facile in connection with usable countertransference communications and our wish to be in a state of readiness to work with our countertransferences. Maybe we have pulled a power ploy on some clients by understanding our depression as a communication of their depression, and there are other problems as well. (I drew up a list of the problems with understanding countertransference as 'an important organ of information' in Samuels 1993: 45–46.)

Alchemy as a metaphor for the therapeutic process

It would be mistaken to take Jung as preoccupied with the relational dimension of therapy to the exclusion of an internal exploration of the unconscious on the part of both persons involved. Rather, Jung's particular contribution may be to have found ways of combining the 'one-person psychology' of Freud in which making the unconscious conscious is the main thing and later, two-person psychologies which, in diverse ways, stress the importance of the relational dimension of psychotherapy. Jung chose a metaphor by which to manage this combination of the interpersonal and the intrapsychic aspects of therapy and his choice has baffled many outside the Jungian professional community. Why choose *alchemy*, of all things, as the root metaphor for the healing process of psychotherapy? Why did he make his most important book on the transference take the form of an elaborated and expansive commentary on a sixteenth-century alchemical tract, the *Rosarium Philosophorum*?

Jung thought that alchemy, if regarded metaphorically, was a precursor of the modern study of the unconscious and therapeutic concern for the transformation of personality. The alchemists projected their internal processes into what they were doing and what they were doing was as much psychological as scientific, according to Jung. Alchemy, in its heyday between 1400 and 1700, was a subversive and often underground current in culture and, in this sense, had a similar relationship to Christianity to the one psychoanalysis developed in relation to Victorian bourgeois morality.

Alchemists had two aims. First, to create something valuable out of base elements in themselves of little value. This is sometimes expressed as 'gold', or 'the philosopher's stone'. Second, to convert base matter into spirit, freeing the soul from its material prison. The connections between these aims and the typical aims of therapy seemed to Jung to be clear. And the interpersonal or relational factor was also present in the alchemical process. The alchemist, usually represented as a male figure, worked in relation to another person (sometimes real, sometimes an imaginary figure), called the *soror mystica*, mystical sister. That is to say, the alchemist needed an 'other' with whom to relate to get his work done at all. There would be no therapist without the client. The alchemist's use of an 'other' may be compared with what Lacan (1949/1977) called the 'mirror stage' of development and to Winnicott's emphasis (1967) on the mother's reflection to an infant of his or her own worth. (See Papadopoulos 1984, 2002 for a ground-breaking review of the theme of 'the Other' in Jungian psychology.)

Putting these perspectives together, one can see how alchemy does manage to straddle the divide between intrapsychic and interpersonal dimensions of therapeutic process and many of the key terms of alchemy find resonance in therapists who feel comfortable with such a wide deployment of one particular metaphor. For example, the *vas* or sealed alchemical vessel puts one in mind of the containing aspects of the frame within which therapy is constructed. The *coniunctio*, an important alchemical symbolic image of sexual intercourse between a man and a woman, refers metaphorically to the deep and pervasive intermingling of the two personalities involved in therapy. At the same time, the image of the *coniunctio* depicts in dramatic form the movements between parts of the unconscious psyches of both therapist and client (Figure 8.1).

The various stages of the alchemical process suggest to a therapist aspects of the therapeutic process: *fermentatio*, when something is brewing up as

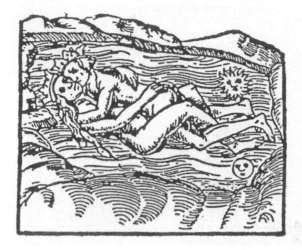

Figure 8.1

the 'chemical' reactions of the therapy process get under way, involving changes in both participants; *nigredo*, a darkening of mood and a realisation of the problems ahead, often taking the form in therapy of a depression occurring soon after its commencement; *mortificatio* – something must die in the client (i.e., change, wither away, shift) and probably in the therapist as well before any healing or change is possible. This is but a partial list of the parallels, intended to whet the reader's appetite. (For a fuller treatment of the topic of alchemy see Samuels 1989: 175–193; Schwartz-Salant 1995; and Chapter 12 by Stanton Marlan in this volume.)

The explicitly sexual nature of the illustrations to the *Rosarium* may puzzle many readers who have not grown up, so to speak, within the Jungian world. Sexuality, intercourse, anatomy, are all intended to be taken as metaphors for aspects of psychological development. Hence eros and psychological transformation are connected. But what does 'eros' mean in Jungian psychology and why is an understanding of the term so important for an understanding of Jungian attitudes to transference and countertransference?

Rather like Freud, Jung uses 'eros' in a variety of ways. Sometimes he equates eros with sexuality or eroticism (*CW* 7: pars. 16–43, written as relatively late as 1943). More often, he writes of eros as an archetypal principle of psychological functioning – connectedness, relatedness, harmony and named for Eros the lover of Psyche and son of Aphrodite. Sometimes the principle of eros is referred to as a 'feminine' principle and this implies a complementary relationship with a 'masculine' principle, logos – the word, rationality, logic, intellect, achievement). Jung's use of 'masculine' and 'feminine' is of course problematic and this becomes marked when he assigns eros to females more than to males. Setting that fiery argument on one side for a moment (but see Rowland 2002; Samuels 1989: 92–122 for discussion of the matter), the point for us here is that *transference-countertransference dynamics and understandings cannot be insulated from eros*. Later, in a section on sexual misconduct, I raise the question of therapeutic work being conducted in reaction and over-reaction to a fear of committing sexual misconduct so that there is a deficit of eros therein, rather than the better-known problem of there being an excess.

The wounded healer

Once we heed Jung's dictum that the therapist is 'in' the therapy as much as the client is, it is possible to begin to theorise about what this might mean. Jungian analysis and therapy has functioned for many years as a laboratory in which the practitioner's role has been scrutinised more thoroughly than in other schools of depth-psychological therapy. As mentioned earlier, therapy is more than a relational process. Each participant has inside themselves a ceaseless unconscious–conscious dynamic or relationship. This means that in a consideration of the therapeutic process one has at least three important relations to consider – the interactive one, and the two internal ones. Critically, *all three are going on simultaneously*.

Being 'in' the therapy also emphasises the woundedness of the therapist. When referring to the idea of 'the wound healer', there is more involved than the ordinary idea that therapists are damaged persons who have become therapists for good unconscious reasons of their own. The idea of the wounded healer implies that the therapist must be wounded, recognise that, and do something constructive stemming from those wounds in relation to the client. Although the notion is present in Jung, the contemporary writer who has best expressed this phenomenon is the psychoanalyst Harold Searles (1975) in his seminal paper 'The patient as therapist to his analyst'. Searles reminds us that healing or helping others is a part of mental health. Hence, when working with a client, the therapist will be aware that the client needs opportunities to help or heal the therapist – without such opportunities, a crucial part of the client's potential cannot develop. The therapist cannot 'play' wounded so as to provide a practice opportunity for healing on the part of the client; he or she really has to be wounded. And, logically as well as psychologically, the therapist has to be open to the possibility of really being healed by the client which may mean accepting at depth that the client's perceptions, far from being 'transference projections', may be accurate. In that earlier example about the client who feels his therapist hates him, the therapist may not reach an insight about the hate within him towards the client that may truly be present without asking himself whom the client reminds him of in his personal history or in his present circumstances, or what it is that he envies in the client.

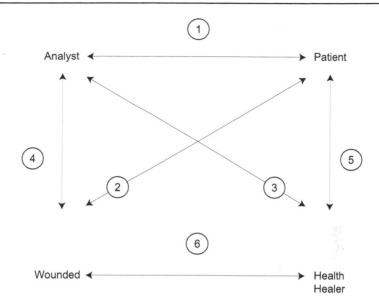

Figure 8.2

Jung presented his ideas on the synthesis of the relational and internal dimensions of therapy in the form of a diagram and many Jungian analysts, including myself, have refined his diagram (see Figure 8.2).

Arrow 1 indicates the conscious connection between therapist and client, where we can see the treatment alliance and the social linkages that make therapy possible. I think that Jung's insistence that analysis be carried out face-to-face, whether taken literally or more metaphorically as a kind of humane principle, means this arrow is much more important than at first seems to be the case. This is the locale for confrontation with the other that was mentioned earlier and sits at the heart of any therapeutic encounter, whether in a consulting room or not. I think it is an important tenet of Jungian analysis and therapy that, in addition to the members of the nuclear family, the client can also be the therapist's ally, enemy, supervisor, therapist, fellow citizen, master/mistress and, on occasion, soul mate.

Arrows 2 and 3 refer to transference projections from the unconscious of therapist and client onto the consciously perceived figure of the other. The therapist projects his or her wounded parts onto the client. The client projects his or her healthy/healer parts onto the therapist. These benign projections seem to me to be the way that therapist and client come to recognise each other *qua* therapist and client. Without these projections, there would not be the heightening of relational tension that makes the therapeutic encounter in some difficult to define way different from an ordinary relationship.

But what happens in arrows 2 and 3 rests to a great extent on what happens in arrows 4 and 5. Arrow 4 signifies the therapist's connection to his or her personal wounds. This should not be limited to whatever has gone on in the analyst's personal analysis (though it is significant that, as Freud (1912) noted, it was Jung who was the first to call (in 1913 – *CW* 4: par. 536) for compulsory training analyses, now a feature of almost every psychotherapy training in some form or other). Rather, we are referring to the therapist's whole apperception of his or her life. Arrow 5 is intended to refer to the client's gradual understanding of his or her potential to be other than a client. The client needs to get in touch, over time, with his or her healthy/healer parts, not only to be able to project them onto the therapist as part of an idealising transference. For there is also the important issue I mentioned earlier – helping and healing others as part of mental health.

Arrow 6 indicates the underlying unconscious connections between therapist and client; this is the level of relationship whose existence makes the idea that countertransference is usable in the client's service possible in the first place. (See the discussion about this, above.)

Some specific issues in connection with transference-countertransference

In the remainder of the chapter, I focus on some specific issues. These are:

- how transference-countertransference dynamics can lead to sexual misconduct on the part of therapists
- transference and countertransference in supervision
- illness in the transference and, in particular, the countertransference
- power issues in connection with transference and countertransference with special reference to transcultural situations
- transpersonal aspects of transference-countertransference.

In the section on alchemy, I included the woodcut from the *Rosarium* that most graphically illustrates the way in which the therapeutic relationship is a kind of marriage with many features in common with such an intense and all-encompassing relationship. It goes without saying that Jungian analysts and therapists do not intend their deployment of such an image to be taken as offering anything other than a metaphorical, as opposed to concrete, comment on the nature of therapeutic work. Nevertheless, in Jungian analysis and therapy, as well as in other approaches to psychotherapy, incompetence and inexperience in handling and understanding processes of transference and countertransference do sometimes lead to *sexual misconduct* on the part of the therapist. This phenomenon must be expressed in such a way – 'sexual misconduct on the part of the therapist' – because, no matter how willing the client might be to enter into a sexual relationship with the therapist, it is by now understood that, despite rationalisations to the effect that there are transferences in all marriages, it is the responsibility of the therapist to conduct the therapy in a continent way.

That said, as I hinted earlier, there is a problem which is the mirror image of sexual misconduct when the therapeutic relationship is overly deprived of some kind of 'erotic' content – meaning something in the areas of warmth, intimacy, intensity and trust rather than overt sexual expression. We must learn to recognise erotic deficit in therapy as well as erotic excess (and the same will be true in families as well, see Samuels 2001: 101–121). It is therefore desirable that considerations of transference and countertransference continue to incorporate psychological explorations of the 'sexual chemistry' or lack of it of the participants. Post-Jungian writers (e.g., Rutter 1989), have been explicit in raising these issues because of a tendency among Jungian analysts of earlier generations (now greatly reduced to the point where the problem is no more serious than in any other school of psychotherapy) to ignore the pitfalls and dangers of rendering concrete what needed to stay on the metaphorical level. It was no accident that among the earliest features of the transference noted by Freud, it was the sexual and loving aspects that caused the greatest difficulties whether of management or understanding. No discussion of transference-countertransference should overlook this segment of the theme and, given the relationship between sexual misconduct and professional ethics, it has become clear that there is an ethical aspect to work that involves an understanding of or working with transference-countertransference dynamics (see Solomon 2000).

Moving on, the second specific topic I would like to address is how the transference-countertransference dynamics of the therapy couple may be addressed in *supervision*. One way, of course, would be for the supervisee simply to present the transference-countertransference material to the supervisor, who would add his or her understandings to those already developed by the worker. Another way, which I think represents the state of the field at the present time, is for the supervisor and supervisee to accept that what is happening in their relationship parallels what is happening in the therapeutic relationship. Sometimes parallel process takes the form of a straight parallel between the transference developed by the supervisee in relation to the supervisor and the countertransference of the supervisor to the supervisee. At other times, the situation will be much more fluid and the relational and intrapsychic themes, feelings, images passing between supervisor and supervisee will have to be scanned in more general terms so as to elucidate what it is they reflect in terms of the transference-countertransference dynamics of the 'official' case.

The theory behind this approach to supervision is that, when one affectively charged relationship is present within another affectively charged relationship (for whatever reason, supervision being but one illustration of the general phenomenon), there will be an overflow of content and dynamics of one into another. This has led to the phenomenon in Jungian and other professional circles of case discussion groups in which transference-countertransference dynamics pertaining to a case under discussion are recognised and elucidated by reference to what is happening within the case discussion group itself. (See Mattinson 1975 for a full account of the 'reflection process' in supervision.)

Regarding the next specific aspect of transference and countertransference, I would like to float the idea that there are genuine risks involved in working with this material in terms of *the psychological and even physical health of the individuals involved.* Here, I am thinking particularly of illness in the countertransference and of the vulnerability of the therapist. Later, I will discuss the power of the therapist. Though many experienced practitioners know about this aspect of transference-countertransference, not much has been written about its role in the production of illness. Therapeutic work is exceedingly stressful for both participants and both are subjected to the usual range of stress-related, psychogenic and psychosomatic illnesses, ranging from disorders of the musculature and the skeleton (the 'bad back' so many therapists suffer from) to heart disease, arthritis and, maybe, some cancers. Not nearly enough research has been done into this topic but, in the intense states of mutual persecution and mutual longing that can arise within the transference-countertransference relationship there may lie some seeds of illness. Recognising this phenomenon and working it through may offer very valuable experiences for therapist and client. Clients are by definition vulnerable; let us not forget the vulnerability of the therapist in which the permeability of his or her ego boundaries that permitted the transference projection to penetrate also contributes to a real and sometimes awful suffering caused by the projection.

The fourth specific issue was *power*, with reference to transcultural situations. Most analytical trainings, and many in psychotherapy generally, do not pay sufficient attention to questions of power. In fact, power is an ubiquitous element in therapy (and sexual misconduct may additionally be understood as an abuse of power deriving from the transference of the client). It is tempting, for the liberally minded people who tend to become therapists, to balk at the idea that, in the conscious and unconscious minds of their clients, they are exceedingly powerful, that this power can be experienced as malign as well as benign, and that, far from being 'Terrible Mothers' or 'Archetypal Fathers' in the transference, they are closer to being experienced as torturers, jailers or cruel arbiters of social hierarchy. When there is a transcultural element to therapy (in succinct terms, when the client is from a different cultural/ethnic background to the therapist), these power dynamics intersect with transference-countertransference issues in a bewilderingly complicated manner. For what might be transferred in the case of a person from a minority ethnic group, receiving therapy from a person of the majority ethnic group in a locale, is the former's entire experience of living under the sway of the majority culture. It is not a personal transference, more of a 'group transference' but the experiences will also have been highly personal, maybe involving prejudice, discrimination and humiliation. How could such experiences not lead, in some cases, to the expectation of a repeat performance in therapy? Nor are these transferences 'archetypal', in the sense of being perennial and typical because such transferences (and the concomitant countertransferences involving unconscious and conscious assumptions on the part of the therapist about a member of such-and-such an ethnic or national group) originate in social organisation and the time-bound political arrangements within a society.

The last specific aspect of transference-countertransference I wanted to discuss was the *transpersonal* aspect. There are many ways to approach this topic which, until recently, with the rise of a transpersonal strand within humanistic and integrative psychotherapy, was a field in which the Jungian presence was overwhelming. The intensity of relational energy in a transference-countertransference situation does give the participants a sense of accessing something beyond what is involved in an ordinary relationship. Clearly, one has to conceptualise this with great caution lest one be seduced into an inflated assessment of what therapy is capable of. Nevertheless, there is undoubtedly a relational dimension that adheres to the transference-countertransference dynamic that is 'larger' than in an ordinary personal relationship. Some, including myself, would argue that this is indeed a simulacrum and a reprise of a relation to the divine. More sceptical and rationalist readers may find this point of view off-putting but numerous writers (e.g., Ulanov 1995) have offered their own narratives of how the therapy conversation moves, seemingly of its own volition, in transpersonal and 'spiritual' directions when the intensity of the transference-countertransference dynamic is not unduly resisted. What is interesting is that the same clinical phenomena – transference-countertransference dynamics – lead *backwards* to origins and roots and *forwards* to an enhanced practical spirituality accessible by both participants in therapy. The alchemists did their work in a *laboratorium* and contemporary pictures and illustrations show us a room or cell recognisable as a modern 'lab'. If the alchemist is a medical alchemist (or 'iatrochemist'), then one can see the clients receiving or waiting to receive their treatments. But the alchemists also prayed for the success of their work in another room – an *oratorium* and written above the door they posted the words *Deo concedente* – God willing.

Mention of divine intervention leads to the following concluding thought: in our concern for the less obvious aspects of the analytical relationship, referred to as transference-countertransference, and clearly the province of the analyst as an expert, we should be careful not to exaggerate the importance of a technical approach. An exaggeratedly professional attitude not only misses the humanity of the analytical encounter but also leads to a state of hubris or inflation on the part of the analyst that can injure the work that she or he believes in.

References

Dieckmann, H. (1974) 'The constellation of the countertransference', in G. Adler (ed.) *Success and Failure in Analysis*. New York: G.P. Putnam's Sons.

Fordham, M. (1978) *Jungian Psychotherapy: A Study in Analytical Psychology*. Chichester: John Wiley.

—— (1979) 'The self as an imaginative construct'. *Journal of Analytical Psychology*, 24(1): 18–30.

Freud, S. (1900) *The Interpretation of Dreams. Standard Edition* 4 and 5. London: Hogarth Press.

—— (1910) 'The future prospects of psycho-analytic therapy', in *Standard Edition* 8. London: Hogarth Press.

—— (1912) 'Recommendations to physicians practising psycho-analysis', in *Standard Edition* 12. London: Hogarth Press.

—— (1913) 'The disposition to obsessional neurosis', in *Standard Edition* 12. London: Hogarth Press.

—— (1925) *An Autobiographical Study*, in *Standard Edition* 20. London: Hogarth Press.

Hauke, C. (1996) 'The child: development, archetype, and analytic practice'. *San Francisco Jung Institute Library Journal*, 15(1): 17–38.

Hobson, R. (1985) *Forms of Feeling: The Heart of Psychotherapy*. London and New York: Tavistock.

Kirsch, J. (1995) 'Transference', in M. Stein (ed.) *Jungian Analysis*. La Salle, IL: Open Court.

Kohut, H. (1971) *The Analysis of the Self*. New York: International Universities Press.

Lacan, J. (1949/1977) 'The mirror stage as formative of the function of the I as revealed in psychoanalytic experience', in *Ecrits*, trans. A. Sheridan. London: Tavistock.

Mattinson, J. (1975) *The Reflection Process in Casework Supervision*. London: Institute of Marital Studies.

Moore, B. and Fine, B. (eds) (1990) *Psychoanalytic Terms and Concepts*. New Haven, CT and London: Yale University Press.

Papadopoulos, R. (1984) 'Jung and the concept of the Other', in R. Papadopoulos and G. Saayman (eds) *Jung in Modern Perspective*. London: Wildwood.

—— (1998) 'Jungian perspectives in new contexts', in A. Casement (ed.) *Post-Jungians Today: Key Papers in Contemporary Analytical Psychology*. London and New York: Routledge.

—— (2002) 'The other other: when the exotic other subjugates the familiar other'. *Journal of Analytical Psychology*, 47(2): 163–188.

Perry, C. (1997) 'Transference', in P. Young-Eisendrath and T. Dawson (eds) *The Cambridge Companion to Jung*. Cambridge: Cambridge University Press.

Peters, R. (1991) 'Transference as a fetish'. *Free Associations*, 35: 56–67.

Plaut, A. (1956) 'The transference in analytical psychology', in M. Fordham with others (eds) (1974) *Technique in Jungian Analysis*. London: Heinemann.

Plaut, A. (1970) 'Comment: on not incarnating the archetype', in M. Fordham with others (eds) (1974) *Technique in Jungian Analysis*. London: Heinemann.

Rowland, S. (2002) *Jung: A Feminist Revision*. Cambridge: Polity.

Rutter, P. (1989) *Sex in the Forbidden Zone*. London: Unwin.

Samuels, A. (1980) 'Fragmentary vision: a central training aim'. *Spring*: 215–225.

—— (1985) *Jung and the Post-Jungians*. London and Boston, MA: Routledge and Kegan Paul.

—— (1989) *The Plural Psyche: Personality, Morality and the Father*. London and New York: Routledge.

—— (1993) *The Political Psyche*. London and New York: Routledge.

—— (2001) *Politics on the Couch: Citizenship and the Internal Life*. London: Profile; New York: Other Press.

Schwartz-Salant, N. (1984) 'Archetypal factors underlying sexual acting-out in the transference/countertransference process'. in N. Schwartz-Salant and M. Stein (eds) *Transference/countertransference*. Wilmette, IL: Chiron.

—— (1995) 'Introduction', in N. Schwartz-Salant (ed.) *C.G. Jung on Alchemy*. London: Routledge; Princeton, NJ: Princeton University Press.

Searles, H. (1975) 'The patient as therapist to his analyst', in H. Searles (1979) *Collected Papers on Countertransference and Related Subjects*. New York: International Universities Press.

Sedgwick, D. (1994) *The Wounded Healer: Countertransference from a Jungian Perspective*. London and New York: Routledge.

Solomon, H. (2000) 'The ethical self', in E. Christopher and H. Solomon (eds) *Jungian Thought in the Modern World*. London: Free Association.

Strachey, J. (1934) 'The nature of the therapeutic action of psychoanalysis'. *International Journal of Psycho-Analysis*, 15: 127–159.

Symington, N. (1986) *The Analytic Experience: Lectures from the Tavistock*. London: Free Association.

Totton, N. (2000) *Psychotherapy and Politics*. London: Sage.

Ulanov, A. (1995) 'Spiritual aspects of clinical work', in M. Stein (ed.) *Jungian Analysis*. La Salle, IL: Open Court.

Williams, M. (1963) 'The indivisibility of the personal and collective unconscious', in M. Fordham with others (eds) (1973) *Analytical Psychology: A Modern Science*. London: Heinemann.

Winnicott, D. (1967) 'Mirror role of mother and family in child development', in D. Winnicott (1971) *Playing and Reality*. London: Tavistock.

Young-Eisendrath, P. and Dawson, T. (eds) (1997) *The Cambridge Companion to Jung*. Cambridge: Cambridge University Press.

Chapter 9

Individuation

Murray Stein

Introduction

The theme of individuation sounds through Jung's writings, like a leitmotiv, from the time of his break with Freud and psychoanalysis onward without pause to his death. All things considered, it is perhaps his major psychological idea, a sort of backbone for the rest of the corpus.

Introducing the term in his esoteric, anonymously published little book *Septem Sermones ad Mortuos* (*Seven Sermons to the Dead*) in 1915, Jung deepened and expanded the idea in the much revised work, also begun in the same period, *Two Essays on Analytical Psychology* (*CW* 7) and in the summary work of the early period, *Psychological Types* (*CW* 6). Later he added further substance to the notion in his studies of archetypes and especially in his researches on alchemy. He detailed individuation clinically in his seminars (*Analytical Psychology, Dream Analysis, Visions* and Nietzsche's 'Zarathustra') as well as in several case studies. It also played an important role in his many writings on religion and culture.

Individuation was taken up as a central theme by nearly all of Jung's important students. Major contributions were made to the theory by Fordham (1969), who studied individuation in children, and by Neumann (1955), who saw individuation as unfolding in three major stages, each containing several sub-phases. Hillman, a Jungian deconstructionist, has vigorously attacked the notion of psychological development in general and individuation in particular, holding a view that such ideas are nothing but fantasies used to construct modern psychological myths. More recently, Jacoby has added refinement and differentiation to the theory of individuation by introducing data from modern infant research. Samuels has introduced the feature of political consciousness and involvement. The debate goes on.

In the following pages, I present a distillation and synthesis of the Jungian tradition on the central theme of individuation, situating this particular discussion in the clinical setting of psychotherapy and showing how the working Jungian psychotherapist may use this developmental idea in practice.

When Jungian psychotherapists face patients for the first time, they try to size them up. One listens to that first outpouring of narrative, of confession or complaint, with an ear cocked to tone. Does this sound like true suffering, or is this person blocked in feeling or cranky in thought? Is this someone who blames others too much, or does she shoulder too much responsibility for what goes wrong? Is this person too passive? Too active?

Within the texture of even the most innocent first narrative, therapists will often spot fragility, entitlement, emotional vulnerability and a host of other telling feelings and attitudes. In the therapist's own emotional responses to this narrative, too, one may detect the pull of a raging demand for help, or the opposite – the pushing away that creates too great a distance. In the first sessions, and indeed throughout a long therapeutic treatment, therapists spin an evolving mental assessment of how their patients are carrying on with life at the particular stage they find themselves in now, as they attempt to settle their old accounts, open new ones, and elaborate their stories.

Jungian psychotherapists hold a notion of psychological development, of 'stages of life', and we ask ourselves questions about the levels of psychological development demonstrated in the narratives offered by the people who come to us. Does a person's discourse show a good match, we wonder for instance, between chronological age and psychological attitudes? The full clinical impression of a person's level or degree of psychological development takes many sessions and much observation to formulate in depth and detail. It is an estimate of their achieved individuation. Individuation is a term used to indicate a person's potential for full psychological development. In the following, I will describe some of the features of Jung's complex vision and estimate of the human potential. In its simplest formula, individuation is the capacity for wholeness and evolved consciousness. The aim of analysis is to increase and to promote individuation in patients.

The Jungian therapist's unspoken reflections on achieved individuation take place within the general context of formulating a diagnosis and assessment of a patient's psychological development. What is the patient's level of everyday functioning? Does physical illness play a role? Is there serious psychopathology? Sometimes these considerations feature prominently in the treatment; in other cases they play no significant role at all. Determining their importance for guiding treatment is the business of the early sessions of psychotherapy, even while these concerns remain a consideration throughout. And just as diagnosis from the clinical perspective of the standard *Diagnostic and Statistical Manual of Mental Disorders* (DSM-IV: this was devised by the American Psychiatric Association and it is now in its fourth edition, revised in 2000) is an ongoing and evolving consideration – which the Jungian psychotherapist, like any other, makes in such terms as major depression, anxiety, the various character

disorders, not to mention addictions, relationship and adjustment problems, etc. – so also the evaluation of individuation is an evolving procedure and ongoing estimation. It is not always so clear exactly where a
particular patient stands on the road to individuation even after considerable time has been spent in therapy, but the experienced Jungian
psychotherapist will have a strong sense of the general picture after even a
few sessions.

This question of how far a person has come on the road toward individuation is different from the usual types of diagnostic question raised in
psychological assessment, although they are not unrelated, as I will try to
show in the following pages. In considering individuation, one has in mind
something more encompassing than only cognitive development, behavioural adjustment, moral attainment, or the presence or absence of
psychopathological features. These are important markers in the complexity that constitutes individuation, but they are not exhaustive. There
are other features that are also determinative. The assessment of
individuation describes a person's conscious and unconscious assumptions
and attitudes: about the basis and sources of identity and sense of self-
worth, about the quality and meaning of relationships to other people and
to the world at large, about the energy (or the absence of it) poured into
personal striving and ambition, about the objects of desire and passions
that lead a person into the highways and byways of life, about the focus of
life's meaning. What the Jungian therapist is looking for in making an
assessment of individuation is how a person's chronological age matches
up with the level of development in these conscious and unconscious
assumptions and attitudes. To take the full inventory of them is a large
and complex study, which includes transferential and countertransferential
sources of information. Of course, cultural factors must also be considered
in making a reasonably fair and accurate assessment of a person's
individuation.

Jung himself, who could be considered (Papadopoulos 1992, vol. 2: 97–
98) to be the first important full lifespan theorist, wrote about two major
stages of life, the first half of life and the second. Each stage has its typical
developmental tasks, sequences and crises. A later Jungian theorist, Erich
Neumann, conceptualised the lifelong development of personality as falling
into three major eras or phases. Neumann's paradigm, which does not
contradict Jung's, adds a useful degree of further differentiation to the first
half of life, and Neumann's model is widely used by Jungian psychotherapists today.

Within the linguistic universe of analytical psychology, the lifelong
development of personality is called individuation. Briefly stated, individuation refers to the process of becoming the personality that one innately
is *potentially* from the beginning of life. The sequence of developmental
stages in almost every individual's life has common features, hazards and

breakdowns. The Jungian psychotherapist has a keen awareness of how this developmental sequence unfolds ideally and how it so often fails to reach its proper destination due to genetic, circumstantial, social and cultural obstacles. There are also some important differences between the genders to be considered.

In summary, then, the patient arriving for Jungian psychotherapy is intuitively and clinically assessed in the mind of the psychotherapist, generally against the DSM-IV standards of normal and abnormal mental and psychological states and specifically against the perspectives of the individuation process as this has been outlined in the Jungian literature (see the bibliography for a selection of key works on this topic). Most likely this assessment never becomes apparent to the patient, nor is it discussed explicitly. It is, however, used by the therapist to guide interpretations, to make interventions, and to establish and maintain the structure of therapy. Much of the therapist's style in a specific case depends on this assessment of where the patient stands on the road of individuation.

In the following pages I will survey the three main stages of the individuation process, its two major crises periods, and its ultimate goal. The efforts made in therapy are fundamentally geared toward promoting and facilitating, or toward unblocking and restarting, the individuation process in patients. The three stages of individuation are, first, the containment/ nurturance (i.e., the maternal, or in Neumann's terminology the matriarchal) stage, second, the adapting/adjusting (i.e., the paternal, or, again in Neumann's terminology, the patriarchal) stage, and third, the centring/ integrating (in Neumann's terminology, the individual) stage. (These can be coordinated with Erik Erikson's seven stages of psychological development, first published in 1950.) The two major crises of individuation fall in the transitions between these stages, the first in adolescence and early adulthood and the second at midlife.

These three stages should be thought of not as discrete and entirely separate rooms that are inhabited for a period of time and then left behind when one enters the next chamber, or as a specific number of miles on life's journey never to be trodden again once passed through. Rather, they indicate emphases and predominant attitudes during the major eras of a person's life. They are stages of growth and development that shade gradually from one into the next, and features of each continue, but in a less predominant way, as a person makes the passage through a whole lifetime. The first stage refers to childhood, the second to early and middle adulthood, and the third to middle and late adulthood and old age. This view of the lifeline is a tool for psychotherapy, useful if applied with a deft touch but damaging if handled too concretely and with blunt force. It is a perspective that gives the Jungian psychotherapist a way of understanding the psychological qualities and some of the troubling deficits of the patients who come for treatment.

The containment/nurturance stage of individuation

Like other mammals, humans start terrestrial life in a maternal womb. This space, bathed in amniotic fluid and kept warm by the surrounding body of the mother, is the archetypal nurturing environment. Passively fed through the umbilical cord, the foetus is required to make little effort to care for itself. For postnatal life, the mother's womb symbolises the psychological environment needed for the first stage of a person's life. It is a protected space, an enclosure in which the vulnerable young can grow relatively undisturbed by toxic intrusions from the surrounding world. For humans, this type of shielded environment is suitable for a lengthy period of time after birth. This is true especially for infants, for unlike many other mammals, human offspring, because of their large head size, are ejected from the mother's womb long before they are prepared to function independently of a nurturing container. Human neonates require an external nurturing environment of extended duration, until their bodies and minds are prepared to cope with the physical and social worlds into which they have been delivered.

Especially in modern developed cultures, this first stage of life, which we casually refer to as childhood, lasts a long time. For most people nowadays, the containment/nurturance stage extends through much of the educational experience, from infancy and the years of primary and secondary school, through university studies and further professional training. During these years, a person, even if physically and to some extent psychologically prepared to assume some of the roles of adulthood, is not fully equipped to deal with the demands of social life and is usually not economically viable as an adult member of society. This period of dependence on parents and parental institutions may last for thirty years or more. In traditional cultures, on the other hand, where initiation rituals into adulthood occur at around the age of 12 or 13, the containment/nurturance stage of individuation/development is typically terminated at the onset of puberty. By that age, a person is considered ready and able to take up the physical and cultural tasks required of young adults in the group. There it is an abrupt and dramatic change of attitude and social identity; in our modern cultures, the change is gradual and takes place over decades.

The quality of the containment/nurturance stage is defined, symbolically speaking, as maternal. The containing environment is constructed socially and psychologically on the model of a womb, in that the basic ingredients needed for survival – food, shelter, highly structured settings of care that are screened and protected – are provided by family and society. At the emotional level, nurturance is delivered (ideally) in the form of warm support and encouragement. Young children are loved unconditionally, appreciated for being rather than doing. The harsh aspects of reality are screened out. Children are held, caressed and comforted by smiling, doting parents who stand guard over them and look out for their well-being. The most that is asked of the young is a cooperative and willing attitude. For the rest, adult supervision and protection prevail. Not much is demanded of young people at this stage in the way of contributing to the general welfare of the family or group. They remain dependent and are nourished by parents and other adults.

Naturally the degree of richness of the matrix in this stage of containment is highly dependent upon the attitudes and resources that happen to be available to the adult caregivers. It is also crucially dependent on their emotional stability and maturity. Instead of screening harsh reality out of the protected environment, anxious parents may amplify threats and worrisome aspects of reality. Absence of adequate containment and serious breaches in the walls of protection surrounding the person at this stage generally put down the groundwork for later psychopathology, such as anxiety disorders and various character disorders. In addition, the frightened or threatened child, in order to replace the absent or breached outer protective shield, develops primitive and massive defences of the self, which also have the capacity to cut the person off from important developments and relationships later in life.

Under the best conditions, the quality and degree of containment gradually changes as a person passes through the sub-phases of childhood. At first there is maximal nurturance and containment. The kind of attention given to the newborn baby, who can do practically nothing for itself, modulates to a less intense level of care as the child grows older. Later the parents will place further limits on the amount and kind of nurturance they provide, and the degree of containment is eased. Expectations for a relative amount of autonomy, independence and self-control are introduced at many points along the way, as the child is able to respond positively to these changes. Normally these shifts are met by a willingness on the part of the child to cooperate if the onset of these new conditions corresponds to growing abilities (cognitive, emotional, motor). As the individual proceeds through the usual sub-phases of childhood development, the nurturing container evolves in order to meet the new needs that appear and to reduce what would become an intrusive type of overprotective care in many areas. By the end of this stage of individuation, people experience only a minimum of nurturing and containment from the environment and are able to do for themselves what others have done for them earlier.

The first and primary nurturing figure is, of course, the mother. From pregnancy onwards, the mother represents as well as symbolises the nurturing container itself. Nurturing and containing can be referred to as the mothering function, whether this is delivered by the actual biological mother, by mother surrogates, by fathers, teachers, or institutions. Symbolically speaking, they are all 'the mother' if they approach the individual in a nurturing, containing mode.

Nurturing, while it grows out of concrete acts of mothering like breast-feeding, is not only physical, and to a large extent it takes on other features as the child grows. Feeding takes place on emotional, cognitive and spiritual levels. Nurturing is an attitude. Symbolically it has been expressed by mother figures since time immemorial. The Great Goddesses of world religions – figures such as Demeter (Greek), Isis (Egyptian), the Virgin Mary (Christian) to name only a few – are identified as nurturers, feeders, containers and comforters. The role of the Great Mother Goddesses extends far beyond the biological and physical feeding functions, although it is rooted in the gestures and rituals of literal feeding. The church, for example, is a classic nurturing, containing institution that feeds its 'children' the bread of heaven, a spiritual type of food. Its primary mission is not to feed people materially, although sometimes it has done so and has dedicated itself to the material improvement of the poor. Yet its main meal is a symbolic and spiritual one. Nurturing institutions are typically represented by mother images. Similarly, containers such as ships are referred to as 'she'. This does not mean that actual mothers or nurturing institutions like the church or ships of the navy do not also have marked fatherly, patriarchal functions and aspects, but when the emphasis falls on nurturing, the images hark back to the mother. Therefore this stage of individuation is referred to as the mother stage, and people within it are seen as living 'in the mother'.

Whether the containing/nurturing function is performed by the actual mother, by another person, or by an institution, the underlying attitude is: 'I am here to help you'. Nurturers are providers, helpers, sustainers. This attitude on the part of the nurturer, in turn, creates or inspires a corresponding attitude in the recipient of nurturance. Nurturers conjure children, and children attach themselves to nurturers. The recipient's attitude is one of radical dependence upon the perceived nurturer. This attitude may be quite conscious or largely unconscious. In the first years of life, it is definitely unconscious. Nurturance and containment are simply taken for granted by the infant and the young child. Recipients often struggle mightily against their caregivers, not realising how profound the real dependence actually is. A child pushing away from its mother and running impulsively out into traffic simply assumes, at an unconscious level, that it will be safe, cared for, protected, and at the end of the day fed, held and comforted. This degree of entitlement is unchallenged in the young child, and the nurturing adult, who may even find it attractive and mildly amusing, freely gives it. The dependency arising out of a good bonding between infant and mother is to be desired, for too much anxiety about the world at this early stage of life would not augur well.

The containment/nurturance phase of individuation serves the psychological purpose of supporting and protecting an incipient ego in the child. The ego complex, which we conceive of as the centre of consciousness with certain executive functions and some measure of innate anxiety about reality, comes into being gradually over the course of early childhood. Its earliest beginnings lie already in the intrauterine experience. There the ego is barely a point of awareness and of reaction to stimuli, a tiny bit of separate consciousness in the darkness of the mother's body. With birth, the ego's world is dramatically enlarged, and the infant's ego responds by registering and reacting to sights, tastes, and touching as well as to sounds and smells. Very quickly a baby is able to recognise its mother's face and to respond. At a profound psychological level, however, infant and mother remain joined in a state of psychological fusion. The ego's separateness is severely limited. This unconscious identification is mutual. The mother is as deeply tied into it as the infant. Jung termed this type of identification *participation mystique*, a phrase that denotes an unconscious psychophysical bond and comes originally from anthropology (introduced by Lévy-Bruhl 1910). What happens to one person in this union happens to the other. They feel each other's pain, hunger and joy. For the infant, this forms the basis of later empathy and eventually will develop into a sense of responsibility for others and an inner conscience. It also creates part of the foundation for later ego identity, especially for female children.

With further motor and cognitive development, the ego is able to begin exercising its executive functions and to exert some control over muscles. Arms and legs become coordinated and speech follows. Soon the whole world becomes a vast theatre of play and learning, a veritable Garden of Eden to explore. The healthy child asserts itself vigorously and with abandon in this perceived safe and protected environment. Serious reality testing is left to the oversight of the parental unit, a nurturing and containing presence hovering above. The boundaries of this paradise are tested soon enough as the child exerts more and more autonomy physically and emotionally. Disobedience and increasing consciousness go hand in hand. Psychological boundaries begin to be erected between child and parental guardian, and the child becomes aware of the differences between self and other and exploits them. Throughout this stage, however, a basic level of unconscious identification remains between child and nurturing environment. *Participation mystique* continues to reign. Jung thought of the child's psyche as largely contained in the parental psyche and reflective of it: 'Children are so deeply involved in the psychological attitude of their parents that it is no wonder that most of the nervous disturbances in childhood can be traced back to a disturbed psychic atmosphere in the home' (*CW* 17: par. 80). The child's true individual personality does not emerge until it leaves the parents' psyche in a sort of second birth, a psychological birth for the ego when it becomes a more truly separate entity.

This psychological containment of the young gives parents enormous influence over their children, not only through the conscious transmission of culture, tradition, teaching and training, but more importantly and deeply through unconscious communication of attitude and structure. Via the unconscious, a kind of psychological programming of the child's inner world takes place, for good or ill. It is not what the parent says, but what the parent is and does, that has the greatest impact on the shape of the child's inner world. The family is the child's adaptive environment, and much of this world's emotional tone enters the child's inner world by introjection.

The testing and challenging of physical and psychological boundaries continues throughout the first stage of individuation. Adolescence, which for most of us falls within this stage, is a transitional time when physically, and to some extent psychologically, a person is ready to leave the nurturing/containing environment and enter the next stage of individuation. In modern developed societies, however, this is complicated by educational and training requirements that often prolong the containment stage to a significant extent. An adolescent of 15 or even 18 is nowhere near being able to take on the tasks and responsibilities of adulthood in modern societies. This prolongation of the first stage of individuation creates the specific problems and attitudes so characteristic of adolescents in these countries: impatience, rebelliousness, feelings of inferiority, being marginalised, and frustration. Ready to leave the world of childhood but not yet prepared for the tasks of adulthood, they are truly betwixt and between. The adult personae that initiation rituals provide in traditional societies are withheld from adolescents in modern cultures, and the dependent state of childhood is artificially prolonged far beyond its natural physical and psychological timeframe. Schools and colleges are the holding pens and containers devised by modern cultures for adolescents and post-adolescents who need to have more time to mature and to become acculturated and ready for successful adaptation to the demands of work and family that are shortly to fall upon them.

The adapting/adjusting stage of individuation

While the mother occupies the symbolic centre of the first stage of individuation, the father assumes this position in the second stage. This transformation comes about not by usurpation but gradually and through psychological necessity. The father is needed by the growing ego to gain freedom from the nurturing containment offered by the mother and to instil the rigor of functioning and performance demanded for adaptation to the world. The father introduces anxiety to the ego, but ideally in amounts that can be mastered by increasing competence.

Again it is necessary to understand the terms 'father' and 'patriarchal' (Neumann) symbolically and metaphorically rather than literally and sociologically. Where the first stage of individuation is characterised by containment and nurturance (the Garden of Eden), the second stage is governed by the law of consequences for actions taken (the reality principle) and by the constant demand for performance and achievement in the wider world. In the second stage of individuation, the person is exposed to a world in which standards of performance are paramount and consequences for behaviour are forcefully and implacably drawn. A person who is living fully in this type of environment of expectation and conditional regard has entered the 'father world'. It is no longer a world in which unconditional love is the norm, but rather one in which strict and even harsh conditions are imposed upon the distribution of all rewards, including love and positive regard. This is not the world as ideal but the world as real. The ego is required to become realistic about itself and about the world at large. This means fitness and competition.

In truth, the reality principle is typically introduced into the life of children long before they leave the containment stage, but there, ideally, it is introduced in doses that are moderate and therefore tolerable to the young and vulnerable ego. The containing environment provides a protective screen that removes the harsh and potentially damaging aspects of reality. The demands for performance and achievement should not be brought to bear too forcefully or too soon in life. If this does happen, the child's ego can be crushed or convulsed with anxiety. Against severe threats such as these, the psyche will erect primitive defences to guard against annihilation. On the other hand, if too few demands for achievement and performance are introduced into a child's Garden of Eden, and if consequences for behaviour are not drawn, the ego does not become accustomed to dealing with stress and tension. It remains underdeveloped, and hence will be unprepared later for the demands and expectations characteristic of the next stage of individuation. A moderate amount of frustration and tension, dosed out at the right times and in the right amounts, is growth promoting for the ego. Jung believed that the ego develops through 'collisions with the environment', and Fordham introduced the notion that the ego develops through cycles of de-integration and re-integration. Both notions feature the element of optimal frustration.

Typically the demand for some measure of control and performance begins already in the first years of life with toilet training and weaning. This may be introduced slowly and subtly, but the timing coincides with the child's ability to make the necessary adjustments. Demands for performance pick up with schooling and gradually increase in seriousness and consequence as a child passes out of primary school into secondary school. The father becomes a more important figure, symbolically speaking, after the early years of childhood have passed. By the time a child reaches high school and college, the adaptive environment induces a good bit of anxiety, and the young person becomes aware of and responsive to the demands of a less forgiving world. Consequences become more life shaping and determinative of action and behaviour. In some countries, the academic tests taken around the age of 13 are decisive for a person's entire career. Grades and academic performance have life-changing consequences for almost all children, and under the pressure of this awareness there comes the realisation that the world will not continue to be the nurturing container that one knew as an infant and a young child.

The decisive passage from the first stage of individuation into the second takes place over a period of time, typically between the ages of early puberty and early adulthood (ages 12–21) in most modern societies. This may be earlier in exceptional cases, and it is later for people who prolong their education into graduate and postgraduate studies. Schools are partially matriarchal holding environments and partially patriarchal adaptive ones. Their job is gradually to prepare a person for life beyond school. (For some people, of course, this does not happen. They may ignore school and drop out of its programmes before they reach any degree of real competence, or they may stay in school all their lives, as perpetual students or teachers.) As bridging institutions, schools play the archetypal role of the paternal parent to a growing child, whose job it is to help the child leave the family container when the years appropriate for nurturing are over and adapt to the demands of adult life in the larger world. This is the role fathers play in traditional cultures for the young men who come of age and need to be introduced into the social structure at a new level. Mothers play a similar role for daughters, who are given new and larger responsibilities and taught the skills of womanhood as they come of age. In modern societies there is no distinction of this sort between sons and daughters. Nowadays both genders go to school with the idea of preparing for a life of work in the world outside the home. In addition, both genders are expected to accept the responsibilities of house-holding and child-rearing. The division of labour between women and men, while still often present to a degree, has been considerably blurred in modern life.

The completion of the passage from the containment stage (childhood) to the adapting/adjusting stage of individuation (adulthood) is, of course, fraught with crisis and emotional turmoil. The largest psychological obstacle lying in the way of making this passage is what Jung discussed under the rubric of the incest wish. Disagreeing with Freud that the incest wish was concretely a wish to have sexual relations with one's closest family members, especially the contrasexual mother and father, Jung interpreted it as the wish to remain a child, to stay in the containment stage of life. The incest wish is the wish never to grow up, to live in a Garden of Eden forever. Peter Pan speaks for this attitude when he announces with vehemence, 'I'll never grow up, I'll never grow up!' and refuses the transition from playful boy full of fantasy to reality-oriented adult. What is required psychologically to overcome this desire to remain a child is the appearance of the heroic, a surge of ambition and energy that pushes one out of the security of Eden to meet the exciting challenges offered by the real world.

The hero is the archetypal energy that kills the dragon (i.e., the incest wish) and frees the princess (i.e., the soul), for the sake of going forward in life. The hero asks for and takes up the challenges of real life with an abundance of confidence that many find unrealistic and almost death defying. The hero shows the confidence, call it bravado, to face up to the father and meet the challenges of the patriarchal world. An inner identification with a hero figure frees the ego from the pull towards regression and towards the comfortable earlier dependency on the 'mother' and energises it to meet the tasks and challenges of adaptation to reality. When a person comes to the conclusion that reality offers greater and finer rewards than fantasy, and that reality can be mastered, that person has passed from the first stage of individuation to the second.

Reality must be understood as the whole world of psychological, physical, social, cultural and economic challenges facing an individual in life, many of which lie beyond anyone's control. To deal with reality means that one faces up to all the issues that present themselves from without and within – love and death, jobs and career, the weather, sexuality, ambition, other people's expectations, the body with its weaknesses and tendencies to succumb to illness, the consequences of smoking or alcohol abuse, and so on. It means recognising that one lives and participates in a world filled with uncertainty and hazard, and that one's area of mastery and control is seriously limited. The hero gladly and even joyfully attacks the problems posed by reality with the confidence that whatever dangers may lurk, there must be some way to surmount them. Every problem has a solution, the hero believes. As the ego sets forth on the hero's journey, it soon enough discovers that in this stage one comes into a world of work and taxes, of pension plans and insurance policies, of long-term relationships and family responsibilities, of success and failure as judged by others, and of often intractable problems with no clear-cut solution. This is what must be faced, adapted and adjusted to, and invested in during the second stage of individuation. This is life outside the Garden of Eden.

Many people shrink away from this because of early psychological traumas that so severely handicap their capacities to cope with anxiety that they can never bring themselves to face reality fully. Moreover, there is a natural enough resistance to facing harsh reality, and the ego's defences push it away. Some people procrastinate and delay so long, and are allowed to do so by extended nurturing environments and circumstances, or by trickery and subterfuge and self-deception, that it becomes embarrassing and nearly impossible to face this transition later in life. This delay produces what Jungians call the *puer aeternus* (i.e., the 'eternal child' or *puella aeterna*, for the female version) neurotic character type. For one reason or another in these people, the hero has never arrived on the scene, or the ego has not identified with a hero figure and its energy, and dependency (conscious or unconscious) on nurturing and containing environments, real or imaginary, has been prolonged into adulthood and even old age. The incest wish goes unchallenged to any serious degree, and the threatening father looms too large and fearsome. The psyche stagnates as a result. A sort of invalidism takes hold, as the person, fearing exposure, challenge, and the normal problems of coping with life, shies away and falls back. The ego remains 'in the mother', symbolically speaking, sometimes even literally acting this out by never leaving home. In these cases, one wonders if there is any individuation beyond the first stage. These people tend to remain childish throughout life. They may be harmless, but they also contribute little. Their potentials remain just that, potentials; they are not actualised. They are always just about to write the great novel but can never bring themselves to the point of putting real words on real paper.

Many of the character disorders described in the *Diagnostic and Statistical Manual of Mental Disorders* would correspond to the failure to separate successfully enough from the containing world of childhood. The borderline personality disorder, for example, seems to relate to remaining stuck in a love–hate relationship with the mother that is typical of children in their early years: now a person succumbs to fusion states of dependency upon maternal others, now he or she attacks them and tries to separate from them with violent gestures of hatred and disdain. This is a person who has not managed to accomplish the transition process from stage one to two and is repeating the drama of separation from the mother endlessly with significant maternal others throughout an entire lifetime. The narcissistic personality disorder also derives from being stuck in the containment stage of individuation, in that a driven need and demand persists that significant others do nothing but offer adoration and mirroring. People with narcissistic personality disorders long to remain the adored baby forever, performing for enthralled audiences who never utter a critical word or render a judgement on their brilliant performance. Their lives are full of open wounds and suffering because the world outside of the contained space of childhood is not set up to accommodate their needs to be seen and totally admired.

Psychotherapy, as it is usually set up and practised, lends itself to the impression that it is primarily a nurturing/containing environment reminiscent of the containment stage of development. The therapist typically accepts and supports a patient, withholds judgement, and offers more or less unconditional positive regard and mirroring. Many people who enter therapy, it must be said, come in so beaten and bruised by the slings and arrows of harsh reality that they need a respite, at least for a time, in order to recover their sense of balance and self-worth. If they are deeply damaged from early childhood abuse and trauma, they will repeat the struggles of psychological birth and development in the therapeutic relationship, fusing with the therapist as infant with mother, then struggling to free themselves from the therapist in the way of the borderline who cannot make this transition, or desiring endless amounts of adoration and mirroring from the all-embracing and accepting mother-like therapist. In these cases, it is the therapist's main task to help these people gradually make the transition from the mother world to the father world. In small doses, the therapist administers, consciously or unconsciously, deliberately or accidentally, the collisions with reality that strengthen the patient's ego and can help to prepare it for the world of adult functioning if these breaches are handled sensitively. From nurturing/containing mother, the therapist changes to another kind of person, a symbolic father, who helps the patient bridge to the world of achievement, work, struggle, competition and interpersonal competence.

The centring/integrating stage of individuation

The most significant and interesting contribution of Jungian psychology to the idea of psychological development is what it says about the part of life that follows the second stage of individuation. This is where most other psychoanalytic theories stop. What is still left to do, they might ask, after a person has successfully passed over from the attitude of dependency upon nurturing environments in the first stage of psychological development and has taken up the responsibility of living like an adult in a world of other adults in the second stage? Is there anything more beyond the psychologically advanced stage of entering the father world of adaptation and adjustment and being willing and able to cope with reality? For the Jungian psychotherapist the answer is 'yes', because in fact many people enter Jungian therapy in the second half of life looking for something more than fine-tuning of their patriarchal attitudes and the further elimination of residues of childish complexes. They are often successful adults who have held jobs, raised families, succeeded in reaching many of their goals, and now wonder if this is all there is to life. It is at this point that Jungian reflection on the individuation process in the second half of life becomes relevant. This is the phase of psychological development described classically by Jung in such works as 'A study in the process of individuation' (in CW 9i), when mandala symbolism, the religious function and the search for individual meaning become important.

The task in this stage of life, if all has gone relatively well in earlier phases, is not to become a responsible member of the community and a relatively independent and self-sufficient personality (this has been achieved in the second stage), but rather to become a centred and whole individual who is related to the transcendent as well as the immediate concrete realities of human existence. For this, another level of development is called for.

The first separation was from the mother, initially from her body (the first birth), then from her nurturing parental psyche (a second birth). At that point the psychological individual stepped forth into the world. Now there is another passage, a third birth, when the ego puts away the primary importance given to the achievement of adaptation, which calls for conformity to the standards and expectations of the collective (the world of the 'fathers') and embarks upon the journey of becoming an individual. The second stage, a stage of conformity, is often entered, paradoxically enough, by violent acts of adolescent rebellion, undergirded by the energy of the hero archetype. The adolescent breaks out of the parental container with determined force. The third stage, on the other hand, is usually entered into with a rather depressed and questioning attitude, as a person in the middle of life begins to shed the trappings of conformity and enters slowly and often painfully into a process of becoming born anew as a whole and integrated individual. Sometimes this stage is entered as the consequence of tragic loss that shatters fixed collective assumptions. Generally synchronicity, defined by Jung as 'meaningful coincidence' (*CW* 8: par. 827), plays an important role in the entry into and in the ongoing process of individuation in the third stage.

Entering the stage of centring and integrating means gradually abandoning the previous collective definitions of identity and persona and assuming an image of self that emerges from within. Of course this does not mean leaving collective reality behind. Social reality does not disappear from the ego's horizon or concern, but coping with it and adapting to its demands absorb less energy. There is a shift of interest and emphasis, toward reaching out to dimensions of living that have less to do with survival and more to do with meaning. Spiritual life becomes more crucially important and individualised.

Much of the identity that is established in the second stage of individuation is derived from collective images and stereotypes, also from parental models. The persona assumed by the ego in the second stage is a structure offered by society and made of a socially constructed set of elements that more or less suit the individual. Personality in the second stage of individuation is largely a social construction. This persona is highly useful for adapting to cultural imperatives and expectations. In the third stage, the ego, which has taken on this persona and largely identified with it, begins to draw away and create a distinction between a true inner self and the social self that has been dominant. As the light between these two psychological structures widens, an element of choice enters with respect to what kind of person one is and is going to become. This new person is more unique and individual, less a social construction.

This does not mean that one can now become anything, or anyone, one wants to be or can imagine. Rather, the truth is that an underlying structure of the psyche – called by Jung the Self (capitalised to denote its transcendence and essential difference from the ego) – comes into play in a new way and takes over the dominant position formerly held by external authority, by the voice of reality and by the 'father' and the social persona.

The ego now begins to answer to an inner demand and call to obedience from the psyche, rather than primarily to an outer one derived from authorities in society. The new structure that emerges from the inner world of the psyche, in the form of dream images, intuitions, inspirations, remembered ambitions, fantasies and a strong impulse toward personal meaning, gradually destroys and replaces the persona. Working to live and to survive is no longer sufficient; one must now find something that is worth living for, and this new direction must be tailor-made to fit the individual. In fact, it grows out of the individual who is deeply and constructively individuating in the second half of life.

For someone entering upon this stage of development, psychotherapy is quite different from what it is for people who have not made it through the first two stages. While everyone, no matter how developed or mature, shows some residual elements from the earlier stages of development – some borderline and narcissistic features, some degree of *participation mystique* with others and the environment, some lingering childishness and puerile qualities and defensiveness – these are not the paramount issues in therapy with a person in the third stage of individuation. What is central is, first, separating from the identification with the persona formed in the second stage, and then finding a personal centre, a point of inner integrity that is free of the stereotypes of collective culture and based on intimations of the Self. What is aimed for is a degree of integration of the inner opposites inherent in the Self, which allows for striking a vital balance in one's everyday life. Jung speaks of integrating the shadow and relating in a new conscious way to the anima or animus.

Transference is fundamentally different, too, in the psychotherapy of people who are entering or pursuing further the third stage of individuation. The therapist is not consciously or unconsciously related to as nurturing mother or guiding father. Instead, the therapist is typically seen (truly or not) as a wisdom figure, as someone who has achieved individuality and wholeness and relates personally to the Self. This projection is cast upon the therapist because this is the unconscious content that the patient needs and must find a model for, somewhere in the world at this stage of life. That job lands at the feet of the therapist. People look for, and seem to find, the models they need for their further growth in their therapists, and an image of psychological wholeness is what is now required by the psyche.

A wisdom figure is someone who is seen to have arrived at an inner centre and lives out of the resource found there. It is not necessarily someone who has all the answers to life's concrete problems. It is a person in whom we see containment of the opposites, who is able to remain relatively intact and balanced in even the most splitting and tension-ridden situations, who maintains an even attitude of connection with others but also detachment from ego preferences. It is a person who has found the Self and lives in relation to that inner reality rather than seeking approval from others or being possessed by desire and attachment to egoistic goals. Most importantly, it is a person who shows spontaneity, freedom and a distinctive personality. This person is vivid and displays a sense of uniqueness based upon having made many clear individual choices in life.

This image is what is found in the transference projection. Much of it is, of course, a projection based on unconscious patterns that are emerging in the field between patient and therapist. One can think of it as a sort of idealising transference, but one that is grounded in the archetype of the Self rather than in the unconscious mother or father images.

The goal of this third stage of individuation is the inner union of pieces of the psyche that were divided and split off by earlier developmental demands and processes. In this stage of integration, a strong need arises to join the opposites of persona (good person) and shadow (bad person), of masculine and feminine, of child and adult, of right brain and left brain, of thinking and feeling, of introversion and extraversion. All of the under-valued pieces of potential development that were earlier separated from consciousness and repressed in the course of the first two stages of indi-viduation, so that one could grow an ego and enter into relation to the world of reality in an adaptive way, now come back for integration. In those first two stages one typically becomes a certain psychological type, one identifies with one gender and one gender preference, one adopts a certain persona from among those offered by family and wider culture and identifies with it. In the centring/integrating stage, on the other hand, one reaches back and picks up the lost or denied pieces and weaves them into the fabric of the whole. In the end, nothing (or very little) that is human is foreign to the Self. And as the ego approximates the Self, it too feels less alienated from all of humanity and from the profound complexities of reality. In short, one becomes more accepting of complexity within and without.

Conclusion

Individuation is sometimes confused with individualism. To some extent these two concepts overlap in meaning, but individuation is in fact much broader in that it is not limited to emphasising only the ego. Individualism often ends up being a kind of narcissism, centred on the importance of the ego and its rights and needs. Thus it is correctly judged to be an exaggera-tion of normal and healthy selfishness. Individuation, on the other hand, includes a large amount of ego development and selfishness, but it does not leave off with this. It goes on to include and integrate the polarities and complexities within and without. It does not ignore the importance of altruism and relationship, but rather includes these elements centrally in its programme. It fosters both self-regard and broad social interest in that it focuses on the Self (not the ego), which is common to all humanity. The individuality that arises from the third stage of individuation is made up of a unique collection of common human elements embodied in one particular life, and this one life is not cut off from others or made more important than any other life on the planet. It is simply affirmed as one experiment in human life that is unique because of its precise position in the common matrix.

Bibliography

Adler, G. (1961) *The Living Symbol: A Case Study in the Process of Individuation.* Toronto: McClelland and Stewart.

American Psychiatric Association (APA) (2000) *Diagnostic and Statistical Manual of Mental Disorders*, 4th edn revised (DSM-IV-TR). Washington, DC: APA.

Beebe, J. (1992) *Integrity in Depth*. College Station, TX: Texas A&M University Press.

Edinger, E. (1972) *Ego and Archetype: Individuation and the Religious Function of the Psyche*. New York: G.P. Putnam's Sons.

Erikson, E.H. (1950) *Childhood and Society*. New York: Norton.

Fordham, M. (1969) *Children as Individuals*. London: Hodder and Stoughton.

Henderson, J. (1967) *Thresholds of Initiation*. Middletown, CT: Wesleyan University Press.

Hillman, J. (1977) *Revisioning Psychology*. New York: Colophon.

Jacobi, J. (1967) *The Way of Individuation*. London: Hodder and Stoughton.

Jacoby, M. (1985) *The Longing for Paradise*. Santa Monica, CA: Sigo Press.

—— (2000) *Jungian Psychotherapy and Contemporary Infant Research*. London: Routledge.

Jung, C.G. (1966) *Two Essays on Analytical Psychology*. Princeton, NJ: Princeton University Press.

—— (1967) *Symbols of Transformation*. Princeton, NJ: Princeton University Press.

—— (1968) 'A study in the process of individuation', in *CW* 9i: 290–354. Princeton, NJ: Princeton University Press.

—— (1984) *Dream Analysis: Notes of the Seminar Given in 1928–1930*, ed. W. McGuire. Princeton, NJ: Princeton University Press.

—— (1988) *Nietzsche's* Zarathustra*: Notes of the Seminar Given in 1934–1939*, ed. J.L. Jarrett. Princeton, NJ: Princeton University Press.

—— (1989) *Analytical Psychology: Notes of the Seminar Given in 1925*, ed. W. McGuire. Princeton, NJ: Princeton University Press.

—— (1997) *Visions: Notes of the Seminar Given in 1930–1934*, ed. C. Douglas. Princeton, NJ: Princeton University Press.

Kalsched, D. (1996) *The Inner World of Trauma*. London: Routledge.

Lévy-Bruhl, L. (1910/1925) *How Natives Think*, trans. L.A. Clare. New York: A.A. Knopf (original French title *Les Fonctions mentales dans les sociétés Inferieures*).

Neumann, E. (1954) *The Origins and History of Consciousness*. London: Routledge and Kegan Paul.

—— (1955) *The Great Mother: Analysis of an Archetype.* London: Routledge and Kegan Paul.

Papadopoulos, R.K. (ed.) (1992) *C.G. Jung: Critical Assessments*, four volumes. London and New York: Routledge.

Samuels, A. (1993) *The Political Psyche*. London: Routledge.

Schwartz-Salant, N. (1989) *The Borderline Personality*. Wilmette, IL: Chiron.

Stein, M. (1983) *In Midlife*. Dallas, TX: Spring.

—— (1998a) *Jung's Map of the Soul*. La Salle, IL: Open Court.

—— (1998b) *Transformation: Emergence of the Self*. College Station, TX: Texas A&M University Press.

von Franz, M.-L. (1964) 'The process of individuation', in C.G. Jung and M.-L. von Franz, *Man and his Symbols*. Garden City, NY: Doubleday.

—— (1977) *Individuation in Fairy Tales*. Dallas, TX: Spring.

Chapter 10

Active imagination

Joan Chodorow

Introduction

To introduce the importance and overall relevance of active imagination in the Jungian opus, I can think of no better source than Jung himself. In a beautifully written passage, he reflects on the significance of active imagination and at the same time conveys a bit of its magic:

> My most fundamental views and ideas derive from these experiences. First I made the observations and only then did I hammer out my views. And so it is with the hand that guides the crayon or brush, the foot that executes the dance-step, with the eye and the ear, with the word and the thought: a dark impulse is the ultimate arbiter of the pattern, an unconscious 'a priori' precipitates itself into plastic form.
> (Jung 1947: par. 402)

To say it again, his 'most fundamental views and ideas derive from these experiences'. Most of the basic concepts of analytical psychology come from Jung's experiences with active imagination. First, he 'made the observations' and only then did he 'hammer out' his views. For example, the shadow, the syzygy (anima and animus), persona, ego, the Self, all of these are concepts, but at the same time they are inner figures and inner events that personify certain structures and functions of the psyche. Affect, archetype, complex, libido – these are words and concepts – but in the deepest sense they are palpable human experiences.

Jung referred to active imagination as his 'analytical method of psychotherapy' (1975: 222). The process involves turning attention and curiosity toward the inner world of the imagination and expressing it symbolically, all the while seeking a self-reflective, psychological point of view. The many creative forms of active imagination include visions in the mind's eye, hypnagogic images that float up not only as visual impressions, but also auditory images, motor images and other somatosensory impressions; dialogue with inner figures; expressing the imagination through any or all of the arts, the symbolic enactment of Sandplay, and many others. Active imagination may include work with the dynamics of the therapeutic relationship, that is, the transference as active imagination (Jung 1916/1958: par. 186; Davidson 1966). Finally, the scholarly process of symbolic amplification (Jung's method of dream interpretation) is based on the same natural process of parallel association as active imagination (Jung 1947: par. 404).

Active imagination opens to and draws from the depths of the unconscious. At the same time, its expressive forms are shaped by the particular tastes, talents and inclinations of each individual, which in turn have been influenced by the cultural atmosphere (Henderson 1962: 8–9). Every creative process requires such a relationship of the conscious and the unconscious. From this perspective, active imagination and creative imagination are basically the same process. Both involve the expression and transformation of the emotions through 'ritual', 'rhythmic harmony', 'reason' and 'relationship' (L.H. Stewart 1987: 138). The main difference has to do with intent. Creative imagination is turned toward the creation of the cultural forms (religion, art, philosophy, society), while active imagination is turned toward the re-creation of the personality.

In Jung's view, life is paradox, so it is seems natural that his important ideas are presented in paradoxical ways. On one hand, active imagination is a meditative procedure and/or expressive process, meant to be done by the patient alone, away from the analyst. On the other hand, by linking active imagination to his symbolic method of dream interpretation and to work with the dynamics of the transference, he seems to be laying the groundwork for a comprehensive analytical method of psychotherapy.

Aligned with and shaped by the image-producing function of the psyche (the imagination), Jung's active imagination is based on an inherent psychic function, and at the same time it is a method of self-healing that can be taught. Active imagination is not so much a technique as it is a natural event: 'I write about things which actually happen, and am not propounding methods of treatment' (Jung 1928: par. 369).

Whether we are conscious of it or not, the autonomous activity of the archetypal imagination goes on all the time. It is expressed through play, dreams, fantasies, and active imagination as well as the age-old forms of creative imagination that shape human culture. For Jung, fantasy is an integrative function, 'the mother of all possibilities, where like all psychological opposites, the inner and outer worlds are joined together in living union' (Jung 1921: par. 78).

> Every good idea and all creative work are the offspring of the imagination, and have their source in what one is pleased to call infantile fantasy. Not the artist alone, but every creative individual whatsoever owes all that is greatest in his life to fantasy. The dynamic principle of

fantasy is *play*, a characteristic also of the child, and as such it appears inconsistent with the principle of serious work. But without this playing with fantasy no creative work has ever yet come to birth. The debt we owe to the play of imagination is incalculable.

(Jung 1921: par. 93)

Jung was far ahead of his time. His early recognition of the creative, integrative, healing function of play and fantasy anticipated future developments in psychoanalysis and psychotherapy (Samuels 1985: 9–11). Similarly, contemporary neuroscientists affirm the interwoven relationship of body, emotion, imagination and consciousness, as well as the multisensory nature of the image (Damasio 1999; Pert 1997).

I turn now to a chronological study of Jung's experiences and ideas, based on his writings.

JUNG'S VIEWS ON ACTIVE IMAGINATION

Jung's views on active imagination seem to fall in a natural way into three overlapping periods of time. First, I look at some early influences and ideas that contain seeds of his future method during 1902–1914. Next come the years of his 'creative illness' (Ellenberger 1970: 672–673) and experiments with self-healing around 1912–1919. In the third section, I take up his basic ideas as well as certain developments and modifications during 1916–1961. With three sections, it seems natural to wonder whether there might be a 'missing fourth'. If so, the roots of active imagination in childhood come to mind. I'm reminded of the young child's imaginary companion (Cwik 1995), the 'invisible friend' and the many ways creative fantasy guides development from infancy on (C.T. Stewart 2001). Although Jung's childhood is not presented in a separate section, his discovery of active imagination is completely interwoven with his re-discovery of symbolic play.

Initial influences and ideas (1902–1914)

Jung's first published work is his medical dissertation (1902). It includes detailed descriptions of a series of séances in which a young medium opens herself to inner figures and embodies them. Although the following description was written perhaps twelve to fourteen years before he discovered active imagination, Jung's observation and analysis of the séances led him to understand that there are many ways to express the inner world of the imagination, including bodily movement.

Gradually gestures began to accompany the words, and these finally led up to 'attitudes passionnelles' and whole dramatic scenes . . . Her movements were free and of a noble grace, mirroring most beautifully her changing emotions.

(Jung 1902: par. 40)

The nature of the image

From the beginning and throughout his long life, Jung recognised that the word 'image' is not limited to visual impressions. He cites Charcot who differentiates auditory images, visual images and motor images (Jung 1902: par. 86, note 35). Auditory, visual and motor images appear again in the fantasies of Miss Miller (Miller in Jung 1912: 447–462). A few years later in his first paper on active imagination, Jung speaks of 'visual types' who experience the unconscious as fantasy pictures, and 'audio-verbal types' who are more likely to hear inner voices (Jung 1916/1958: par. 170). Twelve to fourteen years later, in his seminar on dream interpretation he made the comment: 'Anyone with a motor imagination could make a very beautiful dance out of that motif' (1928–1930: 474).

Complexes and the nature of emotion

Jung recognised early on the significance of the emotions. Whereas Freud emphasised the drives as sources of human motivation, Jung held to the primacy of the emotions. His word association studies measuring physiological changes around psychic disturbance corroborated both Freud's concept of the repression mechanism, and Jung's concept of the emotionally toned complex (Jung 1904–1909). The link to affect is that every complex is organised around an emotional core. As early as 1907, Jung proposed a theory that the emotions are at the foundation of the psyche: 'The essential basis of our personality is affectivity. Thought and action are . . . only symptoms of affectivity' (Jung 1907: par. 78). Here Jung suggests that emotions are not only at the core of our most troublesome complexes; they are primal sources also of the higher functions.

Two kinds of thinking

In 1912, Jung differentiated fantasy thinking and directed thinking:

Whereas directed thinking is an altogether conscious phenomenon, the same cannot be said of fantasy thinking. Much of it belongs to the conscious sphere, but as least as much goes on in the half-shadow, or entirely in the unconscious, and can therefore be inferred only indirectly.

(Jung 1912: par. 39)

In this early passage, Jung links fantasy thinking mainly to the activity of the unconscious whereas directed thinking is linked entirely to the activity of consciousness. In later writings, Jung speculated about the unconscious thoughts and insights that 'lie close beside, above, or below consciousness, separated from us by the nearest "threshold" and yet apparently unattainable' (Jung 1947: par. 362). Here Jung recognises not only fantasy thinking, but also directed thinking as an unconscious function that comes to consciousness through its products. The link between Jung's two kinds of thinking and active imagination is that active imagination requires an ongoing dialectical relationship between these two streams of the life instinct.

Symbolic amplification

Jung's 1912 book about the libido that led to the break with Freud begins with his essay on two kinds of thinking. Most of the book, however, is devoted to Jung's amplification of a series of vivid, creative fantasies that came to a culturally developed young American woman. A distinguished journalist and lecturer, Miss Miller wrote an article about her fantasies. With clarity, intelligence and a gift for self-reflective exploration, she analysed the origin of her own sub-conscious images, tracing them back to certain impressions of life that had settled in her mind. In addition, she amplified some of the images with new information she gathered from ancient and contemporary cultural resources. Having never met her, Jung worked entirely from her article and from his own imagination and ideas, drawing further symbolic parallels to her hynagogic fantasies, associations and amplifications. In a 1925 seminar, he reflects on how absorbed he was in her fantasy images and in hindsight he recognises the degree to which he projected onto her, his own wounded feminine nature (Jung 1925: 27–28; Shamdasani 1990).

In another early formulation, Jung distinguished retrospective understanding from prospective understanding (Jung 1914: par. 391). Retrospective understanding uses a reductive method. It is oriented to the past as it seeks a causal, scientific point of view. By contrast, prospective understanding uses a constructive method. It is oriented toward the future, inviting speculation and valuing subjectivity. 'The constructive standpoint asks how, out of this present psyche, a bridge can be built into its own future' (Jung 1914: par. 399). Jung never denied the importance of reconstructing the past, but made the comment: 'To understand the psyche causally is to understand only one half of it' (Jung 1914: par. 398). Both ways of understanding are essential: 'The psyche at any given moment is on the one hand the result and culmination of all that has been and on the other a symbolic expression of all that is to be' (Jung 1914: par. 405). From the beginning, the passion to *understand* the meaning of the symbol was an essential part of active imagination.

Confrontation with the unconscious (1912–1919)

Jung's book *Symbols of Transformation* (1912) proposed a broader, more inclusive concept of libido than Freud could accept and with its publication, their friendship and collaboration came to an end. Following the break with Freud, Jung became uncertain and disoriented, with fearful and lethargic moods that threatened to overwhelm him. Seeking to discover the cause of his inner crisis, he went over all the details of his entire life, twice, with particular attention to early memories. But he could find no rational explanation and no relief. Finally, faced with a desperate situation and not knowing what else to do, he made the conscious decision to turn his attention toward and to be guided by the images and impulses of the unconscious. In the following passage, Jung tells the story of how he was led to recapitulate the symbolic play of childhood, and how the process took him to the emotional core of one of his deepest complexes.

The first thing that came to the surface was a childhood memory from perhaps my tenth or eleventh year. At that time I had a spell of playing passionately with building blocks. I distinctly recalled how I had built little houses and castles, using bottles to form the sides of the gates and vaults. Somewhat later I had used ordinary stones, with mud for mortar. These structures had fascinated me for a long time. To my astonishment, this memory was accompanied by a good deal of emotion. 'Aha,' I said to myself, 'there is still life in these things. The small boy is still around, and possesses a creative life which I lack. But how can I make my way to it?' For as a grown man it seemed impossible to me that I should be able to bridge the distance from the present back to my eleventh year. Yet if I wanted to re-establish contact with that period, I had no choice but to return to it and take up once more that child's life with his childish games. This moment was a turning point in my fate, but I gave in only after endless resistances and with a sense of resignation. For it was a painfully humiliating experience to realize that there was nothing to be done except play childish games.

Nevertheless, I began accumulating suitable stones, gathering them partly from the lake shore and partly from the water. And I started building: cottages, a castle, a whole village. The church was still missing, so I made a square building with a hexagonal drum on top of it, and a dome. A church also requires an altar, but I hesitated to build that.

Preoccupied with the question of how I could approach this task, I was walking along the lake as usual one day, picking stones out of the gravel on the shore. Suddenly I caught sight of a red stone, a four-sided pyramid about an inch and a half high. It was a fragment of stone which had been polished into this shape by the action of the water – a pure product of chance. I knew at once: this was the altar! I placed it in the middle under the dome, and as I did so, I recalled the underground phallus of my childhood dream.

(Jung 1961/1965: 173–174)

While Jung's building game took him back to his years as a schoolboy, the dream he recalled took him still further back to early childhood when he had a terrifying nightmare about a cannibalistic, phallic God in an underground temple. The dream came around a troubled time when the little boy began to associate Lord Jesus with funerals and death. Overwhelmed with fears, he could no longer find comfort in his prayers and he did not feel free to tell anyone about his anxious ruminations. Long after his nightmare, the terrifying God-image continued to come to mind: 'Whenever anyone spoke too emphatically about Lord Jesus . . . I would think of his underground counterpart, a frightful revelation which had been accorded me without my seeking it' (Jung 1961/1965: 13).

Jung's extraordinarily sophisticated childhood dream haunted him for years, but was then buried and forgotten (Jung 1961/1965: 11–15). Through the process of symbolic play, he remembered and gained a mature understanding of it. It is remarkable to see that just as his early trauma reflected a religious problem in the family atmosphere, so, he was directed from within to discover and develop a school of psychology that offered a way to approach the psyche with a religious attitude. Reflecting on the meaning of his childhood nightmare, he wrote in his memoirs:

Who spoke to me then? Who talked of problems far beyond my knowledge? Who brought the Above and Below together, and laid the foundation for everything that was to fill the second half of my life with stormiest passion? Who but that alien guest who came both from above and from below?

Through this childhood dream I was initiated into the secrets of the earth. What happened then was a kind of burial in the earth, and many years were to pass before I came out again. Today I know that it happened in order to bring the greatest possible amount of light into the darkness. My intellectual life had its unconscious beginnings at that time.

(Jung 1961/1965: 15)

After retrieving his childhood nightmare, Jung's fears subsided and his energy returned. However, a new kind of inner pressure replaced the fears. He opened himself, then, to a long series of fantasies, visions and dreams that flowed in an incessant stream and preoccupied him for years. He wrote them down as carefully as possible. He also drew and painted them (Jung 1961/1965: 170–199, 1925: 40–64 and 88–99, 1912/forthcoming).

In 1916, Jung brought forth some of the first fruits of his ongoing confrontation with the unconscious. *Seven Sermons to the Dead* is not a professional paper, rather it is an example of Jung's own active imagination. It reads as if an ancient Gnostic teacher speaks through Jung's pen. This passionate, rhythmic, paradoxical work contains the seeds that developed eventually into Jung's analytical psychology. At first, it was published anonymously as a booklet that he occasionally gave to friends. Toward the end of his life, he consented to have it published as an appendix to his memoirs (Jung 1961/1965: 378–390). In 1916 he also wrote 'The transcendent function' (1916/1957, 1916/1958), a significant and original work that remained unpublished for many years. Written with the rushing raw energy of a first draft, it presents a multidimensional introduction to his new method.

Before returning to his ideas on active imagination, there is a touching story about Jung as father, reported by Franz, his third-born child and only son. Franz was born in 1908, so he was only 4 or 5 years old when Jung began playing his building game on the shore of the lake by the family home. Many years later when Franz Jung was himself an elder, Swiss analyst Renate Oppikofer asked him whether he remembered anything about the years of his father's 'Confrontation with the unconscious'. Franz replied that he was quite young back then and did not remember much. But he did remember a time when he and his father often played a building game together by the side of the lake. For Franz, the building game was a simple memory of father and son playing together. When C.G. Jung died in 1961 and Franz read his father's memoirs, he realised – for the first time – the game was not only about father and son at play (Renate Oppikofer, personal communication, 1995). I am grateful for her permission to tell this story because it offers a privileged insight into Jung as father. In light of this story, it seems especially fitting that Franz Jung's interest in building never came to an end, as he became a gifted architect.

Jung's ideas on active imagination (1916–1961)

Emotions

Jung never changed his early views about the significance of the emotions. But over the years his interest shifted gradually from affect toward his developing theory of archetype. The shift may well have begun in the midst of his experiments in self-healing when he realised it was possible to 'translate' his own troublesome emotions and moods into symbolic images.

To the extent that I managed to translate the emotions into images –
that is to say, to find the images which were concealed in the emotion –
I was inwardly calmed and reassured. Had I left those images hidden in
the emotions, I might have succeeded in splitting them off but in that
case I would inexorably have fallen into a neurosis and so been
ultimately destroyed by them anyhow. As a result of my experiment I
learned how helpful it can be, from the therapeutic point of view, to
find the particular images which lie behind emotions.

(Jung 1961/1965: 177)

It is in the transformation from affect to image that active imagination
aligns itself with the natural healing function of the imagination. In place of
raw affect, the imagination creates symbolic images and stories that express
the mood or emotion in a way that may be more bearable. This completely
natural process occurs in the spontaneous symbolic play of children and it
guides the continuing process of psychological development. Certain
meditative traditions as well as active imagination, seem to foster a similar
kind of inner development. It involves a shift from a state of being flooded
by affect, toward a new symbolic perspective. Jung describes the development of such a new point of view in his 'Commentary on *The Secret of the
Golden Flower*':

What on a lower level had led to the wildest conflicts and to panicky
outbursts of emotions, from the higher level of personality now looked
like a storm in the valley seen from the mountain top. This does not
mean that the storm is robbed of its reality, but instead of being in it
one is above it. But since in a psychic sense, we are both valley and
mountain, it might seem a vain illusion to deem oneself beyond what is
human. One certainly does feel the affect and is shaken and tormented
by it, yet at the same time one is aware of a higher consciousness
looking on which prevents one from becoming identical with the affect.

(Jung 1929: par. 17)

Attitudes toward fantasy

Ever since his early essay on 'Two kinds of thinking' (1912), Jung remained
engaged with questions about the nature of fantasy thinking, directed
thinking and the dynamic relationship between them. Over the years, he
described also active and passive attitudes toward fantasy: 'It all depends
on the attitude the patient takes toward his fantasies' (Jung 1913/1955:
par. 417).

Whereas passive fantasy not infrequently bears a morbid stamp or at
least shows some trace of abnormality, active fantasy is one of the

highest forms of psychic activity. For here the conscious and the unconscious personality of the subject flow together into a common product in which both are united.

(Jung 1921: par. 714)

As Jung defines active fantasy, it sounds very close to a dialectical relationship between fantasy thinking and directed thinking. Each potentiates the other. Such a union of conscious and unconscious is essential in play, creativity and active imagination.

Starting points of active imagination

Active imagination usually begins with a conflicted, depressed or disturbed state of mind. 'In the intensity of the emotional disturbance itself lies the value, the energy . . . to remedy the state of reduced adaptation' (Jung 1916/ 1958: par. 166). The idea is to begin with the raw material of the unconscious, for example, affect, image, impulse. Everyone gets at it in his or her own way. Some have the capacity to open directly to the inner world of visual and auditory images. Others may turn toward the inner world of bodily felt sensations, movement impulses and psychosomatic symptoms. Some choose (or are chosen by) a poster, photo, painting or other picture or object and concentrate on it until it comes alive. With others, the inner voice is heard, more or less distinctly. People attend inwardly in different ways to discover their own points of departure.

> Take the unconscious in one of its handiest forms, say a spontaneous fantasy, a dream, an irrational mood, an affect, or something of the kind, and operate with it. Give it your special attention, concentrate on it, and observe the alterations.
>
> (Jung 1955: par. 49)

> He must make the emotional state the basis or starting point of the procedure. He must make himself as conscious as possible of the mood he is in, sinking himself in it without reserve and noting down on paper all the fantasies and other associations that come up. Fantasy must be allowed the freest possible play, yet not in such a manner that it leaves the orbit of its object, namely the affect . . . The whole procedure is a kind of enrichment and clarification of the affect.
>
> (Jung 1916/1958: par. 167)

Stages of active imagination

The method has two parts. The first part is *letting the unconscious come up*. The second part is *coming to terms with the unconscious*. The process is sequential by nature, yet there may be times when the stages fluctuate back and forth, or both may occur simultaneously. For example, it is possible to open to the unconscious and give free rein to fantasy, while at the same time maintaining an active, self-reflective point of view. Since everyone is unique, there are many ways to approach the process. Sometimes a single experience includes both stages. Other times, it takes many years: 'It has taken me virtually forty-five years to distill within the vessel of my scientific work the things I experienced and wrote down at that time . . . It was the *prima materia* for a lifetime's work' (Jung 1961/1965: 199).

Closely related to the stages, but not identical with them are two tendencies that arise as a natural part of the process. One is the aesthetic tendency toward artistic elaboration. The other is the scientific tendency toward intellectual understanding.

It hardly seems possible for the one to exist without the other, though it sometimes does happen in practice: the creative urge seizes possession of the object at the cost of its meaning, or the urge to understand overrides the necessity of giving it form. The unconscious contents want first of all to be seen clearly, which can only be done by giving them shape, and to be judged only when everything they have to say is tangibly present.

(Jung 1916/1958: par. 179)

Forms of active imagination

In 1916, Jung had not yet developed his theory of psychological types. However, as he studied the ways spontaneous fantasies arise, he seemed to describe a typology of the senses. 'Visual types should concentrate on the expectation that an inner image will be produced . . . Audio verbal types usually hear inner words, perhaps mere fragments of apparently meaningless sentences to begin with' (Jung 1916/1958: par. 170). There are those also whose 'hands have the knack of giving expression to the unconscious' as well as those who are able to 'express the unconscious by means of bodily movement' (Jung 1916/1958: par. 171). In addition to developing the capacity to produce visual, auditory and motor fantasies, Jung advised the reader to note everything down in writing, as well as to make drawings. In this earliest paper he spoke also of automatic writing and work with plastic materials.

Jung described the powerful therapeutic effect of his building game in his 1925 seminar and again in his memoirs. Although 'building game' and 'symbolic play' are not specifically named in his essays on active imagination, it seems obvious that terms such as ritual, dramatic enactment, and symbolic enactment embrace many forms of symbolic expression.

Although Jung used many synonyms and other names to describe them, the actual expressive forms of active imagination did not change much over the years. The same forms Jung described in 1916 appear and reappear in later writings.

> And so they begin to draw, to paint, or to shape their images plastically, and women sometimes do weaving. I have even had one or two women who danced their unconscious figures. Of course, they can also be expressed in writing.
>
> (Jung 1935: par. 400)

> I therefore took up a dream-image or an association of the patient's, and, with this as a point of departure, set him the task of elaborating or developing his theme by giving free rein to his fantasy. This, according to individual taste and talent, could be done in any number of ways, dramatic, dialectic, visual, acoustic, or in the form of dancing, painting, drawing, or modeling.
>
> (Jung 1947: par. 400)

Late in life, Jung speculated about musical composition as active imagination:

> A musical configuration might also be possible provided that it were really composed and written down. Though I have never met a case of this kind, Bach's *Art of Fugue* would seem to offer an example, just as the representation of the archetypes is a basic feature of Wagner's music.
>
> (Jung 1955: par. 754)

Dangers

Fantasy images are not in themselves pathological, but identification with them can be problematic.

> The characteristic feature of a pathological reaction is, above all, *identification with the archetype*. This produces a sort of inflation and possession by the emergent contents, so that they pour out in a torrent which no therapy can stop. Identification can, in favourable cases, sometimes pass off as a more or less harmless inflation. But in all cases, identification with the unconscious brings a weakening of consciousness, and herein lies the danger. You do not 'make' an identification, you do not 'identify yourself', but you experience your identity with the archetype in an unconscious way and so are possessed by it. Hence in

more difficult cases it is far more necessary to strengthen and consolidate the ego than to understand and assimilate the products of the unconscious.

(Jung 1933/1950: par. 621)

The analyst

Jung's writings on active imagination include his ideas on the role of the analyst, and descriptions of how he worked. He was non-directive in the sense that he distrusted dogmatic ideas and preferred to ask open-ended questions. At the same time he engaged through all of the age-old cultural forms. In addition to creative formulation through the arts and the scientific passion to understand, Jung engaged through two kinds of relationship – intrapsychic and interpersonal. Although I touch on each separately, the practice of analysis involves an integrative process of blending and interweaving, drawing from the rich resources of human culture from a self-reflective, psychological point of view.

The arts

When appreciating the expressive movements of the body, or the vivid colours and shapes that bring a painting to life, or when using poetic metaphor to describe any number of events, it is obvious that Jung's aesthetic imagination mirrored, affirmed and amplified that of his patients. Involved as both mentor and as highly differentiated witness, Jung's intention was not as much about the creation of art, as it was 'the living effect upon the patient himself' (1931: par. 104).

Understanding

For Jung, the contents that emerge in active imagination require understanding, but they do not require interpretation: 'Image and meaning are identical, and as the first takes shape, so the latter becomes clear. Actually, the pattern needs no interpretation; it portrays its own meaning' (Jung 1947: par. 402). His method of symbolic amplification is aligned with the natural process of parallel association, inviting exploration of questions around origins, meaning and purpose.

Encounter and dialogue with the gods

Inner-directed relationship seeks direct experience of the Self. In the deepest sense, the analyst brings conscious and unconscious together through ongoing intrapsychic work. In addition, Jung taught certain analysands to open to, engage with, and differentiate from the ongoing stream of visions in the mind's eye and inner voices.

Relationship

Although active imagination is usually done alone, the therapeutic relationship serves as a container of this process. The analyst 'mediates the transcendent function for the patient' (Jung 1916/1958: par. 146), serving at various times as mentor, scholar and participant-witness. Toward the end of his life, Jung made a brief but significant addition to his 1916 essay, linking active imagination to transference enactments that may emerge or erupt in the analytic hour. Here he points toward an enlargement of active imagination to include work with the dynamics of the transference.

> In most cases a long conflict will have to be borne, demanding sacrifices from both sides. Such a rapprochement could just as well take place between patient and analyst, the role of the devil's advocate easily falling to the latter.
>
> (Jung 1916/1958: par. 186)

DEFINITIONS

It is not a simple thing to define active imagination because Jung used many different names to describe it. Some of the terms are clear, while others are fluid, embracing more than one meaning. At first he called it the transcendent function (1916/1957, 1916/1958). Then for at least nineteen years, Jung and his associates used a variety of names to describe the method. Some names referred to a particular form, for example, 'the picture method' is about drawing or painting symbolic pictures. Other names pointed to meditative procedures, ways to open toward the inner world of hypnagogic images, for example, 'active fantasy', 'active phantasying' and 'visioning'. Further names include technique of the descent, technique of introversion, introspection, technique of differentiation and exercises. It was not until 1935 that Jung used the term 'active imagination' for the first time in public, when he delivered the Tavistock Lectures in London.

Jung's transcendent function is a dynamic, multifaceted concept that encompasses method, function and process. It includes also the final result (Dehing 1993).

> The whole process is called the 'transcendent function'. It is a process and a method at the same time. The production of unconscious compensations is a spontaneous *process*; the conscious realization is a *method*. The function is called 'transcendent' because it facilitates the

transition from one psychic condition to another by means of the mutual confrontation of opposites.

(Jung 1939/1954: par. 780)

While the term 'transcendent function' refers to method, function and more, active imagination generally refers to the method alone. Even so, it is clear the term 'active imagination' is an analytical *method* (active imagination) based on the underlying image-producing *function* of the psyche. Both the transcendent function and the function of the imagination are dynamic, creative, complex, integrative functions that shape and transform the living symbol. For Barbara Hannah (1953), the transcendent function is one of Jung's early ideas that was incorporated gradually into his developing concept of the archetype of unity, the Self.

For Gerhard Adler (1948: 56), active imagination is 'a definite attitude toward the contents of the unconscious, whereby we seek to isolate them and thus observe their autonomous development'. For Barbara Hannah (1953: 38), active imagination can be called 'a scientific form of meditation'. For Rix Weaver:

One of Jung's discoveries was the autonomous creative activity of the unconscious, an activity which revealed itself as having what might be termed a myth-forming propensity. He then found that this tendency could be used analytically, and he named the process active imagination.

(Weaver 1973/1991: 2)

For Andrew Samuels (1985: 12), 'active imagination is a channel for "messages" from the unconscious by any means; for example, by media such as painting, modelling or writing'. For Verena Kast (1991: 161), active imagination is 'the process by which a strong but flexible ego complex allows intangible unconscious material (complexes, dreams, and images) to be expressed in a tangible product such as painting, poetry, or song'. For Murray Stein (2000), active imagination is one of the 'four pillars of analytical psychology'. For Sam Naifeh (personal communication, 2000), 'active imagination defines analysis'.

JUNGIANS AND POST-JUNGIANS ON ACTIVE IMAGINATION

Since Jung's active imagination is based on a natural, creative healing process, it has, inevitably, made its way into the cultural collective where it is alive, well, fruitful and multiplying. In addition to the Jungian literature, there is the growing body of literature in the expressive arts therapies and resurgence of attention to and development of the vast world literature on meditative and contemplative traditions.

Among Jungian authors, I look at four of the major innovations: Joseph Henderson's concept of the cultural unconscious, Louis Stewart's theory of affect and archetype, Dorothy Davidson's transference as active imagination and Dora Kalff's Sandplay.

The abundance of significant developments in active imagination presents an embarrassment of riches. A section of a chapter, or even a full chapter or more, cannot do justice to generations of colleagues who have made and continue to make significant contributions.

Criticisms by Michael Fordham and Elie Humbert bring this section to a close.

Innovations and developments

Cultural unconscious

Joseph Henderson introduced the concept of the cultural unconscious in 1962. A mediating layer between the personal and primordial unconscious, the cultural unconscious is a latent function. As inherent potential is mirrored by certain powerful influences from the environment (via family, education and the *zeitgeist*), the cultural unconscious is awakened and activated.

> Such an educational experience does not necessarily come as an inspiration (though it may originate that way) but is built up through many exposures to cultural canons of taste, of moral principles, of social custom, and of religious symbolism. And it is built upon certain influences from the family life in which an important part of these canons have been passed on from previous generations. Accordingly much of what has been called 'personal unconscious' is not personal at all but that part of the collective culture pattern transmitted through our environment before we were able to affirm its validity for ego consciousness.
>
> (Henderson 1962: 8–9)

Four cultural attitudes, the aesthetic, religious, philosophic and social are organised around a fifth central, self-reflective psychological attitude. Characterising the four traditional cultural attitudes, he describes 'the ethical consistency of a social attitude, the logic of a philosophical attitude, the transcendent nature of a religious attitude . . . the sensuous irrationality of the aesthetic attitude' (Henderson 1984: 49).

As intrinsic ways to experience the life of the spirit, the cultural attitudes may be understood also as intrinsic forms or categories of the imagination.

Affect and archetype

Louis Stewart's (1985–1986) theoretical contribution reframes and extends certain Jungian ideas, offering a deeper, more differentiated understanding of both the nature of the psyche and active imagination. From work with children, Stewart came to understand joy and interest as affects of libido, the life instinct. His hypothesis is that all of the higher functions of the psyche – including the ego functions and the symbolic cultural attitudes – have evolved from joy and interest as they modulate and transform the affects of crisis and survival. Just as Joy energises play and imagination, so, the affect Interest energises curiosity and exploration. The crisis affects then, provide *prima materia* for the natural process of psychological/ symbolic development.

Seeking to identify what the universal dynamisms might be that express the primal self and at the same time shape its development, Stewart proposes the terms Ritual, Rhythm, Reason and Relationship, as a kind of mnemonic device. 'These are the irreducible elements, respectively, of Religion, Art, Philosophy and Society. And . . . these are the Categories of Imagination, and appear as Henderson's Cultural Attitudes, the Religious, the Aesthetic, the Philosophic and the Social' (L.H. Stewart 1987: 138–139). His understanding of affects as primal sources of psychic energy and the archetypal imagination, provides an elegant and useful perspective. In the deepest sense, active imagination is the central, self-reflective, psychological attitude drawing from the creative resources of human culture: the religious (dialogue with the god within), the aesthetic (expressive arts), the philosophic/ scientific (understanding the meaning of the symbols) and the social (work with dynamics of the mutual transference).

Affect and archetype involves a tale of two brothers in closely related fields. Charles Stewart makes an outstanding contribution in *The Symbolic Impetus: How Creative Fantasy Motivates Development* (C.T. Stewart 2001). His systematic study looks at psychological and symbolic development throughout infancy, childhood and adolescence from the perspectives of normal development, stage-specific disturbances and corresponding issues in psychotherapy. Identifying the typical fantasies of each stage, he investigates the symbols that shape development and healing.

Further contributions include Karlyn Ward (1992) on cross-cultural exploration of music, affect and imagery, Anita Greene (2001) on body, mind and consciousness, and my own work on sources in the psyche of expressive movement (Chodorow 1991, 2000).

Transference as a form of active imagination

Dorothy Davidson came to her important idea as she was trying to understand certain countertransference reactions. As she felt herself being pulled 'willy-nilly' into a drama not of her choosing, she was led eventually to see that much of analysis may involve enactment of a patient's 'hitherto unconscious drama' (1966: 135). As the analyst begins to understand the symbolic nature of the vital emerging dramatic enactment, something may shift. The patient does not need pre-mature interpretation, rather the patient needs the analyst's empathic understanding of the subtle and complex dynamics in the emotional atmosphere between them. This kind of relationship at a pre-verbal level is 'the soil out of which true interpretations grow' (Davidson 1966: 143). 'It is in this sense that I think a successful analysis can be thought of as a lived-through active imagination' (Davidson 1966: 135).

Recognising the significance of transference as active imagination, Andrew Samuels (1985) looks at the contribution of Davidson (1966) and also Schwartz-Salant (1982), coining the term 'medial practitioners' to describe analytical psychologists whose work radiates a 'desire to bridge the divide that has grown up between the classical-symbolic-synthetic approach and that of interactional dialectic' (Samuels 1985: 204). Continuing developments in this area include the contributions of Norah Moore (1975, 1986) and Sheila Powell (1985). Building on the idea that the association process is the basic element in all analytic technique (Zinkin 1969; Charlton 1986), Joe Cambray (2001) makes a splendid contribution as he develops symbolic enactment and symbolic amplification, with special attention to the inner experience of the analyst and the therapeutic relationship.

Sandplay

Dora Kalff, a Swiss analyst who worked with children, had her training analysis with Jung and completed studies at the Jung Institute, Zurich in 1955. When Jung encouraged her to develop a method of symbolic play for child therapy, she travelled to London to study Margaret Lowenfeld's 'World Technique' (Lowenfeld 1939, 1979). Jung knew about Lowenfeld's work from a 1937 congress in Paris and it seems natural to imagine he recognised in Lowenfeld's technique his own early discovery of the healing function of symbolic play. Lowenfeld developed her technique from the sandbox, floor and other building games children have played everywhere, from earliest times. Materials consist of a shallow tray filled with sand and a collection of hundreds of miniature human, animal and mythic figures, houses, vehicles, castles, shells, stones, trees and other images, everything needed to create a miniature world. Adapting Lowenfeld's technique to Jungian analysis, Kalff coined the term Sandplay. For Kalff, more important than verbal interpretation is creating an atmosphere she called 'a free and sheltered space' (1980: 29).

In addition to showing the process of Sandplay in a marvellous documentary film made by Peter Amman (1972) and writing a book, Kalff

(1980) presented her work throughout Europe, the United States and Japan. In 1982, the International Society of Sandplay Therapists (ISST) was formed and in the years that followed, affiliate groups were formed in many parts of the world.

An excellent historical review, with a comprehensive English language bibliography through 1994, can be found in the book *Sandplay: Past, Present and Future* (Mitchell and Friedman 1994). An impressive body of literature continues to evolve through the beautifully written and illustrated *Journal of Sandplay Therapy* (www.sandplayusa.org) as well as other publications.

Further developments of active imagination

Marie-Louise von Franz (1980) was the first to suggest a subdivision of Jung's two stages of active imagination. She proposed: empty the mind; let a fantasy image arise; give it some form of expression; reaction by the ego, ethical confrontation; and take it into life, live it. Others have proposed slightly different fourfold stages (Dallett 1982; Johnson 1986). Considering these similar yet at the same time unique perspectives on active imagination seems to point toward a natural dynamic process that invites each person to discover their own way.

Jungian contributions to the healing power of the arts offer rich resources. Anthony Stevens (1986) tells the story of Withymead, a therapeutic community in the United Kingdom. A video by Carolyn Grant Fay (1996) shows her multifaceted approach to active imagination. Essays on music as a way to express the emotions and the imagination include Patricia Skar (1997), Margaret Tilly (1982), Karlyn Ward (1992) and Patricia Warming (1992). Alfred Wolfsohn, a shell-shocked veteran of the First World War, made an original contribution using the voice as therapy (Newham 1992). Joseph Henderson and Dyane Sherwood (2003) relate a series of illuminated alchemical paintings to creative development in life and analysis.

Studies by Jungian authors on the therapeutic value of art include Joseph Henderson (1973), Edith Wallace (1975), Joy Schaverien (1992), Mary Dougherty (1998), Richard Stein (1992), Kate Donohue (2001) and many others. Naomi Lowinsky's gift to active imagination is shaped by the rhythm and rhythmic harmony of poetry (1999). John Allan (1988) and Helmut Barz (1993) are among those who use drama and dramatic enactment as active imagination. The significant contributions of Shaun McNiff, an art therapist who works from a Jungian perspective, include his development of art-based research (McNiff 1998).

Active imagination cannot be separated from its affective origins expressed through visual, auditory, motor and other and somatosensory images. Mary Watkins (1976), Robert Bosnak (1986), Robin van Löben Sels

(2003), Carol McRae (1997), Ruth Fry (1974) and Jeanne Achterberg (1985) as well as Robert Assagioli (1965) are among those who have made significant contributions toward experiencing and understanding the imaginal landscape and its inhabitants. A beautifully written study by Mary Lynn Kittelson (1996) approaches the realm of auditory imagery from multiple perspectives. The writings and teachings of Marion Woodman are all about psyche's home in the body and the healing of early trauma. Anita Greene's significant contributions include 'Embodied active imagination' (2003). Arny Mindell's Process Oriented Psychotherapy can be understood as a development of active imagination applied in diverse fields of study (Mindell 1985).

As far back as 1916, Jung and his associates understood bodily movement as a natural way to express and transform unconscious contents. In the following passage, Tina Keller describes her first experience of this in an analytic hour with Toni Wolff in Zurich, perhaps around 1924:

> When I was in analysis with Miss Toni Wolff, I often had the feeling that something in me hidden deep inside wanted to express itself; but I also knew that this 'something' had no words. As we were looking for another means of expression, I suddenly had the idea: 'I could dance it.' Miss Wolff encouraged me to try. The body sensation I felt was oppression, the image came that I was inside a stone and had to release myself from it to emerge as a separate, self-standing individual. The movements that grew out of the body sensations had the goal of my liberation from the stone just as the image had. It took a good deal of the hour. After a painful effort I stood there, liberated. This very freeing event was much more potent than the hours in which we only talked. This was a 'psychodrama' of an inner happening or that which Jung had named 'active imagination'. Only here it was the body that took the active part.
>
> (Keller 1972: 22, translated by R. Oppikofer)

In the 1950s, pioneer dance therapist Mary Starks Whitehouse developed dance movement as active imagination and today it is a branch of dance therapy as well as a form of active imagination in analysis (Whitehouse 1954–1979; Chodorow 1974–1991). The process involves a mover, a witness, and the dynamics of their relationship (J. Adler 1972–1994; Wyman-McGinty 1998, 2002). In addition to being a valuable form of active imagination in analysis, the mover–witness relationship offers a powerful tool for studying the dialectic of expressive movement that is part of every depth psychological relationship. Jungian analysts Woodman (1982), Greene (2003), Wyman-McGinty (2002), Spitzer (2003), Gerson (2005), Lorentz (1998), as well as Fay (1996), Adorisio (2005), Stromsted (2001) and others continue a process of creative development. A quarterly publication entitled

A Moving Journal: Ongoing Expressions of Authentic Movement (www.movingjournal.org) reports on many aspects of this evolving work.

Arts in psychotherapy

All the creative art therapies can trace their roots to Jung's early contribution. Art therapy, music therapy, dance therapy, drama therapy and poetry therapy emerged in the United States as separate professions in the 1960s and 1970s. Both similar to and distinct from drama therapy, psychodrama is based mainly on the contribution of Jacob Moreno. Each field has its own professional association(s), with formal standards of professional preparation and ethical practice; each offers conferences, books and journal(s) designed to meet the needs of clinicians, researchers and educators. In recent decades, many of the most vital developments are global, with associations, graduate-level training programmes, and publications in many parts of the world. Professional education is usually grounded in studies and practice of a particular form, yet all of the arts interweave in a natural way with each other, as well as with verbal psychotherapy. The International Expressive Arts Therapy Association (IEATA) founded in 1994 does not specialise, rather it is based on an integrative approach to the arts.

Hillman raises and reflects on the question:

> What actually goes on when a patient begins to dance, to choreograph or paint his or her state of soul, to speak aloud freely in a dramatic tirade or a poetic soliloquy, to sculpt it in clay or lay it out in a collage . . . I want to ask about the 'it' that is being presented, expressed, shown, or formed by means of these various arts. Clearly, the 'it' is an emotion, an emotionally tinged state of soul.
> (Hillman 1960/1992: x)

> What else is there besides the art product, the patient, and the emotion? Imagination. Since art therapy activates imagination and allows it to materialize – that is, enter the world via the emotions of the patient – therapy by means of the arts must take precedence over all other kinds.
> (Hillman 1960/1992: xiv)

Criticisms

In a 1956 article and again in 1958, Fordham tried to differentiate between active imagination and imaginative activity. He did not present Jung's view of imaginative activity as the matrix out of which play, dreams, fantasy, active imagination and creative imagination emerge, rather, Fordham presented his own transferential perspective: 'Imaginative activity is usually related to what the patient thinks is required of him or is somewhere an attempt to interest, fascinate, or otherwise manipulate the analyst's affects' (Fordham 1958: 78). Due to the transference, 'so long as a person is a patient we should refer to active imagination only in a qualified sense' (Fordham 1958: 80). As I understand Fordham, active imagination and transferential material are seldom compatible. Based on his ideas, Fordham evaluated the products of active imagination described in a number of early essays by analyst colleagues and concluded that many, if not most of the works presented, were examples of imaginative activity, not active imagination.

Elie Humbert (1971) offered a critical essay of an entirely different nature, raising essential questions about the curious fate of active imagination:

> The form of psychological work called active imagination occupied a considerable place in Jung's life and in the lives of most of his students. Today this seems to be no longer the case. The method is little used and is presented only occasionally in terms which render it either banal or esoteric. Can it be, one may ask, that the school of psychology which calls itself Jungian is in this way manifesting a profound resistance to the unconscious?
>
> (Humbert 1971: 101)

CURRENT STATUS AND FUTURE DEVELOPMENT

For those who seek a comprehensive analytical method of psychotherapy, active imagination offers a way to hold and honor and imagine and think about all the ways different analysts and analysands do their work. I am reminded that it may be human nature to travel long distances seeking the Bluebird of Happiness, only to discover that it is found in one's own back yard.

Active imagination is more than a specific meditative procedure or expressive technique. In the deepest sense, it is the central, self-reflective psychological attitude that draws from all of the symbolic cultural attitudes described by Joseph Henderson (1984): the religious, the aesthetic, the scientific/philosophic and the social:

> I can imagine a group of future analysts teaching a new appreciation of old cultural attitudes not because they set out to do this on purpose in any missionarizing spirit but because this teaching would be an inevitable result of their way of working with their patients.
>
> (Henderson 1962: 14)

In analysis, we are engaged with all of the intrinsic categories of the imagination. Depending on tastes and talents, inclinations and typology, different forms of the imagination will be prominent in the work of different individuals.

Given the nature of the psyche, it seems inevitable that analysis invites the religious imagination, *imagination of the mysteries* expressed as visions in the mind's eye, inner voices and intrapsychic work that develops toward an ongoing dialogue with the god or gods within.

Similarly, analysis invites the aesthetic imagination, *imagination of beauty* expressed through rhythm and rhythmic harmony. Fantasies may be expressed through drawing, painting, sculpting, dance, music, dramatic enactment, poetry and Sandplay, as well as tapestries, stories and many other forms, according to individual nature and preferences.

We engage also through the philosophic, scientific, *scholarly imagination*. Jung's method of symbolic amplification is built upon the natural process of parallel association that draws in part from the rich resources of human knowledge including child development, animal studies, cultural history, mythology and more. In analysis, *scholarly imagination* is all about exploring and understanding the symbol in its personal, cultural and archetypal dimensions.

Analysis is contained by and interwoven with the social imagination, the *imagination of relationship*, empathic imagination and work with the dynamics of the transference and countertransference. Jung referred to the transference as active imagination when he wrote: 'The inner dialogue could just as well take place between patient and analyst' (1916/1958: par. 186).

Finally, analysis leads, inevitably, toward the central, self-reflective *psychological imagination*, which is a quintessence of the other four. By quintessence, I mean that the natural way to create and re-create the personality is through the symbolic cultural attitudes (religious, aesthetic, philosophical, social), shaped by the age-old value inscribed at the Delphic Oracle: *Know Thyself*.

Acknowledgement

Material in this chapter was compiled and presented first as part of a forthcoming book by Joan Chodorow entitled *Active Imagination: Healing from Within* for the Carolyn and Ernest Fay Series in Analytical Psychology, edited by David Rosen, published by Texas A&M University Press.

Bibliography

Achterberg, J. (1985) *Imagery in Healing: Shamanism and Modern Medicine*. Boston, MA and London: Shambhala.
Adler, G. (1948) *Studies in Analytical Psychology*. New York: W.W. Norton.

Adler, J. (1972–1994) 'Janet Adler Papers', in P. Pallaro (ed.) (1999) *Authentic Movement: Essays by Mary Starks Whitehouse, Janet Adler and Joan Chodorow.* London: Jessica Kingsley.

Adorisio, A. (2005) 'Bellezza Orsini and creativity: images of body and soul from a sixteenth century prison'. *Spring,* 72 (special issue on Body and Soul honouring Marion Woodman): 281–297.

Allan, J. (1988) *Inscapes of the Child's World.* Dallas, TX: Spring.

Amman, P. (1972) *Sandspiel* (16 mm film), directed and produced by Peter Amman. Videotaped 1985, available from C.G. Jung Institute of Los Angeles, CA.

Amman, R. (1991) *Healing and Transformation in Sandplay.* La Salle, IL: Open Court.

Assagioli, R. (1965) *Psychosynthesis.* New York: Viking.

Barz, H. (1993) 'The transcendent function and psychodrama', in M.A. Mattoon (ed.) *The Transcendent Function.* Einsiedeln, Switzerland: Daimon Verlag.

Bosnak, R. (1986) *A Little Course in Dreams.* Boston, MA: Shambhala.

Bradway, K. and McCoard, B. (1997) *Sandplay: Silent Workshop of the Psyche.* London: Routledge.

Bradway, K., Signell, K., Stewart, C.T., Stewart, L.H. and Thompson, C. (1981) *Sandplay Studies: Origins, Theory, Practice.* San Francisco, CA: C.G. Jung Institute.

Cambray, J. (2001) 'Enactments and amplification'. *Journal of Analytical Psychology,* 46(2): 275–303.

Charlton, R.S. (1986) 'Free association and Jungian analytical technique'. *Journal of Analytical Psychology,* 31(2): 153–171.

Chodorow, J. (1974–1991) 'Joan Chodorow Papers', in P. Pallaro (ed.) (1999) *Authentic Movement: Essays by Mary Starks Whitehouse, Janet Adler and Joan Chodorow.* London: Jessica Kingsley.

—— (1991) *Dance Therapy and Depth Psychology: The Moving Imagination.* London: Routledge.

—— (2000) 'The moving imagination'. *American Journal of Dance Therapy,* 22(1): 5–27.

—— (2005) 'Multi-sensory imagination'. *Spring,* 72 (special issue on Body and Soul honouring Marion Woodman): 159–166.

Cwik, A. (1995) 'Active imagination: synthesis in analysis', in M. Stein (ed.) *Jungian Analysis,* 2nd edn. La Salle, IL: Open Court.

Dallett, J. (1982) 'Active imagination in practice', in M. Stein (ed.) *Jungian Analysis.* Peru, IL: Open Court.

Damasio, A. (1999) *The Feeling of What Happens.* New York: Harcourt.

Davidson, D. (1966) 'Transference as a form of active imagination'. *Journal of Analytical Psychology,* 11(2):135–146.

Dehing, J. (1993) 'The transcendent function: a critical re-evaluation', in M.A. Mattoon (ed.) *Proceedings of the Twelfth International Congress for Analytical Psychology.* Einsiedeln, Switzerland: Daimon Verlag.

Donohue, K. (2001) 'A transcendent journey through the motherline: a voyage with Helen Hardin, southwest artist'. *The Arts in Psychotherapy,* 28(1): 19–30.

Dougherty, M. (1998) 'Duccio's prayer', in M.A. Mattoon (ed.) *Proceedings of the Fourteenth International Congress for Analytical Psychology.* Einsiedeln, Switzerland: Daimon Verlag.

Douglas, C. (1993) *Translate this Darkness: The Life of Christiana Morgan.* New York: Simon and Schuster.

Ellenberger, H.F. (1970) *The Discovery of the Unconscious.* New York: Basic Books.

Fay, C.G. (1996) *At the Threshold: A Journey to the Sacred through the Integration of the Psychology of C.G. Jung and the Expressive Arts, with Carolyn Grant Fay* (videotape). Boston, MA: Bushy Theater.

Fordham, M. (1956) 'Active imagination and imaginative activity'. *Journal of Analytical Psychology,* 1(2): 207–208.

—— (1958) 'Problems of active imagination', in M. Fordham, *The Objective Psyche.* London: Routledge.

Fry, R.T. (1974) 'Teaching active imagination meditation', doctoral dissertation, Laurence University.

Gerson, J. (2005) 'Wounded instincts, weeping soul: working with embodied countertransference'. *Spring,* 72 (special issue on Body and Soul honouring Marion Woodman): 205–217.

Greene, A. (2001) 'Conscious mind – conscious body'. *Journal of Analytical Psychology,* 46(4): 565–590.

—— (2003) 'Embodied active imagination', in M.A. Mattoon (ed.) *Proceedings of the Fifteenth International Congress for Analytical Psychology.* Einsiedeln, Switzerland: Daimon Verlag.

Hannah, B. (1953) 'Some remarks on active imagination'. *Spring:* 38–58.

Henderson, J. (1962) 'The archetype of culture', in *The Archetype: Proceedings of the Second International Congress of Psychology, Zurich.* New York: S. Karger.

—— (1973) 'The picture method in Jungian psychotherapy'. *Art Psychotherapy,* 1: 135–140.

—— (1984) *Cultural Attitudes in Psychological Perspective.* Toronto: Inner City.

Henderson, J. and Sherwood, D. (2003) *Transformation of the Psyche: The Symbolic Alchemy of the Splendor Solis.* London: Routledge.

Hillman, J. (1960/1972/1992) *Emotion: A Comprehensive Phenomenology of Theories and their Meanings for Therapy.* Evanston, IL: Northwestern University Press.

Humbert, E. (1971) 'Active imagination: theory and practice'. *Spring:* 101–114.

Johnson, R.A. (1986) *Inner Work: Using Dreams and Active Imagination for Personal Growth.* San Francisco, CA: Harper and Row.

Jung, C.G. (1902) 'On the psychology and pathology of so-called occult phenomena', in *Collected Works* (*CW*) 1: pars. 1–165. Princeton, NJ: Princeton University Press, 1975.

—— (1904–1909) 'Studies in word association', in *CW* 2: pp. 1–580, pars. 1–1311. Princeton, NJ: Princeton University Press, 1973.

—— (1907) 'The psychology of Dementia Praecox', in *CW* 3: pp. 1–151, foreword and pars. 1–316. Princeton, NJ: Princeton University Press, 1960.

—— (1912) *Symbols of Transformation. CW* 5. Princeton, NJ: Princeton University Press, 1967.

—— (1912/forthcoming) *C.G. Jung's Red Book,* ed. S. Shamdasani. Zurich: Niedieck Linder, literary agent.

—— (1913/1955) 'The theory of psychoanalysis', in *CW* 4: 83–226, historical note, forewords and pars. 203–339. Princeton, NJ: Princeton University Press, 1961.

—— (1914) 'On psychological understanding', in *CW* 3: pars. 388–424. Princeton, NJ: Princeton University Press, 1960.

Jung, C.G. (1916/1925/1961) 'The seven sermons to the dead', trans. H.G. Baynes. Appendix V, in C.G. Jung, *Memories, Dreams, Reflections*. New York: Random House/Vintage, 1965.

—— (1916/1957) *The Transcendent Function* (booklet), trans. A.R. Pope. Zurich: privately printed for the Students' Association, C.G. Jung Institute.

—— (1916/1958) 'The transcendent function', in *CW* 8, 'Prefatory note' and pars. 131–193. Princeton, NJ: Princeton University Press, 1975.

—— (1921) *Psychological Types. CW* 6. Princeton, NJ: Princeton University Press, 1971/1974.

—— (1925) *Analytical Psychology: Notes on the Seminar Given in 1925*, ed. W. McGuire. Princeton, NJ: Princeton University Press, 1989.

—— (1928) 'The technique of differentiation between the ego and the figures of the unconscious', in *CW* 7: pars. 341–373. Princeton, NJ: Princeton University Press, 1953/1966/1975.

—— (1928–1930) *Dream Analysis: Notes of the Seminar*, ed. W. McGuire. Princeton, NJ: Princeton University Press, 1984.

—— (1929) 'Commentary on *The Secret of the Golden Flower*', in *CW* 13: pars. 17–45. Princeton, NJ: Princeton University Press, 1976.

—— (1930–1934) *The Visions Seminars*, ed. C. Douglas, vols 1 and 2. Princeton, NJ: Princeton University Press, 1997.

—— (1931) 'The aims of psychotherapy', in *CW* 16: pars. 66–113. Princeton, NJ: Princeton University Press, 2nd edn 1966, 3rd printing with corrections 1975.

—— (1933/1950) 'A study in the process of individuation', in *CW* 9i: pars. 525–626. Princeton, NJ: Princeton University Press, 2nd edn 1968.

—— (1935) 'The Tavistock Lectures', in *CW* 18: pars. 1–415. Princeton, NJ: Princeton University Press, 1976.

—— (1939/1954) 'Psychological commentary on *The Tibetan Book of the Great Liberation*', in *CW* 11: pars. 759–830. Princeton, NJ: Princeton University Press, 1958.

—— (1947) 'On the nature of the psyche', in *CW* 8: pars. 343–442. Princeton, NJ: Princeton University Press.

—— (1955) *Mysterium Coniunctionis. CW* 14. Princeton, NJ: Princeton University Press, 1974.

—— (1961/1965) *Memories, Dreams, Reflections*. New York: Random House/ Vintage.

—— (1975) *Letters, Volume Two, 1951–1961*. Princeton, NJ: Princeton University Press.

—— (1997) *Jung on Active Imagination: Key Essays Selected and Introduced by Joan Chodorow*. London: Routledge.

Kalff, D. (1980) *Sandplay*. Santa Monica, CA: Sigo Press.

Kast, V. (1991) *Joy, Inspiration, and Hope*. College Station, TX: Texas A&M University Press.

Keller, T. (1972) *Wege inneren Wachstums: Aus meinen erinnerungen an C.G. Jung*. Erlenbach, Switzerland: Bircher-Benner Verlag.

—— (1982) 'Beginnings of active imagination: analysis with C.G. Jung and Toni Wolff, 1915–1928', in J. Hillman (ed.) *Spring*: 279–294.

Kirsch, J. (1955) '"Journey to the Moon": a study in active imagination', in *Studien zur analytichen psychologie C.G. Jung*, Volume 1. Zurich: Rascher.

Kittelson, M.L. (1996) 'Auditory imagery: the acoustic vessel', in M.A. Mattoon (ed.) *Proceedings of the Thirteenth International Congress for Analytical Psychology, Zurich 1995*. Einsiedeln, Switzerland: Daimon Verlag.

Lorentz, E. (1998) 'Movement as active imagination', diploma thesis, Inter-Regional Society of Jungian Analysts.

Lowenfeld, M. (1939) 'The world pictures of children: a method of recording and studying them'. *British Journal of Medical Psychology*, 18: 65–101.

—— (1979) *The World Technique*. London: George Allen and Unwin.

Lowinsky, N. (1999) 'How Eurydice tells it'. *Psychological Perspectives*: 38: 86–104.

McNiff, S. (1998) *Art-Based Research*. London: Jessica Kingsley.

McRae, C. (1997) 'Learning to listen: a snake calls me to a shamanic path', in D. Sandner and S. Wong (eds) *The Sacred Heritage*. London: Routledge.

Middlekoop, P. (1985) *The Wise Old Man: Healing through Inner Images*. Boston, MA: Shambhala.

Miller, J. (2004) *The Transcendent Function: Jung's Model of Psychological Growth through Dialogue with the Unconscious*. Foreword by Joan Chodorow. Albany, NY: State University of New York Press.

Mindell, A. (1985) *Working with the Dreambody*. Boston, MA: Routledge and Kegan Paul.

Mitchell, R.R. and Friedman, H.S. (1994) *Sandplay: Past, Present, and Future*. London: Routledge.

Moore, N. (1975) 'The transcendent function and the forming ego'. *Journal of Analytical Psychology*, 20(2): 164–182.

—— (1986) 'Amplification, transference analysis and the analyst's inner process'. *Journal of Analytical Psychology*, 31(2): 113–133.

Naifeh, S. (1993) 'Experiencing the self'. *San Francisco Library Journal*, 12(1): 5–27.

—— (2001) 'Images in psychiatry: Carl Gustav Jung, M.D., 1875–1961'. *American Journal of Psychiatry*, 158(12): 1973.

Newham, P. (1992) 'Jung and Alfred Wolfsohn'. *Journal of Analytical Psychology*, 37: 323–336.

Perera, S.B. (1981) *Descent to the Goddess*. Toronto: Inner City.

Pert, C. (1997) *Molecules of Emotion*. New York: Scribner.

Powell, S. (1985) 'A bridge to understanding: the transcendent function in the analyst'. *Journal of Analytical Psychology*, 30: 29–45.

Robertson, R. (1998) 'Active imagination in practice'. *Gnosis Magazine*, Fall: 44–48.

Samuels, A. (1985) *Jung and the Post-Jungians*. London: Routledge.

Sandner, D. (1992) 'The transcendent function: response to Jef Dehing', in M.A. Mattoon (ed.) *Proceedings of the Twelfth International Congress for Analytical Psychology*. Einsiedeln, Switzerland: Daimon Verlag.

Schaverien, J. (1992) *The Revealing Image*. London: Routledge.

Schwartz-Salant, N. (1982) *Narcissism and Character Transformation*. Toronto: Inner City.

Searle, Y. and Streng, I. (eds) (2001) *Where Analysis Meets the Arts*. London: Karnac.

Shamdasani, S. (1990) 'A woman called Frank'. *Spring*, 50: 26–56.

Singer, J. (1972) 'Dreaming the dream onward: active imagination', in J. Singer (1994) *Boundaries of the Soul*. Garden City, NY: Doubleday.

Skar, P. (1997) 'Music and analysis, contrapuntal reflections', in *Proceedings of the Thirteenth International Congress for Analytical Psychology, Zurich 1995.* Einsiedeln, Switzerland: Daimon Verlag.

Spitzer, S. (2003) 'Embodied implicit memory', in *Proceedings of the Fifteenth International Congress for Analytical Psychology.* Einsiedeln, Switzerland: Daimon Verlag.

Stein, M. (1998) *Jung's Map of the Soul.* La Salle, IL: Open Court.

—— (2000) *Four Pillars of a Jungian Approach to Psychotherapy* (audiotapes #448, 2 cassettes). Atlanta, GA: Jung Society of Atlanta, www.jungatlanta.com

Stein, R. (1992) 'The transcendent function as revealed in unconscious drawings', unpublished paper with slides given at the Twelfth International Congress for Analytical Psychology, Chicago.

Stevens, A. (1986) *Withymead: A Jungian Community for the Healing Arts.* London: Coventure.

Stewart, C.T. (2001) *The Symbolic Impetus: How Creative Fantasy Motivates Development.* London: Free Association.

Stewart, L.H. (1985–1986) 'Work in progress: affect and archetype', in N. Schwartz-Salant and M. Stein (eds) *The Body in Analysis.* Wilmette, IL: Chiron.

—— (1987) 'Affect and archetype in analysis', in N. Schwartz-Salant and M. Stein (eds) *Archetypal Processes in Psychotherapy.* Wilmette, IL: Chiron.

Stromsted, T. (2001) 'Reinhabiting the female body'. *The Arts in Psychotherapy,* 28(1): 39–55.

Tilly, M. (1982) 'Margaret Tilly remembering a musical visit with Jung', in F. Jensen (ed.) *C.G. Jung, Emma Jung and Toni Wolff: A Collection of Remembrances.* San Francisco, CA: Analytical Psychology Club.

van Löben Sels, R. (2003) *A Dream in the World: Poetics of Soul in Two Women, Modern and Medieval.* London: Routledge.

von Franz, M.-L. (1980) 'On active imagination', in M.F. Keyes (ed.) (1983) *Inward Journey: Art as Therapy.* La Salle, IL: Open Court.

Wallace, E. (1975) 'For C.G. Jung's one hundredth birthday: creativity and Jungian thought'. *Art Psychotherapy,* 2: 181–187.

Ward, K.H. (1992) 'Music, affect and imagery: a cross cultural exploration'. *Journal of the Association for Music and Imagery,* 1: 19–31.

Warming, P. (1992) 'Psyche and sound: the use of music in Jungian analysis', in D. Campbell (ed.) *Music and Miracles.* London and Wheaton, IL: Quest.

Watkins, M. (1976) *Waking Dreams.* New York: Harper and Row.

Weaver, R. (1973/1991) *The Old Wise Woman: A Study of Active Imagination.* Boston, MA: Shambhala.

Weinribb, E. (1983) *Images of the Self.* Boston, MA: Sigo Press.

Whitehouse, M. (1954–1979) 'Mary Whitehouse Papers', in P. Pallaro (ed.) (1999) *Authentic Movement: Essays by Mary Starks Whitehouse, Janet Adler and Joan Chodorow.* London: Jessica Kingsley.

Woodman, M. (1982) *Addiction to Perfection.* Toronto: Inner City.

—— (2000) *Bone.* New York: Viking.

Wyman-McGinty, W. (1998) 'The body in analysis: authentic movement and witnessing in analytic practice'. *Journal of Analytical Psychology,* 43(2): 239–260.

Wyman-McGinty, W. (2002) 'Authentic movement and witnessing in psychotherapy', in P. Camic and L. Wilson (eds) *Bulletin of Psychology and the Arts*, 2(2): 90–92.

Zinkin, L. (1969) 'Flexibility in analytic technique'. *Journal of Analytical Psychology*, 14(2): 119–132.

Chapter 11

Dreams

Mary Ann Mattoon

> The dream is a little hidden door in the innermost
> and most secret recesses of the soul.
> (C.G. Jung 1933: par. 304)

Is a dream a door to the soul, or is it, as we often hear, 'only a dream'? Sometimes the 'only a dream' statement is an effort at consoling the person who has had a disturbing dream; on other occasions it is a way of saying that a dream has no bearing on reality. Increasingly, however, many people appreciate their night dreams as being not so 'only'; rather, dreams are vital in their lives.

After considering the importance of dreams in Jungian psychotherapy and the history of their role, we will look at the methods of working on a dream. Then we will approach the interpretation: amplifying, seeking its meaning and exploring validation of the interpretation.

Importance of dreams in Jungian psychotherapy

Dreams are a major thoroughfare to the unconscious psyche, which is vastly larger than consciousness. If we do not pay attention to them, we limit our knowledge of the psyche to the relatively small segment that is conscious, while missing an opportunity to expand consciousness.

One reason dreams are ignored is that the dream often is not readily understood. Jung advised that we carry each dream around, turn it over and over, look at it from every perspective. Often it is helpful to tell it to a trusted friend, or to a therapist. An insight may result, or the dreamer may puzzle for years about this nocturnal visitor.

Another major reason that some people ignore (or avoid) their dreams is their assumption that dreams deliver unpleasant messages. Sometimes this assumption is borne out. Often, however, dreams point out our strengths and help us to solve problems of living.

In common speech, dream can mean wish or fantasy, that is, a daydream. I am using the term to mean only the images and other contents that come during sleep.

History of dream interpretation

Is attending to dreams a new idea? By no means. For millennia, people have been informed by their dreams. For example, generally known – at least to persons of Jewish and Christian backgrounds – are the dreams of Pharaoh in the Old Testament. In Genesis 41, dreams of emaciated cows and blighted grain were interpreted as warnings of impending famine. Similarly, in the New Testament (Matthew 1) an angel appeared to Joseph in a dream, telling him that Mary's unborn child was conceived by the Holy Spirit. Even earlier than the Pharaohs were the ancient Egyptians and Babylonians, to whom the Jewish interpreters almost certainly owed the rudiments of their knowledge of dreams to the Egyptians and Babylonians.

Dreams are so important to us humans that, if deprived of them (by being awakened whenever a dream begins), we are likely to hallucinate. Since hallucinations, like dreams, are unconscious contents, it appears that the psyche *needs* to bring such contents into consciousness, and uses hallucinations when the dream route is blocked.

Some people feel that they have no choice about attending to their dreams. As far as they know, they do not dream. However, dream researchers are reasonably sure now that everyone dreams: probably at least once in each sleep period of ninety minutes or more, and four or more times in a night. Thus, when we have the impression that we do not dream it is almost certain that, instead, we are not remembering our dreams. When a person attempts to remember dreams and writes down whatever fragments become available, I have found that the effort to remember is nearly always successful: not every night, but often enough to have plenty of dream material to reflect on.

Do all dreams have meaning? We cannot prove that they do, but many individuals spontaneously record or tell their dreams; to them it seems self-evident that dreams have meaning. Moreover, psychotherapists and other workers with dreams have found meaning in nearly all of those studied. Failure to find a dream's meaning is probably our lack, not the dream's.

Concrete indications that dreams have meaning are found in their having helped philosophers and scientists, such as Friedrich August Kekulé and René Descartes, to make major discoveries. Kekulé deduced from a dream image the structure of the benzene ring, which is a crucial phenomenon in organic chemistry; Descartes had three dreams which turned his life toward philosophy. In literature we find Robert Louis Stevenson dreaming the plot of *Dr. Jekyll and Mr. Hyde* after years of searching for a story that would describe the double being (good and evil) of humans.

Present-day people of many cultures attach importance to dreams. For instance, the Senoi people of Malaya (now Malaysia) are said to discuss their dreams daily. It seems probable that prehistoric peoples also were impressed by their dreams.

Dreams in Jung's opus

Jung broke away from Freud in 1913 as a result of theoretical disagreements between them and, no doubt, personality clashes. Before the break, Jung had accepted many of Freud's ideas, including that of the dream's manifest and latent contents: the dream text and its underlying meaning. After the break, Jung became more forthright in developing his own ideas: regarding dreams as well as many other areas. For example, instead of continuing to accept Freud's notion that the manifest dream is a disguise, Jung stated repeatedly that the dream means what it says.

Another major disagreement with Freud is Jung's frequent statement that dream images are symbols, not signs. A sign is a one-to-one designation, such as Freud's view that the image of a church steeple represents a penis. Jung found the image as pointing to the creative *mana* and, ultimately, not quite determinable. Dream images arise from a variety of sources including physical stimuli, repressed complexes, memories, everyday experiences, subliminal perceptions, even telepathy and anticipation of future psychic contents. Unlike Freud's view that dream images are repressed conscious material, Jung insisted that some of the material never had been present in consciousness. Altogether, the images constitute the dream language.

The elements of the dream language, although they are not signs, still can be relatively fixed symbols:

> typical motifs such as falling, flying, being persecuted by dangerous animals or hostile people, being insufficiently or absurdly clothed in public places, being in a hurry or lost in a milling crowd, fighting with useless weapons, running hard and getting nowhere.
>
> (Jung et al. 1964: 53)

Each element contributes to the translation of the dream language.

A study of Jung's dream theories reveals that virtually all the innovations are enrichment rather than changes. There is modification, development and a process of making the theories more explicit.

Since Freud's (1900) *Interpretation of Dreams* and Jung's writings from 1912 on, many people have been led to look to dreams for information about their unconscious psyches. Indeed, dreams provide – for those who want it – ready access to this important resource.

In addition to Freud's and Jung's approaches to dreams are others. Alfred Adler, although the third of the big three of psychoanalysis, made little contribution to dream theory. Other depth psychologists have shared concepts with both Freud and Jung. Examples are Erich Fromm, with his 'forgotten language' of dreams, and Thomas French's and Erika Fromm's focal conflict theory.

The existential-phenomenological approach does not hypothesise unconscious mental contents, but is compatible with Jung's ideas in other ways. The major theorist of this school is Medard Boss. Others who are well known are Leopold Caligor and Rollo May, as well as Fritz Perls.

Jung's method of interpretation is, in my view, the broadest and most flexible, hence covers the widest range of dreams and appeals to virtually all dreamers. Indeed, this method subsumes virtually all the theories that are compatible with it.

How to work on a dream

Even if we are convinced that dreams have meaning, how do we discover the meaning of a particular dream? There is a process for figuring it out; the dreamer can follow the process independently, with a trusted friend or a group, or with the help of a therapist who has training and experience in dream work.

The first step in working with a dream is to have paper and pencil readily available for writing the dream immediately after wakening and as completely as possible. It is helpful to repeat the dream to yourself while you are still in the half-waking state, even before stirring to reach for the writing materials. To get up and move around before writing the dream is to risk forgetting a great deal of it.

In addition to writing the dream, you may draw or paint it. Since many dreams take the form of stories, there may be multiple scenes. Drawing even one scene can help to make the dream more vivid, to fix it in your mind. To draw or paint a dream, it is not necessary, and perhaps not even desirable, to be a trained artist.

After writing the dream, jot down reflections (facts, thoughts and feelings) that come to mind in connection with the dream images. Write first those that come readily, but add later those that come only with extra effort. For example, many thoughts may come to you about your brother Tom, whom you see frequently, but an image of your long-dead Aunt Nellie requires some digging into your memory. Some dreamers find it helpful to write the dream in one column, facts, thoughts and feelings about it in another.

The image of Tom may remind you of experiences you had with him, how he treated you, attitudes he had/has and what he is doing now. Aunt Nellie's side of the family, whether that of your mother or your father, may be the poor relations, for instance, or they may have held beliefs that were different from your family's way of looking at the world.

Nearly all dreams have human figures. Many have also animals, inanimate objects and scenes. Indeed, the setting of a dream is a factor in its interpretation. The setting may be marked by its vagueness, but often it is quite specific. For example, if the dream takes place in a particular forest, you may recall what were the occasions of your visits to that forest, with what companions, what events occurred there and what you felt about each of these memories. Or the vaguely imaged forest could be reminiscent of a literary work, such as Lillian Hellman's (1973) *Another Part of the Forest*.

All these facts, thoughts and feelings about images in the dream are known to Jungians as *personal associations*. They are usually readily available to the adult dreamer. The dreams of children, however, often reflect their parents' problems and, thus, are illuminated by the parents' associations. All such associations are included in the broader term, 'individual amplifications'.

Personal associations are not to be confused with *free associations*, which Freud advocated. Free association means associations to associations. Such a practice tends to take the attention away from the dream images. Hence, the interpretation is likely to be distorted. Jung advocated staying close to the image, 'circumambulating' it.

In addition to the associations that occur to the dreamer, a therapist often can help the client/dreamer to recall additional individual amplifications: events in the dreamer's life that are connected with the dream images. For example, a middle-aged woman dreamed during the month of May that *she visited her mother, who was crabby and inhospitable*. The dreamer had mentioned that she had been unaccountably depressed for several days before the dream. Knowing that the mother was dead, the therapist asked when the death occurred. The dreamer replied, 'Last summer'. When both therapist and client consulted their notes, they found that the dream occurred almost exactly on the anniversary of the mother's death. The dreamer recalled that one of her children had been very ill at about the same time. Although she had felt very sad about the death, she had not been free to experience it fully; the dream helped her to experience and express her grief.

In addition to personal associations, there is other information about the dream images that does not stem from your individual experience; this information comes from the lore of humanity. Examples are: myths, religious observances and practices of preliterate cultures. The dream forest, for example, may be reminiscent of a forest where the goddess Artemis roamed. Such contents are from the collective unconscious and are known as *archetypal parallels*. Children's dreams, according to Jung and to some other dream researchers, have an especially large proportion of archetypal parallels. Dreams with archetypal parallels to the images are known as *archetypal dreams*.

Many cultures and individuals experience archetypal dreams as especially numinous (awe-inspiring). Thus, they are considered to be *big dreams*, which may carry a message for the community at large, rather than for the individual alone.

Personal associations and archetypal parallels together comprise *amplifications*. Even for a dream with only a few images, the number of amplifications can be quite large. Consequently, it is important to continue to write down all such information.

With the amplifications in hand, we turn to the other major kind of information that is needed: what was going on in your life, outer and inner, before the dream came to you. This information consists primarily of events and experiences that are emotionally significant to you, but their significance may not have been immediately apparent. Begin with the day or two before the dream, but consider also a longer time segment: perhaps the duration of an ongoing event, of a difficulty you were having, or of a decision you were in the process of making. For example, you may have been experiencing conflict in your family, considering changing jobs or wishing for a vacation. Also important is your inner emotional climate. At the time of the dream, were you generally happy? Anxious? Depressed? All these events, experiences and feelings comprise your *conscious situation* – what is going on in your life.

But each dream is one among many. The *series* of dreams preceding the one under consideration may be helpful in understanding it. The series may be composed of all the dreams you can remember, or all those that were especially vivid. Usually, however, you benefit more by considering a smaller number of dreams: for example, the dreams during a prolonged, difficult life situation. Or several dreams in which a particular image appears. If you are in psychotherapy, the series could be all the dreams since the beginning of the therapy, those since a crucial time in the therapy, or those that occur between two successive therapy sessions. The dreams of one night can be considered a series, but they often are so closely linked that they can be treated as one dream.

Recurring dreams – repetitions of essentially the same dream – form a special kind of dream series. The recurrence ordinarily means that the dream is especially important. Usually the recurring dream ceases to recur when it has been interpreted correctly.

There is a name for all the information gathered as amplifications, conscious situation and dream series. That name is the *dream context*.

What do we do with so much material? We look for interconnections among all these facts: common themes that point to a particular problem, complex or question on which the dream may be commenting. For example, a man's dream depicted three human figures: a young woman he had once nearly married, a friend who was in the process of divorce and the minister who performed the dreamer's wedding ceremony. The common theme is marriage. The question may be how to deal with the conflict in his marriage. The underlying complex could be his fear of being an inadequate husband, a failure.

Approaching an interpretation

With so much material, even with interconnections identified, we are still a considerable distance from interpretation. However, there are useful guidelines by which to approach that goal.

The first guideline – that of *avoiding assumptions* – may seem laughable to the novice dream interpreter, who may have no assumptions to avoid. Yet many people have heard of Freud's assumptions (with or without his name) that every dream reveals a sexual conflict and provides a *wish-fulfilment*. Making such an assumption is likely to distort the process of dream interpretation. Jung insisted that the meaning of a dream cannot be known in advance of the amplification and interpretation process.

A popular assumption is that the dream predicts the future. Occasionally it does (as did Pharaoh's dreams, mentioned earlier). More often dreams are oriented to the here-and-now. They describe the current view of the unconscious psyche toward a plan, behaviour or attitude of the dreamer.

In urging the avoidance of assumptions, Jung insisted that the dream means what it says; it is not a disguise. (His view contrasts with Freud's that the 'manifest' content – the dream text known to the dreamer – disguises the 'latent' content, the unconscious wish of the dreamer.) An example of the dream's meaning what it says is the dream of a woman that *she was trying, unsuccessfully, to get her hands clean.* Since the term 'dirty hands' is a metaphor for unethical behaviour, it seems likely that the dream was judging adversely the ethics of some of her behaviour.

Although the dream means what it says, it speaks through the language of *symbols.* 'Symbol' does not mean, here, the items in a 'dream dictionary', which gives a fixed meaning for each dream image. One such dictionary states that the image of a lamp filled with oil 'denotes business activity with gratifying results'. Such a statement is arbitrary; using it would impoverish or even distort the dream analysis.

Jung insists that a symbol is the best possible formulation of a relatively unknown psychic content. Thus, the meaning of the lamp image can be discovered only with knowledge of the context of the dream in which the image appears, including interconnections among images. With this knowledge, the lamp can denote, for example: illumination; a useful object from an earlier era; a decorative object; and/or or a reminder of a particular person, place or time in the dreamer's life. An interpretation is a conjecture about the meaning of such an image.

Although a given dream image usually has a unique meaning for each dreamer, sometimes the image has a relatively fixed meaning. Such a

meaning pertains when there is a general cultural meaning and no contradictory personal significance. For example, a dream image of *a baptismal
ceremony* could be taken as a relatively fixed symbol of spiritual cleansing.
Although that is its established meaning in a Christian subculture, it is only
relatively fixed because baptism predates Christianity. In addition, this
interpretation might not be applicable to an individual dreamer who has no
religious affiliation, or one that does not recognise baptism.

Much as we may want guidance from our dreams, usually the dream does
not tell the dreamer what to do. To be sure, if the dream depicts the
dreamer in a dangerous situation, it may seem to call for action to avoid the
danger. Nevertheless, the dream does not direct an action to avoid danger,
but various avenues may be possible. Thus, the dream describes the
situation as the unconscious 'sees' it and leaves decisions to the dreamer's
consciousness.

The most important guideline in an interpretation is that it is a translation of the dream language, which can be likened to an extinct language
that has been rediscovered. The ancient Egyptian language serves as a
model. Before it was deciphered, no one knew what a particular word in
that language means in English. When modern scholars discovered writing
in ancient Egyptian, they used the entire context and the usage of each
character to identify letters and words, then translated texts. Similarly, in
interpreting dreams, we consult the context and the various ways an image
is used, to get clues as to the meaning of each image and the entire text.

What does the dream mean?

A dream can have different meanings, depending on its focus: *subjective* or
objective. When you dream about Cousin John, whom you have not seen in
ten years, is the dream telling you something about your cousin? Possibly,
but not probably. Because Cousin John is not part of your daily life, it is
more likely that the dream is telling you about a part of yourself that
is reminiscent of Cousin John. Jung called such a message a *subjective*
interpretation.

Used in relation to dreams, subjective does not carry connotations of
insubstantial or illusory. Rather, this description calls attention to qualities
and attitudes that the dreamer shares with the dream figure. Thus, these
images often depict parts of the dreamer's personality, for example, a
shadow quality: unacknowledged, often negative to the dreamer.

The subjective approach is easiest to understand in relation to human
figures in dreams, but the concept applies also to non-human figures, even
inanimate ones. Gestalt therapy has made use of this concept in its method
of the dreamer's acting out each image in the dream.

But what if you dream about your spouse, who is part of your daily life?
The dream interpretation may give you some insight regarding the spouse

or the feeling situation between the two of you. Such an interpretation is an *objective* one.

Objective in this situation does not mean unbiased. It means, rather, that the dream provides a view, from the dreamer's unconscious, of the object – an actual person, animal, place or thing, and the dreamer's relationship to that object.

How does one know when to make a subjective interpretation, when an objective one? A subjective interpretation is indicated, generally, if the dream figure depicts someone (or something) not highly significant to the dreamer in waking life: a remote relative, a long-lost acquaintance, a celebrity, a historical figure or a person who is unknown to the dreamer or imaginary.

A subjective interpretation seemed appropriate, for example, to a dream of a 45–year-old unmarried woman: that *her nephew had died*. The dream context included the facts that the boy was the only son of her only brother and that the nephew and the dreamer were not emotionally close. As the carrier of the family surname, he seemed to personify the family tradition. Since the dreamer tended to conform too much to family expectations, the image of the death of the boy indicated the possible death of her tendency to be tradition-bound.

An objective interpretation is likely to be needed if the dream figure is someone who plays a large role in the dreamer's waking life: a spouse, sexual partner, family member, close friend, employer, co-worker or – in the dream of a psychotherapist or other professional person – a client.

A dream that seemed to call for an objective interpretation was one of a young man who recently had made friends with a certain young woman and was quite enamoured of her. He dreamed that *his new friend was sexually promiscuous*. He and his therapist concluded that the dream was telling him something about the young woman. Thus, his unconscious perception of her was different from his conscious view, so that he decided to move cautiously in the relationship. Later, he learned that she was indeed promiscuous.

In deciding between an objective and a subjective interpretation, it is important to notice whether the figure is depicted photographically, that is, as known to the dreamer in waking life. If so, the figure usually should be considered objectively. If the dream picture is markedly unlike the actual person, the dissimilar qualities are likely to be (subjective) attributes of the dreamer.

A distorted image of someone close to the dreamer may still point to an objective interpretation. An example is a 22-year-old woman's dream that *her mother was one of the witches in Shakespeare's* Macbeth. The dreamer's association to a witch was 'demonic power'. In understanding this image objectively, we need not conclude that the actual mother was totally demonic. Rather, the dreamer became aware that her mother was keeping her (the daughter) emotionally and financially dependent, hence under the mother's power. Her hold was so powerful that the daughter experienced her mother as a witch. Alternatively, the daughter may have had a too-positive view of her mother and lacked awareness that the negative mother is always present.

Distinguishing between subjective and objective meanings is especially important for therapists in working with their own dreams. We must consider: does a dream in which a client appears concern the therapist's psyche–subjective or the client's psyche–objective? To answer this question, we follow the same guidelines as for any other dream. Regardless of the answer I arrive at, it is extremely rarely that it is wise to tell a client about my dream.

In my experience, dreams about clients are infrequent but important. The fact that I dream about a client means that he or she has touched something in me. Thus, the dream may well provide (subjectively) a new insight into my own psychology, or give me a clue about the client: an unrevealed problem, or (objectively) give me a hint about conducting the therapy.

Dreams often have both subjective and objective meaning. The young man's dream of his new woman friend, for example, could keep its objective meaning and still say something about his psyche. One such subjective possibility is that he had a tendency to promiscuity.

Indeed, the subjective and objective meanings are often difficult to distinguish, because the psyche chooses dream figures that have psychological meaning to the dreamer. For example, a woman chooses as a husband a man who matches in some way her inner image of men. Therefore, when she dreams of her husband, the dream figure may personify the inner masculine as well as the actual husband.

Ideally, each dream image should be considered separately. In the same dream, one image may be subjective, another objective. In practice, however, a dream containing only a few images is likely to be primarily subjective or objective. A similar rubric pertains to the dimensions I am about to discuss: reductive/constructive and compensatory/non-compensatory.

Whether subjective or objective (or both), a dream can have different directions of impact on the dreamer: *reductive* or *constructive*. A reductive interpretation is likely to tell us why we have a particular problem; a constructive interpretation points to a solution or a possibility of psychological development.

'Andrew', a successful businessman who was depressed and anxious, dreamed that *he was visiting the town where he grew up. A woman who had lived next-door to his family (in a poor neighbourhood) said to her husband, 'Andrew doesn't come here very often'*. The dream reminded Andrew of his humble origins, evidently commenting on the roots of his anxiety. It pointed to the fact that he had ceased to pay attention to the vulnerable part of himself, the part that had experienced economic insecurity. Such a dream interpretation is reductive.

Reductive, from its Latin roots, means leading back: for dreams, designating root causes, seeking to answer the question why in the sense of what caused the dream? Such causes tend to be unpleasant, repressed contents (pleasant contents usually are not repressed): events, impulses or complexes and other shadow material. Freud's approach to dream interpretation was almost entirely reductive.

Just as some dreams point to unpleasant, repressed origins, other dreams are constructive in their intent. They seek to answer the question 'What for?' That is, 'To what purpose?' The answer is usually one of strengthening attitudes and qualities that are healthy and worth preserving, or pointing to a previously overlooked possibility in the dreamer. Jung tended to emphasise the constructive approach to dream interpretation while not excluding the reductive.

A *constructive* interpretation seems apt for another dream of Andrew, which seemed to indicate that his depression was related to his neglect of his non-business interests. (Many Jungians believe that the psychological basis of depression is a damming of psychic energy.) He dreamed that *he was at an art sale and paid a high price for a painting that he liked very much; he considered it well worth the price.* The dream was constructive in indicating that he had high energy for artistic or other creative ventures. Thus, it pointed to new (or renewed) possibilities in his life.

What do dreams have in common?

Objective/subjective, reductive/constructive. Is there any one rule that we can apply to all dreams? Yes and no. Yes, in that nearly all dreams can be viewed as *compensatory*. No, in that relatively few dreams are *non-compensatory*.

That the dream is compensatory – compensates a conscious attitude – means that, by way of the dream, the unconscious psyche provides information that is needed by consciousness. Such a need could be almost anything in mental life, but most likely is an answer to a question the dreamer has been asking, awareness of an attitude that needs changing, or a complex that has been *constellated* (activated).

Does compensation mean that the dream says the opposite of what the dreamer has in mind? Possibly, but not necessarily. Sometimes compensation even confirms the conscious attitude and tells you that it is a valid one. Such confirmation may be compensatory to your uncertainty about the attitude you hold. Alternatively, the dream says that you are partly right, but . . . On other occasions, by exaggerating the conscious attitude or by opposing it, the dream says that you are totally off the mark. In each case, as Zurich analyst Marie-Louise von Franz has said, 'The unconscious doesn't waste much spit telling you what you already know'.

Confirming the conscious attitude is a dream of a student who was about to take a crucial examination. Knowing that she had prepared well, she was confident – consciously. Nevertheless, she was vaguely anxious, presumably harbouring doubt – unconsciously. In her dream *she was walking across the stage in her graduation robe.* The image seemed to confirm her conscious attitude and deal with her unconscious fear by assuring her of her ability to pass the exam and get her degree.

Opposing the conscious attitude was a dream of an employer who often praised the work of a particular employee. The employer dreamed that *his employee was above him, on a balcony in the office where they both worked; he had to look up to talk with her.* In reflecting on the dream and his feelings about the employee, the employer/dreamer realised that his attitude toward her was, in effect, one of looking down on her. His praise of her evidently had been a defence against acknowledging his condescending attitude.

A dream can challenge the conscious attitude by exaggerating it. For example, a young man dreamed that *he met his boss, Mr Todd, whose ailments became a subject of conversation. The dreamer comforted him, then reflected that Mr Todd's ailments were due to smoking.* Coming after a controversy that had arisen between the two men, the dream seemed to be telling the young employee that he was angrier than he realised, as expressed in his fantasy of 'wishing' Mr Todd to be ill and accusing him (in that the ailments were due to smoking) of being at fault for his illness.

Many dreams compensate the conscious attitude by confirming and contradicting, both partially. That is, they modify it. An example is a man's dream in which *he shot at a wolf and missed.* The wolf – in metaphorical terms an indiscriminate pursuer of women – seemed to embody a predatory attitude in the dreamer. By aiming at the animal, the dreamer expressed his desire to eliminate the wolf in himself. By missing, perhaps deliberately, he expressed a conflicting desire: for the wolf side of his personality to live. Thus, the dream modified the man's conscious attitude that he wanted to destroy the inner wolf.

With all the possibilities that compensation covers, how can there be dreams that are non-compensatory? Some are *traumatic* dreams: those that re-tell, often many times, horrifying experiences, such as battle scenes or severe accidents. When the dream ends or becomes unbearably intense, the dreamer is likely to awaken, perspiring and with heart pounding, an emotional response similar to that which accompanied the actual experience.

There is usually no interpretation possible for a traumatic dream. A friend or therapist can only listen empathically and offer emotional support. Such dreams tend to recur until the emotional impact of the trauma has diminished. Indeed, they seem to be the psyche's way of discharging the emotion; telling the dream after each recurrence probably lessens the dream's emotional charge.

Other non-compensatory dreams reflect *extra-sensory perception* (ESP). Its occurrence in waking life is well established empirically, although the relevant data are not widely known. It can occur also in dreams.

A *telepathic* dream, one of two forms of ESP dreams, brings a message of an event at the time the event occurs. For example, a woman dreamed that *her mother was calling to her*. A few hours later, the dreamer received a phone call telling her of her mother's death – at about the time that the dream had occurred.

Precognitive (prophetic) dreams seem to involve ESP in advance of the event. An example from literature appears in Shakespeare's *Julius Caesar*. Caesar's wife, Calpurnia, calls out in her sleep, 'Help, ho! They murder Caesar.' Caesar was assassinated the following day. Similarly, many people report having had dreams anticipating the assassination of President John F. Kennedy.

Prophetic dreams are assumed in popular opinion to be more common than (in my experience) they actually are. To qualify as prophetic, a dream must depict, ahead of an event, essentially the same happening. In order to know that a dream is prophetic, it would have to be recorded carefully and subsequent events monitored. If this recording is not done and the predicted event fails to occur, the dreamer is likely not to notice the discrepancy. Or the dreamer may remember the dream erroneously, conforming it to the subsequent happening.

Some dreams that anticipate developments are not prophetic. Rather they are *prospective*. Such dreams reflect an expectable result of factors that exist at the time of the dream. An example is a young man's dream that *he was riding his motorcycle very fast and took off, flying; he was about to crash*, when he awoke. Some weeks later, he actually crashed his motorcycle. The crash was less a fulfilment of prophecy than an expectable result of the reckless, grandiose attitude reflected in his dream. Conceivably, the outcome could have been a metaphorical crash: losing his job, failing at business, love or gambling, or becoming depressed.

Nightmares, if they are not re-enactments of traumatic dreams, often seem to be predictive but probably are prospective. The fear accompanying the nightmare draws attention and urges the dreamer to look at the images symbolically.

Hypothesising and verifying an interpretation

Now that we know various guidelines for approaching an interpretation, we can venture to *hypothesise* one. I have found in my work with clients that, for many of them, this is a great moment. They are usually intuitive and have had to restrain themselves from jumping to a conclusion. Now is their opportunity to discover what the dream may mean.

Let us apply our knowledge to an actual dream. A young married woman, 'Margaret', dreamed: *I was married to Dan in a wedding ceremony. Afterward he wouldn't be my husband. He wouldn't live with me.*

Margaret's associations were that 'Dan', a younger man, was very attractive to her; she had had sexual fantasies about him. Marriage, she said, is a lifetime commitment. A wedding is a festive event in which the bride is the central figure. Finally, she associated her observation that for a married couple not to live together means not to have sexual relations.

The conscious situation was that Margaret was not getting along well with her actual husband, Fred, who often was highly critical of Margaret's lack of orderliness. They had spent the evening before the dream with a group of friends, including Dan; he had ignored her. She found herself in an angry mood the day after the dream.

The interpretation (largely objective) began with the image of Margaret's being married to Dan. It can be translated as her wish to consummate her sexual fantasies and, perhaps, to be married to Dan instead of to Fred. Dan's going through the wedding ceremony and then refusing to live with her confirmed her feeling that he was dallying with her and rejecting her. The timing of the dream, following the unhappy evening, helped Margaret to realise how angry she was, from her disappointed hope of a relationship with the actual Dan. Taken subjectively, the dream revealed Margaret's severe self-criticism. (Because her associations were sparse, no interconnections were required.)

When an interpretation has been forged, how do we *verify* it? First, we look for the dreamer's response to the interpretation. Margaret was not enthusiastic but she was receptive. Thus, it 'clicked' with her, albeit in an understated way.

Whether or not it clicks with the dreamer, sometimes the interpretation is verified by subsequent events. As Margaret's analyst I noticed a marked change in her attitude toward her problems. Instead of blaming her husband and children for all her negative emotions, she began to see that her expectations were excessive; frequent disappointments were virtually inevitable. A therapeutic result helped to confirm the dream interpretation. It 'acted for' the dreamer.

Even when the interpretation seems to be supported by the dreamer's response, it may be incomplete or slightly off the mark. We can discover this by checking to see that the setting and the major images have been taken into account. If the wedding had taken place on top of a mountain, for example, another dimension would have been added.

What happens when an interpretation is incorrect? The dreamer's psyche is likely to reject it, either by an immediate, negative ego response ('That doesn't fit') or by a subsequent dream. An example of both avenues of rejection followed an interpretation by a woman dreamer's male analyst. He had interpreted a previous dream as meaning that the dreamer should break off her relationship with her lover. The dreamer objected (verbally) to the interpretation. It became evident that her unconscious was even more dissatisfied; she had a subsequent dream that *she had surgery, which proved to be injurious to her*. The surgeon was the agent of attempted cure and unnecessary injury, just as the analyst had been in his interpretation. Analyst and dreamer concluded that the analyst's interpretation of the previous dream had cut out something healthy, thus damaging the dreamer.

When such a rejection of the initial interpretation occurs, it is important to review the context and try again. When a valid interpretation is reached, it usually goes unremarked by subsequent dreams.

In summary, the steps in dream interpretation are as follows:

1 Record the dream immediately after waking.
2 Write the personal associations and (where known) the archetypal parallels to each dream image.
3 Write the conscious situation: the events and feelings surrounding the dream.
4 Consider what interconnections there may be among the amplifications and between them and the conscious situation.
5 Review the guidelines for approaching the dream: avoid assumptions; the dream means what it says; it speaks the language of symbols; it does not tell the dreamer what to do; interpretation is translation of the dream language.
6 Characterise each dream image as subjective or objective, reductive or constructive, compensatory or non-compensatory.
7 Identify the problem or complex with which the dream is concerned.
8 Hypothesise an interpretation; verify it by the dreamer's response or subsequent events.

Are all these steps necessary? Yes and no. Yes, they are all needed for maximum accuracy in interpretation. No, because an adequate interpretation often can be reached without strict adherence to all the steps. The latter choice often has to be made, at least in psychotherapy, because including them all can require several hours for an interpretation to be reached.

Thus, it is useful to know these steps as it helps in shortening the process. One help is an increasing acquaintance with one's dream history. Such acquaintance gives us a head start on the context of each new dream. Indeed, as dreams accumulate we may see patterns emerging: recurring figures or settings, feelings that reflect interpersonal or inner conflicts in our waking lives, or even a continuing story.

Another factor, especially helpful when we work with dreams in psychotherapy, is that much of the non-dream information brought to a session is useful in dream interpretation. In many therapies, the client routinely tells the therapist what has been going on in the client's life. Consequently, when a dream is introduced, some of the conscious situation is already on the table. Indeed, in my experience as an analyst, the client and I tend to turn to the dreams when we have a sense of what aspect of the client's life is the focus for that session.

Thus, steps in dream interpretation are taken with varying frequency, aided or hindered by intuitive leaps. The possibility of error is considerable, but, as we have seen, errors can be revealed by the dreamer's response and subsequent events.

Our dreams can help us by increasing our consciousness of the otherwise hidden parts of our psyches. Simply paying attention to dreams increases consciousness to some extent. Working through the interpretation process increases it a great deal more. Thus we are aided in understanding ourselves, our motives and purposes; enriched with possibilities for further development, and strengthened in our ability to make valid decisions.

Many people find that understanding their dreams adds depth and richness to their lives . . . and that working – and playing – with dreams is simply fun.

Recommended reading

Freud, S. (1901) *On Dreams. Standard Edition* 5: 633–686.
Mattoon, M.A. (1984) *Understanding Dreams*. Dallas, TX: Spring.
Noone, R. and Holman, D. (1972) *In Search of the Dream People*. New York: William Morrow.
Whitmont, E.C. and Perera, S. (1989) *Dreams: A Portal to the Source*. London and New York: Routledge.
Woods, R.L. and Greenhouse, H.B. (1974) *The New World of Dreams*. New York: Macmillan.

References

Freud, S. (1900) *The Interpretation of Dreams. Standard Edition* 4 and 5. London: Hogarth Press.
Hellman, L. (1973) *The Little Foxes* and *Another Part of the Forest: Two Plays*. New York: Viking.
Jung, C.G. (1933) 'The meaning of psychology for modern man', in *CW* 10: pars. 276–332.
Jung, C.G. and von Franz, M.-L. et al. (eds) (1964) *Man and his Symbols*. London: Aldus.

Part III

Applications

Chapter 12

Alchemy

Stanton Marlan

Introduction

Jung considered alchemy in a way that few if any before him had imagined. Alchemy for the most part had been relegated to the status of an historical anachronism or hidden away within the confines of an esoteric occultism. To the contemporary mind, alchemists were viewed as odd, reclusive and strange old men in their laboratories hopelessly trying to change lead into gold. Their practice was seen as nonsense, or, at best, as a precursor to the modern science of chemistry.

Jung began his reflections with a similar attitude as he describes in *Memories, Dreams, Reflections* (1963). There he notes that when he first desired to become more closely acquainted with alchemical texts, he procured the classic volume *Artis Auriferae Volumina Duo* (1593):

> I let this book lie almost untouched for nearly two years. Occasionally I would look at the pictures and each time I would think, 'Good Lord, what nonsense! This stuff is impossible to understand'.
>
> (Jung 1963: 204)

However, as his inquiry grew deeper, Jung concluded that the alchemists were speaking in symbols about the human soul and were working as much with the imagination as with the literal materials of their art. The gold that they were trying to produce was not the common or vulgar gold but an *aurum non vulgi* or *aurum philosophicum*, a philosophical gold (Jung 1963). They were concerned with both the creation of the higher man and the perfection of nature. In a 1952 interview at the Eranos Conference, Jung stated:

> The alchemical operations were real, only this reality was not physical but psychological. Alchemy represents the projection of a drama both cosmic and spiritual in laboratory terms. The *opus magnum* had two aims: the rescue of the human soul and the salvation of the cosmos.
>
> (Jung, quoted in McGuire and Hull 1977: 228)

This move brought alchemy into the realm of contemporary thought and was the beginning of a sustained psychology of alchemy.

To see alchemy in this way – as a psychological and symbolic art – was a major breakthrough for Jung and a key to unlocking its mysteries. The exploration and development of this insight led Jung eventually to see in alchemy a fundamental source, background, and confirmation of his psychology of the unconscious. The impact of alchemy on his continuing work was so great that: 'A good third of Jung's writings are directly or tangentially concerned with alchemy, proportionately far more than he wrote about typology, association experiments, eastern wisdom, or parapsychology' (Hillman 1980: 30, n. 3). As Schwartz-Salant (1995) has noted: 'C.G. Jung, perhaps more than any other modern researcher of alchemy, is responsible for resurrecting this body of thought as a respectable field of study' (Schwartz-Salant 1995: 2).

Jung's writings on alchemy

The English publication of Jung's *Collected Works* did not follow the order of his original writings or presentations. Some individual volumes have been arranged as collections of papers from different periods and not necessarily in terms of the unfolding of his ideas or the importance of his work. Editorial notes to each volume help to place his original writings back into chronological order. Although the historical unfolding of his ideas can be traced in his autobiography *Memories, Dreams, Reflections* (Jung 1963), it should be noted that Jung's reflections on alchemy are not simply systematic. The development of Jung's theoretical ideas might best be considered as a mosaic of discovery, elaboration and synthesis – of his ongoing exploration of the unconscious and of its connection with alchemical thought.

As noted, Jung's work on alchemy constitutes a considerable field of research. The most obvious resources are to be found in those volumes of his *Collected Works* dedicated specifically to alchemy. These include *Psychology and Alchemy* (vol. 12), *Alchemical Studies* (vol. 13) and his magnum opus, *Mysterium Coniunctionis* (vol. 14). In addition to these major works, important alchemical reflections can be found in *Aion* (vol. 9ii) and in *The Practice of Psychotherapy* (vol. 16). The important paper in this volume related to alchemy is 'The psychology of the transference' (1946). Jung notes that this essay can also serve as an introduction to his more comprehensive account in *Mysterium Coniunctionis*. In addition *The Symbolic Life* (vol. 18) contains a few short reflections: 'Foreword to a catalogue on alchemy' (1946), 'Faust and alchemy' (1949) and 'Alchemy and psychology' (1950). This last piece was written initially for the *Encyclopedia Hebraica* and is a short synopsis of the alchemical work that is more fully elaborated in *Psychology and Alchemy*. Another short synopsis is also detailed in an interview with Jung in *C.G. Jung Speaking: Interviews and Encounters* (McGuire and Hull 1977). The interview was conducted by Mircea Eliade at the Eranos conference in 1952 for inclusion in the journal *Combat* and is reproduced in the above-noted text with corrections and explanatory notes by Jung. The above two synopses give Jung's short but mature overview of the alchemical process.

Beyond these materials Jung's autobiography *Memories, Dreams, Reflections* (1963) contains his recollections of his discovery and elaboration of alchemy. These reflections are amplified in a considerable number of letters reproduced in *C.G. Jung Letters*, Volumes 1 and 2. These letters are a small treasure trove of correspondence with such figures as H.G. Baynes, Karl Kerenyi, Hermann Hesse, Erich Neumann, Victor White, Maud Oakes, John Trinick and others. In addition there are also a collection of unpublished seminar notes containing fifteen lectures from the winter of November 1940 to February 1941, which were compiled by Barbara Hannah with the help of a number of others including Marie-Louise von Franz, Toni Wolff and Jung himself. These notes, though reproduced, have not been made available to the public and were generally restricted to seminar members and analysts. Other tools for researching Jung's alchemical work include the *General Bibliography* (vol. 19) and the *General Index* (vol. 20) of the *Collected Works*. The index contains two sub-indices that focus on Renaissance collections of alchemical texts and their authors; it also contains alchemical themes and symbolic references that locate these ideas and images in Jung's overall alchemical writings. In addition, the student or researcher may find *The Abstracts of the Collected Works of C.G. Jung* (1976) to be of value, as it contains synopses of all of Jung's collected works.

Resources beyond Jung's writings

Beyond Jung's own works noted above, a number of Jung's followers have written about alchemy in a way that helps the reader to enter the complexity of his work with greater ease. Both Marie-Louise von Franz and Edward Edinger have explicitly stated this goal in their works on alchemy. Specifically, von Franz's *Alchemy: An Introduction to the Symbolism and Psychology* (1980) and *Alchemical Active Imagination* (1979) serve as good introductory texts, as does Edinger's *Anatomy of the Psyche* (1985), as well as his other detailed studies which guide readers through Jung's most difficult works: *The Mystery of the Coniunctio: Alchemical Image of Individuation* (1994), *The Mysterium Lectures* (1995) and *The Aion Lectures: Exploring the Self in C.G. Jung's Aion* (1996a). In addition, Nathan Schwartz-Salant has compiled a work entitled *Jung on Alchemy* (1995) which, along with a scholarly introduction, contains carefully selected passages from Jung's major works.

Many Jungian analysts have written on and/or referenced Jung's work with important insights that lend themselves to understanding Jung's alchemical project. Andrew Samuels has dedicated a chapter of his book *The Plural Psyche* (1989) to helping others understand Jung's involvement with alchemy and to showing its relevance for current analytical theory and clinical application. David Holt's (1987–1988) article 'Alchemy: Jung and the historians of science' in *Harvest* provides a reference guide to the historical literature for those who have an interest in Jung's work in relation to the history of science and to scientific ideas. Holt has researched the important journal *Ambix*, a periodical concerned with the history of chemistry and alchemy, which contains many responses to Jung's alchemical writings. Beverley Zabriskie (1996) has also addressed in her work the issue of the relationship of Jung's alchemy to modern science, particularly physics. The continuing importance of alchemy for current Jungian thinkers has been addressed by me in my edited book *Fire in the Stone: The Alchemy of Desire* (1997), which brings together a range of essays by Jungian analysts and scholars who have been inspired by the continuing vitality of the alchemical metaphor in their own work. Containing essays by Hillman, Kugler, Berry, Kalsched, Corbett, Schenk, Churchill and myself, this collection can serve as introductory to the range of application of the alchemical metaphor. Finally, Murray Stein (1992) has produced a series of ten audiotapes entitled *Understanding the Meaning of Alchemy: Jung's Metaphor of the Transformative Process*, and Joseph Henderson has recorded a videotape on the alchemical text, *Splendor Solis*, with his commentary and discussion.

Beyond the references mentioned above, which survey the breadth of alchemy's application, there are a number of Jungian thinkers who have made contributions to the psychology of alchemy and who have addressed and elaborated specific alchemical themes. Each in his or her own way has been carrying on the work originally begun by Jung himself. It would be impossible within the scope of the present overview to include and elaborate every source or contribution from those who have applied Jung's theory to alchemy. However, a number of these contributors – including Marie-Louise von Franz, Edward Edinger, James Hillman, Nathan Schwartz-Salant, Paul Kugler, Stanton Marlan, Jeffrey Raff, Walter Odajnyk, Hayao Kawai, Wolfgang Giegerich and Yasuhiro Tanaka – have been chosen to represent ideas that reflect a wide range of perspectives from classical application to contemporary revisionist themes. The work of these writers will therefore be more fully elaborated later in the text. Many others who have made important contributions are simply noted below and can be pursued by readers interested in the particular themes of their writings.

Michael Fordham (1960) reflected on the relationship of analytical psychology to theory, alchemy, theology and mysticism. In 1967 Aniela Jaffé published a reflection on 'The influence of alchemy on the work of

C.G. Jung', and Robert Grinnel's (1973) book *Alchemy in a Modern Woman* applied alchemy to a clinical case and followed its archetypal dynamics. In the same year David Holt (1973) in 'Jung and Marx' continued the reflection on the importance of alchemy for understanding theory. Joe Henderson (1978) wrote on the 'Practical application of alchemical theory', which reflects on Solomon Trismosin's *Splendor Solis* and considers if in theory or practice we are 'always seeking to heal the split between Spirit and Matter' (Henderson 1978: 251), and in 2003 he and Dyane Sherwood published *Transformation of the Psyche: The Symbolic Alchemy of the Splendor Solis*. K.D. Newman (1981) in 'The riddle of the Vas Bene Clausum' amplified the idea of the closed container 'giving particular attention to the practical application it has for analytical psychotherapy' (Newman 1981: 239). Patrick McGoveran (1981) applied an alchemical model to a therapeutic milieu with psychotic borderline patients.

Mario Jacoby (1984) in his book *The Analytic Encounter: Transference and Human Relationship* wrote about the application of alchemy to the analytic situation, focusing specifically on transference and erotic love. Barbara Stevens Sullivan (1989) in her book *Psychotherapy Grounded in the Feminine Principle* reflected on alchemy and the transference, as did Jean Kirsch (1995) in her paper 'Transference' – both adding important reflection on the nature of the dialectical relationship. Sullivan's particular contribution was to revise the masculine and feminine principles and to offer a renewed understanding of the *coniunctio*. Finally, Irene Gad (1999) published an introductory article on the continuing importance of alchemy entitled 'Alchemy: the language of the soul'.

Before going any further into the development of Jung's ideas about alchemy it is important to turn to the origin of his reflections.

Jung's discovery of alchemy

It is difficult to say precisely where the origin of an idea lies, but it is beyond doubt that Jung's engagement with alchemy was fundamental for the development of his mature psychological theory. The best description of Jung's early encounter with alchemy and his subsequent unfolding ideas about it comes from his autobiography, *Memories, Dreams, Reflections*.[1] In this work it is evident that the role of his inner life – his images, dreams, visions and synchronistic experiences – was of paramount importance. These experiences were the *prima materia* of his scientific work, the 'fiery magma' out of which the goal of the work was to be crystallised and incorporated into a contemporary picture of the world.

Like the figure of Faust in Goethe's classic epic, Jung opened himself to the unconscious, out of which a radically new way of seeing emerged. This vision did not come easily and required an intense confrontation with the unconscious, which initiated him into a period of great uncertainty and isolation. In order to come to terms with his experiences, Jung began to draw mandalas (circular drawings) which he felt corresponded to the whole of his psyche actively at work. He did not know where the process was going, but felt the need to abandon himself to it. Over time, a sense of direction emerged, a path to a centre that seemed to have direction and aim, and to lead to a central and deeper structure of the personality. The existential recognition and articulation of this centre led Jung to postulate a structure of the psyche superordinate to the position of the *ego* (Jung 1963), which he called the *Self*.

A number of Jung's dreams in the 1920s anticipated the receipt of a Taoist alchemical manuscript which later served to confirm his vision of the *Self* as the goal of psychic life. In 1928, Jung received a letter from Richard Wilhelm asking if he would write a psychological commentary on a Chinese alchemical treatise, *The Secret of the Golden Flower*. This was Jung's first real and important contact with alchemy, and the text gave further support to his developing idea of the *Self*. This work stirred Jung to become more acquainted with alchemical texts, and he began a study of Western alchemy and soon obtained an important Latin treatise, *The Artis Auriferae Volumina Duo* (1593), containing a number of classical tracts on alchemy. Around that time, he remembered his crucial and now classic dream from 1926. At the end of this dream, he passed through some gates to a manor house and entered its courtyard. When he reached the middle of the courtyard, the gates flew shut. A peasant jumped down from a horse-drawn wagon and proclaimed, 'Now we are caught in the seventeenth century' (Jung 1963: 203). Jung connected this dream to alchemy, which had reached its height in that century, and concluded that he was meant to study alchemy from the ground up. This process of study absorbed Jung virtually for the rest of his life. For a long while before he found his way about in this labyrinth, and while studying another sixteenth-century text, the *Rosarium Philosophorum*, he noticed expressions that were used again and again. He attempted to decipher them, creating a lexicon of cross-references as if he were trying to solve the riddle of an unknown language. These studies convinced Jung of the parallels between alchemy and analytical psychology. He described this recognition in *Memories, Dreams, Reflections*:

I had very soon seen that analytical psychology coincided in a most curious way with alchemy. The experiences of the alchemists were, in a sense, my experiences, and their world was my world. This was, of course, a momentous discovery: I had stumbled upon the historical counterpart of my psychology of the unconscious. The possibility of a comparison with alchemy, and the uninterrupted intellectual chain back to Gnosticism, gave substance to my psychology. When I pored over these old texts everything fell into place: the fantasy-images, the empirical material I had gathered in my practice, and the conclusions I had drawn from it. I now began to understand what these psychic contents meant when seen in historical perspective. My understanding of their typical character, which had already begun with my investigation of myths, was deepened. The primordial images and the nature of the archetype took a central place in my researches, and it became clear to me that without history there can be no psychology, and certainly no psychology of the unconscious.

(Jung 1963: 205–206)

For Jung a psychology of consciousness could be content with material from the personal life of the patient but, as soon as the processes went deeper and involved the unconscious, something else was needed. Working with the unconscious often required unusual decisions and the interpretation of dreams. For Jung this called for a source in addition to personal memories and associations and a contact with the 'objective psyche', Jung's term for psychic reality that goes beyond the limits of seeing psyche as simply a subjective phenomenon. Edinger's (1985) work *Anatomy of the Psyche: Alchemical Symbolism in Psychotherapy* is explicitly concerned with this point, and it is one of the reasons why alchemical images are so valuable, in so far as they give us an objective basis from which to interpret dreams and other unconscious material.

As Jung deepened his reflections, he came to realise that engaging the unconscious could bring about psychic change. His study of alchemy brought him to an understanding of the unconscious as a process, and he began to clarify his view that the psyche can be transformed in a positive way by the contact between the ego and the contents of the unconscious. This process of development can be seen in an individual's dreams and fantasies, and it leaves its mark on our collective lives in the various religious systems and their changing symbolic structures. Through a study of these collective transformation processes and through an understanding of alchemical symbolism, Jung arrived at the central concept of his psychology: the individuation process.

A vital part of Jung's work soon began to address a concern with the individual's worldview and thus the relationship of psychology and religion. He published these inquiries in his work *Psychology and Religion* (1937) and in a 'direct offshoot', *Paracelsica* (1942). Jung notes that the second essay in that book, 'Paracelsus as a spiritual phenomenon', is of particular importance. It was through this work on Paracelsus that Jung was finally led to discuss 'alchemy as a form of religious philosophy' (Jung 1962: 209). He took this up in his *Psychology and Alchemy* (1944) and thus felt he had reached the ground that underlay his own experiences of the years 1913–1917. He noted that the process he had passed through corresponded to an alchemical transformation (Jung 1963: 209). It was a continuation of these thoughts that opened Jung further to the questions of religion and to his ongoing relationship to Christianity.

For Jung the Christian message was of central importance for Western humankind, but it needed to be seen in a new light and in accord with the spirit of the times, otherwise it would have no practical effect on human wholeness. He found many parallels between Christianity and alchemy and demonstrated a relationship between the dogma of the Trinity and the text of the Mass with the visions of Zosimos of Panopolis, a third-century Gnostic and alchemist. Jung's attempt to bring analytical psychology into relation with Christianity ultimately led to the question of Christ as a psychological figure. In *Psychology and Alchemy*, Jung (1944) demonstrated a parallel between Christ and the alchemist's notion of the 'lapis' or 'stone'. In the midst of these reflections, he had an important vision of a greenish/ gold body of Christ. He felt that the image pointed to a central archetypal symbol and was the expression of the life spirit present in both man and inorganic nature. In this image both are brought together in what amounts to an alchemical vision of Christ. Here the Christ image is also the *filius macro cosmi*, the anthropos whose roots he saw in the Jewish tradition, on the one hand, and the Egyptian Horus myth, on the other. This image was felt to animate the whole cosmos and was fundamental as an archetypal integration of spirit with matter, a conjunction that he felt was not adequately accomplished in Christianity (Jung 1963).

In the alchemical view, Christianity has saved humankind but not nature. Jung had critiqued Christianity for neglecting the body and 'the feminine' and, in so doing, ultimately devaluing 'nature'. Murray Stein takes up an extensive exploration of this issue in his book, *Jung's Treatment of Christianity* (1985). As noted earlier, the alchemist's dream was to save the world in its totality. Its opus magnum had two aims: the rescue of the human soul and the salvation of the cosmos. Alchemy with its emphasis on matter thus compensated for the lack in Christianity and held out the possibility of the further development of the religious psyche.

In *Aion*, Jung (1951) furthered his research, concerned now with the relationship of the Christ figure to psychology and to the structure of the Self. Here, he focused on the 'interplay between conscious and unconscious . . . with the impact of the greater personality, the inner man, upon the life of every individual' (Jung 1963: 221). Jung noted that at the beginning of the Christian era, the ancient idea of the anthropos took possession of the people and that this archetype was then concretised in the Christ image. The image of God's own son stood opposed to the deified Augustus, ruler of the secular world, and represented hope and expectations that tran-scended the oppressive *zeitgeist* of the times. In addition, Jung's aim was to demonstrate the full extent to which his psychology corresponded to alchemy or vice versa. He wanted to discover, side by side with religious questions, what special problems of psychotherapy were treated in the work of the alchemists.

Jung reflected on his earlier demonstration that the *coniunctio* in alchemy corresponded to the transference (1963: 212). This had already been taken up in *Psychology and Alchemy* (1944) and more particularly in his essay 'The psychology of the transference' (1946). In this essay Jung established parallels between the alchemical process as seen in the illustrations of the *Rosarium Philosophorum*, and the psychological problem of the opposites, transference and the *coniunctio*. A fuller treatment of these problems was taken up in Jung's final work, *Mysterium Coniunctionis* (1955–1956). In this work he followed his original intention of representing the whole range of alchemy as a kind of 'psychology of alchemy', and as an 'alchemical basis for depth psychology' (Jung 1963: 221).

In *C.G. Jung Speaking*, Jung offered a synopsis of the alchemical process:

> This work is difficult and strewn with obstacles; the alchemical opus is dangerous. Right at the beginning you meet the 'dragon,' the chthonic spirit, the 'devil' or, as the alchemists called it, the 'blackness,' the *nigredo*, and this encounter produces suffering. 'Matter' suffers right up to the final disappearance of the blackness; in psychological terms, the soul finds itself in the throes of melancholy, locked in a struggle with the 'shadow.' The mystery of the *coniunctio*, the central mystery of alchemy, aims precisely at the synthesis of the opposites, the assimilation of the blackness, the integration of the devil . . . In the language of the alchemist, matter suffers until the *nigredo* disappears, when the 'dawn' (*aurora*) will be announced by the 'peacock's tail' (*cauda pavonis*) and a new day will break, the *leukosis* or *albedo*. But in this state of 'whiteness' one does not *live* in the true sense of the word, it is a sort of abstract, ideal state. In order to make it come alive it must have 'blood,' it must have what the alchemists call the *rubedo*, the 'redness' of life. Only the total experience of being can transform this ideal state of the *albedo* into a fully human mode of existence. Blood alone can reanimate a glorious state of consciousness in which the last trace of blackness is dissolved, in which the devil no longer has an autonomous existence but rejoins the profound unity of the psyche. Then the opus magnum is finished: the human soul is completed integrated [*sic*].
>
> (Jung, quoted in McGuire and Hull 1977: 228–229)

At the conclusion of his work, Jung's imagination was captured by the ideas and metaphors of alchemy, with its dragons, suffering matter, peacock's tail, alembics and athanors; its red and green lions, kings and queens, fishes' eyes and inverted philosophical trees, salamanders and hermaphrodites; its black suns and white earth, and its metals – lead, silver and gold; its colours – black, white, yellow and red; and its distillations and coagulations, and rich array of Latin terms. All became the best possible expression of a psychic mystery as yet unknown which enunciated and amplified his maturing vision of the parallels between alchemy and his own psychology of the unconscious. All this and far more, Jung saw as projected by the alchemists into matter. Their effort was to bring about unity from the disparate parts of the psyche, creating a 'chemical wedding'. This Jung saw as the moral task of alchemy: to unify the disparate elements of the soul, both personal and ultimately cosmic, and thus to create the goal, the lapis or philosopher's stone. Likewise, Jung's psychology works with the conflicts and dissociation of psychic life and attempts to bring about the mysterious 'unification' he called Wholeness.

Finally, with his *Mysterium Coniunctionis* (1955–1956), Jung noted that his psychology was at last 'given its place in reality and established on its historical foundations' (Jung 1962: 221). Thus his task was finished. He felt he had reached 'the bounds of scientific understanding, the transcendental, the nature of the archetype per se, concerning which no further scientific statement can be made' (1962: 221).

Classical development of Jung's ideas

The power of the above sentiment and of Jung's studies strongly influenced his close followers, Marie-Louise von Franz (1915–1988) in Europe and Edward Edinger (1922–1998) in the United States. Both von Franz and Edinger held Jung's work to be fundamental and viewed themselves primarily as elaborators of his ideas, and as commentators who gave students easier access to the work of the master. These rather humble self-assessments do not adequately represent the extent to which their own contributions have extended and contributed to the field of analytical psychology and especially to our understanding of alchemy.

Von Franz has been considered to be the primary developer of Jung's alchemical legacy. She 'became world renowned among followers of Jung and after his death was an eloquent spokesperson for his ideas' (T.B. Kirsch 2000: 11). Von Franz met Jung when she was 18 years old in 1933, just around the time Jung's interest in alchemy was catalysing. He analysed her in exchange for her work on translations of texts from Greek and Latin. She continued as a close collaborator and eventually published what was in essence the third part of the *Mysterium Coniunctionis* called *The Aurora Consurgens* (1966). The *Aurora* is an account of and commentary on an alchemical text that dated roughly from the thirteenth century. The text has been ascribed to Thomas Aquinas, though its authorship is disputed. Jung chose this text as exemplary of medieval Christianity's attempt to come to terms with alchemical philosophy and as an instance of the alchemical problem of the opposites. Von Franz's (1966) commentary shows how Jung's analytical psychology may be used as a key to unlock the meaning of this difficult and very psychological text, and how the traditional practice of alchemy is best understood as a symbolic process.

Von Franz extended her work on alchemy through lectures to students at the Jung Institute in Zurich in 1959. These lectures were transcribed by Una Thomas, a member of the seminar, and published in 1980 under the title *Alchemy: An Introduction to the Symbolism and the Psychology*. The book was designed to be an introduction to Jung's more difficult study and is a 'practical account of what the alchemists were really looking for – emotional balance and wholeness' (von Franz 1980). The text contains lectures on old Greek and Arabic alchemy as well as on later European alchemy and *The Aurora Consurgens*. In giving her course and publishing this book von Franz hoped to enable students to read Jung with more comprehension. She recognised how dark and difficult his alchemical writings were and that even many of his closest students could not follow his work in this area. Nevertheless, she stressed the importance of this work. Her lectures continued in Zurich in January and February of 1969, and her book *Alchemical Active Imagination* was published in 1979. In addition to a short history of alchemy, von Franz concentrated on Gerhard Dorn, an alchemist and physician who lived probably in the sixteenth century. Following his work as a whole, and staying close to the original, she showed the similarity between the alchemist's practice and Jung's technique of active imagination, both of which promote a dialogue with the unconscious.

Von Franz's last direct work on alchemy is an historical introduction and psychological commentary on an Arabic alchemical text, *Hall ar-Rumuz*, or *Clearing of Enigmas*, alternatively translated *The Explanation of Symbols* (1999). The author, Muhammad ibn Umail ('Senior'), lived in the tenth century AD. Two non-professional translators did the translation of the text, and von Franz's interpretation was based on this draft. In order to avoid premature discussion, the work has been printed privately by Theodor Abt with the provision that it not be quoted or reviewed until a rectified and more complete translation is accomplished. Abt is in possession of a valuable collection of Arabic manuscripts that presumably will also be published. The first of these has been entitled *Corpus Alchemicum Arabicum: Book of the Explanation of the Symbols Kitab Hall ar-Rumuz*, a text attributed to Muhammad ibn Umail. This first volume of the Arabic corpus was co-edited by Wilferd Madelung in 2003. These texts represent the missing link within the mystical branch of alchemy, connecting Gnostic-Hermetic Greek alchemy to the mystical Latin alchemy of Europe.

In the above work, von Franz before her death acted as a collaborator, translator and creative developer of Jung's alchemical work. She contributed to the history of alchemy, the dialogue of alchemy with Christianity, and the importance of a symbolic and psychological approach. She also furthered our thinking about the alchemical problem of the opposites and our understanding of the *Unus Mundus*, the unified field upon which the opposites rely. These themes are further elaborated in her book *Psyche and Matter* (1992). In it, she brings together reflections on number, time, synchronicity, and the relationship between depth psychology, contemporary physics and quantum theory. She has also contributed to Jung's view of Christianity and an understanding of the importance of alchemy as a religious contribution to the Christian myth. In an interview (Wagner 1977), when asked what the main value was of Jung's and her own work on alchemy, she stated that:

> civilization needs a myth to live . . . And I think that the Christian myth, on which we have lived, has degenerated and become one-sided and insufficient. I think alchemy is the complete myth. If our Western civilization has a possibility of survival, it would be by accepting the alchemical myth, which is a richer completion and continuation of the Christian myth . . . The Christian myth is deficient in not including enough of the feminine. (Catholicism has the Virgin Mary, but it's only the purified feminine; it does not include the dark feminine). Christianity treats matter as dead and does not face the problem of the opposites – of evil. Alchemy faces the problem of the opposites, faces the problem of matter, and faces the problem of the feminine.
> (Marie-Louise von Franz, quoted in Wagner 1998–1999: 15–16)

If von Franz can be considered to be the pre-eminent follower of Jung's in Europe, few would argue against the same status for Edward Edinger in the United States. For more than forty years, 'in lectures, books, tapes and videos, he masterfully presented and distilled the essence of Jung's work, illuminating its relevance for both collective and individual psychology' (Sharp 1999: 18). Though Edinger wrote on a wide range of topics, including Moby Dick, Faust, Greek Philosophy, The Bible, the Apocalypse and the God image,[2] like von Franz, he had a special passion for alchemy. In the first issue of *Quadrant* (spring 1968), the New York Institute announced its final spring series of lectures by Edinger entitled 'Psychotherapy and alchemy', and the following issue contained a précis of Edinger's lectures, 'Alchemy as a psychological process' (*Quadrant*, 2: 18–22). These lectures, given in New York and Los Angeles in the late 1970s and early 1980s, were serially published in *Quadrant: Journal of the C.G. Jung Foundation for Analytical Psychology*,[3] and were later collected for his book *Anatomy of the Psyche: Alchemical Symbolism in Psychotherapy* (1985). In these lectures and his book, Edinger focused on seven selected images, which he used to organise the typical stages of the alchemical process: *calcinatio, solutio, coagulatio, sublimatio, mortificatio, separatio* and *coniunctio*. By focusing on these images/operations, Edinger (1985: 14) attempts to bring order to 'the chaos of alchemy'. Each of these operations is found to be the centre of an elaborate symbol system. These central symbols of transformation 'provide basic categories by which to understand the life of the psyche, and they illustrate almost the full range of experiences that constitute individuation' (Edinger 1985: 15; cf. Robertson 1999: 54).

In his work, Edinger views Jung's discovery of the 'reality of the psyche' as a new approach to understanding alchemy and other pre- or pseudo-sciences such as astrology. For Edinger, these systems of thought are expressions of a phenomenology that can serve to illustrate patterns and regularities of the objective psyche. As such they serve as archetypal images of transformation. What Edinger considers himself and Jung as presenting are psychic facts rather than 'theoretical constructs or philosophical speculations' (Edinger 1985: preface).

Edinger was also concerned with the practical problems of psychotherapy. His goal was to become familiar enough with archetypal images and to have sufficient enough knowledge drawn from personal analysis that we can discover an anatomy of the psyche, as 'objective as the anatomy of the body' (1985: preface). He contends that psychological theories are often too narrow and inadequate, and that when analysis goes deep, things are set in motion which are mysterious and profound. It is easy for both therapist and patient to lose their way. According to Edinger:

> What makes alchemy so valuable for psychotherapy is that its images concretize the experiences of transformation that one undergoes in psychotherapy. Taken as a whole, alchemy provides a kind of anatomy of individuation. Its images will be most meaningful . . . to those who have had a personal experience of the unconscious.
>
> (Edinger 1985: 2)

For him, as for Jung, the work of alchemy can be equated with the individuation process, but the alchemical corpus exceeds any individual's process in richness and scope. In the end, for Edinger, alchemy was considered to be a sacred work, one that required a religious attitude; and like von Franz, he saw Jung's work in alchemy as a development of the Christian myth.

Edinger's examination of Jung's work on alchemy continued with a number of texts carefully devoted to explicating it. While the *Anatomy of the Psyche* (1985) is an overall look at alchemical processes and the symbolism of the individuation process, Edinger's further reflections focus on particular works of Jung in order to give us further access to and help in understanding them. In 1994 he published *The Mystery of Coniunctio: Alchemical Image of Individuation*. It contains both an introduction to Jung's *Mysterium Coniunctionis* and an essay on the psychological interpretation of the *Rosarium* pictures. These essays were first presented as lectures at the C.G. Jung Institute of San Francisco during 19–20 October 1984. In this work, Edinger takes a somewhat different stance from Jung, suggesting other ways to look at the pictures of the *Rosarium*. He does not oppose Jung's interpretations but suggests that the images have multiple facets, meanings and contexts in which they can be seen.

In 1995, he published *The Mysterium Lectures* based on a course he gave to members of the Jung Society of Los Angeles during 1986–1987. In this text he leads his readers through Jung's most difficult work. He follows his fundamental metaphor of the anatomy of the psyche, suggesting that this is a book of facts described in 'images'. He selects the major images throughout the *Mysterium* and elaborates them with amplificatory material and commentary. Edinger had the capacity to take difficult symbolic material and to translate it into clear, contemporary psychological statements, making it possible to integrate the material into our current psychological worldview.

In 1996 Edinger continued his elaboration of Jung's difficult work in *The Aion Lectures: Exploring the Self in C.G. Jung's Aion*. Here he again worked through Jung's text, suggesting that the reader not approach it with a linear attitude. He stressed that Jung's way of thinking and writing is better understood as presentational and as a kind of 'cluster thinking', likening it to the way a dream presents itself. *Aion* examines the notion of the God image of Christianity and Jung's complex reflections on the archetype of the Self. These concerns are amplified in a number of his other commentaries and books beyond the scope of alchemy proper.

Innovations, criticism and developments

If von Franz and Edinger were major classical disciples of Jung's work, James Hillman is a major critic and innovator in his own right. From one perspective Hillman fundamentally revised Jung's thoughts, but from another he returns to its radical essence, carrying its implications to a new level. His first organised attempts to present his alchemical reflections were in lectures given at the Zurich Institute in 1966. He states that he had been drawn by alchemy's 'obscure poetic language and strange images, and by its amazing insights especially in Jung's introduction to *The Secret of the Golden Flower* and [in his essay on] "The philosophical tree"' (Hillman 2003: 101). Later, in 1968, while at the University of Chicago Hillman continued his lectures and 'expanded [his] library research and collection of dreams with alchemical motifs' (Hillman 2003: 101). These lectures were given in an old wooden chemistry hall and entitled 'Analytic work – alchemical opus'. His approach in these lectures was 'to exhibit a background to analytical work that is metaphorical, even preposterous and so, less encumbered by clinical literalism' (Hillman 2003: 102). This theme had run through Hillman's papers on alchemical themes beginning in his 1970 publication 'On senex consciousness'. In 1978 Hillman published 'The therapeutic value of alchemical language' which set its stage for his continuing reflections. What followed was a series of papers: 'Silver and the white earth', parts 1 and 2 (Hillman 1980, 1981a), 'Alchemical blue and the *unio mentalis*' (1981b), 'The imagination of air and the collapse of alchemy' (1981c), 'Salt: a chapter on alchemical psychology' (1981d), 'Notes on white supremacy: the alchemy of racism' (1986), 'The yellowing of the work' (1989a), *Concerning the Stone: Alchemical Images of the Goal* (1990), 'The seduction of black' (1997) and most recently 'The azure vault: the caelum as experience (2004), a revision and elaboration of his paper on alchemical blue. Like alchemical texts themselves, the content of these papers is complex and difficult to summarise in any unified narrative, but if there are any themes that run through them, it is in his turn to the nuances of language and image, the importance of the imagination and attention to alchemical aesthetics, and to colour as an organising focus for reflection. In addition, Hillman continues to revise and add to this ongoing reflection and is in the process of preparing a book that integrates and expands his vision. For Hillman images speak more directly when their metaphysical coverings can be set aside, then the

> level of collective consciousness can be peeled away, so that the material may speak more phenomenally. Then pagan images stand out: metals, planets, minerals, stars, plants, charms, animals, vessels, fires, and specific locales.
>
> (Hillman 2003: 102)

For Hillman these alchemical images have been obscured by both Jung's psychology as well as by its association with Christian metaphysics. He explained this awareness to the International Congress in Rome in 1977, noting that 'while Jung reclaimed alchemy for the psyche, he also claimed it for his psychology' (Hillman 2003: 102) and that its 'liberation of alchemy from the former traps (mysticism, charlatanism, and pre- or pseudo-science) entangled it in his system of opposites and Christian symbols and thought' (Hillman 2003: 102).

Jung's metapsychology and his reliance on Christian imagery led Hillman to make a distinction between an 'alchemy of spirit' and an 'alchemy of soul', and he notes that the transformation of the psyche can be distinguished from the Christian idea of redemption. He states that when we make this distinction, then

> the subtle changes in color, heat, bodily forms and other qualities refer to the psyche's processes, useful to the practice of therapy for reflecting the changes going on in the psyche without linking these changes to a progressive program or redemptive vision.
>
> (Hillman 2003: 103)

In short, alchemy's curious images and sayings are valuable not so much because alchemy is a grand narrative of the stages of individuation and its conjunction of opposites, nor for its reflection on the Christian process of redemption, but 'rather because of alchemy's myriad, cryptic, arcane, paradoxical, and mainly conflicting texts [which] reveal the psyche phenomenally' (Hillman 203: 103).

For Hillman, alchemy needs to be encountered with the 'least possible intrusion of metaphysics' (2003: 103). He saw Jung, von Franz and Edinger as informed consciously or unconsciously by a metaphysical attitude and attempted to examine alchemy in a scholarly manner in order to find objective meaning. He, on the other hand, sees himself as emphasising the 'matters' of alchemy as metaphorical substances and archetypal principles. He seeks to activate alchemical language and images finding those qualities of human life which act on the very substance of personality.

> The work of soul-making requires corrosive acids, heavy earth, ascending birds; there are sweating kings, dogs, and bitches, stenches, urine, and blood . . . I know that I am not composed of sulfur and salt, buried in horse dung, putrefying or congealing, turning white or green or yellow, encircled by a tail-biting serpent, rising on wings. And yet I am! I cannot take any of this literally, even if it is all accurate, descriptively true.
>
> (Hillman 1978: 37 and 39)

For Hillman, such passages resonate with the complex experiences of the soul. While Jung, von Franz and Edinger worked to develop and extend a 'psychology of alchemy', Hillman makes a critical and innovative move and stylistic shift. His intention is less to extend a psychology of alchemy than to develop an alchemical way of psychologising and to restore an alchemical way of imagining. As noted, this alchemical psychology focuses on images and is highly sensitive to language. On the one hand, he doesn't want to reduce alchemical metaphors to generalised abstractions, while on the other hand, he wants to re-materialise our concepts, 'giving them body, sense and weight' (ibid.: 39).

The alchemical writings of Kugler and myself (Marlan) reflect classical, archetypal and postmodern influences. Kugler, picking up on Hillman's attention to language and his poetic metaphors in *The Dream and the Underworld* (1979), engages these metaphors through a careful attention to linguistics in his own book *The Alchemy of Discourse: An Archetypal Approach to Language* (1983). In this text he integrates Jung's early research in his word association experiments with his later focus on the psychology of alchemy. He analyses the role language plays in the alchemical process of deliteralising matter, asking what is actually involved in the deliteralising of substance and notes that the process is similar to that of moving from an objective to a subjective level of interpretation (Kugler, personal communication, 13 March 2001). This movement from matter to soul is made possible by the inherent polysemy of sound patterns, which have multiple objects of reference, and allow interpretation to move back and forth between their implicit meanings. For Kugler the acoustic image is the crucial intersection between external and internal, between the literal and the metaphoric. 'While the alchemists were working on the soul in matter they were simultaneously working on the "matters" of their soul' (ibid.). Alchemy thus works through the inherent polysemy of the phonetic patterns. In his book Kugler demonstrates how through the acquisition of language we are separated from the external material world of reference and initiated into a shared archetypal system of meaning relations. The acquisition of language enabled man to take 'matters' out of life and transform them into imagination. Shifting the linguistic mode from semantic to phonetic consideration transforms the material of the 'day world' (objects of reference) into the insubstantial poetic images of the 'night world' (image – meanings).

Likewise influenced by Hillman, I have edited two books on the subject, *Salt and the Alchemical Soul* (Marlan 1995) and *Fire in the Stone: The Alchemy of Desire* (1997). The inspiration for the first book was Hillman's (1981d) essay 'Salt: a chapter in alchemical psychology'. The goal of the work was an exercise in reflection on the image of salt, which has had a place in the history of depth psychology and in alchemy. In this work a range of genres of depth psychology were explored, including a Freudian, a Jungian and a Hillmanian approach to the subject. The intention was not so much to juxtapose perspectives in order to find the right or best approach, but to appreciate the particular genius of each author. While this is true, the flavour of this approach draws heavily from the phenomenological/postmodern and archetypal perspectives in its sensitivity to a variety of perspectives and in its attempt to 'restore psychology to the widest, richest, and deepest volume, so that it resonates with the soul' (Hillman 1989b: 26). A second edited book (Marlan 1997b), *Fire in the Stone: The Alchemy of Desire*, was inspired by the continuing vitality of the alchemical metaphor. In my essay, 'Fire in the stone: an inquiry into the alchemy of soul-making' (Marlan 1997a), the focus is on the psyche's intentionality and its complexity, emphasising its often conflicting and multiple intentionalities and reflecting on Hillman's (1983) question 'What does soul want?' My reflections on this question lead to the metaphor of the 'alchemy of desire', which problematises any simple understanding of subjectivity and shifts the concern to a broader view of the dynamism of the soul. The essay seeks to look again at the soul's complexity and the danger of essentialism in psychological theory. It brings to bear the reflections of Hillman and Derrida, showing a relationship between their approaches, in so far as they share the medium of fictional space and articulate a postmodern voice. Both Hillman and Derrida revise our understanding of fiction and destabilise a literal understanding of psychological theory.

The complexity of the soul is not adequately understood by any of the forms of logocentrism but belong to a wider field of psyche (Hillman) or signs (Derrida). In this field, the hard and fast boundaries of the ego are progressively loosened. The essay goes on to reflect on the goal of both depth psychology and the opus of alchemy. The inquiry follows post-modern and archetypal sensibilities along the lines of Hillman's revisioning of the traditional concepts of telos and the goal, and opens a notion of fictional space in which an alchemy of desire is enacted, where we can 'speak meaningfully of a multiplicity of intentions in the play of desire, of a dialectic of desire in which . . . complex intentionalities encounter one another'. The alchemy of desire is 'a subtle field of traces, exchanges, and fictional enactments' from which 'we can develop an ear to the soul's desire' (Marlan 1997a: 14). This field of desire then articulates a shared psychological space opened by postmodernism and archetypal psychology.

Schwartz-Salant's *The Mystery of the Human Relationship* (1998) is both a theoretical and clinical contribution to the Jungian literature. His reflections bear on the philosophical foundation of Jungian analysis as well as on its clinical practice, on transference and beyond to human relationships in general. Schwartz-Salant (personal communication, 2000) notes that Jung employed alchemical symbolism to amplify his theory of individuation process, and dealt with alchemical imagery from the point of view of projection. Projection as an idea requires a number of philosophical and metapsychological presuppositions which are taken for granted in classical analysts such as von Franz and Edinger. Going beyond these assumptions requires a fundamental shift in metapsychology if not ontology and it is this kind of shift that Schwartz-Salant intends to bring about. Rather than beginning with the idea of two separate individuals relating to one another he emphasises an 'intermediate realm' between people in relationships as well as giving attention to the field between subject as object, mind and matter, psychic body. His contribution here is to focus on and deepen our understanding of this field as something more than an inter-subjective event as it is often described in contemporary psychoanalysis (Schwartz-Salant, personal communication, 2000).

It is in his emphasis on the experiential rather than the causal relatedness of the alchemist and his or her work, and in an encouragement of the engagement with one's 'mad parts' and those of patients that Schwartz-Salant feels he goes beyond Jung (Schwartz-Salant, personal communication, 2000). He summarises his contribution as follows. He starts by noting that Jung employed alchemical symbolism to amplify his theory of individuation and that, in the process, he dealt with alchemical imagery from the point of view of projection, in other words, from the point of view that reified the subject–object dichotomy. Schwartz-Salant argues that this dualistic

framework does not adequately capture the complexity of original alchemical imagery because this imagery is the 'residue of centuries of experiences
that do not always, or even primarily, fit into an "inside-outside"' structure.
To this end, he developed the idea of the interactive field, and in so doing he
brings to bear 'correspondence theory, archetypal theory and subtle body
theory' (Schwartz-Salant, personal communication, 2000). In addition, he
draws on the phenomenologists Edmund Husserl and Maurice Merleau-
Ponty as well as Jean Gebser and Henry Corbin, who have all contributed to
understanding this realm (ibid.). For these thinkers our traditional Cartesian
understanding of an observing ego stands in the way of a deeper experiential
awareness of what the alchemists were speaking about. Schwartz-Salant
wants to capture this experience, which goes beyond a rational discursive
approach and requires a kind of 'aperspectival consciousness' (ibid.).

Schwartz-Salant's continuing reflection on the human relationship led
him to reimagine the model of transference found in Jung's 'Psychology of
the transference'. He was also the first one to analyse all twenty pictures of
the *Rosarium*, the interpretation of which translates well to his field
approach. Schwartz-Salant's work opened the door for a comparative psychoanalytic reflection showing how, for instance, what Kleinian analysts
call projective identification can be seen more profoundly as the phenomenology of the field manifesting in a consciousness attuned to projection
and causality (Schwartz-Salant, personal communication, 2000). This
shows how the field is primary and how projective identification could be
seen as part of alchemical imagery. He notes that from this perspective one
can see that Jung was working on the same issues as Melanie Klein was,
both in 1946. Beyond this, he has used alchemical texts to understand
transformations in the field. Rather than seeing the field as an intersub-
jective product (Self-psychologists, Ogden, interpersonal approaches, etc.),
he saw it like an actual field in physics, i.e., something with its own processes. That is why he used the term 'interactive'.

In the above ways and in reimagining human relationships, transference
and in encouraging an experiential entry into the above-described field,
Schwartz-Salant goes beyond Jung. Zabriskie (personal communication,
2000) in her own way but like Schwartz-Salant writes that her study of
alchemy and its antecedents in Egyptian mythology have informed her
'understanding and approach to the psyche as a process capable of transformation and of its images in the dynamic interrelationships to each other
and to the psychic "field" constellated around and within an individual'
(ibid.). Zabriskie is also concerned with the relationship of this field to the
issues of contemporary physics, and writes that the most compelling vector
and amplification of the alchemical world has come from the 'themes and
models of modern physics' (Zabriskie, personal communication, 2000). She
states that she came to this through studying the relationships between Jung
and the Nobel physicist Wolfgang Pauli. This interest led to her paper 'Jung

and Pauli: a subtle asymmetry' (1995a) and to her introduction in *Atom and Archetype: The Pauli/Jung Letters, 1932–1958* (2001). Zabriskie's other interest was in following Jung's study of the alchemist's hypothesis of the relation between psychic and the material dimension and wrote a review of von Franz's (1992) essay in *Psyche and Matter* called 'The matter of psyche' (Zabriskie 1996a). In addition she is interested in the clinical and cultural contextualisation of alchemical imagery as in her 'Exiles and orphans: Jung, Paracelsus and the healing images of alchemy' (1995b) and 'Fermentation in alchemical practice' (1996b). In this latter paper, she questioned why Jung inserted the eleventh engraving of an edition of the *Rosarium* between the fifth and sixth images and speculated on the philosophical and clinical values of this (Zabriskie, personal communication, 2000).

The question of Jung's relationship to contemporary clinical psycho-analysis had earlier been brought up by Andrew Samuels (1989). It was his concern to present Jung as a credible thinker in the mainstream of analytic discourse and as a reliable base for further contributions to analysis (Samuels 1989: 175). For Samuels this concern requires some understanding of why Jung gave so much intellectual effort to a subject considered by many to be pejoratively mystical if not absurd. Samuels counters this judgement by pointing out that alchemy provides important if not central metaphors for psychological activity and that its imagery is well suited

> to capture the almost impossible essence of analysis or any other deep human condition; the play between interpersonal relatedness on the one hand and imaginal, intrapsychic activity on the other.
>
> (Samuels 1989: 176)

Samuels goes on to explore the fecundity of alchemical metaphors as a unique way of imagining psychological processes and their clinical application. To accomplish this he, like many other Jungians, reflects on Jung's (1946) paper, 'Psychology of the transference' and he elaborates how it is that Jung found in the obscure images of the *Rosarium Philosophorum* an important analogue of the archetypal level of experience. While Jung spoke here about the archetypal conceptions of the transference, Samuels also noted that he also spoke of its personal aspects. Thus for him, Jung both contributed something new to the field that had not been picked up before as well as contributing ideas that were later to become standard contemporary themes of psychoanalysis. In Jung's original understanding of the Otherness of the Self to the ego he also anticipated the vision of Lacan. Analysts have often been split over the extent to which they feel Jung should be understood in the tradition of psychoanalysis. Jeffrey Raff is one who would rather place Jung in the context of a larger spiritual perspective.

Raff in his book *Jung and the Alchemical Imagination* (2000) picks up, renews and extends the classical tradition of Jung and von Franz. He sees alchemy as an expression of a long esoteric spiritual tradition of which Jung's work is a contemporary expression. Raff finds three major components of Jung's work important in extending this tradition of 'Jungian spirituality'. These are 'the transcendent function, active imagination, and the self' (Raff, personal communication, 2000). He is not so much interested in psychological interpretation as in 'developing a model for inner exploration and transformation'; and this is what, he feels, primarily connects him to the von Franz tradition (Raff, ibid.).

Like Hillman, but with very different conclusions, Raff puts special emphasis on the imagination and the nature of alchemy as an imaginal experience; and also like Hillman, he links imagination to the Sufi concept of an intermediate realm. He also emphasises the nature and development of inner figures that personify the unconscious and may be worked with in active imagination. Working with these figures for him moves psyche toward the manifestation of the Self, the classical goal of Jung's individuation process. Up to this point Raff is a 'very mainstream classical analyst though he [Raff] emphasizes the inner figures more than is usual and also places an extreme importance on active imagination' (Raff, ibid.).

Where Raff departs from Jung is in stating that Jung did not appreciate what the alchemist Dorn spoke about as a third *Coniunctio*, which is a union with the *unus mundus*. For Raff, Jung's work stopped with his interpretation of the second *Coniunctio*, which is the corporal union and 'which he interprets as the point at which the Self comes fully alive within the psyche and begins to function more powerfully' (Raff, ibid.).

Raff believes that Jung did not go far enough 'because of his bias that all is contained within the psyche' (Raff, ibid.). For him the third *Coniunctio* occurs when the manifested Self, or the 'individuated' person, goes beyond the psyche to face the transpsychic world of the spirit (Raff, ibid.).

Though Jung intuited what he considered to be a metaphysical realm, he always claimed not to be a metaphysician and remained an empiricist.

Raff, on the other hand, following the Sufi alchemists, argues that alchemy is really about the transpsychic world, the world of the Gnostic imagination. For him to access these spiritual dimensions one must go beyond ordinary active imagination to enter what he considers the psychoid realm. In this state, body and spirit are one and spiritual beings manifest as psychoidal figures (Raff, ibid.). The most important of these figures he calls the Self of the psychoid or 'the ally', which is a personification of God. This figure is individually experienced as transcendental and not part of the psyche. For Raff, the alchemy of the psychoid is about the 'interaction of human awareness and feeling with spiritual entities that have taken on form in the psychoid world' (Raff, ibid.).

In his book, he talks about the third *coniunctio* as union of self and ally, and the inclusion of transpsychic forces as part of our worldview. On a personal note, he states that to his knowledge, no one has written about the ally in this way nor studied the third *coniunctio*. Hence, he feels that he differs from others in emphasising the spiritual nature of Jung's work and in putting less emphasis on clinical work or psychological interpretation, Raff extends his model to include the psychoid world as the place where spiritual entities manifest and take on form. For Raff, in the higher states of development the human and divine worlds come together and one can imagine in this the Western equivalent to enlightenment.

Walter Odajnyk (1993) also takes up the theme of the spiritual importance of Jung's alchemical work in his book, *Gathering the Light: A Psychology of Meditation*. Odajnyk's focus is on the importance of the meditative tradition, which he feels has not been given adequate notice in serious psychological reflections. Thus he turns to the East and to the psychological contributions that Jung has made to our understanding and appreciation of Eastern religious thought and practice. Throughout his book, he 'sought to demonstrate and, where necessary, to apply and extend, Jung's contribution to an understanding of psychology of meditation' (Odajnyk 1993: 166).

Odajnyk returns to Jung's commentary on *The Secret of the Golden Flower* and thus also to the relationship between meditation and alchemy. He notes that while Western alchemy is more differentiated in its description of the earlier stages of development, the Eastern tradition is more developed in its description of its final goals. To develop this insight, Odajnyk takes up Jung's discussion of the *coniunctio*, as described in *Mysterium Coniunctionis*, and compares it to the goal of psycho-spiritual transformation in meditation. Odajnyk states that Jung had the tendency to lump together many images relating to the goal of the alchemical process while for him there are many distinctions between these images which may refer to a further differentiation of the goal. In addition, there do not seem to be Western equivalents to certain descriptions found in Eastern alchemy. Jung concludes that psychic wholeness will never be attained empirically, but for Odajnyk further acquaintance with Eastern alchemy and meditation practices raises the possibility of the actual psychological experience of these higher goals as taking place in what he has termed 'the meditation complex'. An additional amplification of this theme is taken up in Harold Coward's (1995) book, *Jung and Eastern Thought*, which also critiqued Jung for not going far enough. Coward (1995: 142) raises the question 'if there can be mystical experience without an individual ego?'

For Odajnyk (1993), this meditation complex is a new way of seeing the new psychological and energetic field, and it is this perspective that forms a ground for new ways of interpreting Jung's ideas. In addition, this perspective lends itself to the consideration that apart from Jung's idea of the goal of wholeness, we can now also reconsider the idea of self-realisation and enlightenment. Besides his comparison of the Eastern and Western notions of the *coniunctio* and his introduction of the meditation complex, Odajnyk's assessment of Thomas Cleary's work is noteworthy. Cleary (1991) critiqued both Wilhelm's translation of *The Secret of the Golden Flower* and Jung's commentary of it (see Cleary 1991; Odajnyk 1993: 191–212).

The theme of Taoist alchemy is also addressed in my paper, 'The metaphor of light and renewal in Taoist alchemy and Jungian analysis' (Marlan 1998).[4] In this work, I noted that light and renewal are important if not fundamental metaphors in both Taoist alchemy and Jungian analysis, and the use of this metaphor is traced in the classical alchemical work, *The Secret of the Golden Flower*, mentioned above. In focusing on the metaphor of light and renewal in the two traditions, the relationship between analysis and spiritual discipline is addressed and a comparison is made between the images of 'turning the light around' and 'the emergence of the spiritual embryo', as well as further reflection on the unity of opposites or the *coniunctio*, themes important to both Taoist alchemy and Jungian analysis.

This reflection on the theme of the metaphor of light was a continuation of issues raised in the paper 'The metaphor of light and its deconstruction in Jung's alchemical vision' (Marlan 2000),[5] in which the interrelationship of light and consciousness and their privileged place in the development of Western metaphysics is considered with the conclusion that consciousness and vision also have a shadow which has been challenged in Jungian and archetypal psychology, postmodern theory, Eastern thought, and alchemy. A new understanding of light and its relation with darkness is essential for the development of consciousness in our time.

Reflection on this theme is deepened in 'The black sun: the alchemy and art of darkness' (Marlan 2005).[6] The Black Sun, *Sol Niger*, is considered here as an archetypal phenomenon having two poles and multiple differentiations. At one end the non-self can be seen in its most literal form, locked into the *nigredo* and mortification of the flesh, while its other pole opens the soul to the dark shine of sacred illumination.

Continued reflection of alchemy and Eastern thought is also taken up by Japanese analyst Hayao Kawai (1996) in *Buddhism and the Art of Psychotherapy*. In this book, Professor Kawai compares the classic series of Ox Herding pictures with illustrations from the *Rosarium Philosophorum* (1996: 52). He notes that both sets of pictures illustrate the individuation process but while there are 'mysterious similarities' between them, he also sees important differences. For him comparing these images amounts to contrasting Eastern and Western styles of consciousness. He agrees with the conclusion of Marvin Spiegelman (1985) who analyses the same sets of images. Kawai notes that in the West, there is a tendency to emphasise a linear, developmental goal-oriented tendency while in the East there is a leaning toward seeing the process as circular, archetypal and infinite. Likewise in the West emphasis is placed on the individual person while the East tends to focus on nature. These styles of consciousness are important with regard to how we see both the individuation and alchemical processes. It is possible to view these processes from either style of consciousness.

Kawai is masterful at resisting the temptation to simply fall into either perspective concluding that when working with a patient it is necessary to be able to see from both orientations, with and without stages. For Kawai, it is important to carry and accept the paradox. In this way, the human person and nature can work in harmony. In concluding, Kawai, himself, ends with such a paradox. He reflects on the question of whether or not it is possible to integrate two orientations, linear/circular, developmental/archetypal, male and female, East and West, and concludes that it is both possible and impossible (Kawai 1996: 141). One is tempted to say that his orientation is typically Eastern, and perhaps comes more out of the recognition of the female principle than of the West's demands for either/or logos. But I believe this would simply fall back into what Kawai deconstructs. His acute observation about the role of contemporary Japanese women in traditional society is a case in point. The soul's alchemy refuses to rigidify into traditional categories.

Wolfgang Giegerich's book *The Soul's Logical Life* (1998/2001) contains an important critical view of Jung's approach to alchemy. Giegerich elaborates both what he feels were Jung's contributions and where he feels Jung did not go far enough (Giegerich, personal communication, 2000). Reflecting on his position, Giegerich acknowledges Jung's accomplishment in the discovery of alchemy as a basis for his depth psychology. He notes that using alchemy as a model had important and interrelated methodological advancements.

Given this appreciation for Jung's contribution, Giegerich is nevertheless critical about some dimensions of Jung's alchemical conceptions. For Giegerich, as noted, but in a way different from others before him, Jung did not go far enough. Alchemy entered Jung's psychology only as a topic or content:

> while trying to hold the structure of psychology itself down in the total incompatible character of a modern science (the neutral empirical observer standpoint). Its semantic content was not allowed to come home to (affect, infect) the logical or syntactical form of psychology.
>
> (Giegerich, personal communication, 2000)

What Giegerich critiques is that Jung's scientific/modernist metapsychology seems to remain the same, maintaining a subject/object split, while at the same time making an object of alchemical ideas that themselves do not fit into these categories. Then Jung would reduce alchemical processes to events 'in' the unconscious or the interior of the personality. Giegerich notes:

> the individual, the personality, the inner, and 'the unconscious' are our names for the 'bottle' in which the mercurial 'substance' had to stay firmly enclosed for Jung.
>
> (Giegerich, personal communication, 2000)

Giegerich continues his reflection by noting that 'because Mercurius remained enclosed in the above way "it" had to stay a substance, an object, and entity' and could not be true to its own nature as a spirit (something intangible and unrepresentable). This interpretation sets the stage for the fundamental thrust of Giegerich's emphasis in *The Soul's Logical Life*: namely, when Jung, and Hillman for that matter, stick to 'images' as fundamental, they are in fact objectifying the spirit of alchemy. The image itself becomes objectified, while the true spirit of alchemy aims at realising the logical life of the soul, which is conceptual, subtle, non-positive, intangible. Throughout Giegerich's critique he juxtaposes images and a 'pictorial form of thinking' which valorises perception and imagination, with what he considers to be the true aim of alchemy which is to achieve the level of dialectical thought and logical expression as he details it in his text cited above. For Giegerich when Jung opts to hold the image as fundamental he steps over the goal of alchemy to release the spirit from its container and ignore the 'self sublation' or death that the alchemical process requires. In doing so he skips 'over the successive psychological development of several centuries' (Giegerich, personal communication, 2000).

> Jung pronounced his psychology of the unconscious to be the immediate successor and redemptor of alchemy. In this way he could declare the previous image-oriented (pictorial) mode of thinking, long overcome by the history of the soul, to still be 'the' psychological mode and decry the later development into which alchemy had dissolved as a mere rationalism, intellectualization, i.e., mere 'ego'. Jung excluded from his psychological reception of alchemy the fact that the telos of alchemy had been the overcoming of itself. He froze it, and psychology along with it, in an earlier phase.
>
> (Giegerich, personal communication, 2000)

In short, for Giegerich, the task of alchemy was to deconstruct itself, or at least, in his terms, to surpass itself as a movement of the historical expression of the soul. Here a Hegelian dialectical understanding of history influences Giegerich. Finally, for him, Jung did not give enough emphasis to the active dimensions of consciousness as constituting the reality of the psyche. That is, alchemy was an active human project, which meant that the observer of the alchemical process was not passive. He notes that even the activity of 'registering, recording, maybe painting, the dream or fantasy images received and in thinking *about* them as a text' (ibid.) there was still the tendency to relate to this text as a finished 'product' delivered by the producing 'nature'. 'But consciousness had to refrain from entering the process of the production of images themselves'. Giegerich qualified this statement to note the 'exception' of active imagination, though even in this instance 'what is to become active and enter the production process is not the reflecting mind, but the empirical ego'. In short the mythos of Jungian work, psychological and alchemical, is that the 'natural process of the production of images was not to be interfered with'. For Giegerich, this was the vestige of fundamental naturalism left in Jung's psychology and in the end 'was contrary to the spirit of alchemy' (ibid.). Finally, one might say that Giegerich's reading is both Hegelian and deconstructive. He notes that in Jung: 'we have the curious spectacle . . . of a singular dedication to and propagation of alchemy "and" its simultaneous repression. His advancement of alchemy as a psychological paradigm was "in itself" the substance of what it was intrinsically about' (ibid.).

Giegerich's ideas have begun to influence other Jungians. A case in point is the work of Yasuhiro Tanaka, a Japanese analyst. Tanaka (2000) has written a paper entitled 'The alchemical images and logic in analytical psychology'. He picks up on Giegerich's critique of 'images' and the limitations of an 'imaginal psychology'. For him, if we remain one-sidedly dependent on such a perspective 'then we fall into the trap of remaining on the horizon of surface-psychology rather than depth psychology' (Tanaka, personal communication, 2000).

For Tanaka as for Giegerich 'we psychologists living after Jung, have to address the alchemical logic in analytical psychology'. His assessment of Jung is that while Jung on a personal level perceived the logical, paradoxical and dialectic dimension of alchemy, he could not 'interiorize it enough' or adequately apply it to his psychology as a theory. Thus, for Tanaka, our work now is 'not to fashion the bridge between alchemy and our clinical practice' but to examine the theoretical limitations of Jung's psychology:

> Alchemy was not only his [Jung's] historical background but also his logical background in the sense that for Jung it was none other than the theoria for sublating his own experience in to his psychology.
>
> (Tanaka, personal communication, 2000)

This then means it was Jung's theory that could dispel the *massa confusa* and it is to this that we must now give our attention.

Current status and trends for future development

Jung's psychological reflections on alchemy helped to forge a number of his fundamental concepts. His idea of psychic reality, the centrality of the archetype, individuation, active imagination, the Self as a superordinate structure and the religious nature of psychic life were all developed and/or deepened through his engagement with alchemy. He linked his experiences with those of the alchemists and, as noted, alchemy became both the historical counterpart and conformation of his thought. Jung thus brought alchemy out of obscurity and into the realm of modern psychology. In addition to the basic theoretical ideas noted above, alchemy provided Jung and Jungian psychology with a rich metaphoric language with which to describe the complex transactions of the unconscious and the transformations of analytical work.

The *prima materia* and *massa confusa* became an image of the disorganised beginnings of analytical work, the *vas hermeticum*, the container and sealed vessel of the analytical relationships. In this vessel the matters of psyche could be heated up, cooked, coagulated, distilled and transformed. These psychological alchemical processes worked on the confusions and splits of the personality seeking to heal them through unifications, the *Coniunctio* and the sacred marriage which eventually could result in a stabilised sense of wholeness, the Self, or philosopher's stone. In this way the metaphors of alchemy lend themselves to the newly developed psychology of the unconscious, the colours of alchemy became the colours of analytical psychology, as alchemy could now be seen in a psychological light.

Jung expressed his ideas in a non-dogmatic and tentative way. He thought of himself as a physician and empirical scientist who was discovering and documenting the objective facts of psychic reality. Classical analysts such as von Franz (1980) and Edinger (1985) epitomise this attitude. Edinger (1985: xix) has stated that what Jung presents are 'psychic facts rather than theoretical constructs or philosophical speculations'. Jung did in fact reject metaphysical claims but for many contemporary thinkers such a rejection of the metaphysical implications of one's thought is considered naive. Even empirical science can be seen to carry ontological or at least theoretical implications. Although science claims to be free of philosophical assumptions, this position has been challenged by many philosophers of science as well in the larger hermeneutic tradition. Science, too, has ontological commitments that often remain unacknowledged. What we see is not simply a given; perspective and context are always part of what is seen. Jung knew this, but in most instances did not apply it to his own theory (Giegerich 1998/2001). Classical analysts have often held that Jung was ahead of his time, and our job is to understand him, amplify his ideas and apply them to new areas of research and practice; but for others the implications in his thought are vestiges of metaphysical attitudes that must be seen and critiqued.

One such idea was his notion of projection. Jung relied on this concept as basic for his understanding of the relationship between psychology and alchemy. For a number of analysts projection as a theory is problematic and at best a limited concept by which to understand psychological transactions and relationships. Schwartz-Salant (1995) noted that going beyond the theory of projection would seem to require a fundamental shift in metapsychology if not ontology. In explicit response to projection theory, Schwartz-Salant (1998) has emphasised a shift in focus to the idea of a 'psychic field' that extends beyond the analytical assumptions that form the basis of the idea of projection. In so doing he echoes a contemporary ethos that imagines psychic life from outside a traditional Cartesian and Kantian paradigm.

Hillman's innovations, noted above, propose a radical revision of 'classical' and 'clinical' paradigms. For him these approaches are filled with presuppositions that lead to reductive and literalised renderings of alchemy's powerful imagistic potential. The interpretation of alchemy in this reductive way leads to what he calls a 'psychology of alchemy'. The problem is that our current notions of psychology are far too limited to do justice to the import of alchemical images and processes. Hillman calls for a total revisioning of psychology and the development of an alchemical psychology, placing the non-reducible language of alchemy first as a marker to note its irreducible quality as a realm of language, imagination and soul.

Kugler (1983) likewise emphasised the contribution of language for a paradigm shift, but while Hillman might be said to emphasise a phenomenological attitude toward the place of soul, Kugler also emphasises the formal structures of linguistics and phonetic patterns. Samuels (1989) also moves toward a new vision of the plural psyche, and Odajnyk (1993) contributes the notion of the medication-complex as an energetic field. Marlan (1997a) describes the field as an 'alchemy of desire' and calls attention to Jacques Derrida's idea of 'differance', which Derrida states is 'neither a word nor a concept' but a playful way to imagine a field of indeterminacy. Giegerich (1998) brings to bear philosophical and psychological criticism and inspired by Hegel introduces a new understanding of the 'logical life of the soul'. Tanaka (2000) followed Giegerich in pushing us toward the importance of theory to dispel our theoretical confusion.

Focusing on a 'field approach' and linking all the above thinkers to this notion in no way is an attempt to suggest that they are all saying the same thing. It is rather to note that in their own way, and from within their own frames of reference, they all are responding to the limitations of a Cartesian/Kantian paradigm and are struggling with a new way of seeing and imagining a path beyond the classical paradigm.

In addition to a critique of the metaphysical remnants that remain in Jung's thought, the issue of Jung's relationship and perhaps dependence on Christianity is a current issue. While classical analysts are critical of the limitation of the present-day Christian model, for many it is something that needs to be developed to achieve a more adequate reflection of psychic reality. Others have turned to Egyptian (Abt, Zabriskie), Greek, pagan (Hillman) or oriental (Odajnyk, Marlan, Kawii) and Sufi (Hillman, Raff) traditions to understand alchemy.

Finally, an issue for current reflection is the developing ideas about the goal of alchemy and analysis. As noted, Odajnyk (1993) and Raff (2000) both see the potential of going beyond what Jung felt to be the possible goals of the individuation processes as Jung imagined it. Odajnyk speaks of the actual experience of self-realisation and enlightenment, and Raff of the third *Coniunctio* and the inclusion of a transpsychic union of self and ally. Hillman would still see these extensions and possibilities as not going far enough. What Hillman calls for is a reimagining of the idea of the goal itself. For him all of the above would fall into a spiritual literalism and his way of thinking breaks with the tradition of the spiritualisation of alchemy and with heroic notions of attainment. For him the goal is the psychological cure of 'me' which means going beyond the desire for improvement. This critique resonates (differences aside) with the work of Giegerich, who sees the negation of the 'me' as essential for the soul. To what extent and the way in which these critiques differ from the surpassing of the ego implied in the more spiritualised approaches is a matter for continued debate and reflection.

As can be seen from the above there are many who extend, apply and/or revise Jung's work. There are many complementarities and differences, but in all the vitality of Jung's work on alchemy remains an essential inspiration to contemporary analysts. Many issues remain to be developed, deepened and dialogued. In the end perhaps the 'true' meaning of alchemy will remain as elusive as the philosopher's stone itself.

Notes

1 Psychoanalytic scholar Sonu Shamdasani has pointed out the limitations of relying on *Memories, Dreams, Reflections*, because of its editorial liberties, but he still suggests that individual paragraphs are accurate though thoroughly recast (personal communication, 25 September 2000).
2 For a bibliography of Edinger's work see *Psychological Perspectives*, 39: 58–59.
3 *Quadrant* (summer, 1978) 2(1): Introduction and *Calcinatio*; (winter, 1978) 3(1): *Solutio*; (summer, 1979) 4: *Coagulatio*; (spring, 1980) 5: *Sublimatio*; (spring, 1982) 8: *Coniunctio*; (spring, 1981) 6: *Mortificatio*; (fall, 1981) 7: *Separatio*; (spring, 1982) 8: *Coniunctio*.
4 This paper was first presented at *The First International Conference on Jungian Psychology and Chinese Culture*, Guangzhou, China, December 1998. Proceedings published in *Quadrant* (summer, 2001).
5 This paper was first presented at the Inter-Regional Society of Jungian Analysts and later published in R. Brooke (ed.) (2000) *Pathways into the Jungian World*. London and New York: Routledge.
6 Paper presented at the symposium: Psychology at the Threshold: An International Symposium of Archetypal Psychology, 31 August–4 September 2000. Audio tape available from *Sounds True Recordings*.

References

Cleary, T. (1991) *The Secret of the Golden Flower*. San Francisco, CA: Harper.
Coward, H. (1985) *Jung and Eastern Thought*. Albany: NY: State University of New York Press.
Edinger, E.F. (1978a) 'Psychotherapy and alchemy: introduction and *Calcinatio*'.

Quadrant: Journal of the C.G. Jung Foundation for Analytical Psychology, 2(1) (summer).

Edinger, E.F. (1978b) 'Psychotherapy and alchemy: *Solutio*'. *Quadrant*, 3(1) (winter).

—— (1979) 'Psychotherapy and alchemy: *Coagulatio*'. *Quadrant*, 4 (summer).

—— (1980) 'Psychotherapy and alchemy: *Sublimatio*'. *Quadrant* 5 (spring).

—— (1981a) 'Psychotherapy and alchemy: *Mortificatio*'. *Quadrant*, 6 (spring).

—— (1981b) 'Psychotherapy and alchemy: *Separatio*'. *Quadrant*, 7 (fall).

—— (1982) 'Psychotherapy and alchemy: *Coniunctio*'. *Quadrant*, 8 (spring).

—— (1985) *Anatomy of the Psyche: Alchemical Symbolism in Psychotherapy*. LaSalle, IL: Open Court.

—— (1994) *The Mystery of the Coniunctio: Alchemical Image of Individuation*. Toronto: Inner City.

—— (1995) *The Mysterium Lectures: A Journey through C.G. Jung's Mysterium Coniunctionis*, ed. J. Dexter Blackmer. Toronto: Inner City.

—— (1996a) *The Aion Lectures: Exploring the Self in C.G. Jung's Aion*, ed. D.A. Wesley. Toronto: Inner City.

—— (1996b) *The New God-Image: A Study of Jung's Key Letters Concerning the Evolution of the Western God-Image*. Wilmette, IL: Chiron.

Fordham, M. (1960) 'The relevance of analytical theory to alchemy, mysticism and theology'. *Journal of Analytical Psychology*, 5(2): 113–128.

Gad, I. (1999) 'Alchemy: the language of the soul'. *Psychological Perspectives*, 39: 92–101.

Giegerich, W. (1998/2001) *The Soul's Logical Life*. Frankfurt: Peter Lang.

Grinnel, R. (1973) *Alchemy in a Modern Woman*. Zurich: Spring.

Henderson, J.L. (1978) 'Practical application of alchemical theory'. *Journal of Analytical Psychology*, 23(3): 248.

—— *The Splendor Solis* (video). Monaco Video, 234 Ninth Street, San Francisco, CA 94103.

Henderson, J.L. and Sherwood, D.N. (2003) *Transformation of the Psyche: The Symbolic Alchemy of the Splendor Solis*. Hove, UK: Brunner-Routledge.

Hillman, J. (1970) 'On senex consciousness [Lead and Saturn]'. *Spring*: 146–165.

—— (1978) 'The therapeutic value of alchemical language', in R. Sardello (ed.) *Dragonflies: Studies of Imaginal Psychology*. Irving, TX: University of Dallas.

—— (1979) *The Dream and the Underworld*. New York: Harper and Row.

—— (1980) 'Silver and the white earth, Part I'. *Spring*: 21–48

—— (1981a) 'Silver and the white earth, Part II'. *Spring*: 21–66.

—— (1981b) 'Alchemical blue and the *unio mentalis*', in C. Eshleman (ed.) *Sulfur*, 1: 33–50.

—— (1981c) 'The imagination of air and the collapse of alchemy'. *Eranos Yearbook*, 59: 273–333.

—— (1981d) 'Salt: a chapter in alchemical psychology', in J. Stroud and G. Thomas (eds) *Images of the Untouched*. Dallas, TX: Dallas Institute of Humanities. Also in S. Marlan (ed.) (1995) *Salt and the Alchemical Soul*. Dallas, TX: Spring.

—— (1983) *Healing Fictions*. Barrytown, NY: Station Hill.

—— (1986) 'Notes on white supremacy: the alchemy of racism'. *Spring*, 46: 29–58.

—— (1989a) 'The yellowing of the work', in M.A. Matoon (ed.) *Proceedings of the*

Eleventh International Congress of Analytical Psychology, Paris. Zurich: Daimon Verlag.

Hillman, J. (1989b) *A Blue Fire*, introduced and edited by T. Moore. New York: Harper and Row.

—— (1990) *Concerning the Stone: Alchemical Images of the Goal. Eranos Yearbook*. Ascona, Switzerland.

—— (1997) 'The seduction of black', in S. Marlan (ed.) *Fire in the Stone*. Wilmette, IL: Chiron.

—— (2003) 'A note for Stanton Marlan'. *Journal of Jungian Theory and Practice*, 5(2): 102–103.

—— (2004) 'The azure vault: the caelum as experience'. Keynote address at the Sixteenth International Congress for Analytical Psychology, Barcelona.

Holt, D. (1973) 'Jung and Marx'. *Spring*: 52–66.

—— (1987–1988) 'Alchemy: Jung and the historians of science'. *Harvest*, 33: 40–61.

Jacoby, M. (1984) *The Analytic Encounter: Transference and Human Relationships*. Toronto: Inner City.

Jaffé, A. (1967) 'The influence of alchemy on the work of C.G. Jung'. *Spring*: 7–26.

Jung, C.G. (1921) *Psychological Types. CW* 6.

—— (1928) 'The relations between the ego and the unconscious', in *CW* 7: pars. 202–406.

—— (1929) 'Commentary on *The Secret of the Golden Flower*', in *CW* 13: pars. 17–45.

—— (1937) *Psychology and Religion. CW* 11.

—— (1942) 'Paracelsus as a spiritual phenomenon', in *CW* 13: 189.

—— (1944) *Psychology and Alchemy. CW* 12.

—— (1946) 'Psychology of the transference', in *CW* 16: pars. 353–539.

—— (1951) *Aion. CW* 9ii.

—— (1953) *Psychology and Alchemy CW* 12.

—— (1955–1956) *Mysterium Coniunctionis. CW* 14.

—— (1958) *Psychology and Religion: West and East. CW* 11.

—— (1959) 'Flying Saucers', in *CW* 10: pars. 589–824.

—— (1963) *Memories, Dreams, Reflections*. New York: Pantheon.

—— (1979) *General Bibliography. CW* 19.

—— (1979) *General Index. CW* 20.

Kawai, H. (1996) *Buddhism and the Art of Psychotherapy*. College Station, TX: Texas A&M University Press.

Kirsch, J. (1995) 'Transference', in M. Stein (ed.) *Jungian Analysis*, 2nd edn. La Salle, IL: Open Court.

Kirsch, T.B. (2000) *The Jungians: A Comparative and Historical Perspective*. London and Philadelphia, PA: Routledge.

Kugler, P. (1983) *The Alchemy of Discourse: An Archetypal Approach to Language*. Lewisburgh, PA: Bucknell University Press.

McGoveran, P. (1981) 'An application of an alchemical model for milieu functioning'. *Journal of Analytical Psychology*, 26(3): 249–267.

McGuire, W. and Hull, R.F.C. (eds) (1977) *C.G. Jung Speaking: Interviews and Encounters*, Bollingen Series XCVII. Princeton, NJ: Princeton University Press.

Marlan, S. (1995) 'Introduction to salt and the alchemical soul', in S. Marlan (ed.) *Salt and the Alchemical Soul*. Woodstock, CT: Spring.

Marlan, S. (1997a) 'Fire in the stone: an inquiry into the alchemy of soul-making', in S. Marlan (ed.) *Fire in the Stone*. Wilmette, IL: Chiron.

—— (1997b) *Fire in the Stone: The Alchemy of Desire*. Wilmette, IL: Chiron.

—— (1999) 'A review of *A Dictionary of Alchemical Imagery* by Lyndy Abraham'. *Harvest*, 45(2).

—— (2000a) 'The metaphor of light and its deconstruction in Jung's alchemical vision', in R. Brooke (ed.) *Pathways into the Jungian World*. London and New York: Routledge.

—— (2000b) 'The black sun: archetypal image of the non-self', unpublished paper presented at the International Symposium of Archetypal Psychology.

—— (2001) 'The metaphor of light and renewal in Taoist alchemy and Jungian analysis'. *Quadrant*, summer.

—— (2005) *The Black Sun: The Alchemy and Art of Darkness*. College Station, TX: Texas A&M University Press.

Meier, C.A. (ed.) (2000) *Atom and Archetype: The Pauli/Jung Letters, 1932–1958*. Princeton, NJ: Princeton University Press.

Newman, K.D. (1981) 'The riddle of the Vas Bene Clausum'. *Journal of Analytical Psychology*, 16(3): 229–243.

Odajnyk, V.W. (1993) *Gathering the Light: A Psychology of Meditation*. Boston, MA and London: Shambhala.

Raff, J. (2000) *Jung and the Alchemical Imagination*. York Beach, ME: Nicolas-Hays.

Raff, J. and Vocatura, L.B. (2002) *Healing the Wounded God: Finding your Personal Guide to Individuation and Beyond*. York Beach, ME: Nicolas-Hays.

Robertson, R. (1999) 'A guide to the writings of Edward F. Edinger'. *Psychological Perspective*, 39(summer): 47–62.

Samuels, A. (1989) *The Plural Psyche: Personality, Morality and the Father*. London and New York: Routledge.

Schwartz-Salant, N. (1993) 'Jung, madness and sexuality: reflections on psychotic transference and countertransference', in M. Stein (ed.) *Mad Parts of Sane People in Analysis*. Wilmette, IL: Chiron.

—— (1995) 'Introduction to Jung on alchemy', in N. Schwartz-Salant (ed.) *Jung on Alchemy*. London: Routledge.

—— (1998) *The Mystery of the Human Relationship: Alchemy and the Transformation of Self*. London and New York: Routledge.

Sharp, D. (1999) 'Tribute for E. Edinger'. *Psychological Perspectives*, 39(summer): 17–18.

Spiegelman, J.M. and Miyuki, M. (1985) *Buddhism and Jungian Psychology*. Phoenix, AZ: Falcon Press.

Stein, M. (1985) *Jung's Treatment of Christianity: The Psychotherapy of a Religious Tradition*. Wilmette, IL: Chiron.

——(1992) *Understanding the Meaning of Alchemy: Jung's Metaphor of Transformative Process* (audiotape). Chicago, IL: C.G. Jung Institute of Chicago.

Sullivan, B.S. (1989) *Psychotherapy Grounded in the Feminine Principle*. Wilmette, IL: Chiron.

Tanaka, Y. (2000) 'The alchemical images and logic in analytical psychology', in H. Kawai (ed.) *Lectures on Psychotherapy Volume 3: Psychotherapy and Images*. Tokyo: Inwanami-Shoten.

von Franz, M.-L. (1966) *Aurora Consurgens*. New York: Pantheon.

—— (1979) *Alchemical Active Imagination*. Dallas, TX: Spring.

—— (1980) *Alchemy: An Introduction to the Symbolism and the Psychology*. Toronto: Inner City.

—— (1992) *Psyche and Matter*. Boston, MA: Shambhala.

—— (1999) *Muhammad ibn Umail's Hall ar-Rumuz ('Clearing of Enigmas'): Historical Introduction and Psychological Comment*, by Dr Theodore Abt, printed at Fotorotar AG. CH-8132 Egg/Switzerland.

Wagner, S. (1998–1999) 'A conversation with Marie-Louise von Franz'. *Psychological Perspectives*, 38(winter): 12–42.

Wilhelm, R. (1931/1962) *The Secret of the Golden Flower: A Chinese Book of Life*, trans. and explained by R. Wilhelm with a foreword and commentary by C.G. Jung. New York: Harcourt, Brace and World.

Zabriskie, B.D. (1995a) 'Jung and Pauli: a subtle asymmetry'. *Journal of Analytical Psychology*, 40: 531–553.

—— (1995b) 'Exiles and orphans: Jung, Paracelsus, and the healing images of alchemy'. *Quadrant*, 26(1 and 2).

—— (1996a) 'The matter of psyche'. *San Francisco Library Journal*, 14(4).

—— (1996b) 'Fermentation in alchemical practice', in M.A. Mattoon (ed.) *Proceedings of the Thirteenth International Congress for Analytical Psychology, Zurich 1995*. Einsiedeln, Switzerland: Daimon Verlag.

—— (1999) 'Review of *Fire in the Stone: The Alchemy of Desire*, ed. S. Marlan'. *Roundtable Review*, 6(3), Jan/Feb.

——(2001) 'Jung and Pauli: a meeting of rare minds', Introduction in C.A. Meier (ed.) *Atom and Archetype: The Pauli/Jung Letters, 1932–1958*. Princeton, NJ: Princeton University Press.

Chapter 13

Religion

Roderick Main

Introduction

Religion is a topic of central importance for understanding not only the personal and professional development of Carl Gustav Jung but also the history of analytical psychology and its contemporary status in relation to psychoanalysis, the academy and culture generally.

Jung's personal interest in religion began in his earliest years and continued until his death at the age of 86 (Jung 1963: 21–103, 320–393). His father and many of his other immediate relatives and ancestors were clergymen (Jung 1963: 58). Moreover, he grew up in a period and location, late-nineteenth-century Europe, where there was widely perceived at the time to be an especial crisis in religion, due to the rise of science and secularisation. With this background, it is hardly surprising that one of the facets of Jung's mature identity should turn out to be as a religious thinker (Homans 1979/1995: 161).

Writings specifically on religion occupy a large portion of Jung's output. Volume 11 of the *Collected Works*, *Psychology and Religion: West and East* (1928–1954), is explicitly dedicated to the topic, and copious further material can be found among miscellaneous articles (e.g., 1928/1931, 1939c, 1944–1957, 1945/1948, 1961), letters (1973, 1976; McGuire 1974), interviews (McGuire and Hull 1978) and seminar notes (Jung 1925, 1928–1930, 1930–1934, 1932, 1934–1939, 1939a). Furthermore, as an 'Editorial Note' to Volume 11 points out (Jung 1928–1954: v), several other volumes of the *Collected Works* could equally be designated as concerned with religion, notably *Aion* (1951a) and *Psychology and Alchemy* (1944b). Indeed, all Jung's numerous writings on mythology, Gnosticism, alchemy and Eastern thought are inextricably bound up with the topic of religion. Then, in addition to Jung's own writings, there is a huge secondary literature on analytical psychology and religion. A bibliographic study published in 1973 already included 442 items (Heisig 1973). Nowadays, a comprehensive list might run into five figures.

Jung's psychology of religion has had a significant influence in several areas. It has contributed to religious thought itself, as theologians, religious adherents, academic students of religion, New Agers and numerous others for whom religion remains an issue of importance have variously drawn on or dialogued with Jung's ideas. At the same time, the religious aspect of analytical psychology has provided grounds for its wholesale rejection by Freud (1914/1993: 118–128) and many subsequent psychoanalysts, with far-reaching implications for the status of analytical psychology within the depth psychological and psychotherapeutic traditions. Similarly, the relationship between analytical psychology and religion has affected the reception of Jungian thought within the academy. While there is interest in studying analytical psychology within departments of religious studies (Ulanov 1997), David Tacey has noted that in most other disciplines the 'fundamentally religious' nature of Jungian thought 'sticks in the throat of the secular academy' and has led to its firm exclusion (1997b: 315–316; see also Tacey 1997a; Main 2003). In general, as James Heisig writes, 'so central and decisive is the religious aspect of Jung's thought that it has become the typical turning point for sympathy with or alienation from Jung's life work' (Heisig 1979: 9).

Jung's positions on religion: a chronological and developmental account

At almost all periods of his life, Jung's actual positions on religion were complex, with seemingly opposed or disparate currents of interest flowing into and out of one another. However, a chronological survey of his work on religion discloses some broadly identifiable phases. In his early years, we see him awakening to the problem of the relationship between traditional religion and secular modernity and coming to value personal religious experience over institutionally sanctioned belief. After an unsatisfying attempt to explain religious phenomena reductively in psychiatric and psychoanalytic terms, he began increasingly to emphasise the positive, prospective function of religion. In his mature years, this strengthened into the conviction that the psyche is naturally religious and religion of some form is therefore a psychic necessity. In his later years, he moved from this general concern with the value of religion *per se* to a specific analysis of Christianity as the dominant religious tradition in Western culture, and he provided recommendations for how this tradition might be helped to transform for the better in the light of depth psychological insights.

Early years (1875–1900)

Jung's father, like many of his other close relatives and ancestors, was a pastor in the Swiss Reformed Church (Jung 1963: 58). According to this form of Protestantism, at least as originally developed by Ulrich Zwingli (1484–1531), religious institutions and systems of belief are much less important than an inner, personal orientation towards the transcendent (Tambiah 1990: 4). However, as Jung perceived it, his father precisely lacked this kind of personal, experiential orientation, and consequently had lost his faith under the impact of post-Enlightenment rationalism and materialism (Jung 1963: 113). His mother, meanwhile, though outwardly also a conventional Protestant, had a disposition towards 'spiritualistic' experiences, as had both of her parents (Jung 1963: 65–69, 120; Jaffé 1984: 40). Jung (1963: 110) acknowledges the influence of this domestic 'surrounding atmosphere' on his developing ideas about religion.

In *Memories, Dreams, Reflections* (1963), Jung recounts several childhood experiences that greatly influenced his attitudes towards religion. He describes how the terror he experienced, aged 3 or 4, at the sight of a blackrobed Jesuit priest constituted his 'first conscious trauma' (1963: 25–26). Recalling the effect on him, at around the same time, of a dream of a huge, man-eating phallus in an underground chamber and how this image coalesced with his image of Jesus, he claims that 'My intellectual life had its unconscious beginnings at that time' (1963: 26–30). Most dramatically, he recounts his unsuccessful attempt, at the age of 11, to resist a vision he had of God defecating on Basel Cathedral and his experience of bliss and grace when he finally admitted the fantasy into consciousness (1963: 52–58). Such vivid personal experiences contrasted sharply with his divinity classes which he found 'unspeakably dull' (1963: 43), his unsatisfactory theological discussions with his father (1963: 59–60) and his disappointment at first communion (1963: 70–72). Together, these experiences and impressions gave Jung a deeply negative image of conventional religion, including of Jesus (1963: 25, 28, 73–74). They stimulated his earliest theological reflections on the problem of evil, the notions of grace and submission to God's will, and above all the importance of personal experience as opposed to conventional faith (1963: 52–60). They also disposed him later to become interested in the then very prevalent phenomenon of spiritualism, which promised experiential proof of the reality and post-mortem survival of the soul (1963: 119–121).

Jung's views on religion during his student days (1895–1900) can be examined in the posthumously published student lectures he delivered to his fraternity, the Zofingia Society (1896–1899). Most of his remarks in these lectures suggest that he is attempting to defend religion against the perceived threat of scientific materialism and secularisation. Thus, he argues that immaterial phenomena exist and can manifest both materially and immaterially (Jung 1896–1899: pars. 57, 65–66); that morality cannot be divorced from science (pars. 68, 138); that matter is animated by a life force that is unconscious, intelligent and beyond space and time (pars. 95–99); and that this vitalistic viewpoint is proven by the data of spiritualism (pars. 112–134). He berates contemporary representatives of religion for succumbing to rationalism and denying mystery (pars. 138–142); suggests that the drive to knowledge (the 'causal instinct') leads to religion (par. 191); and champions a view of Jesus as a mysterious god-man who, contrary to the view of the German protestant theologian Albrecht Ritschl (1822–1889), cannot be rationally explained (pars. 284–291). In this anti-Enlightenment spirit, he even advocates a return to the Middle Ages and rejection of secular modernity (par. 290).

Early professional life (1901–1912)

Over the next few years, Jung's professional commitments as a medical practitioner and researcher served to temper this anti-modernist spirit. He adopted first a psychiatric and then a Freudian psychoanalytic approach to religious phenomena, before his own religious attitude began to reassert itself.

Jung's first professional publication was his doctoral dissertation 'On the psychology and pathology of so-called occult phenomena' (1902). A case study of a mediumistic girl observed during a series of spiritualistic séances, this work clearly emerges out of the preoccupations of his childhood and student years. However, Jung's own religious interests and views have been almost wholly displaced by the aim of presenting himself as a responsible research scientist and psychiatrist. Indeed, there is very little discussion of religion in Jung's work until the publication of 'The significance of the father in the destiny of the individual' (1909/1949). By the time this was written Jung had become deeply involved with Freud and the psycho-analytic movement, and Jung's paper, where it touches on religion, presents a wholly Freudian interpretation. The relationship of humans to God is seen as a sublimation of the relationship of children to their father, with the need to reinforce this sublimation by means of the severe compulsive prac-tices of ceremonials (Jung 1909/1949: pars. 738 n. 21, 741 n. 22; cf. Freud 1907/1990). However, towards the end of the period of collaboration with Freud, Jung's interest in religion gradually gained in prominence again and began to manifest characteristics distinct from and contrary to the Freudian outlook.

These developments came to a head with the publication of Jung's first major work in the psychology of religion, his lengthy study of the trans-formations and symbols of the libido, *The Psychology of the Unconscious* (1911–1912), later heavily revised as *Symbols of Transformation* (1911–1912/1952). The original text still largely operates with Freudian presup-positions and emphases. Religious phenomena are seen as projections of unfulfilled, incestuous wishes. We are told that 'God is to be considered as the representative of a certain sum of energy (libido)'; that 'the religious instinct feeds upon the incestuous libido of the infantile period' (Jung 1911–1912: par. 111); and that the symbolic acts and concepts into which the incest wish is transformed 'cheat men' into remaining infantile (par. 352).

Psychoanalysis is superior to religion because, rather than keeping the personality in an infantile state, it helps the personality to mature and adapt to reality (par. 695). States Jung: 'I think *belief should be replaced by understanding*; then we would keep the beauty of the symbol, but still remain free from the depressing results of submission to belief. This would be the psychoanalytic cure for belief and disbelief' (par. 356; original emphasis).

However, Jung maintained a positive, if somewhat patronising, attitude toward religion. He acknowledges that the religious myth 'was and is the bridge to all the greatest achievements of humanity' (1911–1912: par. 353) and argues that, in the struggle against incestuous longings, 'The religious projection offers a much more effectual help [than "suppressing and forgetting"]. In this one keeps the conflict in sight . . . and gives it over to a personality standing outside of one's self, the Divinity' (par. 117). More importantly, however, Jung never fully agreed with Freud's conception of libido as only sexuality (McGuire 1974: 4–5) and now he argues explicitly for a broader definition as psychic energy (Jung 1911–1912: pars. 219–236). One implication of this is that, in certain circumstances, 'The sexuality of the unconscious is not what it seems to be; *it is merely a symbol*' (par. 635; original emphasis); libido can be 'de-sexualized' (par. 672). Hence, even when religion is, as Jung acknowledged it could be, a neurotic symptom, it need not always be a *sexual* neurotic symptom. For Jung, neurosis resulted from an imbalance in libido in his sense of psychic energy (pars. 230–236). Such an imbalance may be religious in form but there can also, Jung implies, be forms of libido that are religious but not imbalanced and hence not neurotic.

More specifically, Jung, unlike Freud, considered that the regression involved in neurosis can often have a positive aspect inasmuch as the regressed libido can activate a stratum of the unconscious capable of producing symbols that constitute a transformation of the libido into forms useful for further psychic development (1911–1912: par. 250). These symbols, often religious in character, are a 'remnant of ancient humanity and the centuries-old past in all people' (par. 291), 'associations of elements and analogies . . . which formerly constituted the archaic idea of the world' (par. 675) – in brief, what Jung would later designate as archetypes of the collective unconscious. Thus, where Freud interpreted religious symbols as expressions of repressed sexual wishes having their origin in an infantile past, Jung considered that they could often be attempts of the psyche to integrate consciousness with the unconscious in response to present and anticipated future conditions of life. Jung is clearly moving towards his later position that it is not the presence of religious symbols but their absence and the failure to respect and recognise their prospective nature that constitute neurosis (1963: 173–178, 190–191).

In other ways, too, *Psychology of the Unconscious* signalled Jung's divergence from Freud. For example, while Freud emphasised the importance of the father-imago for religious symbolism, Jung concluded from his study that 'the part of the libido which erects religious structures is in the last analysis fixed in the mother' (1911–1912: par. 691). Again, Jung's manner of working with symbols differed from Freud's. Rather than always interpret symbols reductively – 'this is the symbol substituted for the mother and that for the penis' – Jung suggested that symbols sometimes have 'no fixed significance' and that their multiplicity of meanings should be explored (par. 339). This approach later developed into his method of amplification.

Towards a mature psychology of religion (1913–1937)

The publication of *The Psychology of the Unconscious* led to a final break between Jung and Freud, both personally and professionally. In the following period of psychic disorientation, his romantically dubbed 'Confrontation with the Unconscious', Jung came to feel both that he lacked a myth and that the contemporary form of the Christian myth was inadequate (1963: 194–195). However, out of a vivid series of personal experiences that he underwent at this time – dreams, visions, guided fantasies and paranormal events (1963: 194–225) – together with the support he drew both directly and indirectly from William James's and Théodore Flournoy's non-psychoanalytic approaches to the psychology of religion (Shamdasani 1995: 126–127), Jung began to forge the outlines of a new psychological understanding. He first framed this new understanding in the form of a pseudonymous and privately circulated 'Gnostic' myth *Septem Sermones ad Mortuos* (1916). As several commentators have noted, this text prefigures in poetic form most of the ideas of Jung's mature psychological model (e.g., Heisig 1972). In addition, Jung began at this time to paint mandalas (circular images usually divided into quadrants) and to develop his notion of the self as the centre of psychic totality (1963: 220–222).

The major work that marks Jung's emergence from his period of encounter with the unconscious, *Psychological Types* (1921), demonstrates a mature consolidation of both the conceptual and the methodological insights he had begun to adumbrate in *Psychology of the Unconscious*. The notions of the collective unconscious and archetypes, the psychological value of symbols, the method of amplification, and the epistemological principle of according primary reality to psychic phenomena all receive forceful expression in this work (1921: pars. 77–78, 746–754, 814–829, 842, 851 and *passim*). Especially significant for a developmental account of Jung's psychology of religion are his beginning references to the notion of the God-image as distinct from God himself; his paralleling of the God-image not with the unconscious but with the entire subject, conscious and unconscious alike; and his appeal to the *consensus gentium* as proof of the psychological (though not metaphysical) truth of God-images (1921: pars.

62, 412–413). In this work, Jung also several times uses the phrase 'the religious function' (pars. 231 n. 14, 411, 529), a notion to which he appeals at key points in his later accounts of religion (e.g., 1938/1940: par. 3, 1944b: par. 14). Above all, Jung focuses in this work on the notion of opposites and their reconciliation under a guiding principle of wholeness. As Murray Stein (1985) points out, this notion allows Jung to characterise modern secular culture as one-sided for failing to acknowledge its opposite, i.e., religion, and likewise to characterise traditional Christianity as one-sided for valuing extraversion, feeling and intuition above their opposites, intro-version, thinking and sensation, and therefore tending to devalue mystic-ism, speculative philosophy and science (Stein 1985: 97–98). Central to Jung's later project of transforming Christianity will be the recommenda-tion that it acknowledges and attempts to integrate what has been excluded by its perceived one-sidedness.

Between the years 1921 and 1937, Jung's psychology of religion under-went few substantial developments in terms of theory or methodology; however, what did change was the nature and scope of his application. These years saw the growth of his interest in alchemy (Jung 1929), Eastern thought (1929, 1930, 1932, 1935/1953, 1936b), paganism (1936a) and secular alternatives to religion (1934–1939). An important role in this was played by the seminars in analytical psychology that Jung began to hold in 1925 and by the Eranos Conferences that were instituted in 1933 and at which Jung was a regular speaker until 1951 (Hayman 1999: 315–316, 415–416). In some of Jung's writings of this period, one can detect an as yet incomplete move towards equating images of God with images of self. When Jung does eventually make this move, it will have momentous consequences for his psychology of religion, for it will provide him with grounds for expecting of the God-image the same kind of totality through union of the opposites of good and evil, masculine and feminine, and spirit and body as his clinical work and comparative research led him, at a psychological level, to expect of images of the self.

'Psychology and religion' (1937)

Jung's main dedicated statement of his psychology of religion is contained in the three Terry Lectures on 'Psychology and religion' that he delivered at Yale University in 1937 (Jung 1938/1940). These not only sum up his thinking on this subject so far but also look forward to how he will develop it in subsequent works. Accordingly, I shall focus on this work at slightly greater length, outlining first the epistemological and methodological assumptions it articulates, then the psychological concepts at work in it, and finally how Jung understands religion and applies his psychological concepts within that understanding.

Jung's most basic assumption is of the primacy of psychic reality: 'the only form of existence of which we have immediate knowledge is psychic' (1938/1940: par. 16). From this, it follows that we cannot know God or any other metaphysical realities in themselves but can know only the psychological experiences and images we have of them. This provides the grounds for Jung's claimed empirical approach to religion: 'Inasmuch as religion has a very important psychological aspect, I deal with it from a purely empirical point of view, that is, I restrict myself to the observation of phenomena and I eschew any philosophical or metaphysical considerations' (1938/1940: par. 2). A religious idea, such as the motif of the virgin birth, is 'psychologically true inasmuch as it exists'; what gives such an idea objectivity is that it is 'shared by a society – by a *consensus gentium*' (par. 4).

Among the psychological notions that contribute to Jung's understanding of religion are the following. The human personality consists of both consciousness and the unconscious (1938/1940: par. 66). The unconscious is not only personal but also collective or transpersonal, i.e., it contains non-personal, autonomous complexes (archetypes) (pars. 21–22, 88). While the centre of consciousness is the ego, the centre of the psyche as a whole, consciousness and unconscious together, is the archetype of the self (par. 67). However, realisation of psychic totality (the self) is no easy matter (par. 68), for it involves recognising and living with everything about oneself that one has no wish to be, all one's personally and socially unacceptable traits and tendencies, one's 'shadow' (pars. 130–132). A particularly useful resource for gaining insight into one's unconscious is provided by dreams, for these 'mirror exactly the underground processes of the psyche' (par. 37). For Jung, a dream is not, as it is for Freud, 'a crafty device to lead us astray' but 'a natural occurrence' that should be taken 'for what it is' (par. 41). Dreams and other forms of fantasy can personify unconscious states and processes. The aspect of one's psyche that is inferior and unacceptable, one's 'shadow', is often personified as a negative figure. The aspect that helps consciousness to relate to the unconscious is often personified as a contra-sexual image, referred to in a man's case as the 'anima' and in a woman's case as the 'animus' (pars. 47–48). The aspect that represents the potential for psychic wholeness is personified by images of the self (par. 140). So long as these archetypal tendencies remain unconscious, they are likely to be projected onto people, situations and organisations in the external world, resulting in unrealistic hostilities, attachments and idealisations (par. 140). An important psychological task, equivalent to the increasing of consciousness, is to withdraw these projections (par. 141). However, this is not a task that can ever be finally accomplished, for the archetypes will continually generate affectively compelling images and experiences. Among these will be the religious symbols generated by what Jung designates as the religious function (par. 3). The ongoing process of projecting, withdrawing projections and symbolising results in continual transformations of consciousness. Ultimately, for Jung, these transformations are governed by the process of the psyche's development towards ever-greater completeness through the integration of consciousness and the unconscious. This is the process Jung calls individuation, the goal of which is ever-increasing realisation of the self. Among the symbols of the self, Jung specially draws attention to mandalas and other quaternity symbols.

The state of religion that Jung analyses by means of these psychological concepts and processes is characterised as one in which there is a severe loss of faith (1938/1940: par. 148), one marked by God's death and disappearance (par. 149) and by the Church's loss of authority (par. 34). Various attempts to reorient in this condition have been attempted – e.g., materialism, psychologism (Freud), or atheistic iconoclasm (Nietzsche) – but Jung rejects all of these as inadequate (par. 142). Jung's own starting point is to assert the naturalness and importance of immediate religious experience. He provides a broad definition of religion as 'a careful consideration and observation of certain dynamic factors that are conceived as "powers"' (par. 8), as 'the attitude peculiar to a consciousness which has been changed by experience of the *numinosum*' (par. 9), and as 'a relationship to the highest or most powerful value, be it positive or negative' (par. 137). Religious beliefs and dogmas are secondary to this: 'Creeds are codified and dogmatized forms of original religious experience' (par. 10). Jung's interpretation of the problem facing modern religions is that their symbols and myths have lost their connection to experience and hence are no longer capable of evoking a living response in the psyches of adherents. Since the psyche has a religious function that cannot be ignored without damage to psychic health, Jung champions a 'psychological approach' as 'probably all that is left us' (par. 148). For instance, he argues that 'Revelation is an "unveiling" of the depths of the human soul first and foremost, a "laying bare"; hence it is an essentially psychological event' (par. 127). According to his psychological model and as illustrated by his case study in 'Psychology and religion', such revelation takes place above all through the medium of dreams and other forms of unconscious fantasy. In making this point, Jung is not unconcerned with traditional forms of religion. Indeed, he acknowledges the value of traditional religious rituals as ways of mediating between consciousness and the unconscious and compares the strengths and weaknesses of Catholicism and Protestantism in this respect (pars. 75–80). However, his main concern is with the many people for whom these traditional resources no longer work.

Jung's lectures on 'Psychology and religion' introduce, mainly through the case study, one of the themes that is going to play a major role in his subsequent writing in this area. This is the notion that images of God undergo transformation and are currently undergoing one such major transformation, which needs to be recognised and understood. Thus, the quaternity and mandala symbols experienced by the dreamer in Jung's examples spontaneously express a view of divinity that differs markedly from the traditional Trinity through according a place to evil, the feminine and the body. The mandala presents an image of totality rather than perfection, and it is an image at whose centre is the human being rather than a god (1938/1940: pars. 136–139). Jung argues that this is not an idiosyncratic product from the mind of his dreamer but 'the continuation of a process of spiritual development which began in the early Middle Ages [with alchemy], and perhaps even further back [with Gnosticism]' (par. 159).

Transforming religion/Christianity (1938–1961)

Over the next twenty or so years, Jung continued to reflect psychologically on the Eastern spiritual traditions of India, Tibet, China and Japan (1939b, 1939/1954, 1943, 1944a, 1950, 1963: 304–311, 348). However, while in India in 1938 he had a dream in which he was seeking the Holy Grail, a pre-eminent Western religious symbol, and thereafter the focus of his attention increasingly turned to Western culture and in particular Christianity (1963: 311–313).

In 'Transformation symbolism in the Mass' (1942/1954), originally delivered as an Eranos lecture in 1941, Jung attempts to elucidate the central symbol of the Christian Mass, when the bread and wine are transformed into the body and blood of Christ. He draws detailed parallels between the phases of this rite and the psychological process of individuation, for both, he argues, unite the temporal world (bread and wine/ego-consciousness) with the eternal (Christ/the self).

Even more radically, Jung at this time further pursued his idea that because the God-image (as distinct from God himself, who is unknowable) is a psychic fact, it is both open to psychological investigation and subject to change, indeed is currently undergoing a major transformation. This is especially evident in his essay, 'A psychological approach to the dogma of the Trinity' (1942/1948), worked up from an Eranos lecture delivered extemporaneously in 1940. Basing his argument on the premise that 'one can never distinguish empirically between a symbol of the self and a God-image' (1942/1948: pars. 231, 289), Jung finds parallels between the images of God in Christian dogma and stages of development of human consciousness. He sees the doctrine of the Trinity as referring to both 'a process of unconscious maturation taking place within the individual' and 'a process of conscious realisation continuing over the centuries'; more generally, it refers to 'the progressive transformation of . . . the psyche as a whole' (pars. 287–289). Each of the figures of the Trinity has its psychological correlate. God the Father correlates with a state of undifferentiated identification with the unconscious: 'the earlier state of consciousness when one was still a child, . . . a passive, unreflecting condition, . . . without intellectual or moral judgement' (par. 270). God the Son correlates with a state in which consciousness differentiates from the unconscious: it consists in 'conscious differentiation from the father [and requires] a certain amount of knowledge of one's own individuality, which cannot be acquired without moral discrimination' (par. 271). God the Holy Ghost correlates with a state in which differentiated ego-consciousness begins to reconnect with the unconscious: it involves 'recognition of the unconscious' and the relinquishing of both 'childish dependence' on it and 'exclusive independence' from it (par. 273).

Besides this psychological translation, Jung's radical proposal in this essay is that the notion of the Trinity be expanded to become a quaternity, which would include the fourth person of Lucifer, 'the Prince of this world' (1942/1948: par. 290). Just as psychological completeness, symbolised as realisation of the self, requires that the shadow and inferior function be acknowledged, so there is a need to acknowledge evil as an aspect of the God-image. Regarding the figure of Christ, Jung on the one hand designates him as an image of the self but on the other hand argues that he is an unsatisfactory image of the self because he is one-sidedly good, masculine and spiritual. An adequate symbol of the self also needs to encompass in its totality evil, the feminine, and the body. In *Psychology and Alchemy* (1944b), Jung considers some alchemical counterparts to the image of Christ which, he argues, were spontaneous attempts on the part of the medieval mind to compensate for this one-sidedness.

The problem of Christ's one-sidedness as an image of the self is also one of the major themes of *Aion* (1951a). In this work, Jung attempts to trace the way the patterns of symbolism relating to Christ have changed over the course of the previous two thousand years. He makes extensive use of supposed parallels (synchronicities) between the phases of the Christian aeon and the astrological Age of Pisces. In particular, he relates the two fishes of the astrological sign to the two 'Sons of God', Christ and Antichrist. As the spring equinox moved from one fish into the other, so the archetypal symbolism associated with Christ began to give way to that associated with the Antichrist, and human consciousness changed from being preoccupied with spiritual transcendence to being more centred on humanity and the earth. Jung's insistence on the equal reality of Antichrist and Christ, of evil and good, also led him to criticise the Catholic doctrine of the *privatio boni*, according to which evil has no substance of its own but consists of the absence or privation of good. Jung considered that this doctrine both trivialises the reality of evil and fails adequately to represent the psychological reality of moral judgement, where the assertion of one member of a pair of opposites (good) entails the equal assertion of the other member of the pair (evil).

The problems of good and evil and of the transformation of the God-image and its parallels in the development of human consciousness found their most personal and most controversial expression in Jung's 'Answer to Job' (1952a; see also Bishop 2002). In this work, which he describes as 'a purely subjective reaction', Jung explores 'God's tragic contradictoriness' (1963: 243) as a being in whom 'Insight existed along with obtuseness, loving-kindness along with cruelty, creative power along with destructiveness' (1952a: par. 560). This contradictory nature is expressed in the Old Testament in the amorality of Yahweh's treatment of his faithful servant Job, whose life he allows Satan to devastate for the sake of a wager. Jung suggests that Yahweh has less moral consciousness than Job and actually needs humanity in order to become more conscious. As in *Aion*, Jung traces various phases of the development of the idea of God from the time of the writing of the Book of Job to the present day. He suggests that God's experience with Job prompted God to incarnate as Christ. However, while God in the person of Christ succeeded in incarnating his good side, his evil side continued to be projected onto his creatures. Hence, the contemporary need for a fuller realisation of the unconscious through acceptance and integration of the evil side as well as the good. It is for this reason that Jung was so interested in the spontaneous emergence of God-images (especially mandalas) that add to traditional trinitarian thought with its emphases on good, masculinity and the spirit the 'missing fourth' element of evil, femininity and the body. Regarding the feminine aspect of God, Jung suggests that the emergence of this symbol into consciousness signals a union of opposites in the Godhead, a divine marriage (*hieros gamos*) portending that 'God desires to rejuvenate himself' (1952a: par. 624). In Jung's account of the history of the Judaeo-Christian tradition, occasions of this emergence are the idea of Sophia (Wisdom), 'a coeternal and more or less hypostatized pneuma of feminine nature that existed before the Creation', in the Book of Proverbs (par. 609); the Marriage of the Lamb (i.e., of Christ with his Church) in the Book of Revelation (par. 726); and, in Jung's lifetime, the papal promulgation in 1950 of the dogma of the bodily assumption of Mary into Heaven (pars. 733, 748–755).

As mentioned earlier, Jung's writings on religion are inextricably bound up with his writings on alchemy, and the above themes of reconciling opposites and attending to spontaneous psychic images of wholeness are central to Jung's late alchemical works, especially *Mysterium Coniunctionis* (1955–1956). Jung also deploys his theory of religion in attempting to understand current social phenomena such as totalitarianism, which he saw as a form of 'massmindedness' that could be counterbalanced only by religion (Jung 1957), and the widespread sightings of flying saucers, which he saw as a nascent salvation myth compensating for the failure of traditional religions to meet contemporary needs for psychic wholeness (Jung 1958).

Meanings and definitions

Most of the terms involved in Jung's psychology of religion have necessarily already been provided with basic definitions in the preceding section, especially in the subsection on 'Psychology and religion'. However, it may be helpful to elaborate on a few of these definitions as well as to make some more general points.

Religion

In crucial respects, Jung's psychology of religion, indeed his psychological model as a whole, emerged out of his attempt to resolve the tension he experienced between traditional religion and secular modernity (Homans 1979/1995; Main 2004: 91–114). How Jung understood religion therefore will have influenced how he came to understand psychology, as well as the other way around. This is apparent if we look at the actual definitions of religion that Jung provides, which all put the accent on experience rather than belief, ritual or organisation (e.g., Jung 1938/1940: pars. 8, 9, 137). The emphasis on direct religious experience is not only, as one might expect, a prioritising of the psychological dimension. It also reflects the emphasis on a personal orientation towards the transcendent within the religious tradition of Jung's upbringing (Swiss Reformed Protestantism) – however unsatisfactory Jung's own experience of this tradition may have been. Of course, Jung does also use the term 'religion' to refer to traditions identifiable by their beliefs, practices and institutions – whether mainstream current traditions such as Christianity and Buddhism, defunct traditions such as Mithraism, or little-known indigenous traditions such as that of the Pueblo Indians. However, he is always quick to establish that these doctrinal, ritual and organisational dimensions of religious traditions have their taproot in the dimension of experience. This emphasis on experience arguably biases Jung's and subsequent analytical psychologists' discussions of religion. It also helps account for Jung's lifelong interest in spiritualistic phenomena, for in these too the accent is on experience (e.g., Jung 1896–1899, 1902, 1920/1948, 1926, 1934, 1963; see also Charet 1993; Main 1997).

In addition to the specifically psychological concepts of psychic reality, the collective unconscious, archetypes, individuation and the self, two significant notions governing the development of Jung's thinking about religion are the religious function and the numinous. The former signals Jung's increasing sense of the importance, naturalness and necessity of religion. He states that the dream material presented in 'Psychology and religion' is meant to 'demonstrate the existence of an authentic religious function in the psyche' (1938/1940: par. 3). In *Psychology and Alchemy*, he asserts that 'the soul possesses by nature a religious function' (1944b: par. 14). At least two major studies of Jung's psychology of religion have incorporated the phrase 'religious function' in their titles (Edinger 1973; Corbett 1996). Heisig, while cautioning that Jung does not seem to use the phrase as much more than 'a means of focusing attention on the positive role of religion in psychic well-being' (Heisig 1979: 158), nevertheless provides an admirable clarification of what is implied by this. He shows that Jung intends the phrase to designate the psyche's tendency, indeed necessity, to have an absolute and unconditional orientation; the basis of this tendency in the releasing of archaic instincts (i.e., archetypes) by means of fantasy; the nature of this process as essentially one of symbol formation, whereby consciousness is compensated by the collective unconscious; and the distinction between this natural and spontaneous activity and adherence to religious dogmas (Heisig 1979: 35–36).

The concept of the numinous was introduced by the German theologian and historian of religion Rudolf Otto (1917/1950). Jung quickly adopted it to designate the particular emotional quality of archetypal experiences, and it has now become one of the most widely used terms in Jungian writing even when the religious dimension is not being directly addressed. For Otto, the concept refers to the non-rational aspect of the holy. He more fully describes this as the *mysterium tremendum et fascinans* (terrifying and fascinating mystery). It implies an emotional apprehension of God as wholly other, awesome, overpowering, urgent and fascinating. For Jung, the term carries most of these connotations, but there are also important differences. For example, in one place Jung writes that it is 'psychologically quite unthinkable for God to be simply the "wholly other," for a "wholly other" could never be one of the soul's deepest and closest intimacies – which is precisely what God is' (1944b: par. 11, n. 6). Again, as Leon Schlamm (1994) has noted, while Otto emphasises that the appropriate response to numinous experience is unqualified submission, Jung consistently urges that consciousness should be maintained, since individuation requires that the conjunction between consciousness and the numinous unconscious should devalue neither (Schlamm 1994: 26–27). Another difference is that Jung tended to equate the numinous and the holy, whereas for Otto the holy involves a uniting of the numinous with rational experience of the divine (Schlamm 1994: 28).

God

Central to appreciating Jung's use of the term 'God' is his distinction between the archetype in itself and archetypal images. Jung writes of God as an archetype (1944b: par. 15) and of the archetype of the God-image (pars. 11, 14). The former, as with all archetypes, is unknowable in itself and Jung therefore generally declines to discuss it (par. 15). Jung's main concern is with the God-image, the ways in which the God-archetype has manifested itself in actual experience, conditioned as this inevitably is by particular personal, social and cultural contexts. 'In the West,' he writes, 'the archetype is filled out with the dogmatic figure of Christ; in the East, with Purusha, the Atman, Hiranyagarbha, the Buddha, and so on' (par.

20). For Jung, none of these archetypal figures can adequately express the indefiniteness of the God-archetype. Hence, he says:

> I have found myself obliged to give the corresponding archetype the psychological name of the 'self' – a term on the one hand definite enough to convey the essence of human wholeness and on the other hand indefinite enough to express the indescribable and indeterminable nature of this wholeness.
>
> (Jung 1944b: par. 20)

As mentioned in the previous section, Jung's equation of the archetype of the self with the God-archetype, and hence of archetypal images of the self with God-images, enables him to apply to the God-image all the insights he has gleaned from his psychological work concerning images of the self. Both kinds of images are able to transform, spontaneously do transform in the direction of more inclusive wholeness and, specifically, prompt an encounter with neglected qualities such as the shadow/evil, the anima/feminine and the instinctual/matter. The equation also underpins Jung's ecumenical, not to say perennialist, viewpoint 'that God has expressed himself in many languages and appeared in diverse forms and that all these statements are *true*' (1944b: par. 18; original emphasis).

Developments, criticisms, innovations

The secondary literature on Jung's psychology of religion is so vast that only a few notable developments, criticisms and innovations can be mentioned here. Indeed, the connections between Jung's general psychological theory and his psychology of religion are so intimate that probably all of the significant challenges and modifications to the former have implications for the latter.

A considerable amount of work has been done simply expounding and clarifying Jung's ideas on religion. Mostly this has been done from within the ranks of practising Jungians, especially those of a primarily 'classical' orientation, such as Aniela Jaffé (1970/1975, 1989), Marie-Louise von Franz (1975) and Edward Edinger (1973, 1984, 1992). Edinger in particular was a forthright and persistent champion of Jung's argument concerning the transformation of the God-image from Trinity to quaternity, even characterising Jung's contribution as 'the new dispensation' (Edinger 1984). Other prolific advocates of Jung's psychology of religion include John Dourley, a Catholic priest whose theology has been deeply affected by Jung's psychological approach (Dourley 1981, 1984, 1995) and Ann Ulanov, a Jungian analyst as well as a professor in a graduate school of religion and a theological seminary, who generally presents a happy blend of theology and Jungian psychology (Ulanov 1971, 1997, 1999).

An illuminating perspective on the overall intention of Jung's psychology of religion has been provided by Murray Stein (1985). He reviews various prevalent interpretations of Jung's work on religion: that Jung was an empirical scientist who turned his attention to religion; a hermeneutical revitalist concerned to disclose to modern consciousness the underlying meaning of ancient religious traditions; a doctor of souls concerned not so much with religious traditions as with the individuals who were suffering because they had identified themselves with religious traditions that could no longer serve their psychological and spiritual needs; or a modern man attempting to resolve the tension between his dual commitments to traditional religion and secular modernity (Stein 1985: 4–17). He suggests, however, that Jung's relationship to Christianity was more fundamentally a therapeutic one. According to Stein, Jung perceived the Christianity of his time, especially as represented by his father, to be ailing. His copious writings on Christianity can be seen as an attempt to treat this ailing patient. Specifically, in the way Jung writes about religion, we can see at work the various phases of his therapeutic technique: anamnesis and historical reconstruction (e.g., in *Aion*), psychological interpretation (e.g., in the essays on the Trinity and the Mass) and, most interestingly, use of the transference and countertransference relationship (e.g., in 'Answer to Job').

Jung's psychology of religion has attracted criticism at several levels. Mostly, critics have found problems with his general psychological theory, including its underlying epistemological assumptions and its methodology (e.g., White 1952, 1960; Heisig 1979; Nagy 1991; Palmer 1997). Other areas of concern have been Jung's understanding of actual religions, for example of Catholic doctrine (White 1952, 1960) or of Eastern traditions (Clarke 1994); the biases stemming from his socio-cultural conditioning, for example his monotheistic emphasis (Hillman 1971, 1975) and his patriarchal assumptions (Goldenberg 1982; Wehr 1987); and the psychological and social motivations of his approach (Freud 1914; Homans 1979/1995; Noll 1994, 1997).

In Jung's lifetime, critical discussion of his psychology of religion was already plentiful. During his last twenty years, when he was most actively engaged in refining and applying his mature model, Jung corresponded and sometimes publicly debated with many theologians (1939c, 1973, 1976). Several of these subsequently wrote books about Jung's ideas. Among them were both Protestants (Frischknecht 1945; Schaer 1951) and Catholics (White 1952, 1960; Hostie 1957; Goldbrunner 1964). Undoubtedly the most important of the theological commentators was the Dominican Father Victor White, who enjoyed a close, if sometimes strained, friendship with Jung between 1945 and White's death in 1960. Together they aspired 'to integrate the findings of psychology into the ecclesiastical doctrine' (Jung 1973: 385). White's two books, *God and the Unconscious* (1952) and *Soul and Psyche* (1960), the former with a foreword by Jung (1952b), evince a deep and sympathetic appreciation of Jung's psychology of religion and the possibilities for relating it to Catholic theology. However, a fundamental tension remained between White's metaphysical view of God and Jung's psychological view. This emerged especially in discussions of the problem of evil, where White considered Jung to misunderstand the doctrine of the *privatio boni*, the concept of God as *Summum Bonum*, and the notion of opposites (see Charet 1990; Cunningham 1992; Lammers 1994).

A similar dissatisfaction with Jung's psychological view of God underlies the Jewish philosopher and theologian Martin Buber's criticisms of Jung. Buber charged Jung with being a Gnostic, denying the validity of faith, and preaching 'the religion of pure psychic immanence' (1953: 83–84). Jung's (1952c) attempts to rebut the charge and defend his approach had little effect. Among later commentators on this debate, Whitmont (1973) argues that Buber and Jung were largely talking at cross-purposes, and he suggests that present Jungians might avoid repeating such misunderstandings by explicitly formulating their psychological insights into religion in terms of 'symbolic perception', acknowledging both the non-psychic referent of religious statements and that such statements unavoidably involve the psyche (Whitmont 1973).

An especially thorough, thoughtful and balanced account of the development of Jung's thinking specifically about the God-image has been provided by Heisig (1979: 17–100). Based on this account, Heisig incisively evaluates and criticises the style, methodology and theory of Jung's writings on religion (1979: 103–145). He notes that Jung's deliberately ambiguous style serves a double purpose: 'the preservation of the richness of the psyche and the signaling of an intellectual task that remains ever half-done' (1979: 109). However, Jung's method of 'objective amplification' (gathering primary data, searching for parallels, and interpreting the data in the light of the parallels) fails in its aspiration to be scientific, though it may be therapeutically effective (1979: 140–142). Heisig details how almost all the central tenets of Jung's theory are both empirically and logically questionable. Jung's notion of images is ambiguous; he fails to distinguish between the origin and function of projection; his arguments in support of the hypothesis of the collective unconscious do not adequately eliminate the possibilities of cryptomnesia and telepathy; and his treatment of archetypes conflates their functions as logical universals, epistemic preconditions and hermeneutic principles (1979: 130–139). Nevertheless, not wishing to gainsay the 'brilliance and wide-ranging appeal' of Jung's theory, Heisig suggests that it should be viewed as 'a metaphorical model, subject to the canons of a hermeneutical critique but not to the verification procedures required of a theory in the natural sciences' (1979: 144).

This is a more open and positive conclusion than the one reached by Michael Palmer (1997) in his lucid exposition and critique of Freud's and Jung's theories of religion. Palmer finds Jung's definition of psychic reality tautological, since it becomes impossible to think of an experience that is not psychic (1997: 169–170). He questions Jung's appeals to the *consensus gentium* as evidence for the God-archetype on the double grounds that universality does not imply innateness and, in any case, there is no universal consensus that God exists, atheism having existed even within traditional cultures such as Buddhism and some forms of Hinduism (1997: 181–184). Palmer considers Jung's approach vulnerable to the charge of subjectivism, since it provides no objective means for deciding whether something is psychically effective or archetypal (1997: 191–192). He suggests that the parallel imagery that constitutes Jung's chief evidence for archetypes is equally well or better explained by other theories, including alternative psychoanalytic theories, which do not make inferences about a realm outside our possible experience (1997: 176–180). He questions whether, in Jung's understanding of individuation, a religious outlook really is necessary for the fulfilment of the self (1997: 192). He notes the impossibility of recognising genuine revelation, if all that is revealed must take the form of structures already latent in the psyche (1997: 191). In the end, Palmer agrees with White and Buber that Jung fails to deal effectively with the charge that he is psychologising God. Jung's theory has

> so radicalized the notion of God's immanence as an exclusively psychic reality that it becomes . . . questionable whether anything has been left of God at all, and thus whether anything distinctive is meant when we speak of religion.
>
> (Palmer 1997: 196)

Jung's work on religion has also been criticised, most conspicuously by Richard Noll (1994, 1997), for its perceived covert aspiration to make analytical psychology itself into a new form of religion. Specifically, Noll charges that Jung secretly but deliberately established analytical psychology as a religious cult, with its own jealously guarded initiation structure (1994: 291–292) and with Jung himself as the paradigmatically enlightened cult leader or 'exemplary prophet' (1994: 284). In a forum organised to reconsider the question of whether analytical psychology is a religion, the three participants – the psychiatrist Anthony Storr (1999), the scholar of religion Robert Segal (1999a, 1999b), and the historian of psychology Sonu Shamdasani (1999) – all concluded that it is not. However, Shamdasani, who elsewhere thoroughly discredits Noll's central argument (Shamdasani 1998), draws attention to Jung's description of his psychology as 'religion *in statu nascendi* [in a state of being born]' (1999).

Interestingly, some of the major attempts at innovation of Jung's psychology of religion have not just conceded but actually celebrated its status as a religion. James Hillman, for example, has argued that the religious dimension of analytical – or, as he prefers, archetypal – psychology is so fundamental that we should speak not of a psychology of religion but of a 'religion of psychology'. 'Psychology as religion,' he writes, 'implies imagining all psychological events as effects of Gods in the soul, and all activities to do with soul, such as therapy, to be operations of ritual in relation to these Gods' (Hillman 1975: 227). As his use of the plural 'Gods' suggests, Hillman (1971, 1975) has also presented a radical challenge to Jung's monotheistic conception of the God-image. Arguing that the character of Jung's central psychological concept of the self narrowly reflects his Western, Christian, Protestant background, Hillman proposes a model of the psyche without a single dominant centre – a 'polytheistic' model (cf. Miller 1974).

In spite of Jung's theologically radical suggestion that the feminine should be included in the God-image, his theory has been assailed by feminist critics, even ones who are otherwise relatively sympathetic to analytical psychology, for perpetuating a decidedly androcentric understanding of the feminine (see, e.g., Goldenberg 1982). Demaris Wehr has therefore invoked insights from feminist theology, with its sensitivity to how images of the feminine have been patriarchally inscribed, in an attempt to make Jung's psychology more acceptable to and liberating for women (Wehr 1987; cf. Ulanov 1971). In doing so, she embraces Buber's claim that Jung's psychology is a religion of psychic immanence (Wehr 1987: 78–79, 95). Among theologians, Buber (1953: 119) himself considered Jung's inclusion of the feminine in the God-image to be a Gnostic formulation, and Christian theologians have also generally been suspicious of it as unbiblical and pagan (see Heisig 1973: 119–120). White, at least initially, accepted that the opposites of masculine and feminine were both contained in the self as the archetype of human wholeness, but he baulked at equating this archetype with God or with the God-image (see Lammers 1994: 220–221). Mostly, however, theologians seem to have been less preoccupied with Jung's inclusion of the feminine in the God-image than with his inclusion of evil (see Lammers 1994: 215–226; Heisig 1973: 219–221). Howard Philp is among those who have questioned whether, if both evil and the feminine are to be added to the Trinity, Jung should not speak of a quinary rather than a quaternity (see Jung 1944–1957: par. 1601).

The view that Jung's psychology of religion reduces religion to psychology, whether this is conceived as a positive or a negative thing, has been challenged by Robert Aziz in a study of Jung's late theory of synchronicity (Jung 1951b, 1952d; Aziz 1990; see also Main 2004). Synchronistic events indicate that meanings experienced psychically can also non-projectively be experienced outwardly. In Jung's best-known example, the appearance and behaviour of a real scarab beetle at Jung's consulting room window just when his patient was recounting a dream in which she had been given a costly jewel in the form of a scarab demonstrated that the archetypal meaning expressing itself in the dream not only was internal and subjective but also could involve the external, natural world (Jung 1952d: pars. 843, 845). Neither, then, is there any reason to suppose that the archetypal meaning expressed in a person's image of God is only internal and subjective. That meaning too could express itself outwardly, neither caused by nor projected from an individual psyche (Aziz 1990: 179–180).

Current status and likely future developments

Jung's psychology of religion continues to engage actively with many of the areas and issues mentioned above. Areas of particular importance in the near future are likely to include the ongoing challenges from gender studies (Meckel 1990; Capps 1997; Tacey 1997c; Rowland 2002), postmodernism (Hauke 2000) and multiculturalism (Adams 1996); increasing attention to interfaith dialogue and the relationship between religion and science (Main 2004: 91–143); and the burgeoning of both religious fundamentalism (R. Brooke 2000; Zoja and Williams 2002; Beebe 2003) and alternative spirituality (Tacey 2001; Main 2004: 144–174).

Analytical psychology will undoubtedly continue to engage with the major traditional religions, both Western (Ryce-Menuhin 1994; Spiegelman 1994) and Eastern (Coward 1985; Meckel and Moore 1992; Clarke 1994; Ritsema and Karcher 1994). Advances in religious studies since the mid-1960s have made available a much richer and more sophisticated understanding of these traditions (for an overview with bibliographies, see Hinnells 1998), so that almost all of Jung's specific analyses could benefit from updating. Particularly interesting developments could occur as analytical psychology becomes more widely international and encounters traditional religions in other than their familiar European and North American contexts. For example, analytical psychology currently seems to be experiencing a period of rapid growth in Latin America (Kirsch 2000: 194–201). This may result in some productive interactions with Latin American Christianity, which not only numbers more adherents than Christianity anywhere else in the world but also in some cases is already interestingly mingled with indigenous religious traditions (Walls 1997: 88–89). There could also be some interesting engagements with Eastern Orthodox Christianity – a tradition surprisingly neglected by Jung (Papadopoulos 2002).

The relationship between religion and science remains a topical subject within theology, religious studies and the history of science (Barbour 1998; Segal 1999c; J. Brooke and Cantor 1998). It was also a lifelong concern for Jung and played a significant role in shaping his psychological theories (Main 2004). Contemporary work on analytical psychology continues to explore the relationship, together with its extension in the relationship between religion and secularity, both contextually (Homans 1979/1995; Main 2004: 65–114) and theoretically (Mansfield 1995). Precisely because analytical psychology is largely a product of tensions between the claims of religion and science, it arguably embeds important insights about both domains, as well as about how they may productively coexist and interact (Main 2003).

One area that has so far not been very fully addressed by analytical psychology is religious fundamentalism, though signs of interest are beginning to appear (R. Brooke 2000; Zoja and Williams 2002; Beebe 2003). The neglect probably stems from Jung's and subsequent analytical psychologists' prioritising of the experiential dimension of religion over its social and organisational dimensions. However, religious fundamentalism is such an influential social phenomenon that a culturally engaged analytical psychology can scarcely afford to ignore it. Moreover, because analytical psychology is one of the few depth psychological orientations that seriously advocates a religious attitude, it may usefully have readier access than other psychological approaches to the thought world of religious fundamentalists (Main 2003).

There understandably has been much more work on the relationship between analytical psychology and various forms of contemporary alternative spirituality, for these generally share Jung's experiential orientation and frequently have been directly influenced by Jungian thought. The relationship to New Age spirituality is particularly complex and ambivalent. On the one hand, there has been an eager association between analytical psychology and the New Age, especially in the United States. For the tremendous popularity of New Age ideas seems to provide Jungian thought with visible social significance, while the greater cultural respectability of Jungian thought seems to provide New Age ideas with intellectual endorsement (R. Brooke 1997: 286). On the other hand, analytical psychology has shown considerable hostility towards the New Age Movement, with frequent accusations of superficiality and commercialism (see, e.g., Young-Eisendrath and Miller 2000: 2, 4, 147, 176). A richer and more balanced relationship may emerge as in-depth studies begin to appear (Tacey 1999, 2001; Main 2002, 2004: 144–174).

Jungian thought has also been related to other forms of non-institutional, detraditionalised and implicit spirituality. Bani Shorter (1996) has examined how the psychological experience of ritual, personal as well as socially sanctioned, can promote perception of the sacred. Ann Casement has identified 'the common thread' running through her edited collection of post-Jungian essays, none of which is explicitly about religion, as 'a concern with numinous experiences and the Jungian theorization of them' (Casement 1998: 11). Andrew Samuels has attempted to distinguish a whole range of spiritualities – 'social spirituality, democratic spirituality, craft spirituality, profane spirituality and spiritual sociality' – that could help connect spirituality, psychotherapy, and politics (Samuels 2001: 122–134). Polly Young-Eisendrath and Melvin Miller (2000) have edited a set of essays that attempt to articulate a form of 'mature' or 'skeptical' spirituality that places neither gods (as in theism) nor humankind (as in humanism) at the centre of the universe. About half the contributors to the book write from an explicitly Jungian perspective. The emphasis on experience in Jung's psychology of religion is also largely responsible for the continued interest in its relationship to mysticism (Schlamm 2000), transpersonal psychology (Schlamm 2001) and shamanism (Sandner and Wong 1997; Smith 1997).

That Jung's psychology of religion can remain in productive dialogue with such a variety of forms of religion and spirituality is testimony to how deeply and insightfully it has penetrated into this perennially significant area of human experience. Precisely how the dialogues continue will depend on developments within the fields of both religion and analytical psychology. Neither field is likely to remain static.

References

Adams, M.V. (1996) *The Multicultural Imagination: 'Race', Colour and the Unconscious*. London and New York: Routledge.

Aziz, R. (1990) *C.G. Jung's Psychology of Religion and Synchronicity*. Albany, NY: State University of New York Press.

Barbour, I. (1998) *Religion and Science: Historical and Contemporary Issues*. London: SCM Press.

Beebe, J. (ed.) (2003) *Terror, Violence, and the Impulse to Destroy*. Einsiedeln, Switzerland: Daimon.

Bishop, P. (2002) *Jung's* Answer to Job: *A Commentary*. Hove, UK and New York: Brunner-Routledge.

Brooke, J. and Cantor, G. (1998) *Reconstructing Nature: The Engagement of Science and Religion*. Edinburgh: T and T Clark.

Brooke, R. (1997) 'Jung in the academy: a response to David Tacey'. *Journal of Analytical Psychology*, 42: 285–296.

—— (2000) 'Emissaries from the underworld: psychotherapy's challenge to Christian fundamentalism', in P. Young-Eisendrath and M.E. Miller (eds) *The Psychology of Mature Spirituality: Integrity, Wisdom, Transcendence*. London and Philadelphia, PA: Routledge.

Buber, M. (1953) *The Eclipse of God: Studies in the Relation between Religion and Philosophy*. London: Victor Gollancz.

Capps, D. (1997) *Men, Religion, and Melancholia: James, Otto, Jung, and Erikson*. New Haven, CT and London: Yale University Press.

Casement, A. (ed.) (1998) *Post-Jungians Today: Key Papers in Contemporary Analytical Psychology*. London and New York: Routledge.

Charet, F.X. (1990) 'A dialogue between psychology and theology: the correspondence of C.G. Jung and Victor White'. *Journal of Analytical Psychology*, 35: 421–441.

—— (1993) *Spiritualism and the Foundations of C.G. Jung's Psychology*. Albany, NY: State University of New York Press.

Clarke, J.J. (1994) *Jung and Eastern Thought: A Dialogue with the Orient*. London: Routledge.

Corbett, L. (1996) *The Religious Function of the Psyche*. London and New York: Routledge.

Coward, H. (1985) *Jung and Eastern Thought*. Albany, NY: State University of New York Press.

Cunningham, A. (1992) 'Victor White, John Layard and C.G. Jung'. *Harvest: Journal for Jungian Studies*, 38: 44–57.

Dourley, J. (1981) *C.G. Jung and Paul Tillich: The Psyche as Sacrament*. Toronto: Inner City.

—— (1984) *The Illness that We Are: A Jungian Critique of Christianity*. Toronto: Inner City.

—— (1995) 'The religious implications of Jung's psychology'. *Journal of Analytical Psychology*, 40: 177–203.

Edinger, E. (1973) *Ego and Archetype: Individuation and the Religious Function of the Psyche*. New York: Penguin.

—— (1984) *The Creation of Consciousness: Jung's Myth for Modern Man*. Toronto: Inner City.

—— (1992) *Transformation of the God Image: An Elucidation of Jung's* Answer to Job. Toronto: Inner City.

Freud, S. (1907/1990) 'Obsessive acts and religious practices', in The Pelican Freud Library, Volume 13, *The Origins of Religion*, translated from the German under the general editorship of James Strachey. London: Penguin.

—— (1914/1993) 'On the history of the psychoanalytic movement', in The Pelican Freud Library, Volume 15, *Historical and Expository Works on Psychoanalysis*, translated from the German under the general editorship of James Strachey. London: Penguin.

Frischknecht, M. (1945) *Die Religion in der Psychologie C.G. Jungs*. Bern: Paul Haupt.

Goldbrunner, J. (1964) *Individuation: A Study of the Depth Psychology of Carl Gustav Jung*. Notre Dame, IN: University of Notre Dame Press.

Goldenberg, N. (1982) *The End of God: Important Directions for a Feminist Critique of Religion in the Works of Sigmund Freud and Carl Jung*. Ottawa, Ont.: University of Ottawa Press.

Hauke, C. (2000) *Jung and the Postmodern: The Interpretation of Realities*. London and New York: Routledge.

Hayman, R. (1999) *A Life of Jung*. London: Bloomsbury.

Heisig, J. (1972) '*The VII Sermones*: play and theory'. *Spring: An Annual of Archetypal Psychology and Jungian Thought*: 206–218.

—— (1973) 'Jung and theology: a bibliographical essay'. *Spring*: 204–255.

—— (1979) *Imago Dei: A Study of Jung's Psychology of Religion*. Lewisburg, PA: Bucknell University Press.

Hillman, J. (1971) 'Psychology: monotheistic or polytheistic?'. *Spring*: 193–208.

—— (1975) *Re-Visioning Psychology*. New York: Harper and Row.

Hinnells, J. (ed.) (1998) *A New Handbook of Living Religions*. London: Penguin.

Homans, P. (1979/1995) *Jung in Context: Modernity and the Making of a Psychology*, 2nd edn. Chicago, IL: University of Chicago Press.

Hostie, R. (1957) *Religion and the Psychology of Jung*. London: Sheer and Ward.

Jaffé, A. (1970/1975) *The Myth of Meaning: Jung and the Expansion of Consciousness*, trans. R.F.C. Hull. New York and Baltimore, MD: Penguin.

Jaffé, A. (1984) 'Details about C.G. Jung's Family'. *Spring*, 45: 35–43.

—— (1989) *Was C.G. Jung a Mystic?* Zurich: Daimon Verlag.

Jung, C.G. (1896–1899) *The Zofingia Lectures*, in *The Collected Works of C.G. Jung*, ed. Sir Herbert Read, Michael Fordham and Gerhard Adler, executive ed. William McGuire, trans. R.F.C. Hull, 21 volumes (hereafter *CW*). London: Routledge and Kegan Paul; Princeton, NJ: Princeton University Press, 1983.

—— (1902) 'On the psychology and pathology of so-called occult phenomena', in *CW* 1: pars. 1–150. London: Routledge and Kegan Paul, 1970.

—— (1909/1949) 'The significance of the father in the destiny of the individual', in *CW* 4: pars. 693–744. London: Routledge and Kegan Paul, 1961.

—— (1911–1912) *The Psychology of the Unconscious: A Study of the Transformations and Symbolisms of the Libido*, trans. B. Hinkle. New York: Moffat, Yard, 1916.

—— (1911–1912/1952) *Symbols of Transformation. CW* 5. London: Routledge, 1995.

—— (1916) '*Septem Sermones ad Mortuos*', in R. Segal (ed.) (1992) *The Gnostic Jung*. Princeton, NJ: Princeton University Press.

—— (1920/1948) 'The psychological foundations of belief in spirits', in *CW* 8: pars. 570–600. London: Routledge, 1991.

—— (1921) *Psychological Types. CW* 6. London: Routledge, 1991.

—— (1925) *Analytical Psychology: Notes of the Seminar given in 1925*, ed. W. McGuire. Princeton, NJ: Princeton University Press; London: Routledge, 1989.

—— (1926) 'Spirit and life', in *CW* 8: pars. 601–648. London: Routledge, 1991.

—— (1928–1930) *Dream Analysis: Notes of the Seminar Given in 1928–1930*, ed. W. McGuire. London: Routledge and Kegan Paul, 1984.

—— (1928/1931) 'The spiritual problem of modern man', in *CW* 10: pars. 148–196. London: Routledge and Kegan Paul, 1981.

—— (1928–1954) *Psychology and Religion: West and East. CW* 11. London: Routledge and Kegan Paul, 1986.

—— (1929) 'Commentary on *The Secret of the Golden Flower*', in *CW* 13: pars. 1–84. London: Routledge and Kegan Paul, 1967.

—— (1930) 'Richard Wilhelm: in memoriam', in *CW* 15: pars. 74–96. London: Routledge and Kegan Paul, 1984.

—— (1930–1934) *Visions: Notes of the Seminar Given in 1930–1934*, ed. C. Douglas, 2 volumes. London: Routledge, 1998.

—— (1932) *The Psychology of Kundalini Yoga: Notes of the Seminar given in 1932*, ed. S. Shamdasani. Princeton, NJ: Princeton University Press; London: Routledge, 1996.

—— (1934) 'The soul and death', in *CW* 8: pars. 796–815. London: Routledge, 1991.

—— (1934–1939) *The Seminars: Volume 2: Nietzsche's 'Zarathustra'*, ed. J. Jarrett, 2 volumes. Princeton, NJ: Princeton University Press, 1988.

—— (1935/1953) 'Psychological commentary on *The Tibetan Book of the Dead*', in *CW* 11: pars. 831–858. London: Routledge and Kegan Paul, 1986.

—— (1936a) 'Wotan', in *CW* 10: pars. 371–399. London: Routledge and Kegan Paul, 1981.

—— (1936b) 'Yoga and the West', in *CW* 11: pars. 859–876. London: Routledge and Kegan Paul, 1986.

Jung, C.G. (1938/1940) 'Psychology and religion', in *CW* 11: pars. 1–168. London: Routledge and Kegan Paul, 1986.

—— (1939a) '*Exercitia Spiritualia* of St Ignatius of Loyola: notes on lectures'. *Spring*, 1977: 183–200; 1978: 28–36.

—— (1939b) 'Foreword to Suzuki's *Introduction to Zen Buddhism*', in *CW* 11: pars. 877–907. London: Routledge and Kegan Paul, 1986.

—— (1939c) 'The symbolic life', in *CW* 18: pars. 608–696. London: Routledge, 1993.

—— (1939/1954) 'Psychological commentary on *The Tibetan Book of the Great Liberation*', in *CW* 11: pars. 759–830. London: Routledge and Kegan Paul, 1986.

—— (1942/1948) 'A psychological approach to the dogma of the Trinity', in *CW* 11: pars. 169–295. London: Routledge and Kegan Paul, 1986.

—— (1942/1954) 'Transformation symbolism in the Mass', in *CW* 11: pars. 296–448. London: Routledge and Kegan Paul, 1986.

—— (1943) 'The psychology of eastern meditation', in *CW* 11: pars. 908–949. London: Routledge and Kegan Paul, 1986.

—— (1944a) 'The holy men of India: introduction to Zimmer's *Der Weg zum Selbst*', in *CW* 11: pars. 950–963. London: Routledge and Kegan Paul, 1986.

—— (1944b) *Psychology and Alchemy*. *CW* 12. London: Routledge, 1989.

—— (1944–1957) 'Psychology and religion', in *CW* 18: pars. 1466–1690. London: Routledge, 1993.

—— (1945/1948) 'The phenomenology of the spirit in fairytales', in *CW* 9i: pars. 384–455. London: Routledge, 1991.

—— (1950) 'Foreword to the *I Ching*', in *CW* 11: pars. 964–1018. London: Routledge and Kegan Paul, 1986.

—— (1951a) *Aion: Researches into the Phenomenology of the Self*. *CW* 9ii. London: Routledge, 1991.

—— (1951b) 'On synchronicity', in *CW* 8: pars. 969–997. London: Routledge, 1991.

—— (1952a) 'Answer to Job', in *CW* 11: pars. 553–758. London: Routledge and Kegan Paul, 1986.

—— (1952b) 'Foreword to White's *God and the Unconscious*', in *CW* 11: pars. 449–467. London: Routledge and Kegan Paul, 1986.

—— (1952c) 'Religion and psychology: a reply to Martin Buber', in *CW* 18: pars. 1499–1513. London: Routledge, 1993.

—— (1952d) 'Synchronicity: an acausal connecting principle', in *CW* 8: pars. 816–968. London: Routledge, 1991.

—— (1955–1956) *Mysterium Coniunctionis: An Inquiry into the Separation and Synthesis of Psychic Opposites in Alchemy*. *CW* 14. London: Routledge and Kegan Paul, 1963.

—— (1957) 'The undiscovered self (present and future)', in *CW* 10: pars. 488–588. London: Routledge and Kegan Paul, 1981.

—— (1958) 'Flying saucers: a modern myth of things seen in the skies', in *CW* 10: pars. 589–824. London: Routledge and Kegan Paul, 1981.

—— (1961) 'The function of religious symbols', in *CW* 18: pars. 560–577.

—— (1963) *Memories, Dreams, Reflections*, recorded and edited by A. Jaffé, trans. R. Winston and C. Winston. London: Fontana, 1995.

—— (1973) *Letters 1: 1906–50*, selected and edited by G. Adler with A. Jaffé, trans. R.F.C. Hull. London: Routledge and Kegan Paul.

Jung, C.G. (1976) *Letters 2: 1951–61*, selected and edited by G. Adler with A. Jaffé, trans. R.F.C. Hull. London: Routledge and Kegan Paul.

Kirsch, T.B. (2000) *The Jungians: A Comparative and Historical Perspective.* London and Philadelphia, PA: Routledge.

Lammers, A.C. (1994) *In God's Shadow: The Collaboration between Victor White and C.G. Jung.* New York: Paulist Press.

McGuire, W. (ed.) (1974) *The Freud/Jung Letters: The Correspondence between Sigmund Freud and C.G. Jung*, trans. R. Manheim and R.F.C. Hull. Princeton, NJ: Princeton University Press.

McGuire, W. and Hull, R.F.C. (eds) (1978) *C.G. Jung Speaking: Interviews and Encounters.* London: Thames and Hudson.

Main, R. (ed.) (1997) *Jung on Synchronicity and the Paranormal.* London: Routledge; Princeton, NJ: Princeton University Press.

—— (2002) 'Religion, science, and the new age', in J. Pearson (ed.) *Belief Beyond Boundaries.* Aldershot: Ashgate; Milton Keynes: The Open University.

—— (2003) 'Analytical psychology, religion, and the academy', in R. Withers (ed.) *Controversies in Analytical Psychology.* London: Brunner-Routledge.

—— (2004) *The Rupture of Time: Synchronicity and Jung's Critique of Modern Western Culture.* Hove, UK and New York: Brunner-Routledge.

Mansfield, V. (1995) *Synchronicity, Science, and Soul-Making: Understanding Jungian Synchronicity through Physics, Buddhism, and Philosophy.* La Salle, IL: Open Court.

Meckel, D. (1990) *Jung and Christianity in Dialogue: Faith, Feminism, and Hermeneutics.* New York: Paulist Press.

Meckel, D. and Moore, R. (eds) (1992) *Self and Liberation: The Jung–Buddhism Dialogue.* New York: Paulist Press.

Miller, D. (1974) *The New Polytheism.* New York: Harper and Row.

Nagy, M. (1991) *Philosophical Issues in the Psychology of C.G. Jung.* Albany, NY: State University of New York Press.

Noll, R. (1994) *The Jung Cult: The Origins of a Charismatic Movement.* Princeton, NJ: Princeton University Press.

—— (1997) *The Aryan Christ: The Secret Life of Carl Jung.* New York: Random House.

Otto, R. (1917/1950) *The Idea of the Holy*, trans. J. Harvey. Oxford: Oxford University Press.

Palmer, M. (1997) *Freud and Jung on Religion.* London and New York: Routledge.

Papadopoulos, R. (2002) 'The other other: when the exotic other subjugates the familiar other'. *Journal of Analytical Psychology*, 47: 163–188.

Ritsema, R. and Karcher, S. (trans.) (1994) *I Ching: The Classic Chinese Oracle of Change.* Shaftesbury: Element.

Rowland, S. (2002) *Jung: A Feminist Revision.* Cambridge: Polity.

Ryce-Menuhin, J. (ed.) (1994) *Jung and the Monotheisms: Judaism, Christianity and Islam.* London and New York: Routledge.

Samuels, A. (2001) *Politics on the Couch: Citizenship and the Internal Life.* London: Profile.

Sandner, D. and Wong, S. (eds) (1997) *The Sacred Heritage: The Influence of Shamanism on Analytical Psychology.* London and New York: Routledge.

Schaer, H. (1951) *Religion and the Cure of Souls in Jung's Psychology*. London: Routledge and Kegan Paul.

Schlamm, L. (1994) 'The holy: a meeting-point between analytical psychology and religion', in J. Ryce-Menuhin (ed.) *Jung and the Monotheisms: Judaism, Christianity and Islam*. London and New York: Routledge.

—— (2000) 'C.G. Jung, mystical experience and inflation'. *Harvest: Journal for Jungian Studies*, 46(2): 108–128.

—— (2001) 'Ken Wilber's spectrum model: identifying alternative soteriological perspectives'. *Religion*, 31(1): 19–39.

Segal, R. (1999a) 'Comments on Storr's and Shamdasani's articles'. *Journal of Analytical Psychology*, 44(4): 561–562.

—— (1999b) 'Rationalist and romantic approaches to religion and modernity'. *Journal of Analytical Psychology*, 44(4): 547–560.

—— (1999c) *Theorizing about Myth*. Amherst, MA: University of Massachusetts Press.

Shamdasani, S. (1995) 'Memories, dreams, omissions'. *Spring: Journal of Archetype and Culture*, 57: 115–137.

—— (1998) *Cult Fictions: C.G. Jung and the Founding of Analytical Psychology*. London and New York: Routledge.

—— (1999) '*In statu nascendi*'. *Journal of Analytical Psychology*, 44(4): 539–546.

Shorter, B. (1996) *Susceptible to the Sacred: The Psychological Experience of Ritual*. London and New York: Routledge.

Smith, M. (1997) *Jung and Shamanism in Dialogue: Retrieving the Soul/Retrieving the Sacred*. New York: Paulist Press.

Spiegelman, J.M. (1994) *Catholicism and Jungian Psychology*. Las Vegas, AZ: New Falcon.

Stein, M. (1985) *Jung's Treatment of Christianity: The Psychology of a Religious Tradition*. Wilmette, IL: Chiron.

Storr, A. (1999) 'Jung's search for a substitute for a lost faith'. *Journal of Analytical Psychology*, 44(4): 531–538.

Tacey, D. (1997a) 'Jung in the academy: devotions and resistances'. *Journal of Analytical Psychology*, 42(2): 269–283.

—— (1997b) 'Reply to responses'. *Journal of Analytical Psychology*, 42(2): 313–316.

—— (1997c) *Remaking Men: Jung, Spirituality and Social Change*. London and New York: Routledge.

—— (1999) 'Why Jung would doubt the New Age', in S. Greenberg (ed.) *Therapy on the Couch: A Shrinking Future*. London: Camden Press.

—— (2001) *Jung and the New Age*. Hove, UK and Philadelphia, PA: Brunner-Routledge.

Tambiah, S. (1990) *Magic, Science, Religion, and the Scope of Rationality*. Cambridge: Cambridge University Press.

Ulanov, A. (1971) *The Feminine in Jungian Psychology and in Christian Theology*. Evanston, IL: Northwestern University Press.

—— (1997) 'Teaching Jung in a theological seminary and a graduate school of religion: a response to David Tacey'. *Journal of Analytical Psychology*, 42(2): 303–311.

—— (1999) *Religion and the Spiritual in Carl Jung*. New York: Paulist Press.

von Franz, M.-L. (1975) *C.G. Jung: His Myth in our Time*. London: Hodder and Stoughton.

Walls, A. (1997) 'Christianity', in J. Hinnells (ed.) (1998) *A New Handbook of Living Religions*. London: Penguin.

Wehr, D. (1987) *Jung and Feminism: Liberating Archetypes*. Boston, MA: Beacon.

White, V. (1952) *God and the Unconscious*. London: Collins.

—— (1960) *Soul and Psyche: An Enquiry into the Relationship of Psychotherapy and Religion*. London: Collins.

Whitmont, E. (1973) 'Prefatory remarks to Jung's "Reply to Buber"'. *Spring: An Annual of Archetypal Psychology and Jungian Thought*: 188–195.

Young-Eisendrath, P. and Miller, M. (eds) (2000) *The Psychology of Mature Spirituality: Integrity, Wisdom, Transcendence*. London and Philadelphia, PA: Routledge.

Zoja, L. and Williams, D. (2002) *Jungian Reflections on September 11: A Global Nightmare*. Einsiedeln, Switzerland: Daimon.

Chapter 14

The arts

Christian Gaillard
Translated from the French by Laura Winn

> One can only make poetry
>   with the anti-poetic;
> one can only make music
>   with the anti-musical.
> (Charles Ferdinand Ramuz to Igor Stravinsky)

THE ARTS: SECTION ONE

This chapter was assigned by the editor of this *Handbook* to be in the 'Applications' part of Jungian psychology. I would like to claim from the start that Jung's relationship to the arts is not in fact an 'application' of his analytical psychology. On the contrary, this relationship was for Jung, and is today for us, a propitious occasion to question, stimulate and renew his thought at each stage of its development, and is thus one of the essential foundations of his clinical practice and his conception of the relationship to the unconscious.

Following the history and evolution of Jung's relationship to the arts means rereading his work through the dynamic of its development as inspired by the nurture and most intimate provocations he felt right from his first childhood experiences. This implies revisiting his successive and often unexpected encounters with the works of art that marked each step of his life and his own work, and that made him keep his distance from Freudian psychoanalysis. Thus we can discover and develop progressively, at the rhythm of his work on the cultural diversity that precedes or surrounds us, his own position on decisive questions such as sexuality, incest, clinical transference and countertransference. And we will be retracing the personal debates Jung engaged with the progress – or the ups and downs and setbacks – of contemporary creation, while he sought, at first through trial and error, then with increasing confidence, to recognise his own place and to shoulder his own responsibilities in the heritage and destiny of our civilisation and culture.

We will see how Jung's encounters, practice and finally his analysis of the arts in their diverse forms were an opportunity to reconsider and deepen his research as a clinician and a psychologist. The importance of such research was made apparent gradually, and is fully developed in his last writings.

The analysis of his most explicit writings on the arts as they were developed during the 1930s will allow us to draw out the essential, most nodal and steadfast characteristics of his thinking on the subject, through the similarities and differences with the other great trends of contemporary psychoanalysis. The focus will be placed on the presentation and analysis of his texts on James Joyce's *Ulysses* and the work of Picasso (Jung 1932a, 1932b). These texts have been considered, even in Jungian circles, as rather weak aspects and moments in Jung's thinking; we, however, will see how these texts bring us to the heart of Jung's analysis of the processes of creation, and from there to the heart of his conception and practice of the unconscious.

We will then consider in turn his encounters, before and after the 1930s, with the arts of Antiquity and of the Orient, iconography and the literature of alchemy, Christian art, and the modern era and contemporary creation.

Finally, we will explore some of the main themes of current research on the arts and their development in the Jungian and post-Jungian movement.

The heart of the debate

We discover in Jung's 'autobiography' (*Memories, Dreams, Reflections*, 1963) that the presbytery where he lived as a child on account of his father's pastoral functions contained old works of art (Gaillard 2003b). Among the paintings in this house, the one that most impressed him, to the point of passing many long hours contemplating it, was a copy of a work by Guido Reni, whose original is at the Louvre (Jung 1963: 16).

This large painting (2.2m high by 1.45m wide) is entitled *David with the Head of Goliath*. It portrays the biblical David as a youth, full-length, facing the spectator, holding the decapitated head of the giant Goliath by the hair. The peculiar characteristic of this canvas is that although the hero is represented as the stronger of the two, evidently victorious over the giant, at the same time he is paradoxically fragile and vulnerable in his young age.

Even without invoking the family name of the young Carl Gustav – the word *jung* in German means 'young' – or evoking the later debates and battles with his mentor Freud, nineteen years his elder, one can only be struck by this evidence whose significance we will explore: David is not Moses. No more than Guido Reni is Michelangelo.

It is possible that there exists between these figures, David and Moses, Reni and Michelangelo, the same disparity as between Jung and Freud, at least in their respective relationships with the arts, and definitively in their respective concepts and practices of psychoanalysis.

Ulysses and Moses

The David of Guido Reni is presented as a cousin Ulysses, the clever and skilled hero, or anti-hero, in Homer and in Joyce's novel which Jung made his subject when he wrote in 1932 one of his main essays on the arts. This essay reveals with great tension and fruitfulness the way he struggles with the culture and traditions that formed us, with our heritage, and equally with the disturbing progression of our contemporary world.

Indeed Jung will write of Joyce's *Ulysses*:

> In its destruction of the criteria of beauty and meaning that have held till today, *Ulysses* accomplishes wonders. It insults all our conventional feelings, it brutally disappoints our expectations of sense and content, it thumbs its nose at all synthesis.
>
> (Jung 1932a: par. 177)

He further clarifies:

> Everything abusive we can say about *Ulysses* bears witness to its peculiar quality, for our abuse springs from the resentment of the unmodern man who does not wish to see what the gods have graciously veiled from sight [for] it is only modern man who has succeeded in creating an art in reverse, a backside of art that makes no attempt to be ingratiating, that tells us just where we get off, speaking with the same rebellious contrariness that had made itself disturbingly felt in those precursors of the moderns (not forgetting Hölderlin) who had already started to topple the old ideals.
>
> (Jung 1932a: pars. 177–178)

When we read Joyce we see that the ideals that we have inherited, often the most dear to us, have been given a good going over. And Jung ends up by following in Joyce's footsteps, himself rejoicing in a deconstructive process that is as deliberate and violent as deliberately violent.

Moreover, he begins to attack the figure of Moses. The constantly accelerating movement of thought and writing soon escalates from deconstruction to revolt, an essentially enthusiastic revolt, and from there again to an open denunciation that makes him declare: 'ideals are not beacons on mountain peaks, but taskmasters and jailers, a sort of metaphysical police originally thought up on Sinai by the tyrannical demagogue Moses and thereafter foisted upon mankind by a clever ruse' (par. 182).

The remark is extraordinarily denunciatory and violent. Extraordinarily because it is in stark contrast to the image that is willingly made of Jung, often represented as a wise old man who seeks perfect self-control, and achieves harmony, integration and synthesis in the manner of the masters of the arts who through their statements, writings and attitudes – think about Michelangelo's *Moses*, so admired by Freud, at San-Pietro-in-Vincoli – devote themselves to proving that such an ideal is at least virtually possible. It must be noted that his writings on the arts reveal an unexpected, unforeseen, and decidedly disturbing Jung.

This is worth noting because we might well have here a concept of the unconscious in action, indeed a relationship to the unconscious in actuality, that highly contrasts not only with the promise – often oriental – of wisdom and salvation, but also with the most widely prevalent psychoanalytical theories of art, those that find their source, their life force and their perspective from the founding texts of Freud on this subject.

The good, the beautiful and the insurrection

In Jung's (1932a) text, curiously there is no reference to Freud's essay – written in 1914 – on Michelangelo's *Moses*. But the violence of his treatment of the effects of art, frankly iconoclastic, places Jung in almost diametric opposition to a conception of the creative processes that wishes to see in them a particularly ideal aim for impulses, an aim which Freud will call 'sublimation'. Without citing directly, Jung assails, deconstructs and definitively denounces the Freudian concept of art and sublimation. He proceeds in the same manner regarding Moses himself and the entire edifice of feelings, thoughts and practices established in his name.

On the universe of *Ulysses* and for those who want to listen, he states even more explicitly:

> Even though the evil and destructive elements predominate, they are far more valuable than the 'good' that has come down to us from the past and proves in reality to be a ruthless tyrant, an illusory system of prejudices that robs life of its richness, emasculates it, and enforces a moral compulsion which in the end is unendurable.
>
> (Jung 1932a: par. 182)

Jung follows Joyce's art so closely – this Joyce in exile, struggling as best he can to detach himself from his excessively Catholic Irish origins – that his own pen rises up in rebellion, and writes in such an enflamed style that we are made to question the kind of art, and above all the concept of the arts towards which this movement can take him. For the undercurrent is not the Freudian lesson on wish fulfilment (*Wunscherfüllung*) and the sublimation of impulses, but quite the opposite: it is his attention and passionate, if not terrifying attraction to the most astounding and manifestly disturbing effects of art. Certain works of art, at least.

A change of scale

It is worth bearing in mind that Jung does not refer to the classic authors and artists. The quotations in his text on *Ulysses* are clear testimonies to this. If he cites Goethe, it is not in referring to *Wilhelm Meistre's Apprenticeship* or to his *Iphigenia*, but to *Faust II*. This in turn brings him to recall, during his reflections on the most acutely disturbing later events of our art history, Nietzsche's most provocative imprecations in *Thus Spoke Zarathustra* and *Ecce Homo*, texts that we know Jung had been familiar with for a long time, since his school years in Basel (Gaillard 1996/2001). He evokes in quick succession the effects, during our collective history, of the 'perverse change of style under Ikhnaton' that, he reminds us, paves the way for the first monotheism; the 'the inane lamb symbolism of early Christians' which is inscribed in the passage from the Roman Empire to the establishment of a Christian State; the 'doleful Pre-Raphaelite figures' that are nevertheless real precursors of a corporeal beauty that had not yet been represented, and 'late Baroque art, strangling itself in its own convolutions' in its own way anticipating the surpassing of medieval dogmatism by the scientific spirit. From here, Jung finally evokes the risks that were taken in the paintings of Tiepolo, or closer to us, Van Gogh (par. 175). With these examples, he argues that the formal innovations of the artists, as devastating as they might seem for previously practised modes of representation, cannot be reduced to the consequence of difficulties they had experienced in their personal lives.

All these works come from a completely different art movement than that which Michelangelo authoritatively established in the marble of his *Moses* at San-Pietro-in-Vincoli. Here it is not a question of sublimation, a concept that Freud elaborated in his admiration for this work. And we find ourselves on a completely different scale. The attention manifestly shifts from the celebration of an exemplary Moses, who each of us ideally could become, to the crisis that could affect *an entire world*, or at least, *a culture*.

Resistance

We can get used to it. But not without reticence, uneasiness, even fear. We must question, especially today, the sense – or nonsense – in the way the arts are progressing, with troubling doubt in, and such dangerous damage to the most widely shared and reputedly sound values.

Jung poses these same questions. Initially with irritation: 'Nothing comes to meet the reader', he states bad-temperedly on the subject of *Ulysses* right from the first pages that he devotes to this strange and unclassifiable novel, 'everything turns away from him, leaving him gaping after it. The book is always up and away, dissatisfied with itself, ironic, sardonic, virulent, contemptuous, sad, despairing, and bitter. It plays on the reader's sympathies' (par. 165). He adds: 'Yes, I admit I feel I have been made a fool of'. 'Joyce has aroused my ill will' (par. 167).

This is his reaction as a clinician. Or more exactly, and for the moment, as a psychopathologist. In his first reading, Jung tries to face the torturous, chaotic and apparently senseless torrent that is *Ulysses*, the evocation of a chain of such destabilising events, by bringing what he sees and reads back to the familiar phenomena of his clinical practice. 'I am a psychiatrist, he writes, and that implies a professional prejudice with regard to all manifestations of the psyche' (par. 172). He expands:

> I must therefore warn the reader: the tragicomedies of the average man, the cold shadow-side of life, the dull grey of spiritual nihilism are my daily bread. To me they are a tune ground out on a street organ, stale and without charm . . . But that is not the half of it – there is also the symptomatology! It is all too familiar, those interminable ramblings of the insane who have only a fragmentary consciousness and subsequently suffer from a complete lack of judgment and an atrophy of all their values.
>
> (Jung 1932a: pars. 172–173)

Thus 'Even the layman would have no difficulty in tracing the analogies between *Ulysses* and the schizophrenic mentality'. And the case seems closed: 'The resemblance is indeed so suspicious that an indignant reader might easily fling the book aside with the diagnosis "schizophrenia"' (par. 173).

However, Jung concludes that such a diagnostic, clearly very tempting even today, when dealing with our doubts and debates, our disagreements and resentments when confronted with a large proportion of the contemporary arts, cannot be justified under these circumstances.

He arrives at this conclusion for at least three reasons – all three are present but unequally developed in this text – which will bring us progressively to enlarge the field of our examination of his writings on the arts.

Some characteristics and manifest effects of these works

First, Jung notes that in the work of Joyce, and the same is true for many comparable examples today, a specific characteristic of schizophrenia is missing: the stereotype. He points out that

> *Ulysses* may be anything, but it is certainly not monotonous in the sense of being repetitious . . . The presentation is consistent and flowing, everything is in motion and nothing is fixed. The whole book is borne along on a subterranean current of life that shows singleness of

aim and rigorous selectivity, both these being unmistakable proof of the existence of a unified personal will and directed intention.

(Jung 1932a: par. 173)

Of course we will have to re-examine this 'subterranean current of life', which here appears almost surreptitiously like a metaphor in the text. We will see that it is in fact at the heart and core of Jung's concept of art, because of its central importance in his practice of the unconscious. We will discuss all its 'collective' dimensions: impersonal, or transpersonal and therefore transgenerational, even transhistorical, if not transcultural; we will also consider the curious scale of such a reality, as well as what Jung calls its 'final intentions'.

But let us look for the moment at a second decisive characteristic of Joyce's *Ulysses*, a characteristic that according to Jung is shared with those works that are formally comparable through the upheavals they induce in the generally accepted criteria of sense and beauty, pushing us to the painful, unsupportable limits of nonsense:

> They are drastic purgatives whose full effect would be dissipated if they did not meet with an equally strong and obstinate resistance. They are a kind of psychological specific which is of use only where the hardest and toughest material must be dealt with.
>
> (Jung 1932a: par. 179)

He writes of purgatives and psychological specifics. Which is to say that the consideration of our resistance to these works and to what it entails is decisive for his reflections on art. This is eminently the consideration of an analyst, for what is at stake here is our resistance to a reality that we would prefer to know nothing about, to an unconscious that functions at its own pace, with its own rhythm and timescale, strength and substance, and which claims its dues.

Jung points out that in fact these works of art, openly negative, apparently insensitive, and mercifully objective, attack our profusion of feelings, our sentimental state. This is the positively destructive effect that works such as these tend to create. He writes in 1932, when memories of the First World War were still fresh in the minds of many:

> there is a good deal of evidence to show that we actually are involved in a sentimentality hoax of gigantic proportions. Think of the lamentable role of popular sentiment in wartime! Think of our so-called humanitarianism! The psychiatrist knows only too well how each of us becomes the helpless but not pitiable victim of his own sentiments.
>
> (Jung 1932a: par. 184)

Jung's conclusion, almost Joyce-like, in the light of the German prepara-
tions at that exact same time for events even more dreadful than anything
that Europe and the world had yet experienced, arrives like a bombshell:
'Sentimentality is the superstructure erected upon brutality' (par. 184).

Another angle

The third decisive characteristic of these works, although their effect is
fairly difficult to gauge for the psychologist, and even for the psychoanalyst, is that they elude and even radically opposes all psychobiographical analysis (par. 186).

Certainly, the author James Joyce can be found in the book, on each
page and even in each character of his 'novel'. But, Jung writes,

> the ego that embraces them all appears nowhere. It betrays itself by
> nothing, by no judgment, no sympathy, and not even with a single
> anthropomorphism. The ego of the creator of these figures is not to be
> found. It is as though it had dissolved into the countless figures of
> *Ulysses*.
>
> (Jung 1932a: par. 188)

So through his encounters with and interrogation of the arts, we see that
Jung has turned his back on the concepts of 'wish fulfilment' and sublimation as they appear in Freud's 'The Moses of Michelangelo' and has
taken the opposite view. Moreover, he has irrevocably excluded from his
approach the tool of psychobiography, which has been and remains the
most largely practised method of research in the psychoanalysis of art since
Freud's *Leonardo da Vinci and a Memory of his Childhood* (published in
1910). This method consists of looking for the meaning of a work of art in
the author's experiences from childhood, if possible right from the cradle.
This method of psychoanalysis of art cannot be applied to Joyce's text
because, as Jung notes, the work itself cannot be grasped.

And yet in 1932 Jung must have known James Joyce, or at least have
heard about the author's trials and tribulations at the close of the 1910s
when he was in Zurich. Joyce's sponsor Edith McCormick, John D.
Rockefeller's daughter and a close supporter of the Jungian circles, had
suddenly decided to cut the financial support she had given Joyce until
then. Joyce may have even suspected at the time that Jung was not completely innocent with regards to his sponsor's decision (Salza 1987: 189–
190, n. 7 and 191, n. 11; Ellmann 1959: 714–715). We also know that in
1934, two years after the publication of the essay on *Ulysses*, Joyce sought
out Jung to treat his daughter Lucy. At first she was treated with some
apparent success, but Jung did not truly believe in her recovery. It finally

transpired that the treatment had been to no avail, most notably due to the fact that the ties between the daughter and her father had never really been broken (Salza 1987: 189–190, n. 7 and 191, n. 11; Ellmann 1959: 684).

But we could search in vain for the slightest reference to Joyce's life in Jung's text on *Ulysses*. Jung has no use for it. He is in no way tempted to indulge in a 'wild analysis' of James Joyce, neither in this text nor, more generally, in any other advancement he makes in the psychoanalysis of art. Nor does he, at any other moment, stop to paint the 'psychological' portrait of Ulysses, the hero, or rather the anti-hero, of this book.

This is obviously not the focus of Jung's approach to the arts. The analysis of a work of art does not at any moment serve as a pretext for him to become the author's clinician or the characters' psychologist. He does not work at this scale. The focus is collective:

> Who, then, is Ulysses? Doubtless he is a symbol of what makes up the totality, the oneness, of all the single appearances in *Ulysses* as a whole – Mr. Bloom, Stephen, Mrs. Bloom, and the rest, including Mr. Joyce. Try to imagine a being who is not a mere colourless conglomerate soul composed of an indefinite number of ill-assorted and antagonistic individual souls, but consists also of houses, street-processions, churches, the Liffey [the river that flows through Dublin], several brothels, and a crumpled note on its way to the sea – and yet possesses a perceiving and registering consciousness!
>
> (Jung 1932a: par. 198)

Ulysses looks at our world and each and every one of us in a pretty strange way. From elsewhere, from various angles and viewpoints. And so it makes us look at ourselves and our ordinary lives from another angle, plural and multiplied. The angle is definitively plural, and so lacking in lenience that it can be implacably objective. *Ulysses*, Jung writes, 'wants to be an eye of the moon, a consciousness detached from the object, in thrall neither to the gods nor to sensuality, and bound neither by love nor by hate, neither by conviction nor by prejudice' (par. 186). He dared to

> take the step that leads to the detachment of consciousness from the object; he has freed himself from attachment, entanglement, and delusion, and can therefore turn homeward. He gives us more than a subjective expression of personal opinion, for the creative genius is never one but many, and he speaks in stillness to the souls of the multitude, whose meaning and destiny he embodies no less than the artist's own.
>
> (par. 193)

Dreams and creation

Jung approaches and analyses the arts in the same manner as dreams. The dream is in fact far from being only 'disguised wish fulfilment', such as Freud viewed it. The attention Jung gives to a dream, the littlest dream, does not lead him to exercise suspicion as to the distortions due to any practice of censorship. He is inspired by the *surprise* experienced on waking, when we discover ourselves at grips with unexpected representations, reactions and emotions whose consistency and insistence we cannot deny, and that are evidently manifestations of our current preoccupations, be they close or somehow distant, even though we would prefer to know nothing about them.

A dream of course is enigmatic, and a work of art even more so. But this enigma is often the best possible expression of something that we could not express or experience in any other way. In this sense a dream is an interrogation, a provocation. It provokes us to think and react in the face of its presentations and representations. We are not only surprised but often also perplexed and stunned, unless we can accept the imposed *confrontation*. Jung's text on *Ulysses* testifies to this confrontation and to the brutal yet crucial self-questioning that can be arrived at through interpretive work.

'A great work of art', Jung wrote as early as 1930,

> is like a dream; for all its apparent obviousness it does not explain itself and is always ambiguous. A dream never says 'you ought' or 'this is the truth'. It presents an image in much the same way nature allows a plant to grow, and it is up to us to draw conclusions.
>
> (Jung 1930: par. 161)

Here there is bewilderment. But let us take note of the organic, natural metaphor of the plant growing and blooming. Like that of the subterranean current, this is a frequent metaphor in Jung's universe. It brings our attention to a movement of expression and development that is at work, and that could be observed and studied in order to pinpoint its different moments, steps, perhaps even laws.

Here we are at the heart of the question of the arts and, more radically, of the unconscious itself. This is also the heart of a reversal of point of view, of a revolution, at once epistemological and clinical, that Jung implemented in psychoanalysis through his own concept and practice of the unconscious, or more precisely the relationship to the unconscious.

Experience of plural animation

Freud had already taught that the ego 'is not the master of his own house' (Freud 1917: 143): it is questioned and deprived of all pretensions to mastery, common conceptions, ideal representations and values, be they inherited or constructed. Freud was actually the first to have talked about *regression*, *dramatisation* and *symbolisation* in relation to dream work, starting with his *Traumdeutung*. But Jung, having conducted his own research in Zurich even before meeting Freud, undermines the foundations of the Freudian lesson using his own auto-clinical and clinical experience, and threatens the edifice that Freud so patiently and, it must be said, so jealously constructed (Gaillard 2003a).

Following Jung and the path he opened to psychoanalysis, the unconscious is no longer approached only through the effects of the repression of sexuality, above all infantile sexuality, or primal repression. The unconscious is received, observed and most importantly practised from a position of surprise that implies accommodation, accompaniment and finally confrontation. For the unconscious precedes consciousness, is initial and in constant renewal, highly autonomous and radically autochthonous, which is to say, whatever we do, it lives its own life on its own means and terms.

Jung shows that the unconscious is thus endowed with its own means of expression. It is work in progress that advances at its own pace and has its own timescale, which can encompass an individual's past, from one stage of life to another, or a transgenerational period, or in a wider dimension even a cultural era (Gaillard 2001, 2003a). Therefore the work of a Jungian psychoanalyst will concentrate on *becoming-conscious*, at all these levels, rather than only on why and how some impulses and representations become unconscious through repression in each individual's personal history.

This concept and practice of the relationship to the unconscious, through a work of art or a dream, is naturally *dynamic* and *dialectic*. The opening of this angle, underpinned by a power struggle, involves everything from the provisory negotiation of our ordinary neuroses, to irrepressible outbursts, most notably those of psychosis. The ego defends itself. It struggles as best it can. And of course it tries to get the upper hand, as we were able to see in Jung's text when, grappling with Joyce's overwhelming and unacceptable novel, he tries at first to reduce this work to the expression of a well-known pathology, schizophrenia.

But frequenting such works of art can also mean acquiring a taste for the debates they provoke. Moreover, as this text shows, one can passionately question what is sought and found in such a work of art. One can acquire a taste for this plurality, live, disturbing and uncanny, that seems impersonal while out of proportion with the ego's guidelines, criteria and ideals, but that turns out to be rich and animated by unpredictable life-forces, never previously experienced, when it expresses itself here and now, and from the most distant, foreign parts of ourselves demands to be realised.

The relationship to such a work of art can be experienced by the unilateral and unidimensional ego as a menace and a danger, like that of a merciless insurrection. But it can also lead to the evidence and experience of plural animation, situated and deployed in opposition to Moses' monolithic erection, Michelangelo's Moses that Freud so greatly admired, but nevertheless leading to a development that we can learn to welcome, in the form it chooses to take and with our intervention.

Processes and structures

It remains that we must ask ourselves where are we going with this line and how are we to progress. A study of the further developments of this text on Joyce's *Ulysses*, combined with that of another text Jung wrote a few months later on Picasso's work, inspired by a retrospective exhibition in Zurich the same year, will show us the way (Jung 1932b).

We saw that in the essay on Joyce's book Jung wrote at first with irritation, almost with aggression. It is only after a full-blown debate where the psychopathologist tried to impose himself that Jung came to change his stance and be driven, almost in spite of himself, to the point of becoming engaged in an enthusiastic or frenzied reading, almost prophetic at times, where the main themes of his psychoanalysis of art were outlined and progressively became more assertive.

In this text Jung tried, in fact, to express as best as he could and without too much accent on theory the tension that comes to exist in such a work of art between the supposedly most assured values of our cultural heritage and the disconcerting strangeness of the unconscious work that, below or perhaps beyond all personal psychology, takes these values, puts them to the test, and harms them.

The style of the text on Picasso's work is more compact and better controlled. Here Jung does not let himself be carried away or seduced. He progresses with the reserve, experience and fastidious attention of an analyst and psychologist who surprises and questions himself, but who has seen worse and is very careful not to be led astray by the movement of what he observes. So his thinking on the arts becomes more precise, endowed with decidedly more theoretical expression, in order to achieve clarity.

The current dialectics between the ego and the unconscious

Jung evidently remembers his annoyed and irritated initial reactions to Joyce's novel when he writes, this time of Picasso's paintings,

> nothing comes to meet the beholder, everything turns away from him; even an occasional touch of beauty seems only like an inexcusable delay in withdrawal . . . an obscurity, however, which has nothing to conceal, but spreads like a cold fog over desolate moors; the whole thing quite pointless, like a spectacle that can do without a spectator.
> (Jung 1932b: par. 209)

In both cases, when he approaches and tries to understand the central tenets of Picasso's work or of Joyce's writing, the thing that strikes him immediately is the unfair lot given to the reader or spectator.

So he concludes that it is clearly *the ego* that suffers, and severely so, because it is left on the sidelines, rejected, and mistreated by the work of art. The ego is deprived of its predilection for mastery, notably through thought, and Jung emphasises how its efforts are dismissed, despite being benevolent, normally equitable and open to comprehension. This must indeed be accepted.

If Jung insists in this manner on the observation of the fate that befalls the ego in these circumstances, it is because his reflections on Joyce's novel and Picasso's paintings give him the opportunity to inform us more explicitly, as methodologically as possible, and then as theoretically as possible but in his own way, of the debate that he finds himself engaged in, as do we, when confronted with such works of art.

So we are brought to the *relationship between the ego and the unconscious*, a question that belongs to what is classically called in psychoanalysis 'metapsychology'. But Jung does not like to play the metapsychologist. His reflection on this subject is elaborated only in response to his discoveries and encounters, and at the pace and rhythm of the debates that they incite. His clinical practice provides the everyday opportunity for such encounters, but his discoveries in the arts are often privileged and even decisive.

This is the way Jung's analysis of Joyce's and Picasso's work advances. However, after his long account of his manifestly negative reactions to *Ulysses* or the paintings of Picasso, his stance changes. The central focus soon shifts to become the objective, formal and precise observation and description of the form taken by these works, and the tentative exploration of the world they present. A decidedly different world, an other world, an elsewhere. What can we know and say about this world for the sake of a more complete theoretical understanding?

At first this world, foreign to the ego, and refractory to the conscious to the extent that we call it the unconscious, appeared to Jung as so dark, gloomy, cold, fragmented, disrupted, chaotic, despairing and disastrous in the almost crazy autonomy of its expression, that he was tempted to see in it nothing other than a new avatar of a reality that he knew only too well, that of schizophrenia.

But we see that his ensuing reflection still progresses in the rhythm of his debate with this work, which is the rhythm of the writing itself. He writes about Joyce's *Ulysses* in a quasi-visual mode that is '"cubist" in the deepest sense because it resolves the picture of reality into an immensely complex painting whose dominant note is the melancholy of abstract objectivity' (par. 174). Jung notes that the fragmented lines in Picasso's paintings, the internal collisions of colour and form that disappear almost as soon as they appear, oppose the ideals of beauty and of right and wrong with the evidence of a grotesque, quasi-Neolithic primitiveness which leaves some indifferent and frightens others by its brutality or the outpouring of Dionysian evocations drawn from Antiquity (pars. 208 and 212).

It is here, in Jung and Freud's respective relationships to the arts, that the most radical difference between their concepts and respective practices of the unconscious is made apparent. While Freud approaches the unconscious through repression – repression of sexuality and above all, of infantile sexuality, and of primal repression, as we have seen – for Jung the unconscious is the constantly renewed origin of a consciousness, from which it only partially and provisory breaks off and disengages; it is an original state always present and highly impersonal – we find here, in a more elaborate mode, the 'subterranean current of life' evoked earlier – that can occupy the most common course of our lives at every moment and in the most unexpected and often unforeseeable ways: we can always return and re-evoke this state, unexpectedly or in a more deliberate manner, especially when we encounter the arts or when we are ourselves involved in a creative process.

This is the source of Jung's conception of the libido that, from the publication of his book entitled *Wandlungen und Symbole der Libido* in 1911–1912, places him in opposition to the Freudian theory of sexuality. According to Jung (1911–1912), despite its specification in differentiated impulses and thus in every choice of object, the libido can potentially show itself as animated, polymorphous, elementary and sensorial as it always was, through the organic and most archaic pulsations that are experienced in the body.

Freud, and this is his strength, looks constantly to childhood. As a clinician, he seeks to find and relive in the conditions of transference, as circumstantially and emotionally as possible, the moments that marked, formed and deformed us from earliest childhood, and from there on, in one stage of our lives or another. Then he sets out to produce the theory of the 'stages' that we have all passed in the course of our sexuality. His psychoanalysis of art is inscribed in the same retrospective movement. This is the source of his predilection for psychobiography and his explicative, more or less hypothetical, reconstructions of what might have happened in the past, as his text *Leonardo da Vinci and a Memory of his Childhood*, and his analysis of *Moses* at San-Pietro-in-Vincoli show.

Jung, for his part, in his clinical practice and theoretical reflections, shows himself to be more a man of the present. A developing present that he seeks to liberate from its inherited shackles of earliest childhood, and more importantly whose tensions and current potentiality he tries to follow. We see this clearly in the two texts on the psychoanalysis of art that we are dealing with. Each of them reveals a different dimension of Jung's method and thought.

From the focus on countertransference to the introduction of 'functions'

In his study of Joyce's *Ulysses*, Jung not only accepted the shock and destabilisation he felt when encountering this work, but also explicitly expressed these reactions that, if left to their own movement, could have easily have led him to reject this work and all those that are similar to it. His attention was deliberately placed on the vivid and violent counter-transference that seized and animated him, mobilising the reactions of his thoughts both as someone from the upper middle class trained in classical humanities, and as a psychiatrist quick to recognise and qualify without complaisance the disorders of psychopathology. Simultaneously and in the same countertransferential manner he mobilised the reactions of his feelings, including the most negative. Feelings of self-defence, self-preservation and rejection, all the more virulent since the menace that he then perceived threatened not only his personal culture and his hereditary culture, but also his most intimate values, his predilection for and his engagements in equilibrium and ideally peaceful, harmonious happiness.

Further, in the act of writing, Jung is brought to state more and more precisely that Joyce's work decidedly does not place him on the side of thinking and feeling, but rather on the side of the exercise of perception, or more exactly sensation, which his literary and artistic perusals, the common expectations of his intellectual training, and his moral and aesthetic values had as good as failed to acquaint him with.

Inspired by his own reactions as a reader, Jung (1932a) writes that Joyce presents 'a case of visceral thinking with severe restriction of cerebral activity and its confinement to the perceptual processes' (par. 166). And in such a way that in reading this author 'one is driven to unqualified admiration for Joyce's feats in the sensory sphere: what he sees, hears, tastes, smells, touches, inwardly as well as outwardly, is beyond measure astonishing' (ibid.).

So now Jung is just as admiring of this work as he is reticent and irritated by it. But how can he negotiate such ambivalence and progress like the novel itself? He progresses and deepens his exploration and his reflection because it is his intuition that guides him. He is entreated, having made room for his immediate countertransferential reactions in order to be more aware of them, to go beyond and thwart them. This will allow him to locate and perhaps even accept to explore the unfamiliar regions, registers, and modalities of experience of himself, others, and the world.

This exercise of intuition manifests itself in the text through the bid he makes for the importance of the work despite knowing the impact that it had, and still has, on the course of contemporary literature (par. 181). And, more immediately, because it is his bad temper that incites him to think (par. 168). Above all, because he sees himself more or less in the shadows, waiting for the sense such a text can bring to the reader, for whatever Ithaca he might find while following as best as he can this *Ulysses* (par. 191).

Here, the Jungian reader will have evidently recognised the Jung's psychology of the 'functions that orientate the consciousness': thinking, feeling, sensation and intuition. This psychology had been outlined by Jung as early as 1916, and it is to be found already highly developed in one of his early, cardinal works entitled *Psychological Types*, published in 1921. So we can be surprised. Why does Jung not cite this book? Why does he not cite himself? Why, in his text on Joyce, does he not recall, even in passing, this theory of 'functions' which was one of the ways he used to develop his own 'metapsychology'?

Jung has other things to do than to resort to invoking or evoking theory, even his own. He does not care to brandish, or even simply mention, his methodological and theoretical acquisitions. Jung goes back to work, remobilises and reworks his thought at each stage, even if he has to remodel and reformulate his most established acquisitions in sometimes rather markedly different modes. Actually, this is one of the constant difficulties in reading Jung's written works and also in teaching his analytical psychology, notably in university.

Jung truly works on his texts and on himself in the present. We must then determine, locate and renew these acquisitions and tools, in the progression of his texts. The first consequence of this is that concerning his approach to the arts nothing is more foreign to him than the temptation, so frequent in psychoanalysis, to proceed to 'applied psychoanalysis'.

A second consequence is that for Jung, and for those who follow him, the tension that manifests itself, notably through our countertransferential reactions when faced with a work of art or a patient, between the ego that suffers and defends itself and the unconscious that menaces, does not bring him, as the Freud of the first 'topography' might have liked, to deal directly with the opposition between 'impulses of self-preservation' and 'sexual impulses', such as they can be identified by theory and clinically found in one's life story, if possible from as early as childhood.

Jung's approach takes another turn. It offers another hold on this tension and contradiction, derived from the perceptively and theoretically different dialectic and dynamic of the relations between the ego and the unconscious, more immediately present. This is the source of his concept and his practice of the involvement of the 'functions' that orientate our consciousness.

In the case of his debate with Joyce, we see Jung progress. Initially he experiences the heights of misguided thought shocked by its own reasoning, categories and expectations, the hurt reactions of feeling that finds its appreciated, accepted and acclaimed values usurped, and thus seeks its own means of evaluation. Then sensation is mobilised, progressing through sometimes the most elementary of tastes, touch, scents, bringing him finally to play off the senses against sense.

Inspired and guided by Joyce's writing, which comes to progressively modify his own, and also by his clinical practice and the anterior acquisitions of his analytical psychology, Jung rejoins one of the most manifest and most disturbing themes of modernity – or postmodernity – which, not without clashes with or violence against our cultural heritage, seeks to make feeling live through sensation.

Images down below

A displacement of the central focus of the attention given to a work of art and the accompaniment it requires can hardly be self-motivated, even taking into consideration a sufficiently Jungian clinical practice of the relationship to the unconscious. A way must be found to execute the passage from one function to another through an axial mobilisation of sensation. These texts on Joyce and Picasso show how.

Our reader will have understood that the psychoanalysis of art committed to following in Jung's footsteps cannot become yet another applied psychoanalysis. But an assiduous reader of Jung's writings and Jungian literature could be tempted all the same to ask what role in Jung's approach will be played by the complementary, compensatory and even contradictory movements not only between thought and feeling, between intuition and sensation, but also between an extraverted attitude and an introverted attitude. These movements are another axis of Jung's reflection and theory on our everyday relationships to the exterior world and to our interior world.

Jung does not call up his concepts of complementarity, compensation and contradiction in these texts, any more than he explicitly uses his psychology of functions. He does not think about his approach. He observes it. He observes himself. And what does he see? That at page 135 of Joyce's enormous novel, after having defended, wrestled and stuck with it, he suddenly fell asleep. Suddenly, but not without having located the precise moment when this incident occurred and sleep interrupted his debate with the work in question: in his text he painstakingly indicates the page where this event took place. Furthermore, he cites in a footnote, the sentence that contained 'the narcotic that switched off my consciousness, *activating a still unconscious train of thought which consciousness would only have disturbed*' (par. 165, n. 5; the emphasis is mine). What does this sentence say? It describes 'a man supple in combat: stonehorned, stonebearded, heart of stone, . . . that stone effigy in frozen music, horned and terrible, of the human form divine, that eternal symbol of wisdom and prophecy'. The figure is immediately recognisable: it is Moses! The Moses, Jung specifies in the same note, 'who refused to be cowed by the might of Egypt'.

And from here on Jung's text on *Ulysses*, which he had announced in the subheading as 'a monologue', becomes in fact a text with two voices. The first voice still expresses, in the top of the pages, his initial irritated reactions. From this footnote onwards, written as if with the left hand, comes from afar the second voice, from his distant self, in the depths of his sleep, presenting the emblematic figure of Moses, who is decidedly at the heart of his ambivalence towards *Ulysses*.

Jung's contradictory debate with this work, and with an entire part of contemporary art, will of course continue. But from here on, after sudden appearance of the figure of Moses in his reading of Joyce, the form of the debate will change. Jung can now follow closely on Joyce's heels, understand and accompany him in his revolt and his revolution against traditional thoughts, morals and aesthetics. For Joyce these were Thomist Aristotelian and Irish-Catholic; for Jung, who had to leave Vienna after having left the religion of his fathers – as Joyce was in exile from Dublin – they were the values at the heart of his debate with Freudian psychoanalysis, and with Freud himself, where the tall figure of Moses appeared more and more clearly.

At the risk of seeming Lacanian, it must be noted and emphasised here that the backdrop of Jung's debate with Joyce's *Ulysses* is composed of Freud's avowed admiration of Michelangelo's *Moses*. Moreover – how can it not have been seen or heard as so, even if Jung apparently does not say anything about it? – *Freud*'s name in German, and that of *Joyce* in English are so closely related by their meanings that they overlap, one being able to hide the other; they can be superimposed, or even brought to signify each other. In such a way that Jung's debate with Joyce is revealed to be also a debate with Freud, Freudian psychoanalysis and most notably with the Freudian psychoanalysis of art.

But he struggles and debates with it as a psychoanalyst. In his own way, of course. This manner is patently and voluntarily figurative. The figure of Moses embodies Jung's debate with *Ulysses* and allows him to advance. Especially when one examines the succession of images that from here on come to support, contain, and feed Jung's thought.

Jung (1932a) initially wrote that *Ulysses* appeared to him as 'infernally nugatory', like 'a brilliant and hellish monster-birth' (par. 165). Then he noted that this 'novel' can be read backwards for each phrase presents itself as a whole, self-contained, and even stopping mid-sentence 'the first half still makes sense enough to live by itself, or at least seems to'. He continues this sensorial metaphor, or rather lets it live its own life: 'The whole work has the character of a worm cut in half, that can grow a new head or a new tail as required' (par. 165). Then he adds:

> There we have it, the cold-blooded unrelatedness of his mind which seems to come from the saurian in him or from still lower regions –

conversation in and with one's own intestines – a man of stone, he with the horns of stone, the stony beard, the petrified intestines, Moses, turning his back with stony unconcern on the flesh-pots and gods of Egypt, and also on the reader, thereby outraging his feelings of good will.

(Jung 1932a: par. 168)

Finally, the

inexpressibly rich and myriad-faceted language unfolds itself in passages that creep along tapeworm fashion, terribly boring and monotonous, but the very boredom and monotony of it attain an epic grandeur that makes the book a *Mahabharata* of the world's futility and squalor.

(par. 194)

Thus Joyce's writing provokes these images of a hell of stone, monsters and saurians, of solitary worms, which are returned to and adjusted over and over, centring around the figure of the terrible stone prophet. These images lead him to the close recognition of the art of a writer to smell, taste, listen, look, feel, and so to write and compose his 'novel', to create an unprecedented work without equal, and a truly initiatory impact. Through this succession of images that are at first opaque, cumbersome, inopportune, frankly deranging, clearly archaic and always intimately tied to Joyce's writing, the progressive understanding and then the intelligence of the work which Jung failed to perceive at first, rise up and gain substance as he writes.

This process of trial and error, a figurative, prospective and quasi-visionary approach – though initially nocturnal and always weighed down by sensation – shows Jung's method to be in stark contrast with the retrospective reconstruction Freud undertook in front of the *Moses* at San-Pietro-in-Vincoli. Jung deliberately allows himself to dream; this is the starting point of his thought as he methodically seeks and finds in the images that emerge from the darkness of his night, his own mode of progressively controlled objectivity.

This strange way of proceeding, uncanny, deliberately dramatised and inevitably adventurous, undermines the Freudian lesson and opens up another direction for psychoanalysis. Admittedly, this might seems unsurprising to the clinician accustomed to ask of theory only orientation and support in the best possible relationship to the work of unconscious, but might seriously disorientate the intellectual who worries about the architecture of his understanding. Especially because Jungian thought, 'analytical psychology' as practised by Jung and his followers, is itself necessarily influenced by this way of proceeding.

The development of Jung's thought was manifestly and deliberately figurative and dramatised, notably in his encounters with the arts. And this is the way we think ourselves, following his lead.

Figures and presences

Jung's essay on Picasso's work will allow us to draw out more precisely his approach in his relationship to the arts. In this essay, Jung shows the same initially negative bewilderment over the paintings that he expressed regarding Joyce. But here he is also concerned.

His concern is that of a clinician. For what does he observe in 1932 in the continuing work of Picasso? That the dominant colour in the first period of Picasso's paintings, such as they were exposed at Kunsthaus in Zurich, is blue. A midnight blue, in fact. Night is approaching.

So there is plenty to be concerned about. At least for the artist, if not the analyst who through his own practice knows full well that once we allow the experiences and the representations that come out of our darkest interior regions to emerge, we risk losing our light as well as our bearings and perspectives. An analyst also knows that this process, once we go along with it and accept it, can happen over sometimes a very long time, at an extremely slow pace.

But Jung's observation and reflection continue. Jung (1932b) emphasises that this blue strangely resembles 'the Tuat-blue of the Egyptian underworld' (par. 210), and that disturbing figures present themselves in the painter's work. First, we see a clearly distraught woman who seems to look at us, her child in her arms; then a young prostitute, apparently tubercular and syphilitic. Soon both figures give way to a multitude of 'fragments, fractures, discarded remnants, debris, shreds, and disorganized units' (par. 210), and finally the tragic figure of the Harlequin appears. He is sometimes represented in full, but forcibly in pieces, sometimes merely suggested here and there, from one painting to another, by the bottle of wine or the lute that are his exclusive possessions, or still more erratically by the 'bright lozenges of his jester's costume' (par. 212).

This frightens Jung. He wonders how it is possible not to see here, as in Joyce's novel, the all too familiar ruptures of which schizophrenics are so commonly victims. What will become of Picasso, he who has chosen to frequent so many literally deconstructed figures and forms, such hopelessly fatal debris and ruin?

Will Jung's approach become psychobiographical, contrary to what we have seen up until now? Indeed not. For he does not at any time in this text make the smallest allusion to the artist's life, to his childhood trials and tribulations, or to his adventures of the moment, notably that of meeting young Marie-Thérèse Walter. Just as he paid no attention to Joyce's life throughout the critique of his novel. Jung's observations and interpretations do not go in this direction.

On the contrary, what attracts and maintains his attention is the dynamics of the work as seen through its manifest and actual expressions, especially the figures presented and represented. He knows the virtue of images when one finds oneself in such a universe, so dark, cold, lugubrious and primitive as to risk mortal decomposition. He even learned for his own guidance (cf. *Memories, Dreams, Reflections*, ch. VII) and as a therapist to allow images to take form, including images such as these, that they can be the foundation of a method that helps to contain overly dangerous, menacing scissions (par. 207), while allowing the ego to face them and better understand what it is dealing with.

Following his first observations on 'feeling tone complexes' and *imagos*, this attention given to the dramatic figuration of the relationship to the unconscious leads Jung to propose concepts that are themselves figurative, dramatised and even – surprisingly for concepts – gendered. These concepts of *shadow, anima, animus,* and the *self* present themselves like so many *figures of the other*; they serve to give the clinician, or if need be the analysand, a concrete, sensitive hold on the diverse states and stages of the confrontation with the unconscious (Gaillard 2003a).

In these essays on the arts, Jung rarely mentions these concepts of his analytical psychology. He does not state them, but he does use them. They become methods of scrutiny in his exploration and attempts at analysing the works of art that have imposed themselves on him at various points of his life and work. Moreover, as we will see further on, this way of thinking, which is *imaging* in the fullest sense, characterises each stage of his development, and also provides the basis for the use Jungian clinicians still make of drawn, painted, sculpted or modelled images in the course of a psychoanalysis. More generally, this way of thinking can also be found in many contemporary methods of art therapy.

We will come back to this intimate interaction between art and therapy, but for the moment let us return to Jung's relationship to the arts. We must understand what it means in his clinical practice and then in his theory to accompany the figures and presences that can take shape and form and can even have a voice, once we accept them as they are and, if need be, take part in their expression and possible evolution.

This attention given to the *personification* of initially autochthonous expressions of the unconscious work in a dream, fantasy or work of art, and even in psychoanalytical theory, evidently proceeds from the personal experience of the analyst in this matter, and at the same time from a constant bid for the spontaneous competence of the unconscious to express itself – as Chomsky, after Jung, will show.

Further, if one wants to advance in this mode, one must first learn to see things in perspective, which entails learning in practice to consider a painting, a sculpture, or any work of art – or a dream for that matter– not as a punctual, isolated event to be individually interpreted, but as *a moment in a process* whose end remains uncertain, but whose manifestations demand to be considered and accompanied at the rhythm, sometimes slow, of their transformations.

Sharing work in progress

This consideration of a work of art, within a *series* of works that precede and follow it, is one of the important lessons to be learnt from these texts on the arts. We see that the Jungian approach is clearly distinguished from the types of psychoanalysis of art that, on the contrary, following Freud's first works on slips of the tongue, and the more contemporary interest of Lacanian analysts for the interpretation of the key signifiers of an entire life's work, and tend to isolate the event, or even the incident, as if it could make sense in and of itself.

As for the often uncertain outcome of such work in progress, Jung when faced with Joyce's *Ulysses* and Picasso's paintings, as we have seen, shows concern. His concern is real. He wonders how far we can go in such a descent towards the most archaic and dangerously fragmented part of ourselves, and at what price.

Which is to say that here, the preoccupation of the psychoanalyst is *ethical*. Jung's psychoanalysis of art is that of an engaged observer who feels that he is party to, and even in his role as clinician responsible for, what is manifestly produced so close to him. Jung's capacity to seize the central themes of a process at quite a different scale from that of a lone individual – the artist in the trials and tribulations of his own life – now has the full impact of his analysis of the arts.

As his article on Picasso's painting progresses, we see that Jung, while firmly anchored in his experience as psychopathologist and psychoanalyst, again evokes the descent into hell, the *nekyia*, structurally similar to the versions in Homer, Goethe or even Nietzsche. By combining his reading of *Ulysses* with that of Picasso's paintings, he now restates with increasing insistence the necessity of a merciless destruction of the ancient worlds, their convictions and aesthetics, when another dynamic seeks to be tried out in the contradictions of the moment. His considerations of the price of a process of becoming are doubly specified.

He shows that only the clash of opposites can give birth to a revival, which is why we must activate willingly, or at least with necessary consciousness, our most primitive, crudely archaic, elementarily bestial underbelly in its tension with the always somewhat disembodied heights of the mind – and Joyce certainly knows how to apply this! Jung also emphasises that the unity or totality which seeks to be tried out will not be achieved by an ideal, perfectly balanced individual, but can only be the effect of a different, multiple consciousness, shared by many, towards the diversity of the world in movement.

Here we re-encounter the widening of scope of Jungian psychoanalysis with respect to the question of the unconscious. Indeed if Jung allows himself comparisons like those between the manifest themes of Joyce's novel or Picasso's painting on the one hand, and on the other the figures and presences that can be observed in many works of art other than these, and in completely different cultural spheres, it is because these themes spontaneously depicted by the author or the painter seem to be recurrent, reiterated in endless similar adventures.

They are in fact *typical*. That is to say they are not only the expression of work which can be observed in progress in many times and places, but also the mark of a common *structural organisation* of representation right from its creation in the most archaic regions and forms of expression of the psyche. Which is why Jung calls them, from the late 1910s onwards, *archetypes*.

However, in these texts on the psychoanalysis of art, Jung never dwells on the development of his thoughts on this subject, neither does he develop the other major articulations of his psychology. Once again it is the most appropriate accompaniment of the works he is considering which presides over the establishment of any theory, be it his own.

From anxious accompaniment to acquiescence

In the spirit of this not indulgent but deliberately open accompaniment, Jung remarks on Picasso's paintings that he has rarely or perhaps never seen among his patients a case that 'did not go back to Neolithic art forms or revel in evocations of Dionysian orgies' (par. 212). And indeed we observe in Picasso's paintings a jubilation, at first black, but also progressively translated by the colours already contained in the Harlequin's costume, that is born of the trial that had led to the edge of death, or at the very least to the doors of Hades. Jung himself experiences this jubilation that he qualifies as Dionysian in the last pages of his two texts, above all in the one that he devoted to Joyce. (May I point out here that jubilation, enjoyment and joy are in the root of the writer's name!). 'O *Ulysses*', he finally writes in the last page of the essay,

> you are truly a devotional book for the object-besotted, object-ridden white man! You are a spiritual exercise, an ascetic discipline, an agonizing ritual, an arcane procedure, eighteen alchemical alembics piled on top of one another, where amid acids, poisonous fumes, and fire and ice, the homunculus of a new, universal consciousness is distilled!
>
> (Jung 1932a: par. 201)

A new universal consciousness? This is a new and wide perspective, perhaps a promise, of which we could dream. But let us note that the operation in question is far from simple or calm. Trial, crisis and incertitude as to the outcome rest at the heart of the matter. Jung's own writing testifies to that.

What is more, Jung may well create a truly wide perspective (Gaillard 2000b: 146), he is nonetheless preoccupied by the experience and suffering of the artist who is engaged in such a process. His concern for Picasso's fate is present and insistent throughout the text devoted to his art. He writes:

> As to the future Picasso, I would rather not try my hand at prophecy, for this inner adventure is a hazardous affair and can lead at any moment to a standstill or to a catastrophic bursting asunder of the conjoined opposites.
>
> (Jung 1932b: par. 214)

Jung cannot really know what could be the fate of Pablo Picasso. But let us note in passing that time will not prove him wrong for the painter's work will have to endure a time of crisis and disturbing lack of productivity after 1932, until he launches himself into his series of etchings centred on the figure of the blind Minotaur.

Of course Jung's attention is focused essentially on the processes being undertaken in the work of art. But the price the artist has to pay, meanwhile, is also the object of anxious attentions that lead to the ambivalence that openly marks the end of the text on Picasso's work. Jung does not know whether he can content himself with his interest in the process that he is observing and analysing, or whether he should be more immediately concerned with the difficult predicament of the artist.

The text on *Ulysses*, for its part, goes much further. It concludes in a movement of writing that becomes increasingly more vivid and dynamic, and that testifies Jung's adherence to the *yes* that in turn ends Joyce's novel. A *yes* that Jung himself quotes fully in his text, and which we cannot resist the pleasure of citing here:

> O and the sea the sea crimson sometimes like fire and the glorious sunsets and the fig trees in the Alameda gardens yes and all the queer little streets and pink and blue and yellow houses and the rose gardens and the jessamine and geraniums and cactuses and Gibraltar as a girl where I was a Flower of the mountain yes when I put the rose in my hair like the Andalusian girls used or shall I wear a red yes and how he kissed me under the Moorish wall and I thought well as well him as another and then I asked him with my eyes to ask again yes and then he asked me would I yes to say yes my mountain flower and first I put my arms around him yes and drew him down to me so he could feel my

breasts all perfume yes and his heart was going like mad and yes I said yes I will Yes.

(Jung 1932a: par. 200)

This is a woman's *yes*. It is possible that the accompaniment of the processes of creation that Jung urges us to follow, demands the approval, the agreement, and the participation of the senses and rhythms of the body in which Moses is hardly experienced. But Ulysses, who is differently mobile and inventive, who knows how to create his own route in order finally to return home, and who notoriously takes pleasure in his encounters and associations with women, can show us the way.

THE ARTS: SECTION TWO

Thus the attention Jung gives to the arts, far from being overawed by the promise of mastery and the sublimation of urges, is turned towards distinctly disturbing events which undermine the most sure and reputable of heritages, the most entrenched values, the most generally admitted criteria of beauty and meaning.

His psychoanalysis of art is situated within a concept and practice of the relationship to the unconscious that constantly bids for the possible positive effects of a dynamic of deconstruction, denouncement and reversal, and that does not retreat before the probability of crises, disorder, destruction or even chaos.

What is more, his concept of creation is immediately placed at a scale far beyond the individual. Jung can of course show himself to be preoccupied by the personal fate of an artist, as we saw with regards to Picasso, but the most important undertakings in art happen elsewhere. They are for the very least transgenerational, which is to say that art is linked to the advances – or setbacks – of a culture throughout its long-term transformations, from one generation to another and at a rhythm and timescale that are greatly different from those of an individual life.

One of the consequences of this is that his psychoanalysis of art is hardly exposed to the risk of becoming psychobiography. Rather than wanting to present explications founded on the interpretation of works of art with reference to the ups and downs of the life of the artist right from the cradle, Jung's approach means he receives and analyses these works of art in the same manner as dreams. According to Jung, what should be considered in the role of the unconscious in art and dreams is how it affects the present. One of the major effects is that the unconscious presents itself as an invitation, or a provocation to open another perspective, plural or at least prospective, onto our everyday existence.

This invitation provokes at least surprise, more likely resistance, defensive or even offensive reactions, in the face of contemporary creation. Jung's own debate with the work of Joyce and Picasso in the 1930s testifies to this.

This sometimes raw and violent debate does not seek appeasement by resorting to the ready-made knowledge of some theory that could be applied. It seeks rather to weigh up irritated and defensive reactions, which we call countertransferential, in terms of thought and feeling. Then we can become attentive to and appreciate the images, figures and presences which can emerge, sometimes from our most archaic depths, to help us orientate, support and nurture the recognition of the event, initially so disturbing.

In fact, through his debate with Joyce's novel and Picasso's paintings, Jung rediscovers, or more exactly reinvents, the virtues of imaging thought. He must be highly familiar with this mode of thought, for his own psychological elaborations, even the most theoretical, proceed in this fashion. And as a therapist he knows its usefulness when trying to open access to emotions, sensations or intuitions that have been especially insistent and over-absorbing because they are without face or form.

But here he discovers this mode of thought on another plane, that of literature and painting. And so he discovers the internal and intimate relation between his thinking as a psychologist, psychotherapist and analyst, and the advances of the arts. He finds that the central questionings in art and in psychoanalysis are so close that he can recognise in works of art and the processes of creation his own experience of the relationship to the unconscious.

From one encounter to another

Let us now explore how these positions, which we have extracted from two major texts Jung devoted to art in the 1930s, were formed, developed and transformed before and after the 1930s. In this way we will come to consider more widely his successive encounters with the arts of Antiquity, of the Orient, with Christian art, iconography and the literature of Western alchemy, and then with the modern era and contemporary creation.

The arts of Antiquity

In 1909 Jung comes across and reads passionately two poems, a sort of drama composed in what at the time was called a hypnagogic state, and several fantasies and brief commentaries written by the 19-year-old Miss Miller, a rich and cultivated young American.

This young woman was the patient of Dr Flournoy in Geneva. To accompany and explore her confused feelings of love, and at the same time to express her attachment to her mother and her childhood, she had exposed for her doctor her most troubling and ambiguous emotions accompanied by references to her reading matter, quotations of Byron, Longfellow and Milton.

Jung did not know her, and he did not seek to know any more about her. At no point did he attempt to found an interpretation of her writings on what the young woman could have lived in her childhood, as a faithful disciple of Freud should have done. It is worth remembering that Jung had discovered Freud's *Traumdeutung* at the moment of its publication, and had immediately become its defendant in the face of a more than reticent psychiatry; he had met Freud enthusiastically at Vienna in 1907 and had almost straight away assumed his eminent and privileged place in the psychoanalytic movement. Most importantly, Freud's *Three Essays on the Theory of Sexuality* had been published the previous year.

But Jung, rather than pursuing this direction, limits his view of Miss Miller to that of Dr Flournoy's publications. From this starting point, reading the literary essays and other writings of the young woman, he opens his mind and his page to an advancing tide of myths, rites and stories with strange, distant, uncanny forms. These often violent narratives are associated with the themes of Miss Miller's writings and collected together into cultural ensembles that for the most part were not aware of the existence of the others, and so he composes finally in 1911–1912 the first edition of *Symbols of Transformation*. This first edition will be followed by a second, greatly reworked, in 1952, which indicates just how the questions posed by the young American woman and the wide investigation that ensues will follow Jung almost throughout his life and work.

Now what do we find at the heart of this book which marks his rupture with Freud and the foundation of his subsequent works? What is the guiding axis for all his research? A sculpture, frequently reproduced in various forms in Antiquity. It represents Mithra sacrificing the bull, and an example can be seen today in the Vatican Museum in Rome (Gaillard 1998: 25).

Jung uses this highly physical representation of the hero struggling with the sacrificial animal to oppose Freud's theory of sexuality. He presents his concept of the debate, sometimes a full-blown combat, each person is engaged in with a libido that, over and above its specificity and differentiated urges, remains haunted by the bodily memory of an inclusion, ideally without history, fundamentally incestuous, in the archaic union with the mother, and even more radically with nature.

Jung also shows how, in sacrificing the bull, the hero – here Mithra – ambivalently sacrifices a large part of himself, to the extent that the brutality and savagery of his act can be transformed into a slightly sickly sentimentality that can be read on the face of the antique sculpture, and which a certain Christianity, Roman at first, turned to its advantage. In such a way that the path to be taken, not without obstacles, is that which will allow the unconscious identification with one or other of the positions or tendencies, heroic and animal, to be disengaged, so as to accept, internally and as consciously as possible, the tension between opposites and their intimate links.

This book, *Symbols of Transformation*, is punctuated throughout by references to other works of art from Antiquity, often reproduced next to the text thanks to Marie-Louise von Franz, who offered Jung the use of her classical knowledge. For example, Jung is able to evoke *Sphinxes* and *Lamias* whose representations go back further than 500 BC (Gaillard 1998: 68, 70, 72) to help himself and his reader gauge the fear we can feel when faced with the power of the mother, in fact archetypal and far outweighing the reality of a natural mother. Again, when he wants us to give attention to the strange, uncanny proximity between the 'divine' and the most archaic animality, he shows us Egyptian art or the figure of *Endiku* in Gilgamesh's epic (Gaillard 1998: 70, 71). And concerning the double and contradictory tendency of the libido to go at once forwards and backwards, he lets us discover or re-examine the *Priapus* from the Verona Museum of Antiquities, whose finger points to a serpent eating his penis (Gaillard 1998: 79).

In *Psychological Types*, published nine years after the first edition of the *Symbols*, he establishes and develops his concept of types of attitude, extraverted and introverted, and the different functions of orientation of consciousness – thinking, feeling, intuition and sensation. Here again he has recourse to numerous works of art and literature from Antiquity to help him elaborate his thought alongside his perusal and discussion of the aesthetic theories of Schiller and Nietzsche.

In fact, this book which is so important for the establishment of Jung's analytical psychology is also an occasion for him to establish the theory of the use of painting, sculpture and dance. He had been considering these media since 1916 with regards to giving form (he writes *gestalten*) to that which occupies us and demands to be expressed, and avoiding the untimely intervention of a desire to understand (*verstehen*) that can dry up the relationship to symbolic life.

These considerations are entirely practical concerning the relationship to the unconscious. Their first outburst evidently came from Jung himself sculpting as a child (Ma vie), then from his experiences of calligraphy, drawing, and painting. He returned to sculpture again when, after his break with Freud, he had to get back in touch with his furthest interior animations, and had not yet found the words to express himself.

From his earliest writings, the review of the arts of Antiquity provides Jung with an occasion to give form (*gestalten*) to the discoveries he made even in childhood. In Jung's work we can follow the evolution of this truly imaging thought process that knows how to harness the power of image, and increasingly serves to better recognise and transform overly individual experiences by putting them back into the context of experiences shared by many, which artists have often known best how to express.

When Jung worked with the Hellenist Karl Kérényi on his *Essays on a Science of Mythology*, he came back to the arts of Antiquity, notably Greek and Roman, to give us all the possible chances to recognise our everyday dramas by re-examining and reliving the relationship between *Demeter* and his daughter *Kore*, as it has been dramatised in the Eleusinian Mysteries and carved in stone in archaic Greek sculpture.

Overall, the dialogue Jung engages in with the arts of Antiquity widens and nourishes his psychology while inscribing each of our personal lives in the movement of collective history, and thus in historical continuity, a subject that will progressively become one of the major objects of his research.

Furthermore, this is a privileged opportunity to make his readers aware of the virtues and risks of regressions, often necessary, which can lead us back to our most archaic experiences that never cease to seduce, frighten and haunt us.

The arts of the Orient

In the spring of 1938 Jung is returning from a journey to Ceylon, which he visited from Colombo to Kandy both in heavenly sunshine and pouring rain. His boat stops in the port of Bombay. But rather than enter the town, he stays on board ship to continue his engrossed reading of a collection of texts by the early-seventeenth-century writer Gerardus Dorneus, an author almost completely unknown at the time and whose thought Jung wanted to explore and analyse.

In his autobiography he wrote:

> Toward the beginning of spring I set out on my homeward voyage, with such a plethora of impressions that I did not have any desire to leave the ship to see Bombay. Instead, I buried myself in my Latin alchemical texts. [Jung added:] But India did not pass me by without a trace; it left tracks which lead from one infinity to another infinity.
>
> (Jung 1963: 284)

This is a condensed version of the double movement that will constantly mark his relationship with Oriental traditions, arts and ways of life. On the one hand, Jung discovers a whole world of impressions, sensations and interior experiences and thoughts, where he can almost feel at home. Only almost, however. For on the other hand he has to mark a certain distance, the space necessary for him to find and recover his own point of view in the face of his discoveries and the multiplicity of his encounters. He is aware that this point of view belongs to a different history, and that it perhaps opens onto entirely different perspectives.

Jung is not really on unfamiliar territory (Maillard 1996). He has been reading and studying Eastern literature for a long time, and citing passages since 1921. He is most acquainted with the *I Ching*, some of the *Upanishads*, the *Athara-Veda* and the *Tibetan Book of the Dead*. And he has had many occasions to meet oriental scholars before 1938, notably at the Eranos Circle in Ascona.

Most importantly, in 1928, ten years prior to his trip to India, he was given a translation of the Taoist treaty *The Secret of the Golden Flower* by the sinologist Richard Wilhelm. The discovery of the text at this time, when his psychology seemed too dependent on his personal experience and he was having difficulty envisaging how it might progress, came almost as a revelation. He wrote in his autobiography: 'That was the first event which broke through my isolation. I became aware of an affinity; I could establish ties with something and someone' (Jung 1963: 197).

This event was all the more astonishing for Jung because he had just painted a seemingly incomprehensible mandala that borrowed part of its architecture from the Vauban-style fortifications which he had known since adolescence, but that nevertheless had a distinctly Chinese air to it.

Comforted by the discovery of the Taoist text, Jung almost immediately wrote a 'European commentary' of this Chinese treaty, which was the start of a long series of works devoted to the Oriental traditions and their expression in the arts (Jung *CW* 11). He was to study many different mandalas, starting with those he drew and painted himself from 1916 onwards, followed by those made by his patients, finally and especially Oriental mandalas.

He pointed out that these Oriental mandalas, mainly tantric, are very different from each other. Some put a cockerel, snake or pig at the heart of the concentric organisation to signify the central role that can be played by sensuality, jealousy and unconsciousness. But the tertiary system they observe can be transformed and accomplished in a quadratic organisation, in which case the centre is emptied and makes space for a diamond. In the Oriental traditions these quadratic mandalas are held to be the most perfect, and the diamond at the centre is hailed and celebrated as 'the kingdom of supreme joy', the 'golden castle', the 'celestial heart', or the 'land without frontiers'.

What a tempting promise! We could let ourselves be led, convinced, even. We want only to believe it. Except, Jung writes with obvious regret, we must renounce it. Renounce this colourful metaphysical language of the Orient (Jung 1950). And we must also more radically renounce the desire to make the paths of meditation and wisdom our own, for they so tend towards and promise perfect liberation from the 'ten thousand things', from the course of history and all interior contradictions that they end up by dissolving the individual in the eternal emptiness of the great One.

When he discovers the *Secret of the Golden Flower*, Jung (1929) shows an almost fascinated interest in the promises translated by Oriental arts. However, his 'European commentary' of this treaty already puts the accent on the shadow parts that we cannot fail to encounter ourselves when we let ourselves be led entirely by the hands that draw, paint or sculpt.

In his 'Psychological commentary on the *Tibetan Book of the Dead*', Jung (1935/1953) reinforces the necessity of a passage where we recognise our most animal urges, and he emphasises the manifest correspondence between the *Sidpa Bardo* and the most Freudian dimensions of an analysis.

Finally in his 'Psychological commentary on the *Tibetan Book of the Great Liberation*' and his 'Foreword to Suzuki's *Introduction to Zen Buddhism*' in 1939, the central focus of his interpretations is the necessary and often conflicting involvement of the spontaneous expressions of the unconscious.

So his long perusal of Oriental arts helped Jung to better express, define and progressively readjust his concept of the relationship between the ego and the self. When he discovers the *stupas* on the Sanchi site, he is amazed, almost overwhelmed by its perfect harmony. This enables him to grasp Buddhism more than ever before, and especially to comprehend the historical and idealised figure of the Buddha, who is portrayed everywhere in sculpture. But he repeats his observation that our cosmic and cosmo-gonic consciousness must always make room for our own most near and intimate tensions and contradictions.

Jung returns in a dream in 1950 to the *Divan-I-Kaas* of Fathepur Sikri that he visited at the end of the 1930s. This journey perhaps best represents the relationship as a Western analyst to the Oriental arts. The architecture of the place is entirely centred on the sultan who sits on high, surrounded by his councillors and philosophers (Gaillard 1998: 100–101). But in Jung's dream there is a differently important presence that resides above even the sultan. This is the General Uriah who according to the Bible was shamefully betrayed and sacrificed by his master, King David, who wanted to get rid of him and lay his hands on his wife, the beautiful Bathsheba. Thus nothing is perfect, not even the most apparently admirable king. The venerable figure turns out to be a destitute and sacrificed soldier. And we know that it is following this dream that Jung (1952) wrote his 'Answer to Job'.

In his autobiography Jung tells another of his dreams which during his travels in India in 1937–1938 called him back to research his own culture and heritage: 'I was taken out of the world of India, and reminded that India was not my task, but only a part of the way – admittedly a significant one – which should carry me closer to my goal' (Jung 1963: 282).

Christian art

In 1887 when Jung was still a child of 12 years old, as he was going home for lunch to the Presbyterian college of Klein-Hüningen he was struck by the beauty of Basel Cathedral whose coloured tiles were shining in the sunshine on the other side of the Rhine:

> I was overwhelmed by the beauty of the sight, and thought: 'The world
> is beautiful and the church is beautiful, and God made all this and sits
> above it far away in the blue sky on a golden throne'.
>
> (Jung 1963: 36)

This moment of bedazzlement recalls and renews the equally enthralling
experience and sensation that he had from a young age of the beauty of
Nature and the joy of being alive (Jung 1963: 6–7). This explains his
decision to build his house at Küsnacht, on the shores of Lake Zurich, and
to construct his own 'tower' at Bollingen, in an isolated spot near the same
lake, where he would often retreat to live the changing yet permanent
harmony of these Swiss landscapes and to devote himself in solitude to
stone sculpture and wall-painting (Hannah 1976: ch. 1) Jung's watercolour
landscapes also testify to his enjoyment of this region (Gaillard 1998: 207).

The architecture and position of Basel Cathedral in the sunshine on the
bank of the Rhine when he was 12 years old can be seen as an exemplary
condensed version of the ideal that Christian art wants to express, notably
through sculpture, stained glass and the painting of the Middle Ages, all of
which Jung was familiar with (Jung et al. 1964: 7).

However, this quasi-visionary bedazzlement on seeing Basel Cathedral
was not, as readers of Jung will know, to be prolonged but rather cut short.
A vision of catastrophe followed when, despite the boy's attempt to preserve
his ignorance, a terrifying and unforeseeable thing happened: from the
divine throne, far above the world, fell an enormous excrement that landed
on the roof of the cathedral and destroyed it. The temple was crushed.

This scene presents us with a large part of Jung's debate with Christian
art. Founded on the joy of being in the world, and at certain moments live
experience of the harmony of the world, the question is to know or think
about what is excluded from such an accomplishment, what is so menacing
as to destroy it altogether.

Jung was haunted by Nietzsche, who represented a catastrophic counter-
example to his own research; he was marked by the idealised figure of
Goethe whom he liked to call his putative ancestor; equally, the Christian
figure that marked him the most was the fifteenth-century mystic and
patron saint of Switzerland, Nicolas de Flüe. Why? Because this man, who
left his wife and children to live his meeting with God alone in an isolated
hermitage, was a visionary. And an efficient visionary. On returning from
his retreat, he managed to reconcile his compatriots who were so violently
divided by their internal quarrels that civil war seemed inevitable.

The saintly hermit had himself experienced tensions and contradictions
that can lead to chaos. And he had experienced the reorganisation that
allows a new harmony to be created. In his solitary retreat he had had a
vision of violence so terrifying that he was thrown to the ground and his
face was deformed. He could not give name or meaning to this violence

until he finally recognised, perhaps through his remembering the Christ of the Apocalypse, the Holy Trinity as explained in the religious teaching of his period. Then he was able to paint his vision, or commission its painting, on the wall of the village church, but calmed, clarified and reorganised like a Christian mandala centred on the celebration of Eternal Love (Jung 1934/1954: pars. 1–18).

All of this shows once again that giving form (*gestalten*) through the arts to that which we cannot grasp, or which on the contrary overwhelms us, means we can face it, orient ourselves around it, even find within it new strength. It also demonstrates how Christian art has been determined to find the best possible balance between the message of love of the New Testament and the stories of the Old Testament which recount the indiscriminate violence of Yahweh, and more radically between the desire for goodness and the evidence of evil.

Jung then passionately throws himself into the observation of representations of the Trinity and the theological elaborations that accompany them. Why this idealisation of Christ that wants him to be free from all sin, when his story is of incarnation and when the cross is to be found at the heart of his symbolism?

Moreover, he points out that the Trinity of Christian dogma remains obstinately masculine. And this despite the many medieval mandalas that manifestly try to include the Virgin (Gaillard 1998: 170). Which is to say that the arts try to correct and compensate for a universal blindness and repression, but in vain.

These works of art are food for thought. So much so that Jung develops a tight critique of this Christianity that refuses to pass from its tertiary logic to a quadratic dynamics by finally opening up to the presence of evil, and of the feminine. He also elaborates and clarifies soon afterwards his own concept of an 'individuation process' and therefore a 'self-realisation' (*Selbsverwirklichung*) that knows full well that transformation, for a culture as for an individual, comes from realities and forces – largely unconscious – previously repressed, unknown, or left fallow.

Iconography and the literature of Western alchemy

One night in 1939 while Jung was preoccupied by his seminar on Saint Ignatius of Loyola's *Spiritual Exercises*, and notably one of these meditations centred on the soul of Christ, he saw at the bottom of his bed a green-gold Christ, magnificently awesome but frightening, and he became aware of his need to complete and renew his thought about Christianity and the figure of Christ by referring to the thoughts and experiences of the alchemists.

This green gold, which resembles the natural and organic *viriditas* (or greenery) so familiar to these visionary researchers, expresses their concept of a saviour who is not purely spiritual, but actually lives in metal or stone and in matter.

In 1939 Jung had been working in secret and with some difficulty for four or five years on the illustrations and texts of alchemical manuscripts. Some were sent to him by a specialist bookseller in Munich, others he sought out himself in the least visited reserves of libraries in Zurich and Saint Gall. Jung worked in secret because these works, which are now published and studied in various disciplines, were at the time considered to be spell-books of dubious interest, and in any case hopelessly pre-scientific. Jung himself found them abstruse, grotesque and manifestly incoherent. And so he was irritated by them. But very slowly, with the patience of an iconographer and the fastidious attention of a lexicographer, he started to recognise in the recurrent figures and the vocabulary of the alchemists that which he himself had experienced in his relationship to the unconscious, and which his patients often showed him.

Jung's relationship with the world had always been actively sensorial. He had always liked to pass from his library or consulting room to the garden where he would happily chop wood or sculpt a stone on the shore of the lake, just as the alchemists passed from their oratory to their laboratory. And his mind, animated by figures and presences so clearly dramatised that he manages to talk with them, was not without connections with the most insistent themes of alchemic imagery (note on active imagination).

When Jung sees the terribly green Christ, he doesn't think of Christian works of art – Grünewald's *Crucifixion* at Isenheim for example, which he certainly knows – but of that counterpart of Christianity, often judged to be grossly heretical, Western alchemy. Which means that although his study of the strange enigmas of alchemical iconography shows a confusing erudition, due notably to the quality of the documents, its greatest virtue is to lead him, from 1935–1936 until the end of his life, to a reworking of the principal concepts of his psychology, both deepening them and widening their scope.

His psychology of the *shadow* is the first to be renewed when he discovers the alchemists descriptions and representations of the *nigredo* (black phase) which is the first phase of their work, so obscure and hard that they often talk of *mortificatio*, translatable as being put to death (Gaillard 1998: 151).

The alchemists describe this as a seemingly endless period in a dark night without landmarks, where the researcher is left as prey to wild animals that tear him apart, or has to withstand the fumes of the blackest lead and the heaviest mercury. By reading their spell-books Jung understands better the humiliation, but also the defeat, the smashing (*Zerstükelung*), the long and repeated death that the *ego* must live and suffer in order to gauge its neurosis, or even worse where it is caught and withheld even though it wants to escape, until finally it accepts the new balance and approach that will lead to the mobilisation of the *self*.

He sees that this is *a process* that has to be undertaken in order that the next phase can emerge from disaster and this new potential building site. And this despite the uncertain outcome of the process, for the worst trials often come right at the end of a journey, as if the things acquired thus far must be once again lost, broken, pulverised, returned to their initial state of confusion, or even deliberately attacked – the alchemists talk of *separatio, putrefacio, calcinatio, incineratio*. The reader will have noticed the similarity between the expression of such an experience and of some of Jung's comments on *Ulysses* and Picasso's paintings, written three or four years before his work on alchemy.

His work on alchemy also gives more objective and historical weight to his critical analysis of Christianity. For Jung the alchemists opposed Christianity's refusal to give thought and life to the terms excluded from its elaboration – evil, and the feminine. At their own risk they searched for spirit in matter, engaging often in solitude with the underside of the high dogmas where the Church reigned. They played a compensatory role in our history and the structural dynamics of our culture. And present-day psychoanalysts can recognise in the experiments they recount an archaic pre-exercise to their own clinical work.

Just as Jung never lost sight of young Miss Miller while he collected wide-ranging testimonies of myths and rites organised around sacrifice and incest for his book *Symbols of Transformation*, he immersed himself in the iconography and literature of Western alchemy during the last decades of his life in order to better conceive and lead his clinical practice.

So it is not by chance that each chapter of the book most evidently dedicated to psychoanalytic practice, *The Psychology of Transference*, is introduced and nourished by engravings from a sixteenth-century alchemical treaty called *Rosarium Philosophorum*. In his work on the iconography and literature of the alchemists, and notably in their representations of the *vas bene clausum* necessary to their operations, Jung finds the means to support and clarify his experience of the rules to apply and observe to achieve a right relation between the analyst and his analysand. In their representations of the aim of their work Jung finds material to further his thought on what can be expected from a clinician, and the overtly sexual nature of these representations provides yet another occasion for him to debate Freud's positions on sexuality.

The modern era and contemporary creation

Figuration, personification and dramatisation are essential to Jung's thought and his psychoanalytical practice, so how will he react to the transformation, deformation and abstraction of creation in the modern and contemporary era? Jung's work replies to this question in three steps, or rather from three different angles.

First of all, from 1911–1912 onwards, he praises and enthusiastically comments on the revival of nature and the senses in the Renaissance, after centuries of a Christianity highly occupied by its liberation from the dangerous attacks of the instincts and any fascination for nature. He notes the foolish rationalism that from then on tends to denigrate attention given to the realities of the soul, to the extent that even now the psychology of the unconscious has great difficulties getting itself heard. But at least we have acquired an autonomy of thought that prevents us from returning to an unconsidered celebration of the elementary forces of springs, trees and mountains, as was the case in the myths and rites of Antiquity. At the beginning of the modern era we were able to rediscover the path to rejoicing in ourselves and in the world that had long been forbidden by Christianity's desire to banish nature.

Jung finds a joyful example in Titian's *Country Concert* where symbolic life can finally be represented and deployed outside the constraints of dogma, but without being subjected to an immediate realism or the direct experience of the power of nature. An interior space is created, especially in painting, which gives us a whole world of new representations to experience with feelings and sensations of a different order, and which now demonstrates a capacity for surprising, accelerated transformation (Gaillard 1998: 180–181).

This makes it possible for us to understand how at the beginning of the 1930s Jung became fascinated by the literary progress of Joyce as he grappled with the weighty remnants of the Middle Ages in twentieth-century Ireland, or the evolution of Picasso who, not without danger to himself, engaged his painting in a powerfully creative debate between his familiar joy over the most classical arts of Antiquity and his audacious formal inventions, perhaps the most perilous in contemporary art.

In fact, just prior to these essays on Joyce and Picasso, during the 1920s, Jung had already taken a marked step back from the transformations of the arts so as to attempt a more general reflection on artistic creation that he elaborated in two works of particular interest for our subject. He wrote the first text, 'On the relation of analytical psychology to poetry' in 1922, the second, 'Psychology and literature', in 1930.

These two texts both explicitly turn their back on any attempt at causal explanation of a work of art, and choose instead a phenomenological approach which takes the work of art to be a radically enigmatic fact, to be observed in its own attire and which is beyond the intention of the artist, obeying the activation of structures and processes of formation largely independent of the artist's decisions, and so highly autonomous.

Jung therefore pens a differentiation now very enlightening for the psychoanalysis of art, between the specific objects and methods of *psychobiography*, the *analysis of works of art*, and the *analysis of processes of creation* (Gaillard 1984b).

In order to be better understood, and to better understand the importance of his ideas himself, Jung evokes and cites in both these texts Dante's
works, Francesco Colonna's *Hypnerotomachia*, Goethe's second *Faust*,
Nietzsche's *Thus Spoke Zarathustra*, Wagner's *Parsifal*, the novels of
Spitteler, William Blake's paintings, the writings of Jacob Boehme, and the
stories of E.T.A. Hoffmann. He calls these works visionary and opposes
them to those that he calls psychological. A visionary work is evidently not
nourished by our ordinary human experience. If the effect of such a work is
striking to the extent that it seems opaque and resists all comprehension it
is because through 'the proliferation of monstrous, daemonic, grotesque,
and perverse figures', the work appears as a 'frightening revelation of
abysses' (Jung 1930: pars. 144, 146).

Jung notes how our modern and especially contemporary era is repelled
by these abysses. There is a vigorous defence against the anguish and chaos
of the night that we evidently could not control. This defence is not without
cause, for evidence would show that yesterday and today's worst destroyers
and demons come and go from there, as current affairs, including political
events, show full well.

But it remains that an artist can sometimes catch sight

> of the figures that people the night-world – spirits, demons, and gods;
> he feels the secret quickening of human fate by a suprahuman design;
> . . . he catches a glimpse of the psychic world that terrifies the primitive
> and is at the same time his greatest hope,

and tries tentatively to give it form (par. 149).

Here we come back to a reactivated and reworked version of the distinction established by Jung in 1916 between the double necessity in which
we find ourselves both to understand, at the risk of becoming abstract, and
to give form to our experiences, even the most unusual, so as to contain
them (he was already using the terms *verstehen* and *gestalten* in 1916).

Reading Jung, we particularly understand that this structural unconscious,
as well as being highly emotional, is not the effect only of an individual
repression, but is in fact largely impersonal: through the artist's play between
immediate psychological worries and the creative passion that inspires him, a
whole era is confronted by things unwanted and unknown that are obsessive
and menacing, but could in fact be vivifying and compensatory.

So the reader of Jung will not be surprised to find that in the late 1950s, at
over 75 years old, Jung revives his debate with modern and contemporary
artistic creation in a work that seemingly has nothing whatsoever to do with
the subject, because it stems from rumours, generally considered marginal
and of little interest, of flying saucers appearing in the sky (Jung 1958).

Of course these rumours interest Jung precisely because they are
unbelievable: who today would attribute these appearances or epiphanies to

gods or demons? We can, and some do, purport the existence of aliens. But their existence is no more sure than that of gods or demons, so who today can believe in it? Nevertheless this visionary rumour persists and spreads. It is reborn from its own ashes, and demands attention. How can we listen to it? What can we see in it? What can we do about it? Jung opens the inquiry.

Going back in history he discovers visions of this type in sixteenth-century engravings and narratives that he found in the collections of the Zurich central library. He even finds a twelfth-century example in Hildegarde de Bingen's *Rupersberg Codex*, which had just been published in German. He notes that all of these documents relate to particularly critical moments of our collective history (Gaillard 1998: 173).

Scrutinising our contemporary arts, he finds such shapes in paintings, notably those of the surrealist Yves Tanguy, where we also see organically organising forms emerge or disappear in such an inchoate or decomposed universe that it must be the beginning or the end of time, in regions so foreign to any differentiation that it frightens human consciousness. We happen to know, from various photographs, that a painting by this artist remained for a long time in Jung's library (Jaffé 1989: 146–147).

Returning once again to the visionary rumour that so intrigues him, Jung emphasises and repeats that he could not, out of principle, take a stance as to the existence or not of a physical reality concerning this phenomenon, just as he cannot pronounce on the transcendent existence of God when he writes about religious experiences. His interest is for the highly emotionally charged experiences and the typical elaborations that accompany such rumours; these provoke his explorations and questionings. And the running theme of his reflection on this subject is that of unbalance, confusion, and more radically, *distress*. This is the last word in his book. An ordinary distress, but on this occasion open to the event and the most unsuspected joys of the moment.

From this point onwards his attention is given over to the forms and figures described by the documents he consults: holes, circles, balls, that are composed into abstract and tantalising arrangements, including the expression of a 'fourth dimension', actually unthinkable, but alive. Here emerge, appear or disappear nameless beings or things, formally incomplete, uncertain, and even frankly pathetic ('flying saucers'!). All of which would be less incomprehensible if we were to accept them as the expressions of a *becoming*, sketched or escaping, and that all this is but mere beginnings, still informal, hardly started, as yet unrealised.

Jung thus rejoins, or rather precedes, Anton Ehrenzweig's research in Great Britain which is capital to the psychoanalysis of contemporary art. Ehrenzweig was fascinated by the processes of creation as we can learn to perceive them in a work of art, or a series of works. He also considered the most unarticulated, least differentiated states which despite their apparent disorder manifest a 'hidden order of art' (Ehrenzweig 1967).

Jung's approach is also similar to that of Didier Anzieu in France, although expressed in a completely different conceptual language. Both show how creative work is intimately close to the operation of destruction, at least when old forms must be rejected so as to arrive at a new form of expression (Anzieu 1981).

Jung, as we will have seen thus far, is a practitioner and thinker of beginnings and processes rather than accomplishments, despite what some would have him say. His approach to modern and contemporary creation, and more generally his study of the arts which preceded our era, testify to this. Indeed so does his vocabulary throughout his work, as he seeks to best express the surprises and fluctuations of a unity which is attempted within itself, with others, in the world, but which always refuses to speak of totality. The very term *Totalität* – which in German evokes a whole with nothing left out or excluded – is almost completely absent. Meanwhile there is a constant, insistent use of the terms *Ganzheit, Ganzwerdung*, or *ganzwerden* which apply to a completeness in process, and *Vollständigkeit*, which expresses an ensemble reaching towards this completeness, as opposed to *Vollkommenheit*, which promises perfection.

This is the way Jung approaches, analyses and discusses the arts. In fact, he proceeds on this subject in the same way that he proceeds in the context of his clinical practice. He is always attentive to the dynamics of compensation and contradiction, which can turn out to be more than simply disturbing, but overwhelming, and even destructive, which in this case, however, can bring new momentum.

He shows us how the arts, and more especially contemporary art, do as much and as best they can, often taking our most archaic and primal elements as their starting point, to oppose our certitudes of the moment in order to better appeal to us. And at the same time they precede us. Concerning Jung himself and his work, encounters with the arts often allowed him to prove, and particularly to renew, deepen and revive his thought on the relationship to the unconscious.

Faced with creative work, so manifestly and necessarily connected both to destruction and to becoming, we can be anxious, even overwhelmed. This is for the better, for, Jung writes, 'anguish aspires to culture' (Jung 1931).

And today?

A large section of the research which is currently being developed in the Jungian and post-Jungian movement clearly follows on from the work of the first generation of Jungians, those who were Jung's initial students, as they were then called.

The work of Marie-Louise von Franz, Aniela Jaffé, Jolande Jacobi and Joseph Henderson, to name only four, is characterised by the fact that their encounters with the arts had the special function of supporting, nourishing and 'amplifying' what they had learnt of the relationship to the unconscious, in particular the processes of individuation, through their own experience of analysis and their clinical practice. The major work which represents this relationship to the arts is *Man and his Symbols*, published in 1964, four years after Jung's death, and widely circulated in many languages. The work of Erich Neumann, who was very close to Jung but later distanced himself especially after moving to Israel, has and continues to mark many Jungian researchers who are influenced by his analysis of works of art, including those of Leonardo da Vinci, and by the breadth of his interpretation of our collective history.

From this double foundation, still very much alive, many lines of research have been built up and differentiated. Sometimes these lines of research are in ignorance of each other, as is the case with other subjects of recent development in the orientations of the Jungian and post-Jungian movement (Samuels 1985). Often, as we will see, they intersect and interconnect. It is evident that the following overview, far from being a complete or systematic picture of the works published to this date, serves only to highlight some of the particularly typical current progress on the subject of the psychoanalysis of the arts. To maintain a more readable and flowing text, I have not included the references within the body of the text itself. Instead, the books or papers written by the authors I refer to will be found in the bibliography. The bibliography should also allow for wider reading and the discovery of other authors.

Writing and publishing in the service of beauty

Among the Jungian authors who have integrated the intimate relationship between artistic creation and analytical psychology into their way of life and their work, Francesco Donfrancesco takes pride of place. In parallel to his clinical practice he devotes a large part of his time and attention to artists whose work he follows closely, and who he likes to visit in their studios. In fact, he wants to examine artistic experience with the eye of an analyst, and analytic experience with the eye of an artist. And always in close-up, in the manner of a truly remarkable and private encounter.

This is where writing gets involved, understood and practised as an operation, a process which, particularly through the use of image, seeks to merge the individual and the general, subjective and objective, the psychological and the spiritual. For this kind of writing beauty is indeed the aim of all art. But not a beauty that obeys the canons of good taste. A beauty that mobilises Eros through the active myth-defining elements in a work of art, including the most contemporary creation, and thus supports the exchange of aesthetic emotion.

His work as a writer is also the work of an editor. We must note the formal and sensory qualities as well as the contents of the journal *Anima* which he edits, and his active participation in the choice of works published by Moretti e Vitali, where he collaborates with Carla Stroppa, who is herself a clinician, a writer and an editor Her work in these three fields seeks to accompany and express the tight intermingling in images between memory and evolution. She emphasises how these images can use their own artistic language to tell of the worst human wounds, and at the same time permit emotional expression and offer an occasion to heal.

Both these authors often refer to Henry Corbin and James Hillman. The latter initiated the international encounters which they organise together in Italy, and they collaborate closely in the editorial choices which lead them to publish authors whose works are related, even if their individual approaches differ greatly: Peter Amman or Ingrid Riedel as well as Arturo Schwartz, Basileo Reale, Augusto Romano, Luigi Zoja or myself, William Willeford, Paul Kugler and Donald Kalsched.

The analyst in the service of artists

Mary Dougherty is equally convinced that artistic creation and psycho-analysis are related, for in both cases we are dealing with processes of symbolisation. She upholds that one of the functions of a work of art is to move from an individual debate to a more shared meaning. But the main axis of her work is to help artists in the fluctuations of their creation. For her it is very clear that an artist cannot deal only with conscious intentions or solely privilege the movements of the unconscious. This induces the risk of taking refuge in aesthetics to create a fanatical defence against under-developed infantile feelings or an unlimited identification with the unconscious processes.

She is therefore critical of those who want to believe in the therapeutic virtues of the processes of creation left to their own will, and as a therapist she puts the accent instead on the importance of sufficiently good inter-personal relationships, and on the elaboration of an artistic language which allows the artist to share personal experience with others.

She takes Jung's works as a starting point, especially *Symbols of Transformation* and *Psychological Types*, and she also uses the work of Kohut, Marion Milner, Kalsched and Neumann. Her most notable predecessor was Joseph Henderson who accompanied Jackson Pollock in the progress and difficulties of his creation over half a century ago.

The arts in the service of therapy

These days there are many Jungian analysts and Jungian-oriented therapists who use painting, sculpture, drawing, dance and music, in a more or less

elaborated and exclusive fashion, to support and nourish their clinical practice, either in the context of one-to-one therapy, or in a group. Numerous
congresses and conferences are devoted to this kind of group practice, which
offer valuable occasions for participating analysts and therapists to live a
more emotional relationship to themselves and others, and to exchange their
experience and thoughts.

Nise da Silveira in Brazil was a pioneer in this subject. From the 1940s
onwards she created workshops where patients often with seriously psychotic tendencies could express themselves very freely in all sorts of media,
and without any attempt on the part of the people accompanying them to
propose an interpretation. Nise da Silveira, who did not like the term 'art
therapy', or even worse 'psychopathological art', created the *Museu de
Imagens do Inconsciente* in Rio de Janeiro at the beginning of the 1950s to
conserve and make known the works produced in her workshops, notably
at the *Casa das Palmeiras*, a day clinic where expression through painting,
drawing and sculpture were highly encouraged. She went to Zurich in the
late 1950s and met Jung there. She was also close to the work of Bachelard,
and was in contact with the French speakers and promoters of *art brut*,
especially with Jean Dubuffet. Her work and her collections are increasingly well known and admired.

In England, Irene Chapernowne, who had analysed with Jung and was
also his friend, was the pioneer of the therapeutic community approach
with psychotic patients, where the main work was done through art and
creative media; her work, which is recognised in Britain as ground-
breaking, was based on Jungian principles (Stevens 1991).

Among dance therapists, Joan Chodorow has become widely and internationally known for her own interventions as well as those of her many
students of different nationalities. Her practice and teaching are fed by the
classical Jungian practice of active imagination and by her attentive study
of the iconography of the alchemists.

Joy Schaverien has acquired attention through her publications on the
use of painting and drawing in therapy and through her university
teaching. Her books and articles mostly refer to clinical cases (of
psychotic, anorexic, depressed or sexually abused patients), and often
reproduce drawings and paintings created during therapy. Her reflection
makes her mobilise diverse theoretical approaches to let them confront
each other; she explores the setting and the rhythm of sessions of therapy
where artistic expression is central, the importance of the gender of the
therapist and his/her countertransferential reactions, and also the
transgenerational permanence of certain traumas, notably in the case of
post-Holocaust Jews. Joy Schaverien often refers to Jung's *The Psychology
of Transference*, to Winnicott and Bollas, but also consults Cassirer, Freud
and Lacan, and her work follows the recent developments of post-
Feminism.

From therapy through art to the interpretation of works of art

Some therapists who use art in their clinical practice are also authors of essays on the interpretation of works of art. This is true of Ingrid Riedel. She has devoted many books to the use of painting and especially the meanings colours can acquire during therapy. She generally puts an accent on series of images to highlight the transformations of an individual psychotherapy or the evolutions of a group. Parallel to this she has undertaken the analysis of works of contemporary art, for example those of Chagall, Paul Klee and Louise Bourgeois. Her writing is widely read, as is that of Verena Kast, who also recounts the effects of expression through drawing or painting in her work as a therapist. In fact, a whole group of works by Jungian authors writing in German characteristically uses a classical archetypal approach to explore and analyse modern or contemporary creation, from Hans Dieckmann, who has contemplated the works of Gauguin, Chagall and Rilke, to Kathrin Asper, who explores the work of Frida Kahlo.

Indeed this movement from an investigation of the use of painting, drawing or sculpture in therapy to the interpretation of works of art can also be extended, so the analyst becomes an artist. James Wyly is an example of this; after having published essays on the works of Picasso and Rembrandt, he progressively detached himself from his clinical practice to devote himself to his own painting, and in particular to the art of playing the harpsichord. To practise the arts in this way is to take a choice that Jung himself shied away from when he decided to devote himself to his work as a psychologist rather than to more deliberately undertake the arts of painting, sculpture, or even, after writing his *Septem Sermones ad Mortuos*, literature.

Such a radical life choice remains rare. More generally we can observe in the Jungian community, as in the other traditions of the psychoanalytic movement, clinicians who are especially attentive to the expressions of symbolic life produced at intervals, alongside their clinical or theoretical writing, an essay or two on a work of art or an artist that particularly touches or obsesses them. Thus Murray Stein has worked on Rembrandt, Rafael Lopez-Pedraza and Mary Wells Barron on Kiefer, and Monique Salzmann on Giacometti, while Beverley Zabriskie has concentrated on the analysis of the processes of creation.

We can also note that cinema has inspired some work – especially by Aimé Agnel, John Beebe and Christopher Hauke – whereas music remains as underrepresented in Jungian and post-Jungian essays as in those of our Freudian colleagues, with the work of Aimé Agnel, Arthur Colman, Paul Newham, Joel Ryce-Menuhin, Enrique Pardo, Augusto Romano, Jörg Rasche, Patricia Skar or Karlyn Ward remaining rather isolated.

Another timescale

Analysing works of art in the Jungian manner can also serve to put them into the perspective of our collective history. This entails not only following the evolution of creation in the rhythm of one artist's life, but also observing and analysing formal and structural transformations over several generations, a century, or from one period to another. This analysis of the arts demands the elaboration of a methodological approach with enough internal coherence to be able to be used for each of the works of art considered. Equally, the research must be focalised on a typical theme or structure whose evolution can thus be observed from one work to an other.

This is how, through teaching the psychoanalysis of art at the Ecole Nationale Supérieure des Beaux-Arts de Paris and in my publications, I have come to work, hesitantly at first and then in a more thoughtful and organised manner, on certain Roman paintings, works from the international Gothic and the Italian Renaissance, works by Caravaggio, Dürer, Cranach, Courbet, Pollock, Anselm Kiefer, and more recently Rebecca Horn, Jenny Holzer and Gérard Garouste. I did not proceed in the order of their appearance in our history of art, preferring to follow the path of encounters apparently without any connection between them, and in a manifest chronological disorder. Only progressively could a sort of order be established as to the history of our culture, and this only because it slowly became apparent that these works – or at least a large selection of them – showed the transformations of one theme, the representation of the feminine through the ages, with a common structural organisation that was called in the Middle Ages *hortus conclusus* (in French *jardin clos* and the English translation 'enclosed garden').

So my attention has been focused at once on processes of transformation and on the structural organisation of representation. No doubt this practice of the analysis of the arts is not unrelated to the development of my work that seeks to better understand and present Jung within the internal dynamics of his work from one stage of its creation to another, as well as in his place in the history of our culture and his connections and differences with other trends that have been developed in psychoanalysis.

Of the books which can accompany this approach, other than Jung's own – those from 1935 onwards in particular – let me cite Peter Homans' *Jung in Context*, and *C.G. Jung and the Humanities* published under the direction of Karin Barnaby and Pellegrino d'Acierno.

Postmodern concerns

Christopher Hauke also poses questions as to the great transformations that affect our culture. He focuses his analysis, particularly in architecture, on the advent, notably since the 1980s, of what we can call postmodernism.

The designs of Frank Gehry, which apparently live off a development without a ready-established structure or hierarchy, quite contrary to what we call 'modern' constructions, make Hauke renew the discussion about Jung's relationship with history, and with his cultural heritage. He reconsiders Jung's complex relationship with Joyce's *Ulysses* to show how, on this occasion and also in the actual physical construction of his tower at Bollingen, Jung is far from attempting to find refuge in an outdated past, but lives and realises in his writing or in stone a dialogue where the revival of his heritage in turn constantly revives the invention of the present. In the same way, unlike Freud, he does not construct a psychology, and certainly not a metapsychology, but produces animated concepts to deconstruct the rigidities of the conscious and accompany the diverse moments and aspects of a live relationship with the unconscious.

For John Beebe also, one of the major challenges to contemporary creation is to move from modern art, with its minimalist aesthetic that Jung certainly did not predict, to our postmodernity that often manages to offend public taste. He proposes that this movement can be analysed in Jungian terms as a passage to a new relationship between the ego and the unconscious. For a long time this relationship had functioned at the level of transpersonal objectivity; this is still the case in the work of Miro for example. The most recent works of Kiefer, in their intimate affinity with the verses Celan wrote about the concentration camps, serve as evidence of a certain new vulnerability or suffering experienced much more personally and in the body, to the point of fragmentation and dislocation.

Beebe develops this analysis by rereading the *Septem Sermones ad Mortuos*, which Jung wrote in 1916, and insisting on the passage that is actually taking place from an idealised Self – the *pleroma* – to a more unique self of everyday proportions – the *creatura*. He also shows how the alchemists' project to animate Christianity's exclusions can be recognised and is being realised in the insistence of today's arts on working with the most elementary media, and on giving attention to the feminine and questioning evil. He notes how the work of Max Ernst and Schwitters marks this rediscovery and the actualisation of the alchemists' preoccupations.

Beebe suggests that if Modern arts exposed the tension that Nietzsche analysed so well between Apollo and Dionysus, the contemporary arts try to let those of us who seek this sensibility live and emotionally share the tension between the facetious and provocative games of Hermes and the calling of Hestia. This latter tension always begs the question of whether we find ourselves well and at ease in our ordinary environment, as we can see in Gerhard Richter's landscapes and portraits (personal communication, spring 2003).

He has notably worked on films by Alfred Hitchcock, Steven Spielberg and Spike Lee, on Robert Arneson's sculpture, and more generally on the figure of the *trickster* in the arts. He was the editor of the *San Francisco*

Jung Institute Library Journal over a long period, which is devoted to the critical presentation of books, films and other cultural events.

With Hermes and the *trickster*, we are brought back to *Ulysses*, who was our guide in the first pages of this presentation. And with the provocations and progress of postmodernity we come back with more evidence than ever to the disturbances as well as the fruitful discoveries and encounters of our relationship with the unconscious, all of which we have never lost sight of during these pages. For the analyses and practices of the arts developed by present-day Jungian authors, despite their diversity and differences, are well inscribed in the direction opened to psychoanalysis by Jung as he frequented the works of art that had marked him.

This present work poses a few major questions. The good use of art and plastic expression in therapy is different from the relationship between beauty and displeasure or evil. One of the most important, however, is the question of the timescale of unconscious processes as they manifest themselves on the occasion of works of art that come to punctuate the history of a culture. These questions are at the heart of Jung's works and return insistently in Jungian and current post-Jungian works. This is work in progress, to be followed closely in the developments of our contemporary arts as well as in the evolution of our diverse questionings.

Acknowledgements

I would like to thank warmly John Beebe, Francesco Donfrancesco, Mary Dougherty, Jörg Rasche, Ingrid Riedel, Joy Schaverien, Carla Stroppa, James Wyly, Beverley Zabriskie, and especially Renos Papadopoulos, for the information, thoughts and advice they have offered me.

Bibliography

Adams, M.V. (2001) *The Mythological Unconscious*. New York and London: Other Press.
Agnel, A. (1999) 'L'ombre et le soi dans la musique contemporaine'. *Cahiers Jungiens de Psychanalyse*, 96.
—— (2002) *L'Homme au tablier: le jeu des contraires dans les films de Ford*. Rennes, France: La Part Commune.
Alister, I. and Hauke, C. (eds) (1998) *Contemporary Jungian Analysis: Post-Jungian Perspectives from the Society of Analytical Psychology*. London: Routledge.
—— (2001) *Jung and Film: Post-Jungian Takes on the Moving Image*. London: Routledge.
Ammann, P. (1999) 'Music and melancholy', in M.A. Mattoon (ed.) *Destruction and Creation: Personal and Cultural Implications. Proceedings of the Fourteenth International Congress for Analytical Psychology*. Einsiedeln, Switzerland: Daimon Verlag.

Ammann, P., Riedel, I. and Dougherty, M. (1999) *Fra destructione e creazione*. Bergamo, Italy: Moretti e Vitali.

Anzieu, D. (1981) *Le Corps de l'oeuvre*. Paris: Gallimard.

Aulbach-Reichert, B. (1995) *Annette von Droste-Hülshoff. Der Spiritus Familiaris des Rosstäuschers: Ein Deutungsversuch auf der Grundlage des Analytischen psychologie von C.G. Jung*. Münster, Germany: Rüschhaus Verlag.

Barnaby, K. and D'Acierno, P. (eds) (1990) *C.G. Jung and the Humanities: Toward a Hermeneutic of Culture*. London: Routledge.

Barron, M.W. (1998) 'Breaking the vessels', in M.A. Mattoon (ed.) *Destruction and Creation: Personal and Cultural Transformations. Proceedings of the Fourteenth International Congress for Analytical Psychology*. Einsiedeln, Switzerland: Daimon Verlag.

Beebe, J. (1980) '*The Shining* by Stanley Kubrick and Diane Johnson'. *San Francisco Jung Institute Library Journal*, 1(4).

—— (1981a) 'The trickster in the arts'. *San Francisco Jung Institute Library Journal*, 2(2): 48.

—— (1981b) '*Blow Up* by Brian de Palma'. *San Francisco Jung Institute Library Journal*, 2(4).

—— (1987) *The Ante has Gone Up: The Conscience of the Post-modern Artist*. Chicago, IL: private printing.

—— (1989) 'Do the right thing, by Spike Lee'. *San Francisco Jung Institute Library Journal*, 8(4).

—— (1990) 'The notorious post-war psyche'. *Journal of Popular Film and Television*, 18(1).

—— (1992) *Integrity in Depth*. College Station, TX: Texas A&M University.

—— (1995) 'L'anima dans les films'. *Cahiers Jungiens de Psychanalyse*, 83.

—— (2001) '*A.I.* by Steven Spielberg'. *San Francisco Jung Institute Library Journal*, 2(4).

Bruschi, R. (2001) *Il tempio buddista e la via del Sè: una lettura junghiana del simbolismo di Borobudur*. Milan: Vivarium.

Carotenuto, A. (1999) 'E se fosse vero?'. *Rivista di Psicologia Analitica*, 59.

Casement, A. (ed.) (1998) *Post-Jungians Today: Key Papers in Contemporary Analytical Psychology*. London: Routledge.

Chodorow, J. (1986) 'The body as symbol: dance/movement in analysis', in N. Schwartz-Salant and M. Stein (eds) *The Body in Analysis*. Wilmette, IL: Chiron.

—— (1991) *Dance Therapy and Depth Psychology*. London: Routledge.

—— (1997) *Jung on Active Imagination: Key Readings*. London and New York: Routledge.

Christopher, E. and Solomon, H. (eds) (1999) *Jungian Thought in the Modern World*. London: Free Association.

Colman, A. (2003) 'Music and the psychology of pacifism: Benjamin Britten's *War Requiem*', in J. Beebe (ed.) *Terror, Violence and the Impulse of Destroy: Papers from the 2002 North American Conference of Jungian Analysts and Candidates*. Einsiedeln, Switzerland: Daimon Verlag.

Colonna, M.L. (1994) 'La fonction transcendante à l'oeuvre dans *Les Fleurs du Mal*'. *Cahiers Jungiens de Psychanalyse*, 79.

Cosso, S. (1992) *Significato e corrispondenza delle teorie sulla negatività in Freud e in Jung*. Pisa, Italy: Tipografica Editrice Pisana.

Daniel, R. (1993) *Archetypische Signaturen in unbewussten Malprozess*. Fellbach, Germany: Bonz.

Da Silveira, N. (1981) *Imagens do inconsciente*. Rio de Janeiro: Alhambra.

—— (1992) *Omundo das imagens*. Sao Paulo: Atica.

Dieckmann, H. (1981) *Archetypische Symbolik in der modernen Kunst*. Hildesheim, Germany: Gerstenberg Verlag.

Donfrancesco, F. (1996) *Nello spechio di psiche*. Bergamo, Italy: Moretti e Vitali.

—— (1998) *L'Artefice silenziosa e la ricostruzione di uno spazio interirore*. Bergamo, Italy: Moretti e Vitali.

—— (2000) 'Life inside death: through the art of Zoran Music'. *Harvest*, 46(1).

—— (2001) *Una poetica dell'analisi*. Bergamo, Italy: Moretti e Vitali.

—— (2003) 'The care of art', in *Proceedings of the Fifteenth International Congress for Analytical Psychology, Cambridge 2001*. Einsiedeln, Switzerland: Daimon Verlag.

Dougherty, M. (1999) 'Duccio's prayer', in M.A. Mattoon (ed.) *Destruction and Creation: Personal and Cultural Implications. Proceedings of the Fourteenth Congress for Analytical Psychology*. Einsiedeln, Switzerland: Daimon Verlag.

Dyer, D.R. (1991) *Cross-currents of Jungian Thought*. Boston, MA and London: Shambhala.

Edinger, E.F. (1978) *Melville's Moby Dick: A Jungian Commentary*. New York: New Directions.

—— (1986) *Encounter with the Self: Commentary on Blake's Illustrations of the Book of Job*. Toronto: Inner City.

—— (2000) *The Psyche on Stage: Individuations Motivs in Shakespeare and Sophocles*. Toronto: Inner City.

Ehrenzweig, A. (1967) *The Hidden Order of Art*. London: Weidenfeld and Nicolson.

Ellmann, R. (1959) *James Joyce*. New York: Oxford University Press.

Falcone, S. (1998) *Francis Bacon*. Milan: Vivarium.

Fay, C.G. (1996) *At the Threshold: A Journey to the Sacred through the Integration of Jungian Psychology and the Expressive Arts* (video). Houston, TX: C.G. Jung Education Center of Houston, Texas.

Freud, S., *Gesammelte Werke*. London: Imago. *Standard Edition*. London: Hogarth Press.

—— (1917) 'A difficulty in the path of psycho-analysis', in *Standard Edition* 17.

Furth, G.M. (2001) *The Secret World of Drawings: A Jungian Approach to Healing through Art*. Toronto: Inner City.

Gaillard, C. (1977) 'Notes sur deux contributions germaniques à la psychologie de l'art et de la culture. Première partie: T.W. Adorno. Deuxième partie: C.G. Jung'. *Cahiers de psychologie de l'art et de la culture*, 1 and 2.

—— (1978) 'Ulysse et Moïse'. *Cahiers de psychologie de l'art et de la culture*, 3 and 5.

—— (1980) 'L'étrange histoire d'un petit pétersbourgeois: une lecture du *Double* de Dostoïevski'. *Cahiers de Psychologie Jungienne*, 26.

—— (1984a) 'Alchimie et modernité', in *Carl Gustav Jung*. Paris: L'Herne.

—— (1984b) Psychanalyse à l'Ecole?, in J. Gatard (ed.) *La Mémoire de l'art*. Paris: Sgraffite/Ministère de la Culture.

—— (1985) 'Propos croisés sur la Villa des Mystères à Pompéi', avec G. Sauron, *Cahiers de psychologie de l'art et de la culture*, 11.

Gaillard, C. (1986) 'Espace pictural et espace intérieur', *Cahiers de Psychologie Jungienne*, 50.
—— (1987) 'Ovid's Narcissus and Caravaggio's Narcissus', in M.A. Mattoon (ed.) *The Archetype of Shadow in a Split World: Proceedings of the Tenth International Congress for Analytical Psychology*. Einsiedeln, Switzerland: Daimon Verlag.
—— (1990) 'La palette d'Anselm Kiefer'. *Corps Ecrit*, 32.
—— (1991) 'Yesterday's myths to today's creation: genesis of a work' (on Anselm Kiefer), in M.A. Mattoon (ed.) *Personal and Archetypal Dynamics in the Analytical Relationship: Proceedings of the Eleventh International Congress for Analytical Psychology*. Einsiedeln, Switzerland: Daimon Verlag.
—— (1993) 'Leonardo's mother revisited', in M.A. Mattoon (ed.) *The Transcendent Function: Individual and Collective Aspects: Proceedings of the Twelfth International Congress for Analytical Psychology*, Einsiedeln, Switzerland: Daimon Verlag.
—— (1996/2001) *Jung*. Paris: Presses Universitaires de France (the book has been translated into several languages).
Gaillard, C. with others (1997a) *Les Evidences du corps et la vie symbolique*. Paris: Ecole nationale supérieure des Beaux-arts.
—— (1997b) 'Whatever happened to Paradise?', *San Francisco Jung Institute Library Journal*, 16(2).
—— (1998) *Le Musée imaginaire de Carl Gustav Jung*. Paris: Stock; (2003) *Il museo imaginario di Carl Gustav Jung*. Bergamo, Italy: Moretti e Vitali.
—— (2000a) *Donne in mutazione: Saggi di psicoanalisi dell'arte*. Bergamo, Italy: Moretti e Vitali.
—— (2000b) 'Otherness in the present'. *Harvest*, 46(2).
—— (2001) 'Amplification et pensée après Jung'. *Topique: Revue Freudienne*, 76.
Gaillard, C. with Bourreille, C. and Henry-Séjourné, M. (2002) 'Autour de *La Lumière Bleue* de Leni Riefenstahl'. *Cahiers Jungiens de Psychanalyse*, 104.
—— (2003a) 'La psychanalyse jungienne', in M. Elkaïm (ed.) *A quel psy se vouer? Psychanalyses, psychothérapies: les principales approches*. Paris: Le Seuil.
—— (2003b) 'On defining words, some scenarios and vectors in the "autobiography" of C.G. Jung'. *Journal of Analytical Psychology*, 48(5).
—— (2003c) 'Don Quixote in the analyst's consulting room', in H. Solomon (ed.) *The Ethical Attitude in Analytical Practice*. London: Free Association.
Gaillard, C. Gagnebin, M. (eds) (1995) *A corps perdu*. Paris: Revue d'Esthétique/ Jean Michel Place.
Galimberti, U. (ed.) (1987) *Il linguagio simbolico*. Modena, Italy: Mucchi editore.
Giegerich, W. (1987) 'Die *Exercitia Spiritualia* des Ignatius von Loyola und die Unterschiede zwischen einer "theologischen" und einer "psychologischen" Einstellung zur religiösen Erfahrung'. *Analytische Psychologie*, 18.
Goldstein, R. (ed) (1999) *Images, Meanings and Connections: Essays in Memory of Suzan Bach*. Einsiedeln Switzerland: Daimon Verlag.
Grabenhorst-Randall, T. (1990) 'Jung and abstract expressionism', in *C.G. Jung and the Humanities: Toward a Hermeneutic of Culture*. London: Routledge.
Guggenbühl-Craig, A. (1992) *The Old Fool and the Corruption of Myth*. Dallas, TX: Spring.
Hall, J. and Howell, P. (2003) *Self Through Art and Science*. Bloomington, IN: First Books.

Hannah, B. (1976) *Jung: His Life and Work*. New York: Putnam.

Hauke, C. (2003) 'Jung and the post-modern', in *Proceedings of the Fifteenth International Congress for Analytical Psychology, Cambridge 2001*. Einsiedeln, Switzerland: Daimon Verlag;

Henderson, J. (1956) 'Stages of psychological development exemplified in the poetical works of T.S. Eliot'. *Journal of Analytical Psychology*, 1(2).

—— (1967) *Thresholds of Initiation*. Middletown, CT: Wesleyan University Press.

Hillmann, J. (1975) *Revisioning Psychology*. New York: Harper and Row.

—— (1992) *The Thought of the Heart and the Soul of the World*. Dallas, TX: Spring.

—— (1999) *Politica della bellezza*. Bergamo, Italy: Moretti e Vitali.

Hollis, J. (2002) *The Archetypal Imagination*. College Station, TX: Texas A&M University Press.

Homans, P. (1995) *Jung in Context: Modernity and the Making of a Psychology*. Chicago, IL: University of Chicago Press.

Humbert, E.G. (1987) *C.G. Jung: The Fundamentals of Theory and Practice*. Wilmette, IL: Chiron; (2004) *Jung*. Paris: Hachette Litératures.

Jaffé, A. (ed.) (1979) *C.G. Jung: Word and Image*, Princeton, NJ: Princeton University Press.

—— (1989) *From the Work and Life of C.G. Jung*. Einsiedeln, Switzerland: Daimon Verlag.

Jung, C.G. *Gesammelte Werke*. Zürich and Stuttgart: Walter Verlag; *Collected Works*. Princeton, NJ: Princeton University Press.

—— (1963) *Memories, Dreams, Reflections*. New York: Pantheon.

Jung, C.G., Henderson, J. von Franz, M.-L. and Jacobi, J. (1964) *Man and his Symbols*. London: Aldus.

Kast, V. (1991) *Sisyphus: A Jungian Approach to Middle Crisis*. Einsiedeln, Switzerland: Daimon Verlag.

Kirsch, T. (2000) *The Jungians: A Comparative and Historical Perspective*. London and Philadelphia, PA: Routledge.

Krapp, M. (1989) 'Gestaltungtherapie als Beitrag zur Psychotherapie psuchotisher Patienten'. *Analytische Psychologie*, 20.

Lopez-Pedraza, R. (1989) *Hermes and his Children*. Einsiedeln, Switzerland: Daimon Verlag.

—— (1991) 'Picasso's Belle Epoque and Blue period', in M.A. Mattoon (ed.) *Personal and Archetypal Dynamics in the Analytical Relationship: Proceedings of the Eleventh International Congress for Analytical Psychology*. Einsiedeln, Switzerland: Daimon Verlag.

—— (1996) *Anselm Kiefer: After the Catastrophe*. London: Thames and Hudson.

—— (2000) *Dionysus in Exile*. Wilmette, IL: Chiron.

Lowinski, N.R. (2000) *Red Clay is Talking*. Oakland, CA: Scarlet Tanager Books.

—— (2003) 'The poet and the analyst', in *Proceedings of the Fifteenth International Congress for Analytical Psychology, Cambridge 2001*. Einsiedeln, Switzerland: Daimon Verlag.

Maffei, G. (1986) *I linguagi della psyche*. Milan: Bompiani.

—— (2001) *Le metafore fanno avanzare la conoscenza?* Milan: Vivarium.

Maillard, C. (1996) 'L'apport de l'Inde à la pensée de Carl Gustav Jung', in M. Hulin and C. Maillard (eds) *L'Inde inspiratrice*. Strasbourg: Presses Universitaires de Strasbourg.

Marlan, S. (ed.) (1995) *Salt and the Alchemical Soul. Essays by Ernest Jones, C.G. Jung and James Hillman*. Woodstock, CT: Spring.

—— (1997) *Fire in the Stone: The Alchemy of Desire*. Wilmette, IL: Chiron.

Martin, S.A. (1990) 'Meaning in art', in K. Barnaby and P. D'Acierno (eds) *C.G. Jung and the Humanities: Toward a Hermeneutic of Culture*. London: Routledge.

Mattoon, M.A. (ed.) (1999) *Destruction and Creation*. Einsiedeln, Switzerland: Daimon Verlag.

Mazzarella, A. (2001) *In Search of Beatrice: Dante's Journey and Modern Man*. Milan: Vivarium.

Neumann, E. (1959a) *Art and the Creative Unconscious*. Princeton, NJ: Princeton University Press.

—— (1959b) *The Archetypal World of Henry Moore*. Princeton, NJ: Princeton University Press.

Newham, P. (1994) *The Singing Cure: Introduction to Voice Movement Therapy*, foreword by Andrew Samuels. Boston, MA: Shambhala.

O'Neill, T.R. (1979) *The Individuated Hobbit: Jung, Tolkien and the Archetypes of Middle-earth*. Boston, MA: Houghton Mifflin.

Pallaro, P. (ed.) (1999) *Authentic Movement: Essays by Mary Starks Whitehouse, Janet Adler and Joan Chodorow*. London and Philadelphia, PA: Jessica Kingsley.

Papadopoulos, R.K. (2002) 'The other other: when the exotic other subjugates the familiar other'. *Journal of Analytical Psychology*, 47(2): 163–188.

Pardo, E. (1984) 'Dis-membering Dionysos: image and theatre'. *Spring*.

—— (1988) 'The theatres of boredom and depression: two gateways to imagination'. *Spring*.

Philipson, M. (1963) *Outline of a Jungian Esthetics*. Evanston, IL: Northwestern University Press.

Pignatelli, M. (1999) 'Ritagli psicodinamici nella disposizione artistica'. *Rivista di Psicologia Analitica*, 59.

Raff, J. (2000) *Jung and the Alchemical Imagination*. York Beach, ME: Nicolas-Hays.

Rasche, J. (1991) 'Die späte Klaviersonaten von Ludwig von Beethoven'. *Analytische Psychologie*, 22(1).

—— (2004) *Das Lied des Grünen Löwen: Musik als Spiegel der Seele*. Stuttgart, Germany: Walter Verlag.

Reale, B. (1998) *Le macchie di Leonardo: Analisi, immaginazion, racconto*. Bergamo, Italy: Moretti e Vitali.

Ribbi, A. (1990) *Die Dämonen des Hieronimus Boech: Versuch einer Deutung*. Küsnacht, Switzerland: Stiftung für Junsche Psychologie.

—— (1999) *Die Suche nach der Eigenen Wurzeln: Die Beteutung von Gnosis, Hemetik and Alchemie für C.G. Jung und Marie-Louise von Franz und deren Einfluss anf das moderne Verständnis dieser Disziplin*. New York, Paris and Vienna: Peter Land Verlag.

Riedel, I. (1983) *Farben: In Religion, Gesellschaft, Kunst und Psychotherapie*. Stuttgart, Germany: Kreuz.

—— (1985) *Marc Chagall's Grüner Christus*. Olten, Switzerland: Walter Verlag.

—— (1992) *Maltherapie: Eine Einführung auf der Basis der Analytischen Psychologie von C.G. Jung?* Stuttgart, Germany: Kreuz.

—— (1999) 'Destruction and creative interplay in artistic and therapeutic processes', in M.A. Mattoon (ed.) *Destruction and Creation: Personal and Cultural Transformations. Proceedings of the Fourteenth International Congress for Analytical Psychology.* Einsiedeln, Switzerland: Daimon Verlag.

Riedel, I. (2000) 'Louise Bourgeois: die Kunst einer neunzigjährigen', in H.M. Emrich and I. Riedel (2001) *Formen: Kreis, Kreuz, Dreieck, Quadrat, Spirale.* Stuttgart, Germany: Kreuz.

—— (ed.) (2003) *Im Farbenkreis der Emotionen. Festschrift für Verena Kast zum 60. Geburstag.* Würzburg, Germany: Königshausen and Neumann.

Romano, A. (2002) *Musica e psiche.* Turin, Italy: Bollati Boringhieri.

Rosen, D.H. (1996) *The Tao of Jung: The Way Integrity.* New York: Viking Penguin.

Rougeulle, J. (1987) 'Jung et Hermann Hesse: Convergences et divergences'. *Cahiers Jungiens de Psychanalyse,* 53.

Rowland, S. (1999) *C.G. Jung and the Literary Theory: The Challenge from Fiction.* London: Macmillan.

Russak, N. (2003) 'Animals in art, animals in life', in *Proceedings of the Fifteenth International Congress for Analytical Psychology, Cambridge 2001.* Einsiedeln, Switzerland: Daimon Verlag.

Ryce-Menuhin, J. (1992) 'The performing musician as analyst: a shift in depth interpretation'. *Journal of Analytical Psychology,* 37(1): 49–60.

Salza, F. (1987) *La Tentatione estetica: Jung, l'arte, e la letteratura.* Rome: Borla.

Salzmann, M. (1988) 'Le complexe-mère chez un homme: essais de théorisation à partir de l'oeuvre et de la vie d'A. Giacometti'. *Cahiers Jungiens de Psychanalyse,* 59.

Samuels, A. (1985) *Jung and the Post-Jungians.* London: Routledge.

Schaverien, J. (1991) *The Revealing Image: Analytical Art Psychotherapy in Theory and Practice.* London and New York: Routledge.

—— (1995) *Desire and the Female Therapist: Engendered Gazes in Psychotherapy and Art Therapy.* London and New York: Routledge.

—— (ed.) (1997) *Art Psychotherapy and Psychosis.* London and New York: Routledge.

—— (1998) 'Art within the analytic relationship', in M.A. Mattoon (ed.) *Destruction and Creation: Personal and Cultural Transformations. Proceedings of the Fourteenth International Congress for Analytical Psychology.* Einsideln, Switzerland: Daimon Verlag.

Schenk, R. (1992) *The Soul of Beauty: A Psychological Investigation of Appearance.* Lewisburg, PA: Bucknell University Press.

Schwartz, A. (1975) 'L'uomo dalle braccie alzate'. *Rivista di Psicologia Analitica,* 6(2).

Schwartz-Salant, N. and Stein, M. (eds) (1986) *The Body in Analysis.* Wilmette, IL: Chiron.

Sells, B. (ed.) (2000) *Working with Images.* Woodstock, CT: Spring.

Serrano, M. (1997) *C.G. Jung and Hermann Hesse: A Record of Two Friendships.* Einsiedeln, Switzerland: Daimon Verlag.

Singer, J. (2000) *Blake, Jung, and the Collective Unconscious: The Conflict between Reason and Imagination.* York Beach, ME: Nicolas-Hays.

Skar, P. (1997) 'Music and analysis', in M.A. Mattoon (ed.) *Open Questions in*

Analytical Psychology. Proceedings of the Thirteenth International Congress for Analytical Psychology. Einsiedeln, Switzerland: Daimon Verlag.

Spitzer, S. (2003) 'Embodied implicit memory', in *Proceedings of the Fifteenth International Congress for Analytical Psychology, Cambridge 2001*. Einsideln, Switzerland: Daimon Verlag.

Stevens, A. (1991) *Withymead Center, a Jungian Community for Healing Arts*. Boston, MA: Sigo Press.

Stroppa, C. (2003) 'L'acrobata nel vuoto', in *Figure della devozione*. Bergamo, Italy: Moretti e Vitali.

Taylor, C. and Finley, P. (1997) *Images of the Journey in Dante's Divine Comedy*. New Haven, CT: Yale University Press.

Trevi, M. (1986) *Interpretatio duplex*. Rome: Borla.

Ulanov, A. (1987) *Picturing God*. Cambridge: Cowley.

Ulanov, A. and Ulanov, B. (1999) *The Healing Imagination: The Meeting of Psyche and Soul*. Einsiedeln, Switzerland: Daimon Verlag.

Vitolo, A. (1975) 'A proposito di inconscio e letteratura'. *Rivista di Psicologia Analitica*, 6(2).

von Franz, M.-L. (1998) *C.G. Jung: His Myth in our Time*. Toronto: Inner City.

Ward, K. (2000) 'Music and the archetypal ground of the psyche' (review of Alain Danielou's *Music and the Power of Sound: The Influence of Tuning and Interval on Consciousness*; Laurence Bernan's *The Musical Image: A Theory of Content*; Helen L. Bonny and Louis M. Savary's *Music and your Mind: Listening with a New Consciousness*; Linda C. Cutting's *Memory Slip: A Memoir of Music and Healing*). *San Francisco Jung Institute Library Journal*, 19(1).

Wilmer, H. (2000) *Quest for Silence*. Einsiedeln, Switzerland: Daimon Verlag.

Wyly, J. (1987) 'Jung and Picasso'. *Quadrant*, 20(2).

―― (1991) '"The sculptor's studio": Picasso's images of transference and trans-formation', in M.A. Mattoon (ed.) *Personal and Archetypal Dynamics in the Analytical Relationship. Proceedings of the Eleventh International Congress for Analytical Psychology*. Einsiedeln, Switzerland: Daimon Verlag.

―― (1993) 'Minotauromachia', in M.A. Mattoon (ed.) *The Transcendent Function: Individual and Collective Aspects. Proceedings of the Twelfth International Congress for Analytical Psychology*. Einsiedeln, Switzerland: Daimon Verlag.

―― (1997) 'Picasso's mirror', in M.A. Mattoon (ed.) *Open Questions in Analytical Psychology. Proceedings of the Thirteenth International Congress for Analytical Psychology*. Einsiedeln, Switzerland: Daimon Verlag.

Young-Eisendrath, P. (1997) *Gender and Desire: Uncursing Pandora*. College Station, TX: Texas A&M University.

Zabriskie, B. (2000) 'Orpheus and Eurydice: a creative agony'. *Journal of Analytical Psychology*, 45(3): 427–447.

Zoja, L. (1995) *Growth and Guilt: Psychology and the Limits of Development*. London: Routledge.

Index

Note: page numbers in **bold** refer to diagrams

Printed in Great Britain
by Amazon